T0389336

Merging Interests

Why do governments open their economies to multinational enterprises (MNEs)? Some argue democratic forces promote this openness, but many citizen groups view multinational business with suspicion. Using quantitative and qualitative analysis, Bauerle Danzman demonstrates how large domestic firms push to liberalize foreign direct investment (FDI) policies to ameliorate financing constraints, often to the detriment of smaller competitors. MNE investment comes with substantial risks, such as higher labor costs and increased productivity pressures, so well-connected domestic firms will prefer to limit access to local markets when the costs of debt financing are relatively low. However, when local environments make debt financing increasingly expensive, firms will be more willing to dismantle restrictive investment policies so that they may overcome liquidity constraints with equity financing from abroad. Bauerle Danzman includes comparative analysis of Malaysia and Indonesia from 1965 to 2016 to illustrate how governments undertake investment policy reform, and to indicate the interest groups that influence the outcomes of these regulatory changes.

SARAH BAUERLE DANZMAN is an assistant professor of International Studies at Indiana University. She is also a 2019–2020 Council of Foreign Relations International Affairs Fellow, working in the U.S. State Department's Office of Investment Affairs. She has published in various outlets including *International Relations Quarterly*, *Perspectives on Politics*, and *Business and Politics* and consults regularly with the World Association of Investment Promotion Agencies and the World Bank Group on investment promotion policy.

Business and Public Policy

This series aims to play a pioneering role in shaping the emerging field of business and public policy. *Business and Public Policy* focuses on two central questions. First, how does public policy influence business strategy, operations, organization, and governance, and with what consequences for both business and society? Second, how do businesses themselves influence policy institutions, policy processes, and other policy actors, and with what outcomes?

Other Books in the Series

Merging Interests

When Domestic Firms Shape FDI Policy

Sarah Bauerle Danzman
Indiana University

CAMBRIDGE
UNIVERSITY PRESS

CAMBRIDGE
UNIVERSITY PRESS

University Printing House, Cambridge CB2 8BS, United Kingdom

One Liberty Plaza, 20th Floor, New York, NY 10006, USA

477 Williamstown Road, Port Melbourne, VIC 3207, Australia

314-321, 3rd Floor, Plot 3, Splendor Forum, Jasola District Centre,
New Delhi - 110025, India

79 Anson Road, #06-04/06, Singapore 079906

Cambridge University Press is part of the University of Cambridge.

It furthers the University's mission by disseminating knowledge in the pursuit of
education, learning, and research at the highest international levels of excellence.

www.cambridge.org
Information on this title: www.cambridge.org/9781108494144
DOI: 10.1017/9781108657143

First published 2019

A catalog record for this publication is available from the British Library.

ISBN 978-1-108-49414-4 Hardback

For Robarn, Sophia, and Julien.

Contents

Figures

Tables

Acknowledgments

I frequently tell my students that scholarship is never done in a vacuum but instead is the product of a community that provides inspiration, encouragement, sustained critical dialogue, and a host of supportive care work that gives researchers the physical, intellectual, material, and emotional support necessary to think deeply about one small thing for a sustained time. *Merging Interests: When Domestic Firms Shape FDI Policy* reflects the reality that we never accomplish anything of value in isolation, and I have many people to thank for their support over the years during which this book went from the seed of an idea to a fully formed manuscript.

First, *Merging Interests: When Domestic Firms Shape FDI Policy* is an outgrowth of a much-changed dissertation project. I must thank my academic advisers for their support and guidance during my doctoral studies and beyond. Layna Mosley encouraged me to embrace the challenge of studying what was most interesting and important to me. She uncannily knew when to offer a pep talk and when to push me to make my ideas clearer and my empirical methods stronger. When I needed to get some fresh air, she was more than willing to meet me on a running trail. I am so grateful for her advice. Thomas Oatley challenged me to find my voice as a scholar. Through him, I learned how to best frame my question and articulate my argument to contribute to a larger literature without drowning in it. Eddy Malesky, in his unfailing enthusiasm for methodological rigor, provided me with early critiques that led me to stronger analytic techniques. He also sussed out a theoretical affinity in my project to the law-finance-growth nexus literature, which greatly elevated the theoretical contribution of the book and helped me sharpen my analytic focus. Graeme Robertson and Mark Crescenzi provided much needed theoretical breadth and alternate perspectives that helped avoid the myopic tendencies that accompany sustained focus on a narrow question.

Second, I owe a debt of gratitude to many exemplary scholars who read drafts, provided comments, and encouraged me to press on through the project. I am especially grateful to Nathan Jensen and David Leblang, who read entire drafts and provided me excellent comments, critiques, and advice. Helen Milner, Hussain Banai, Benjamin A. T. Graham, Jessica Steinberg, Alissandra T. Stoyan, and William Kindred Winecoff read (often multiple) drafts of various portions of the project and gave me excellent suggestions about how to improve the research design. Participants at various conferences and seminar talks at Princeton University, Elon University, Emory University, Lewis and Clark College, and Indiana University also provided valuable feedback and suggestions. My 2014–15 Niehaus Fellows cohort generously gave their time to providing feedback during our time together: Florian Hollenback, Giovanni Mantilla, Shahrzad Sabet, and Geoffrey Wallace. Richard Solomon provided excellent research assistance. Aseem Prakash, my editor at Cambridge, guided me through the review and publishing process with aplomb; the two anonymous reviewers of the manuscript provided excellent suggestions for how to improve the final manuscript.

I would also like to acknowledge the considerable support I have received from the three academic affiliations I have had the privilege to hold over the course of this project: The University of North Carolina (UNC) at Chapel Hill, The Niehaus Center for Globalization and Governance at Princeton University's Woodrow Wilson School of Public and International Affairs, and the Hamilton Lugar School of International Studies at Indiana University. The Hamilton Lugar School was generous in its support of this project and provided funding for a book workshop in the fall of 2017 that was instrumental in shaping the manuscript in its current form. My predissertation research was supported in part by a UNC departmental grant made possible by the generous support of Thomas Ulhman. While in graduate school, I was fortunate to participate in Sara Mitchell and Kelly Kadera's National Science Foundation-supported Women in International Relations conference in May 2013; I thank these women for their continued efforts to support female scholars in the field.

I have also benefited greatly from an extensive network of scholars who have offered their friendship and scholarly perspectives. I would like to specifically thank Ali, Will, Andy, Amanda, Alex, Kris, Shahrzad, Xander, Geoff, Noel, Ida, Ben, Rachel, Erica, Jess, Jessy,

Stephen, and Huss for making academia a little less lonely and a lot more fun.

Finally, I would like to thank my family. James and Mary Beth Bauerle have encouraged and assisted my educational development my entire life. Their love and sacrifice is immeasurable and I remain forever grateful to them. My sisters, my grandparents, and my large extended family have shown me great care and compassion throughout my studies. My spouse, Robarn, has demonstrated unending patience, love, and trust in me and my endeavors. I thank him for all he has done and continues to do to support my journey. My children Sophia and Julien remind me that I am more than my occupation and that joy comes from many, seemingly limitless, directions.

1 | *Introduction*

We have no horror of **FOREIGN CAPITAL** – if subjected to (domestic) management (Niles' Weekly Register, cited in Wilkins, 1989: 85)

We are always prepared to provide the necessary security to foreign capital *on the condition that its profits be regulated by law* [emphasis added] (Mustafa Kemal Atatürk, quoted in Lipson 1985, 72).

In June 2016, the Indian government announced sweeping changes to its foreign investment laws that eliminated government approval processes for most sectors and substantially increased the maximum foreign equity allowed for firms in several sectors, including retail, food, defense, airlines, broadcasting, and pharmaceuticals. In response, several Indian trade unions voiced their strong disapproval. Unions representing government employees announced an indefinite strike.[1] Far-left and far-right affiliated trade unions issued strong condemnations of the proposed liberalizations, arguing such moves would not increase employment but would lead to increased labor law violations and push small firms out of business.[2]

In contrast to labor unions, business groups reacted positively to investment policy changes. Indian pharmaceuticals expressed support for loosened restrictions on foreign direct investment (FDI) in that sector, arguing decreased scrutiny of foreign funded mergers and acquisitions (M&A) would benefit domestic firms.[3] Industry watchers emphasized the fact that private Indian firms would be more able

---

[1] "1L Central govt staff to go on indefinite strike." *The Times of India.* June 27, 2016.
[2] "Trade unions slam govt's FDI policy initiatives." *Daily News and Analysis,* June 22, 2016.
[3] Mishra, Lalatendu. "M&As to be an active ingredient in pharma." *The Hindu,* June 21, 2016.

to monetize their shares. And, in 2016, the value of inward pharmaceuticals M&A deals increased by over 80 percent year-over-year.[4]

In the wake of the 1997 Asian financial crisis, Malaysian manufacturing firms made similar arguments that embracing policies of openness to FDI, and the financial capital foreign firms could bring, were necessary to ensure the viability of the entire industry.[5] But domestic firms do not always support policies of openness toward multinationals. Indonesian firms largely opposed liberalizing direct entry in the years following the Asian financial crisis, instead advocating for a Chinese-style approach to foreign firms in which governments allow select investors into priority sectors while reserving the majority of industries for domestic and state-owned firms.[6]

The patterns of protest against and support for changes to foreign investment laws in India challenge conventional wisdom regarding the politics of FDI.[7] The most prominent existing explanations of FDI liberalization use factor proportion models from international trade theory to argue that domestic capital is disadvantaged by multinational entry while workers benefit from the jobs new investment creates. These models predict liberalization will occur when workers gain political power over capital – mainly through democratization. Yet, as the above example illustrates, workers can oppose liberalizing reforms to investment law while domestic firms may support these changes.

In contrast to the widespread coverage the Indian reform received, the minutiae of investment policies rarely generate popular political action. A search of news stories about "Foreign Investment" and "Protest" returned 21,326 articles globally between 1970 and April 6, 2016. In comparison, "Trade" and "Protest" returned 448,819 articles over the same time period. If reformist pressures came from publics,

---

[4] Ernst and Young (2017), 20.
[5] Toh, Eddie. "Businessmen Urge Malaysia to Ease Foreign Equity Cap in Key Sectors; They Also Seek to Mothball Foreign Investment Panel." *The Business Times Singapore*, April 9, 2002.
[6] "Indonesia Commerce Body Urges Government to Restrict Foreign Investment." *BBC Monitoring Asia Pacific*, October 25, 2013.
[7] FDI is defined as "an investment involving a long-term relationship and reflecting a lasting interest and control" by an enterprise domiciled in a different jurisdiction. United Nations Conference on Trade and Development (2006), p. 293.

we might expect far greater popular mobilization over investment policy. It therefore seems unlikely that public opinion and voting behavior drive decisions to liberalize investment laws. Instead, most of the time foreign investment laws remain in the purview of what Pepper Culpepper aptly dubs "Quiet Politics," meaning the political dynamics that characterize policymaking when "highly organized interest groups dominate the policy process in arenas shielded from public view."[8]

The Question

What, then, explains governments' decisions to pursue policies that loosen restrictions on FDI? This is an important question because FDI is the primary mechanism through which multinational enterprises (MNEs) expand overseas. MNEs direct the vast majority of global trade, either through trade among affiliates or through trade among intermediate suppliers. Trade among MNE affiliates accounts for approximately one-third of world trade.[9] Some estimate MNEs orchestrate as much as 80 to 90 percent of all trade globally.[10]

Rules governing MNE entry to local markets powerfully influence the ways in which countries' economies are integrated into the global economy. These regulations affect both the type of economic activities that take place within a country and the degree to which the country's economy is integrated into global supply chains. For example, Thailand and Malaysia have undergone extensive liberalization of entry requirements in most sectors, including semiconductors, that allow foreign firms to establish wholly owned subsidiaries in these countries. These laws, and the clarity they provide, have encouraged leading electronics MNEs to locate high value-added activities in these jurisdictions.[11] In contrast, China's complicated and frequently shifting regulations on FDI have made foreign firms hesitant to transfer lucrative intellectual property to subsidiaries in the country. This has resulted in a massive growth in inward investment in low value–added

---

[8] Culpepper (2011), p. xv.
[9] Antras (2003).
[10] United Nations Conference on Trade and Development (2013a), iii.
[11] See Moran (2005).

activities, such as assembly, but less investment in high value–added activities, such as semiconductor wafer fabrication.[12]

This book considers the conditions under which local capital may benefit from, and consequently advocate for, investment policy liberalization. It articulates a process of economic reforms in which incumbent economic elites initiate and manage structural reforms rather than become victims of disrupted economic and political structures of power. Domestic firms' preferences over openness to foreign equity investors depend on domestic financing conditions, which in turn are a function of both global forces and local politics. Because MNE entry comes with substantial risks, such as higher labor costs and increased productivity pressures, well-connected domestic firms will prefer to limit access to local markets when the costs of debt financing are relatively low. However, when local environments make debt financing increasingly expensive – for example, when governments end practices of directing subsidized credit to key industries and businesses – firms will be more willing to dismantle restrictive investment policies so that they may overcome liquidity constraints with equity financing from abroad.

I argue transformations in the ways in which credit is intermediated in local financial markets disrupt economic elites' access to capital and therefore create incentives for local industrial interests to support loosening restrictions on foreign equity ownership. Access to cheap alternative sources of capital makes elites likely to block regulatory reform. Economic conditions and policy developments that limit access to short-term investment and debt financing will cause elites to re-evaluate the costs and benefits of openness. In particular, governments will be more likely to pursue policies of openness to FDI

---

[12] Despite promotional policies designed to attract FDI in the semiconductor industry, and despite becoming the largest semiconductor market, China has failed to capture much global front-end production of semiconductor chips. In 2008, the country accounted for 1/227 of the value of global production of integrated circuits. While the country has successfully attracted investment in low valued–added and labor intensive "back-end" microchip production, it still had only two foreign firms invested in front-end production by the end of 2007. See Yinug (2009) for an extended study. Today China remains an industry laggard in high-end chip manufacturing. Its well-publicized China 2025 initiative is designed to foster substantial government investment in advanced semiconductors because foreign firms have been unwilling to transfer high-end production to the country. See Lewis (2019) for further discussion.

when domestic sources of private credit are limited and governments do not manipulate credit costs through tools of financial repression such as interest rate controls. Consequently, FDI liberalization may be driven less by a need to respond to popular pressures for job creation and more by a desire to provide domestic firms with access to global financing channels.

We should care to explore whose interests are mollified by investment liberalization because who benefits from FDI has important distributive implications. This book provides substantial evidence that openness toward foreign investment is often pursued for the benefit of large domestic business interests, which is an important corrective to dominant narratives that opening markets to foreign investors, capital, and goods dislodges economic elites to the benefit of ordinary citizens, particularly in developing countries. If investment liberalization reflects the preferences of large firms, opening economies to FDI may benefit the largest and most politically influential firms in a local economy while disadvantaging smaller firms and workers. Accordingly, the theory and evidence presented here demonstrates that FDI liberalization can make markets less rather than more competitive. Rather than provide access points to small firms to participate in global value chains or break down structures of crony capitalism, FDI liberalization may benefit a select few well-connected domestic firms while making it increasingly difficult for smaller and newer firms to compete in local markets. In a liberalized FDI environment, large and politically connected domestic firms may cast their lot with MNEs that can provide them greater access to finance and external markets, while smaller firms, potential start-ups, and entrepreneurs disconnected from ruling coalitions may be largely left out of newly formed networks of global production.

The distributive implications of elite-driven liberalization are enormous and troubling, both from an equity and an institutional perspective. If MNE entry benefits elites more than smaller business owners and workers, liberalization does not act as a mechanism to reduce rent seeking and to shift economic power toward labor. Much of the political economic research on FDI emphasizes its upward pressure on wages, at least for skilled labor. This has led most mainstream scholars of economic openness to view FDI as largely having positive implications for ordinary people. But the distributive effects of such investments may be more nuanced. Scholars have become increasingly focused on explaining the rise of within-country economic inequality, a trend that has worsened in recent years despite the decline in between-country inequality. The theory I present here aids our understanding of how processes of economic liberalization may augment inequalities by disproportionately benefiting the upper echelons of domestic economic and political society. And while scholars continue to argue about the direction of any consistent relationship between inequality and political institutions such as democracy, the current global political environment suggests that international political economy scholars must more rigorously interrogate the widely shared perspective that economic integration largely benefits workers in developing countries to instead reexamine the ways in which engagement with a global economy can perpetuate persistent economic and political inequality.

Conceptualizing Regulation

Before delving deeper into the politics of FDI regulatory reform, it is useful to spend some time defining what we mean when we talk about regulation in the context of FDI. FDI regulatory statutes are multifaceted and encompass a diverse set of rules regarding equity restrictions, screening requirements, licensing laws, legal provisions regarding profit repatriation, export balancing requirements, nationalization, and legal resource for aggrieved firms. Governments engage in various forms of incentive programs such as the development of export processing zones, the granting of special work visas for firm managers, and the granting of tax holidays to new investments. Governments also frequently use entry controls and incentive programs to encourage or require MNEs to contribute to a range of industrial priorities such as generating employment, contributing to foreign exchange, transferring technology to local partners, and cultivating local suppliers. We can broadly classify the range of foreign-investment-related regulation into three categories: (1) entry and establishment, (2) treatment and operation, and (3) promotion and facilitation. The complexity of FDI policy has been a contributing factor to the lack of study of this topic, as measurement remains a challenge to researchers.

While I explore the patterns and politics associated with each type of FDI regulation, particularly in Chapters 2 and 5, my main analytic focus concerns rules related to entry and establishment of foreign firms. I do so for a variety of conceptual as well as practical reasons, which

I outline in greater detail in Chapter 3. However, it is worth providing an overview of the conceptual focus here. The primary question of this book is: Why and under what conditions would local firms support policies of openness to foreign investors? Regulations on establishment are the cornerstone of a government's policy stance toward FDI. Even if a government has an expansive network of treaties designed to provide legal protections to foreign investors, equity restrictions can prevent MNEs from entering specific industries either at all, as majority partners, or as wholly-owned foreign subsidiaries.

Thus, the impact of any other FDI policy depends on whether foreign firms are allowed to enter a given industry, and, if so, to what extent. Governments also sometimes use various screening mechanisms to retain the flexibility to reject investment projects that are politically problematic and to provide governments with leverage over foreign firms who must retain the good graces of government officials to invest. Investment approval requirements can create legal environments in which economies are statutorily open to FDI but foreign firms remain largely excluded from participation. From the perspective of domestic firms, laws that decrease restrictions on foreign equity ownership of local businesses and laws that reduce regulatory flexibility to deny entry to specific foreign entities circumscribe the statutory space reserved for local capital. Therefore, the passage of liberal FDI laws and the promulgation of executive decrees that open the economy to more foreign investment represent important moments in political battles over the role of the state, local firms, and global capital in the domestic political economy. The policy preferences over whether to restrict foreign ownership in the local economy have profound implications for economic development, the distribution of economic benefits from growth, and the ways in which different societal groups can exert political influence. For these reasons, I am primarily interested in the politics of laws regarding the entry and establishment of FDI.

Existing Explanations of FDI Policy

The first wave of scholarship on governments' regulation of foreign investment occurred when many countries embraced state-led development strategies to varying degrees and were relatively antagonistic toward multinational firms. Scholarship on foreign investment in the 1960s through the mid-1980s often placed the development financing needs of states as central to understanding government policies toward foreign investors. Writing on the cusp of the Latin American debt crisis, Jeffry Frieden marveled at less developed countries' (LDCs) swift and unprecedented ability to attract massive foreign portfolio capital inflows.[13] The rapid growth of LDC commercial bank debt to foreigners changed the nature of how development was financed. Rather than rely on multinational corporations to bring industrial development and integration into a global economic system, governments could support the development of indigenous firms owned by locals and financed by international capital channeled through state banks. Under these conditions, many developing countries set about limiting direct investment, often in response to domestic elite pressures for protection and buttressed by popular nationalistic opposition to foreign firms.[14] Prominent scholars subsequently pointed to the ensuing debt crises that swept much of the developing world as the cause of liberalizing policies in the 1980s and 1990s.[15]

In comparison, recent research on investment policy has taken an open economy politics approach. Drawing on distributive models of economic conflict, researchers have extended models of trade openness to explain FDI liberalization.[16] This research has typically focused on factor proportion models to anticipate the distributive effects of FDI and then consider how domestic institutions influence the relative political power of capital and labor. In this framework, the labor market effects of FDI inflows are central. There is robust evidence that

[13] Frieden (1981).

[14] See Frieden (1981); Lipson (1985). The sense that policies toward FDI had substantially and permanently changed is perhaps best encapsulated by Lipson's stark assessment: "the rules dealing with foreign investment have changed significantly and irreversibly. Regardless of the incentives for new foreign investment or the existing regulations, there are no real long-term guarantees ... What has been lost, perhaps irretrievably, is a sense of certainty about the way investments will be treated in the future" (Lipson, 1985, 24).

[15] Feenstra (1999); Lipsey et al. (1999).

[16] Others have emphasized policy diffusion as driving liberalization among countries competing for capital (Simmons et al., 2006). While there is evidence that policy innovations do tend to spread regionally, a diffusion theory is incomplete on two accounts. First, it is unclear if governments are responding to the policy innovations of competitors or if governments are simultaneously responding to similar structural changes that shift domestic coalitions' willingness to support restrictiveness or liberalization. Second, if FDI policy innovations occur due to cross-border diffusion, what instigates the decision by the leading state to liberalize?

MNEs pay wage premiums to comparable domestic firms. A lot of research in the literature on wage spillover effects suggests the labor market competition that MNEs engender also places upward pressure on wages in domestic firms.[17] Skilled labor frequently has the most to gain from FDI inflows as MNEs tend to employ more capital-intensive production techniques that require more highly skilled workers.[18] These insights suggest workers, especially highly skilled workers, will benefit from FDI openness. Sonal Pandya finds evidence from mass opinion polls in Latin America that more highly educated individuals are more likely to report support for FDI than are their less educated peers.[19] She interprets this as evidence that more highly skilled workers support FDI. From this microfoundational basis, she argues democratization leads to FDI liberalization as skilled workers gain more political voice and demand openness to MNEs in order to facilitate job creation. Using data on equity restrictions from 1970 to 2000, she finds that democracies restrict about 6 percent less of the manufacturing and services industries on average than do nondemocracies.[20] Starting from a similar theoretical framework in which FDI benefits labor and erodes domestic capital's rents, Pablo Pinto develops a partisan theory of political risk in which left governments incentivize FDI when in power in order to generate jobs, and right governments favor restrictions on FDI so that they can protect domestic firms.[21]

Scholars who place their analytic focus on developed countries have, conversely, emphasized the disruptive effect of FDI flows on workers. In their study of British manufacturing workers in the 1990s, Kenneth Scheve and Matthew Slaughter find employees who work in industries with higher levels of FDI perceive their jobs to be less secure.[22] The effect they measure is quite large substantively; a one standard deviation increase in industry-specific gross FDI flows is associated with a larger deleterious effect on perceptions of job security than is education, income, or even union membership. Erica Owen argues concerns about job security dominate workers' preference formation over FDI policies, and that FDI liberalization is driven by the erosion of union

---

[17] Aitken et al. (1997); Feenstra and Hanson (1997).
[18] Driffield and Firma (2003).
[19] Pandya (2010).
[20] Pandya (2014).
[21] Pinto (2013); Pinto and Pinto (2008).
[22] Scheve and Slaughter (2004).

power. She finds that industries that are more highly unionized also are more protected from foreign ownership in the United States.[23] Among developed countries more broadly, she finds evidence that countries with higher labor union density are less open to FDI.[24] Scholarship on the development of government screening programs such as the US Committee on Foreign Investment in the United States suggests political leaders can use such screening mechanisms to placate economic nationalist sentiments of voters.[25]

Why We Need New Theory

Moving beyond a factor-based theory of liberalization is important because existing arguments have trouble explaining several empirical regularities that characterize FDI policies and the politics they engender, say little about why advanced democracies were also relatively closed to FDI in the mid-twentieth century, and overemphasize the rise of manufacturing investment in shifting perceptions of FDI's value to local economies.

First, democracy-oriented theories of FDI liberalization are unable to explain three characteristics of FDI policy and politics: the prevalence of FDI liberalization among nondemocracies, that labor groups very rarely engage in rhetoric or activities that champion policy reform policies, and that it is often business groups that support such liberalizations. And while factor proportion models predict capital inflows will reduce returns to capital, FDI can bring with it technology, know-how, capital, and purchasing needs that may benefit at least a subset of domestic firms. Accordingly, we need a theory of MNE regulation that pays greater attention to the complex interest of domestic firms. In his seminal work on the role of FDI on the Brazilian development model, Peter Evans argues states can construct a mutually (though not equally) beneficial alliance between MNEs and domestic firms, mediated by state-owned enterprises that offer foreign firms market access in exchange for technology transfer.[26] Others have also pointed to domestic firms' desire to access technological developments to explain why few countries have historically banned

---

[23] Owen (2013).
[24] Owen (2015).
[25] Kang (1997).
[26] Evans (1979).

FDI outright but instead have sought to restrict and manage MNE entry.[27] And governments experiencing economic hard times may be more amenable to FDI than they would otherwise.[28] But these accounts tend to emphasize the role of the state in driving a development agenda, while there has been little analytic attention afforded to the precise conditions under which domestic firms may proactively agitate for more open policies toward foreign investors.

Extant theories of FDI liberalization also tend to ignore policy developments toward FDI in advanced economies. This is problematic because advanced economies host the majority of global FDI stock. While much of the analytic focus of FDI research has adopted, either explicitly or implicitly, a model of advanced economies as home states exporting FDI to developing host states, the majority through establishing new wholly owned subsidiaries, the reality of FDI flows is quite different. Most of the time, FDI occurs between developed countries and is driven by cross-border M&As.[29] Cross-border M&As are less prevalent in developing countries because these deals have smaller book values, local governments frequently block such acquisitions, and multinational firms are often wary of their legal protections regarding such deals. However, the relative importance of greenfield investment to the composition of FDI flows declines as the investment environment becomes more open. As local firms in developing countries amass increasingly large valuations and become more desirable M&A targets, cross-border deals will become increasingly important components of FDI activity.[30] Indeed, we see that in some recent years M&A activity in developing countries is larger than new greenfield equity investments.[31] Even when greenfield FDI outpaces M&As in developing countries, much of these flows are actually follow-on investment from retained earnings. Moreover, these retained earnings are often reserved in cash rather than put toward productive investment.

As developing countries increasingly become sources of FDI, the distinction between home and host countries, however tenuous in original construction, progressively breaks down. The growing importance of state-owned enterprises and sovereign wealth funds as international

---

[27] Dominguez (1982); Pandya (2014).
[28] Meunier (2014); Meunier et al. (2014).
[29] United Nations Conference on Trade and Development (2013b).
[30] United Nations Conference on Trade and Development (2000).
[31] United Nations Conference on Trade and Development (2013b), xx.

direct investors has made developed economies increasingly wary of their own FDI inflows.[32] As the sources and targets of FDI merge, it is important to return to thinking about the ways in which the politics of FDI in developed and developing countries are similar rather than assuming they are distinct. This imperative is all the more central to making our understanding of the politics of FDI policy more complete given historical patterns of policies toward foreign investment. Most countries were largely permissive of direct foreign investment through much of the nineteenth century, when there were few consolidated democracies.[33] A democracy-driven explanation of FDI liberalization cannot explain why policies toward direct investment were largely permissive until the middle of the twentieth century. Nor can they explain why many advanced democracies increased FDI regulation in the postwar era.

Another prominent argument for why FDI is more acceptable to localities today than it was in 1970 is that FDI to developing countries in particular has shifted from extractive and market-seeking investments to export-oriented manufacturing. Current characteristics of FDI are not as fundamentally distinct from historical forms of FDI as some analysts suggest. The majority of FDI in both developed and developing localities occurs in the service sector.[34] Manufacturing FDI certainly increased through the 1960s and 1970s, but it is not the model form of FDI. Just-in-time multinational production chains have also led to substantial increases in subcontracting, which allow local firms in developing countries in particular to partake in international production networks without taking on foreign equity partners. FDI in developing countries before the 1960s was also frequently characterized by export-oriented enclave production, though often of agricultural products, which generated foreign exchange.[35] And FDI began primarily as investments in service sectors, particularly infrastructure development such as railroads.[36] In other words, the types of activities in which FDI concentrates have changed much less than popular perceptions lead many to believe.

---

[32] Marchick and Slaughter (2008); United Nations Conference on Trade and Development (2006).

[33] Lipsey et al. (1999); Scott and Rooth (1999); Wilkins (1970).

[34] United Nations Conference on Trade and Development (2013b), p. 8.

[35] Frieden (1981); Lipson (1985).

[36] Lipsey et al. (1999).

A Financing Constraints Theory of FDI Policy

I argue countries are likely to undertake FDI liberalizations when structural conditions at the global and local levels reduce domestic firms' access to alternative sources of investment finance and that they do so to satisfy the policy preferences of large domestic firms. In general, domestic firms prefer to restrict foreign entry because MNEs push up local wages and create productivity pressures that force less efficient firms to exit. These economy-wide threats from FDI to domestic firms are more certain and affect local businesses more widely than do the firm-specific and less certain benefits to local capital from FDI – mainly, positive spillovers accrued through M&A and subcontracted vertical integration.

However, local firms' desire to limit FDI is contingent on their access to corporate finance. Firms' construct their strategies toward economic openness within the constraints of a central optimization problem – how can they maximize their managerial control (and the private benefits that accrue from such control) while also securing sufficient working capital and finance for capital investment? MNEs may generate competitive pressures in product and labor markets, but they also bring corporate balance sheets flush with cash and increased access to global investment banking. Thus, local firms' willingness to block FDI depends on their broader financing environment. As the availability of other sources of investment declines – and the costs of such capital increases – powerful local business elites will become more willing to support policies that open the local economic to foreign owners. They will do so in order to gain greater access to foreign firms' investment financing. If this is true, we should expect alternative financing constraints to be associated with FDI liberalization, while access to other forms of investment like portfolio or debt flows will impede reform.

Dramatic changes to the way in which capital is intermediated domestically can shift elite lobbying strategies toward favoring more liberal FDI policy environments. In particular, politically influential firms often obtain privileged access to finance – a status once won they fight hard to maintain. By privileged access, I mean conditions under which credit allocation decisions are made through political or personal connections rather than through market discipline. Privileged access provides benefitting firms with increased volume of investment at lower cost – either in terms of interest rates or investor oversight.

When business elites benefit from different forms of financial privilege, the opportunity cost of restricting FDI is relatively low – they have access to other forms of finance, cheaply, and in ways that help guard against competition from new entrants. But when these mechanisms of financial privilege recede, business elites' analysis of the costs and benefits of openness shift. Below, I briefly sketch the main sources of financial privilege in domestic economies and their effects on economic elites' support for FDI. In later chapters, I expand on this analysis and also explore more fully the sources of changing access to privilege.

Formal Financial Privileges

Governments have often managed domestic financial markets and channeled capital to prioritized industries and firms through policies of financial repression. When governments exhibit high levels of control over the financial sector through interest rate controls, directed credit requirements, and large state-owned banks, lending decisions are based on political calculus and therefore provide powerful firms with preferential access to subsidized credit. Under such conditions, business elites most likely to have the power to pressure governments effectively for their preferred policies will be happy to restrict FDI. With access to subsidized credit, these firms will not view foreign direct equity as necessary to fuel their growth. However, when the banking sector undergoes substantial reform, the link between politically powerful firms and subsidized credit diminishes. Under tighter local financial constraints, large and powerful firms will be more willing to bear the costs associated with foreign entry in order to gain access to investment financing through foreign direct equity.

Informal Financial Privileges

Privileged access to finance can also be obtained through informal channels. In particular, in environments characterized by weak formal institutions of corporate governance, minority shareholders are poorly protected. In these circumstances, the private sector often responds through developing informal mechanisms of holding owner-managers accountable to their financiers – especially through bloc-holding and the creation of closely held industrial-financial conglomerates that internalize credit markets.[37] Conglomeration intensifies market distortions in credit markets as the financial arm of these groups loan to connected corporations at below-market rates.[38] The rise of powerful conglomerates thus further entrenches local firms' capacity to use domestically intermediated sources of finance while retaining managerial control over firm assets. Thus, local firms can achieve financial privilege even without direct government intercession in credit markets. This suggests large domestic industrial-financial conglomerates will oppose openness to FDI because they do not need capital injections from MNEs. Conversely, the breakup of conglomerated firms, or increased regulatory scrutiny over connected lending practices, reduces elites' informal financial privileges and makes dominant firms more likely to view FDI liberalization positively.

Structural Constraints on Financial Privilege

Finally, access to financial privilege – especially since the dismantling of the Bretton Woods monetary system – depends upon the global credit environment. When borrowing costs are high, firms will view equity investments more favorably, despite concerns about loss of ownership and control. Indeed, Rajan and Zingales find short-term capital account liberalization is more likely in the context of low global interest rates because local industrial elites are likely to value access to portfolio investment and international lenders when the cost of borrowing is lower in foreign markets than it is in local markets.[39] We may expect an opposite relationship between world interest rates and FDI openness for a similar reason – when global interest rates are high, access to debt instruments is costly and therefore firms may be more willing to finance operations and expansion through equity arrangements rather than debt. However, the relationship between interest rates and FDI policy is likely more complex because of time horizons. FDI is, by definition, a long-term investment stake. Firms engaging in FDI often take as long as two or more years to execute on investment

---

[37] See Ross Schneider (2013), an extensive analysis of what he calls "hierarchical capitalism."
[38] Akerlof and Romer (1993); La Porta et al. (2000).
[39] Rajan and Zingales (2003).

decisions.[40] Consequently, capital injections through FDI are not short-term solutions to credit crunches. Instead, they reflect more long-term considerations. Policies toward foreign equity ownership, therefore, may become more liberal during sustained periods of high interest rates, but we should not expect ownership restrictions to be highly sensitive to short-term fluctuations in global credit markets.

FDI and Other Financing Mechanisms

A financing-based explanation of FDI policy has several advantages over theories that emphasize the redistributive politics of domestic institutions. But embracing this explanation requires us to assume direct investment is largely substitutable for other kinds of cross-border capital flows. For some, this may be a Herculean assumption. The study of FDI originated in the field of industrial organization, and subsequent research has often focused on the multinational firm's choice between direct investment and some other form of international operation.[41] Economists largely cleaved to this firm-level insight that direct investment is in some way superior to indirect investment for the technology transfer and organizational insight multinational investments convey as well as the high redeployment costs that make FDI less "footloose" than easily transferred portfolio investment. However, many of the advantages of FDI are not really "intangible" because local firms can and frequently do obtain technology and organizational innovations through licenses and management contracts. In a liberalized policy environment, the fixed nature of FDI is overstated because investors could sell localized assets, withdraw from operations, and repatriate earnings. At the firm level, there may be important distinctions between modes of investment. However, in the aggregate, FDI and other forms of foreign investment exhibit characteristics of substitutes. In studies across developed and developing countries as well as studies across long periods of time, FDI and other forms of foreign investment are consistently negatively correlated. More generally, a focus on what makes FDI special obscures the reality that FDI is fundamentally a flow of investment capital that finances domestic economic activity.

[40] See, for example, Graham and Wada (2000).
[41] See Hymer (1960), and Dunning and Rugman (1985), for an orientation.

By embedding the politics of FDI policies into the broader financing context, this research project is an attempt to explain how financial regulation affects the strategies of economic actors in seemingly unrelated policy domains in an economically interdependent global system. The global financial crisis led many International Political Economy scholars to call for increased emphasis on the role of financial regulatory systems in explaining patterns of international investment flows and in explaining policy outcomes.[42] This book answers that call by combining insights from earlier work on FDI and the literature on financial repression and reform to consider how local access to financing influences domestic firm strategies with respect to FDI.

Scope Conditions

A financing constraints driven theory of firms' preference realignment should apply generally across time and place. That is, domestic firms' preferences over foreign entry should generally respond to the availability and cost of alternative sources of investment and operational finance. The precise ways in which this connection between changes in domestic credit allocation processes and firm preferences over MNE entry, and ultimately enacted policies, will manifest differently in particular historical and local contexts.

By focusing on shifts from state-directed credit systems to more market-driven banking, however, I concentrate attention on perhaps the most important shift in domestic credit allocation systems in the postwar era. In this sense, the tested observable implications of my theory are subject to some important scope conditions. In particular, the relationship between financial repression and investment policies is a historically bounded argument. As I discuss in greater detail in Chapter 2, the large shift in FDI policies through the 1970s and 1990s occurred in a sociohistorical context in which many governments pursued state planning of economic activities to varying degrees.[43]

Accordingly, we should expect shifts in banking sector policies to induce changes to FDI policies when the following conditions are present. First, this theory is most applicable to countries that entered

---

[42] Mosley and Singer (2009).
[43] See the section entitled *Investment Policies in Historical Perspective* in Chapter 2.

the postwar period with a substantial degree of state direction of credit markets. However, this condition is not particularly limiting. Most countries, even advanced economies, used state-owned banks and heavy-handed banking regulations to direct credit in the postwar era, in large part because the Bretton Woods exchange system created conditions at the global level that made such policies feasible. Capital controls allowed governments more leeway to require banks operating domestically to maintain substantial reserves in local government notes and to provide below-market interest rates to preferred industries and firms. Indeed, advanced economies regulated their banking systems in 1973 to the same extent, on average, that developing countries did in 2005.[44] For example, France's banking sector fundamentally transformed in the 1980s, from one that was mostly closed, highly regulated, and designed to allow the state to direct low-cost credit to priority sectors to one that was largely open and in which interest rates were set by market forces.

Second, the theory applies most directly to countries that have a domestic business class large and powerful enough to influence government policies. Again, this condition is hardly limiting, but we might anticipate that countries vary in the size and strength of capital interest groups. Most governments that pursued state-led industrialization strategies subsidized the growth of domestic industries and shielded them from foreign competition developed such interest groups. However, we might expect that countries with larger economies and industries, for example, Brazil and Indonesia, would have more vocal and powerful business interest groups than poorer countries with less established industries, such as least developed countries in sub-Saharan Africa.

Implications

A financing constraints theory of FDI liberalization contributes at least three insights that have implications for scholars of FDI and more generally to our understanding of the causes and consequences of economic integration. First, it connects the politics of FDI regulation to a more general understanding of how heterogeneous firm preferences over integration generate lobbying efforts that push for complex, layered, and contradictory policy. As the growth of global

---

[44] Abiad et al. (2010).

supply chains further complicates the role of locally operating firms in domestic and international policy advocacy, the theory advanced here can help make sense of the economic policies firms are likely to champion, and the channels through which changes to these policies may generate distributive outcomes. Second, this theory identifies shifts in the domestic financial system as a source of preference updating among relevant societal actors. In doing so, it helps explain how elite groups can shift their preferences over economic integration over time. It accomplishes this by extending existing frameworks from the varieties of capitalism and finance-law-growth literatures to consider the role of FDI as a financing source for firms. Third, a financing constraints theory complicates standard understandings about the distributive implications of economic integration and consequently provides new prisms through which to view the normative implications of globalization. When elites drive liberalization processes, and when such processes help large economic actors to further entrench their power, it becomes harder to assume that ordinary people benefit from such policies. I address each of these implications in more detail below.

Heterogeneous Preferences and Interest Group Politics

The theory presented and tested here combines a previously identified insight – that domestic firms may be more willing to allow FDI inflows when negative shocks constrain their access to credit[45] – with a theoretical approach that centers on firm lobbying that has been employed extensively in the trade literature but has not previously been applied to investment policy. At least since Gene Grossman's and Elhanan Helpman's seminal contribution on lobbying for tariffs,[46] the trade literature has emphasized the outsized role of domestic firms in setting trade policy. Because the gains from trade are diffuse, but the losses are concentrated, firms are better able to overcome collective action problems and expend effort and treasure on influencing tariff policy.[47] While initially the analytic focus of interest group politics explanations of trade policy rested on protectionist coalitions, a second wave of research used factor-based and sector-based models of

---

[45] Aizenman (2005).
[46] Grossman and Helpman (1994).
[47] Olson (1965); Baldwin (1985); Hillman (1982); Mayer (1984); Trefler (1993).

trade policy preference formation to generate predictions over the conditions under which *industries* would support trade openness.[48] More recent work has expanded new-new trade theory (NNTT) to explore the conditions under which *firms* will lobby for openness rather than protection,[49] and the characteristics of firms most likely to influence economic policymaking.[50]

An important insight that emerges from this literature is that trade policy is complex and that business interests take advantage of this complexity. For example, Daniel Kono argues democracies use non-tariff barriers to trade to obscure their protectionist policies.[51] They do so because consumers – who are also voters – benefit diffusely from trade openness, and producers find success lobbying for more opaque protectionist policies. Sean Ehrlich's access points theory predicts that democratic institutions that provide interest groups with multiple access points increase lobbying activity, which leads to more complex trade and tax policies that are biased toward particularly active interest groups.[52] Like trade, policies toward FDI often display contradictions, such as layers of confusing entry restrictions coupled with aggressive tax incentives for certain investments. In Chapter 2, I present an overview of the major trends in FDI policy and measures of openness to show how complicated and seemingly incoherent FDI policies often are. FDI and trade policies, therefore, share some important similarities – most countries have increasingly embraced more open policy environments toward both since the 1970s, but complexity and variation across industries and countries remain. Thus, the presence of investment incentive programs should not be interpreted as evidence of an open policy environment but rather one in which governments have incentives to attract and manage specific kinds of investment projects.[53]

An interest group approach to FDI policy offers a useful way forward to conceptualize and make predictions over the conditions under which domestic and foreign firms generate shared interests. This is

---

[48] Hiscox (2002); Gilligan (1997); Hansen and Mitchell (2000); Milner (1987); Milner and Yoffie (1989).
[49] Kim (2017).
[50] Osgood (2017); Osgood et al. (2017).
[51] Kono (2008).
[52] Ehrlich (2011).
[53] Pandya (2016); Jensen et al. (2014); Li (2006).

important because factor proportion models often assume that domestic and foreign capital have clashing preferences and therefore are not able to address or explain patterns of economic and political cooperation that describe a more integrated global system of ownership and production. As some domestic firms become increasingly integrated into global supply chains, their interests may align more closely with global firms than with local businesses. A focus on interest groups provides the flexibility and framework necessary to approach these emerging research questions. It is also poised to help integrate the analysis of FDI and trade into a study of multinational production.[54] This research pushes the field toward a theory of FDI policy that can incorporate insights into NNTT more fully. As such, it provides an argument space on which scholars can build in the future to examine more fully the competing interests of different types of firms. In Chapter 5, I make the first steps in this direction by providing evidence that capital-intensive industries are more likely to liberalize in the wake of banking sector reforms. Future work can explore other key dimensions such as size and degree of internationalization.

Financing Constraints and Preference Updating

My analysis also has important implications for the ways scholars of economic integration conceptualize and explain the politics of change. While comparative historical institutionalism has increasingly developed rich conceptions of various processes of institutional change, IPE scholars have continued to attribute substantial changes to economic policies as a function of alterations to domestic political institutions that shift the bargaining strength among societal actors with fairly fixed preferences. In their most spare form, these approaches determine – either from theory or from microfoundational evidence – societal preferences, demonstrate how domestic political institutions aggregate those preferences, and then attribute changes in levels of trade and financial openness to changes in the relative weight domestic institutions of governance give to mass groups versus elites. These relatively simple models of policy variation and change have performed quite well in providing a base of knowledge of the distributional

---

[54] Pandya (2016).

political underpinnings of macroeconomic policy orientations and governments' stance toward economic integration.

However, as the global economy becomes increasingly integrated, we need theories that explain changes in underlying preferences of relevant societal actors. This imperative is reflected in a growing emphasis in the IPE literature on the sources of differing preferences among firms, such as what industry and firm-level characteristics are likely to affect attitudes toward trade, monetary policy, and other economic issues. Economic integration should also alter the ways in which individuals calculate and perceive their interests. As workers gain employment in increasingly global value chains, voter attitudes toward globalization become progressively complex. In other words, previous shifts in both the structure of the world economy and the precise way in which individuals and firms are integrated into global trading and financing patterns influence actors' preferences over openness in future periods. Actors update their beliefs; preferences and strategies are not static. As global and local forces place various pressures on different interest groups, their strategies can shift. This may be because their underlying preference structures shift, leading to ideational transformations, or because the constraints that structure their utility functions change.

I point to one particular factor that can shift preferences over FDI specifically, and other economic policy more generally – finance. In doing so, I build on and extend both the finance-law-growth (FLG) nexus literature and the varieties of capitalism (VoC) literature to develop expectations over the ways in which financial access influences firms' interpretation of their interests. The FLG literature focuses its analytic attention on the distinction between ownership and control and considers how different societal cleavages and political institutions lead to variation in the protection of minority shareholder interests, which in turn affects firms' choices between raising capital through debt or through diffuse shareholding. I integrate FLG's emphasis of the firm-level choice between financial access and managerial control, but I make explicit the difference between portfolio equity, which is diffuse and carries no managerial component, and FDI, which is concentrated and defined by the acquisition of a full or partial management stake. This framework allows us to consider FDI as solving the problem of weak corporate governance by internalizing the market for control and relates to arguments about the role of conglomerates. FDI can be an informal, private mechanism of enforcing property rights in countries that have weak protections. Seen in this light, solving financial access problems through liberalizing FDI laws can be more politically expedient than overhauling laws around minority shareholder protections because doing so allows business elites to retain private benefits of control.

My framework also has implications for scholars of varieties of capitalism. The VoC literature emphasizes how domestic firms shape the political economic structures that undergird political, corporate, and labor interactions and outcomes. In doing so, it identifies patient – meaning bank-based – versus shareholder capital as a key component in explaining firms' behavior. In other words, financing is important mainly in terms of how it affects time horizons; patient capital allows firms to pursue long-term strategies of investment in worker skills and high levels of market penetration, while shareholder capital requires firms to prioritize short-term earnings reports. I follow VoC frameworks that view the investment environment as crucial in shaping firms' behavior and policy preferences, but I extend my conceptualization of finance beyond banks and diffuse shareholders to consider also foreign sources of corporate finance. By incorporating foreign investment into the menu of financing choices firms face, I identify a mechanism through which the local financing environment can change over time, which in turn alters firms' policy preferences. Since VoC approaches have typically provided stronger explanations of cross-national differences in domestic capitalist systems than of how domestic institutions develop or change, the dynamism a financing constraints theory provides can help scholars address questions of how domestic political economies undergo substantial changes over time.

Distributive Implications

Finally, an interest group approach can help scholars consider more fully the normative effects of the rapid expansion of MNEs and global supply chains. Factor-based models of FDI liberalization assume that labor actively agitates for FDI liberalization, but this is not consistent with how the policy reform process happens. I argue and demonstrate that it is necessary to think more capaciously about the complex and shifting interests of firms, and how they actually drive these reform processes, in order to push back against the assumption that such processes must automatically benefit workers.

The framework I use to to examine the underpinnings of elite-driven reform incorporates arguments about business power in issue areas characterized by technical complexity and therefore low salience. Taking "Quiet Politics" seriously requires that we not assume that publics have the capacity or interest to organize around investment regulation policies or other technically complex issues related to economic openness. Citizens may pressure governments for economic growth and jobs, but their ability to lobby for specific policies related to industrial economic management is limited. Therefore, we should consider more precisely what firms' policy preferences are. This requires an attention to heterogeneity in firm preferences across firm-level and sector-level attributes as well as the national institutional and economic context. Such an approach also requires creativity in empirical design to uncover variations in behavior that reasonably relate to expectations over preferences, and my research strategy leverages quantitative data at multiple levels of analysis along with comparative case studies to uncover these preferences.

But a firm-centered theory is not a theory devoid of distributive implications. When firms drive policy change processes, labor groups can go unheard, and consequently workers may benefit little or even be harmed by these policy changes. If FDI policy is driven largely by the preferences of domestic firms, and if FDI openness has the effect of aligning local and foreign firms' interests, then openness toward MNEs may generate challenges for democratic institutions and processes in local contexts. Across many industries and in many countries, market power has become increasingly concentrated in the hands of just a few large firms.[55] To the extent that these firms can then use their economic power to amass political power, multinationalization presents critical challenges to democratic values of the separation of economic and political power and the importance of localized accountability.

One implication of the theory is that openness to FDI does not disadvantage all capital but in fact can help large firms thrive while small firms wither. This suggests the IPE literature must do more to conceptualize and explain sources of adaptive power in the global economy. It is already commonplace in the literature to discuss power as a function of who is able to force adjustment costs onto others. But power also has an evolutionary component. Thinking about adaptation requires IPE

---

[55] Zingales (2017).

scholars to examine when size is an asset and when it is a detriment. Theorizing in this way will move us beyond one of the big blind spots in NNTT, which has rapidly become a dominant approach among IPE scholars. NNTT mostly assumes that bigger is better, and in the case of FDI liberalization, bigger firms generally do win out vis-à-vis small firms. If what gives large firms an edge in an NNTT world is the capacity to adapt to new circumstances, however, it is likely that in some circumstances smaller units have greater adaptive capacity than larger ones. Future work should address this possibility in greater depth.

Plan of the Book

In Chapter 2, I provide a comprehensive overview of attempts to regulate and attract FDI. I conceptualize FDI regulation as a constellation of legal restrictions on establishment, regulatory measures designed to impede or facilitate foreign firms' business freedoms postestablishment, property rights protections, and incentive schemes designed to attract "priority" investments and disincentive less desirable foreign firms. By combining existing and newly generated datasets on various dimensions of FDI regulation from 1970 until 2016, I describe global and regional trends in investment regulation over this 46-year period as well as patterns of continued variation in national policies toward FDI across up to 180 countries. These data also allow me to explore how different dimensions of regulatory policy relate to each other. For example, I examine the relationship between equity restrictions and incentive programs.

The emergent properties of FDI regulation are striking; governments retain and use far more policy space than one would imagine possible in a globally integrated system. FDI regulation is best characterized as a complex amalgam of establishment restrictions and allowances and frequently changing targeted incentives for priority sectors. I also compare patterns of FDI regulation with disaggregated measures of capital account openness to examine how regulation of direct investment corresponds with policy postures toward other forms of global capital. The data show regulations around FDI continue to be distinct from patterns of liberalization and closure that characterize other components of the capital account.

Chapter 3 develops and articulates more fully my financing constraints theory and considers its observable implications. FDI creates a variety of pressures on local firms that cause domestic business to prefer policies that protect local markets from foreign entry. However, this preference is conditional on easy access to credit. When highly influential firms become increasingly credit constrained due to the breakdown of state-directed credit markets, the decline of conglomerated financial and industrial corporate forms, and sustained periods of high interest environments, business elites will be more likely to view FDI positively because MNEs can provide financing to their subsidiaries and suppliers.

What matters here is the financing environment for large and politically important firms. Financial repression, state-directed credit provision, connected lending through conglomerated businesses, and bank intermediation of global credit to domestic firms all place large and well-connected local businesses in a privileged position while limiting the financing opportunities for smaller and outsider firms. These firms, however disadvantaged by such financing environments they may be, are not in the position to influence government policy effectively. Nor are they likely to benefit from inward FDI since MNEs will target larger and politically connected firms for acquisition and as suppliers. Instead, the degree to which large and politically influential businesses benefit from privileged financial access or are constrained by less easy access to credit matters for how they perceive the risks and benefits of MNE entry and therefore their decision to support or oppose more open investment policies.

A financing constraints theory of FDI policy predicts investment policies will liberalize in the wake of disruptions to elites' privileged access to finance, as credit environments become increasingly constrained for lengthy periods of time, and that the political support for liberalization will emanate from large domestic firms. It also predicts financing constraints will disproportionately lead to liberalization of more capital-intensive industries and that financing-constraints-induced policy changes will be more pronounced in countries with political institutional environments that amplify business interests.

Chapter 4 presents a series of quantitative tests of the effect of financing constraints on changes in foreign equity restrictions. By leveraging a variety of measures of FDI restrictions across a series of models, I am able to cover a total of 180 countries from 1970 to 2015. I use both national aggregates of foreign investment restrictions for 68 countries from 1973 to 2000, measured both as a percentage of industries in which foreign firms are denied majority stakes and as a simple indicator for policy environments that impose substantial restrictions on inward FDI, and changes to investment regulations from 2000 to 2015 to model the relationship between privileged access to finance, FDI policy, and a variety of other political, economic, and demographic factors that may influence government policies toward foreign investment. To confront concerns about endogeneity and confounding variables, I use error correction and Granger causality techniques to strengthen confidence in the relationship between declining privileged access to finance and FDI liberalization. I also explore how the relationship between changes in financing constraints and FDI policies are conditioned by domestic political institutions. I find evidence that decreases in privileged access to credit are associated with subsequent liberalizations of FDI policy, but only when domestic political institutions favor business interests.

Chapter 5 leverages firm- and industry-level data sources to probe more carefully the causal mechanisms that may lead from changes to domestic credit allocation process to FDI policy reforms. Specifically, I explore two questions. First, I consider how firm-level characteristics and country-level variations in banking sector and FDI policies influences firms' perceptions of financing constraints. Second, I use industry-level data on policy reforms to explore whether and how the capital intensity of industries affects the propensity to liberalize FDI policy. Jointly, these additional tests help to disentangle the mechanisms that tie banking sector reforms to subsequent FDI policy changes.

Chapters 6 and 7 use a comparative case study design to trace the development of FDI policy in Malaysia and Indonesia from 1965 to 2013. I demonstrate how different banking sector policy developments through three distinct periods of these countries' economic histories affected elite interests, and accordingly elite lobbying and ensuing policy outcomes, over restrictiveness toward FDI. Over the time period I cover, Malaysia has more consistently pursued banking sector deepening that has supported gradual liberalization of FDI policies with limited backsliding. In contrast, Indonesian governments have more often pursued policies designed to maintain substantial control over domestic credit allocation decisions and therefore have had less elite support for loosening restrictions on FDI. However, while the *level* of FDI openness in Indonesia has consistently shown protectionist bias, a period of rapid banking sector deregulation in the 1980s did lead to a period of limited liberalization. These policy developments, along with documentation of elite lobbying activities toward FDI policy at the time, provide further evidence that declining elite access to subsidized lending affects FDI policy *changes*. Subsequent state consolidation of the banking sector in Indonesia has led to reform stagnation and reversal, illustrating FDI policy can be subject to a partial reform equilibrium as well as increased protectionism even in a global environment of overwhelming economic integration.

While regime management of interethnic political cleavages initially led the Malaysia government to cautiously embrace highly regulated foreign investors as a way of limiting the economic dominance of non-*bumiputera* capitalists, Indonesia's tight alliance between the military, ruling party, and ethnic Chinese financiers provided the political logic for largely excluding foreign capital from direct investment in the local economy. The Indonesian government's policy of banking deregulation in the 1980s in response to tight global credit conditions and elite interest in establishing private banks linked to powerful domestic conglomerates, however, created local elite support for limited FDI reforms so that, by 1997, Indonesia's FDI polices were slightly less restrictive than were Malaysia's. Divergent crisis response strategies to the 1997 Asian financial crisis led to substantial liberalization of credit allocation in Malaysia, while Indonesia's foreign-bank-led financial-sector restructuring did little to force fundamental changes in the way banks make debt financing decisions and insulated the state from needing to privatize its extensive state-owned banking system. As a result, Indonesian business interests have successfully blocked attempts to implement large-scale liberalization of FDI beyond the initial IMF-imposed policy changes in 1998 and 1999. In contrast, the Malaysian business community has largely supported, and in many cases driven, more fundamental liberalization of FDI policy. These findings point to micro-level support of the expectation that financial-sector liberalization shifts preferences of politically important business interests toward favoring opening to FDI.

In the final chapter, I consider the implications of the financing constraints theory and evidence for our broader understanding of the distributive politics that undergird governments' treatment of MNEs and inward FDI. Unlike previous theories of FDI liberalization, this book provides substantial evidence that openness toward foreign investment is often pursued for the benefit of large domestic business interests. Rather than disrupting incumbent advantages, investment liberalization may benefit the largest and most politically influential firms in a local economy while disadvantaging smaller firms and even workers.

These distributive implications are important. They suggest political economy scholarship on economic liberalization should pay closer attention to how actors' size and power resources influence their adaptive capabilities. Adaptation is a privilege of the powerful and well connected. Therefore, large changes in the regulation of the local economy may reinforce inequalities as actors with the resources to adapt to changing environmental conditions gain further advantages over actors too vulnerable to acclimate meaningfully to changing economic structures. The ability to realize large increasing returns to scale may reinforce the dominance of industry giants and large diversified conglomerates over smaller economic units. If correct, these dynamics will require political economists and policymakers to consider more carefully the ways in which globalization disadvantages small units over large and reinforces and accelerates preexisting inequalities rather than moderating them, and potential policy options that may help reverse the worse excesses of globalization-induced inequalities in order to provide continued support for economic integration and an open global society.

2 | *Describing FDI Policy through Time and Space*

A defining feature of our current globally integrated economy is the ubiquity of multinational enterprises (MNEs) and a general consensus among policy elites that foreign direct investment (FDI) is broadly beneficial to local development. Disaggregated production networks increasingly define the patterns and trajectories of economic activities and FDI flows. Trade in intermediate goods and services now comprise 70 percent of global trade.[1] Participation in global value chains is associated with economic growth rates two percentage points above the global average.[2] And FDI stocks and global value chain participation are strongly correlated, particularly in developing countries.[3] This suggests that the extent to which a country permits and attracts foreign direct investors is central to its economic fortunes. Indeed, the general sense among scholars of capital markets and macroeconomic management is that FDI constitutes the "good cholesterol" of a capital flows diet.[4]

Despite all the reputed macroeconomic health benefits of FDI, most governments still retain a surprising degree of regulatory authority over inward direct investment. And while the general trend from the 1970s to the early 2000s was a large and sustained liberalization of FDI restrictions, substantial variations – particularly at the industry level – remained throughout the period. In today's climate of anti-globalization and anti-Washington Consensus backlash, we may even be seeing a rise in barriers to particular kinds of FDI. According to the United Nations Conference on Trade and Development's (UNCTAD) continual monitoring of investment policies globally, new restrictive policy measures increased from 6 percent of all investment

---

[1] Organisation for Economic Co-operation and Development et al. (2014).
[2] United Nations Conference on Trade and Development (2013b).
[3] United Nations Conference on Trade and Development (2013b).
[4] Hausmann and Fernández-Arias (2000). In this analogy, portfolio investment and foreign bank lending constitute the "bad cholesterol."

regulation changes in 2000 to 27 percent in 2013.[5] Thus, at the policy implementation level, considerations other than technocratically-guided macroeconomic management influence laws and practices related to FDI.

In this chapter, I provide contextual and descriptive information to help readers better understand how FDI policy fits into broader decisions about how a country chooses to integrate into global capital markets, how FDI policy has changed over time, what regulation over FDI policy actually entails, where regulatory authority tends to reside, and how various researchers have chosen to measure the FDI policy environment. In doing so, I provide readers a richer understanding of the contours of regulation over multinational firms before proceeding to theory and hypothesis testing.

In the remainder of the chapter, I discuss the relationship between FDI policy and the capital account, and then I explain why it is useful to think about the politics of FDI reform separately from the rationale and political economy that explain policy decisions over the short-term capital account. Next, I provide a brief overview of general trends in FDI policy from the early twentieth century to today. In this section, I demonstrate that the politics of FDI regulation is not a story of liberalization from a starting state of closure. Instead, like other components of economic activity, FDI goes through liberalizing and protectionist cycles. Third, I explain how governments generally regulate FDI, emphasizing the relationship between legal codes that are normally within the purview of the legislative branch and regulatory implementation, which is often characterized by substantial deference to the bureaucracy. I then describe and compare different measures of FDI regulation. No single existing measure is perfect either in concept construction or country and temporal coverage. However, used collectively, they cover over 180 countries and have temporal coverage from 1970 until 2015.

Capital Account Openness and FDI Policy

Why should we consider policies of openness toward FDI as part of a separate logic of liberalization than capital account openness more generally? In contrast to the relatively small literature on the politics

---

[5] United Nations Conference on Trade and Development (2014), xxii.

of FDI policies,[6] there is a much larger literature on capital account liberalization more broadly. Scholars have debated extensively both the macroeconomic effects of an open capital account and the political economy of capital controls and liberalizations. Much of these debates have focused primarily, either explicitly or through implicit mental models, on short-term capital account openness. Accordingly, the questions and theories that the literature on capital account openness tend to address are closely tied to the determinants and consequences of policies that allow "footloose" investment to slosh around the world. Frames of hypermobile and faceless capital investors map onto a collective mental model of what it means to live in a globalized world.

But the politics of regulations over FDI, or the long-term capital account, are distinct from those that influence the short-term capital account in several important respects. First, while there is much debate about the technocratic value of short-term capital account openness,[7] FDI is widely accepted as the most beneficial financial flow for development and the flow most robust to crisis. Some argue that FDI is not only resilient to macroeconomic shocks but can also accelerate recovery because of its ability to access home country finance when domestic credit is constrained. Thus, it is harder to argue that deviations from full FDI liberalization represent "good" policy.

Second, despite widespread technocratic agreement on the benefits of FDI, policies over FDI restrictions are both common and varied in ways that theories of aggregate capital account liberalization have a hard time explaining. While the nature of short-term capital restrictions are broad-based and affect all short-term financial

---

[6] The politics of FDI literature has tended instead to focus on questions of what entices firms to invest in particular locations and on the effects of FDI inflows on local economic growth and development.

[7] First, openness increases allocative efficiency by both increasing the supply of available capital and by correctly pricing debt (King and Levine, 1993). This is the primary benefit of openness – the increased availability of financial intermediation at market prices. Second, financial openness allows governments in low-savings countries to borrow internationally without negatively affecting domestic investors (Quinn and Inclan, 1997). There are other consequences that are less positive. First, increased volatility of capital flows can create costly exchange rate instability (Hays et al., 2003; Rojas-Suárez and Mathieson, 1993). Second, capital account liberalization may enhance the bargaining power of globally mobile firms vis-à-vis governments' taxation and macroeconomic policy (Hays et al., 2003; Przeworski and Wallerstein, 1988; Swank, 1992).

flows indiscriminately, FDI restrictions are often made at the industry level. This means that while countries may move toward liberalizing their long-term capital accounts, they may do so only partially and in distinct ways. Countries that pursue policies to liberalize FDI in many industries may still impose substantively important restrictions on direct investment into key domestic industries. Studying capital account liberalization in the aggregate makes it difficult to suss out the societal interests that underpin these industry-level variations in FDI policy as well as the political and institutional dynamics that lead to policy change.

Third, the most prominent theories in the capital account liberalization literature do not translate well to FDI. First, many scholars of capital account liberalization argue right-leaning politicians pursue more open capital accounts to constrain future (presumably leftist) governments from profligate spending.[8] According to these scholars, the consequences of capital account openness accrue primarily through the role that international investors play in discouraging governments from enacting fiscal policies that require high levels of borrowing and that often lead to inflationary pressures.[9] Thus, the politics of opening the capital account historically has been driven by partisanship and the political power of relatively unskilled labor.[10] Second, other scholars have emphasized the role of financial crises in forcing governments to open their capital accounts to ameliorate balance of payment problems quickly. While such a dynamic makes sense with respect to short-term, liquid financial flows, it is less relevant in the case of FDI. The primary reason is that direct investment deals take a long time to arrange and execute. With perhaps the exception of "fire-sale" FDI, meaning the quick acquisition of a local firm by a multinational during a crisis, FDI generally is not a good solution to short-term macroeconomic liquidity problems.

Finally, data indicate FDI policies and flows are not well correlated with short-term capital regulations and flows. A recently compiled dataset on disaggregated capital control measures for 100 countries

---

[8] Brooks (2007).

[9] Mosley (2003).

[10] Quinn and Inclan (1997). But note that Quinn and Inclan also find that partisanship receded in systematic importance in the 1980s, which they attribute to technological innovations and economic convergence that blunted both the costs and benefits of financial openness over time.

from 1995 to 2013 illustrates the extent to which FDI restrictions are relatively decoupled from other capital account policies.[11] This data source uses the International Monetary Fund's (IMF) *Annual Report on Exchange Arrangements and Exchange Restrictions* (AREAER) to determine the presence or absence of *de jure* restrictions on ten categories of financial assets for both inward and outward flows.[12] Comparison of direct investment restrictions versus restrictions in other asset classes reveals FDI regulation tends to diverge significantly from regulation of other financial vehicles. While money market, bond, equity, collective investment securities, and derivatives regulations display correlations with each other at or above 70 percent, regulations on direct investment inflows correlate at roughly 40 percent with these same asset classes.[13] When restricting comparisons to the 48 countries defined as "gate" countries, that is, countries that are most mixed in terms of their openness to financial flows, the correlation between regulations on direct investment inflows and money markets, bonds, and derivatives drops to 29, 23, and 19 percent, respectively.[14] While most asset classes display very high correlations between inflow and outflow regulations, the correlation between direct investment regulations on inflows and outflows is only 37 percent. This is the second lowest correlation among all asset classes,[15] and represents a significant departure from the more short-term financial asset classes I mention above, which all display correlations in policies toward their inflows and outflows above 70 percent.[16] Finally, examination of disaggregated gross and net capital flows finds that FDI flows behave quite differently from other more short-term financial flows and that FDI inflows are often negatively correlated with both portfolio equity and portfolio debt flows.[17] Clearly, FDI policy seems to follow a different logic from the regulation of short-term capital flows.

---

[11] Fernández et al. (2015).

[12] These categories include: money market instruments, bonds or other debt instruments with an original maturity of over 1 year, short-term equity, collective investment securities, financial credit, derivatives, commercial credits, guarantees and sureties, real estate, and direct investment.

[13] Fernández et al. (2015), 15.

[14] Ibid., 17.

[15] The lowest is real estate, which displays a 30 percent correlation between restrictions on inflows and outflows.

[16] Fernández et al. (2015), 15.

[17] Bluedorn et al. (2013), 20.

All of this suggests the politics of FDI regulation is sufficiently distinct from those of capital account regulation more generally to warrant separate analysis. Because FDI policy is set at the industry level, empirical analysis of the correlates of FDI liberalization can more tractably consider the heterogeneous preferences of societal interests to foreign direct investors. Changes in FDI policy occur frequently. The experience of many developing countries with FDI liberalization in the last 30 years has been a sweeping overhaul of FDI restrictions followed by partial policy reversals cast mostly at the industry level. Thus, the policies of FDI liberalization and restrictions provide a particularly rich environment to consider how particularistic interests affect policies of financial openness. In the sections that follow, I more fully address the history of FDI regulation across time and space, the mechanics of FDI regulation, and various approaches to measuring FDI restrictiveness.

Investment Policies in Historical Perspective

It is important to remember that strict regulation of foreign investment is a relatively novel phenomenon. International law has long protected foreign investors' property rights, particularly with respect to expropriation and compensation.[18] Right of establishment was hardly controversial through the nineteenth century, when much of the world was under colonial rule and when patterns of cross border investment typically sent capital from developed Western Europe to the cash-poor periphery. Most of this investment often took the form of investments in government bonds and was used for large-scale infrastructure projects.[19] Direct investment, although always the preferred method of cross-border capital flows for the United States, did not become an important source of international investment until the end of the nineteenth century and did not dominant portfolio flows until World War I.[20]

By the 1920s, the generally permissive stance toward inward FDI began to erode. As governments embraced varying degrees of statist

---

[18] Lipson (1985).

[19] Lipsey et al. (1999). However, see Lewis (1938) and Svedberg (1978) for arguments that direct investment figures for this time were much higher.

[20] Dunning (1970), Lipsey et al. (1999).

intervention in domestic economic development, foreign firms were viewed as impediments to domestic capital accumulation.[21] The rise of state-led industrialization entailed national planning; state-owned enterprise development; and state-driven, finance-created conditions conducive to powerful anti-FDI coalitions. State-owned banks created the capacity for local economies to marshal development finance without direct participation of foreign firms. These banks quickly took over foreign-owned companies. Governments increasingly declared that foreign investment could be undertaken only if firms could demonstrate how such projects would contribute to national development. In this new period of anti-FDI policy, Mexico and Turkey led the way.[22] Most starkly, Turkey's first president, Mustafa Kemal Ataturk, declared, "[W]e are always prepared to provide the necessary security to foreign capital *on the condition that its profits be regulated by law* [emphasis added]."[23] The era of FDI regulation had arrived.

The political coalitions fostered by state-led development strategies ossified resistance of locally operating firms to foreign control. Local firms profited from high tariffs and did not want domestic market-oriented foreign entrants to erode their profits. Where labor was well organized, workers benefited from the high wages earned in protected industries.[24] Managers of state-owned enterprises gained advantages from soft budget constraints that weakened competitive pressures and ensured the continued existence of even highly inefficient enterprises. State politico-bureaucrats who guided development policy benefited from their gatekeeper status. The 1960s saw additional erosion of international investment norms that protected foreign firms. Expropriation of foreign investment peaked in the early 1970s when governments began to target specific industries and firms. During this time, 75 percent of all takeovers were of enterprises that were wholly owned by foreigners. Only 4 percent of nationalizations during this time were of firms in which foreign investors held a minority stake.[25]

---

[21] Frieden (1981), Lipson (1985), Moran (1978).
[22] Lipson (1985).
[23] Quoted in Lipson (1985), 72.
[24] Teichman (1995, 2001).
[25] Lipson (1985).

Financial Repression and Statist Development

Antipathy toward FDI was supported and reinforced by government repression of the financial sector. Repressed financial systems are characterized by policies that give governments control over credit allocation either directly through state-owned banks or indirectly through guiding the lending portfolios maintained and interest rates charged by private banks.[26] State guidance of domestic banking and capital allocation was typical. A confluence of factors contributed to this, including postwar reconstruction efforts in Europe, economic nationalism in the wake of decolonization, the prevalence of statist development policies, and the Bretton Woods system of exchange rates that relied on extensive capital controls. Many states, both developing and wealthy, had large state development banking systems. Those that did not nonetheless often retained great control over the financial sector by maintaining bank licensing restrictions that led to highly concentrated, wholly domestically-owned banking sectors and excessive reserve requirements that channeled credit to favorite domestic industries, financed government spending, and generated seigniorage.[27]

The precise mechanisms through which governments maintained this system of financial repression varied across regions and states. In much of Latin America, state-owned development banks were the backbone of government repression of the financial sector. In some countries in the region, highly concentrated private banks characterized the financial sector, but the region experienced multiple large-scale bank nationalizations during the mid-twentieth century. In East Asia, governments often preferred to use interest rate controls and targeted subsidies to support large conglomerates of financial and industrial interests.[28] The *chaebols* of South Korea and the *keiretsus* of Japan are prominent examples. In communist Eastern Europe and Central Asia, central planning channeled all investment decisions through the state.[29] In resource-rich countries, financial repression was easier as governments were able to use their royalty payments to establish state banks and sovereign wealth funds.[30] In Africa, the continued weakness

---

[26] McKinnon (1973).
[27] Brooks and Kurtz (2012).
[28] Haggard (1990), Haggard et al. (1993).
[29] Denizer et al. (1998).
[30] Zarra-Nezhad et al. (2012).

of domestic banking sectors across the region is often considered to be the direct result of high levels of repression.[31] Regardless of the precise method, the outcome was largely the same – government control over investment allocation decisions.

Financial repression was not just a tool of authoritarian regimes. Theories that emphasize median voter dynamics often argue democracies will be less able to pursue financial repression because borrowers, who face high interest rates under financial repression, have more political voice in such regimes. However, there remain many prominent examples of financial repression under democracy, and this may reflect both the complexity of domestic interests over financial liberalization and collective action dynamics.[32] In particular, large industrial firms may have preferences complementary to those of the financial sector. Large industrial incumbents have a financing advantage over smaller rivals and may prefer higher borrowing costs as a way to freeze out potential competitors.[33] If borrower preferences are not homogenous, effective mobilization to end the use of policies of financial repression will be difficult. Furthermore, financial repression may be a particularly useful tactic of industrial control for democracies because technical policies such as interest rate controls and high reserve requirements are likely to be opaque and of low salience to voters.[34]

FDI Liberalization Trends

While most accounts of domestic and international politics surrounding FDI place the bulk of analysis on developing host states and developed home economies, the majority of FDI occurs among developed countries, and these countries also have a history of regulating foreign direct entry.[35] Many European countries promulgated investment screening mechanisms mid-century in order to minimize foreign acquisitions.[36] For example, Sweden made all foreign acquisitions subject to government review in 1973 and also required foreign investors

---

[31] Andrianaivo and Yartey (2010).
[32] Pepinsky (2013a).
[33] Rajan and Zingales (2003).
[34] Ibid.
[35] Seminal analyses of FDI policy regimes include Vernon (1971), Evans (1979), Lipson (1985).
[36] Blomstrom and Kokko (1997), Michalet (1997), Safarian (1999).

to source at least 50 percent of capital overseas.[37] France had similar investment screening provisions that were only relaxed for non-EU-originating FDI in 1992.[38] Japan also greatly restricted inward FDI for much of this period.

The neoliberal period, however, saw a general movement toward decreased restrictions on foreign equity globally. Starting in the 1970s and accelerating through the 1990s, wealthy and developing countries alike across various regions substantially liberalized their FDI policy regime as they largely abandoned central planning and indigenous development models in favor of economic liberalization and structural adjustment. Moves toward openness were not confined to developing countries. Figure 2.1 illustrates the average level of foreign equity openness, defined as the percentage of industries that restrict FDI to minority ownership, as well as the sample standard deviation for the time period 1973 through 2000.[39] Over this time, FDI policies across developed and developing countries experienced convergence toward a policy environment more statutorily open to direct investment by foreigners.

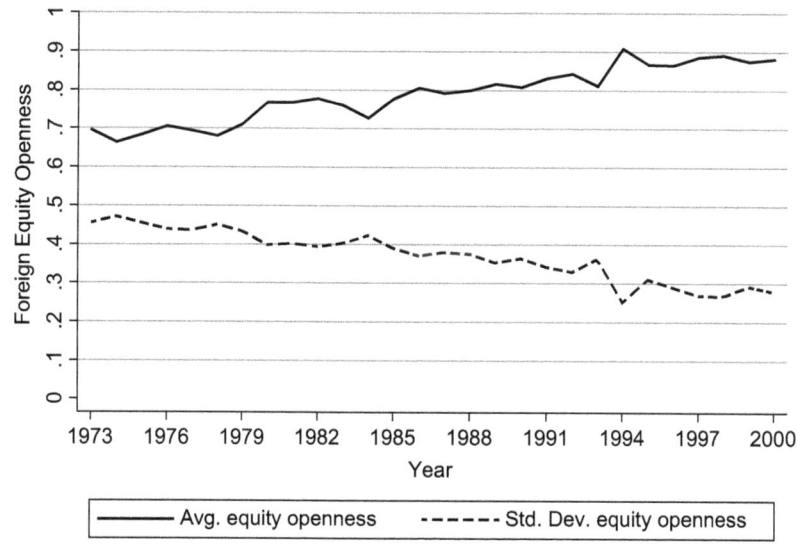

Figure 2.1 Equity restrictions over time

[37] Blomstrom and Kokko (1997), 367.
[38] Michalet (1997), 330.
[39] Pandya (2013).

Despite this macro-level convergence, variation continues to persist. Most countries pursue a complex set of investment policies designed to attract certain types of FDI inflows, particularly manufacturing, while repelling foreign investment in other areas of the economy.[40] Since 2000, the percentage of yearly changes in national investment policies that are more restrictive has steadily risen from 6 to 25 percent. Restrictive investment policy changes are not isolated to developing countries. In 2012, the largest share of restrictive policy changes occurred in developed countries.[41] Countries also vary in the extent to which they use centralized screening mechanisms to approve investment projects with foreign participation; such approval processes tend to have a chilling effect on cross-border mergers and acquisitions.[42] Figure 2.2 shows how screening processes had progressively liberalized

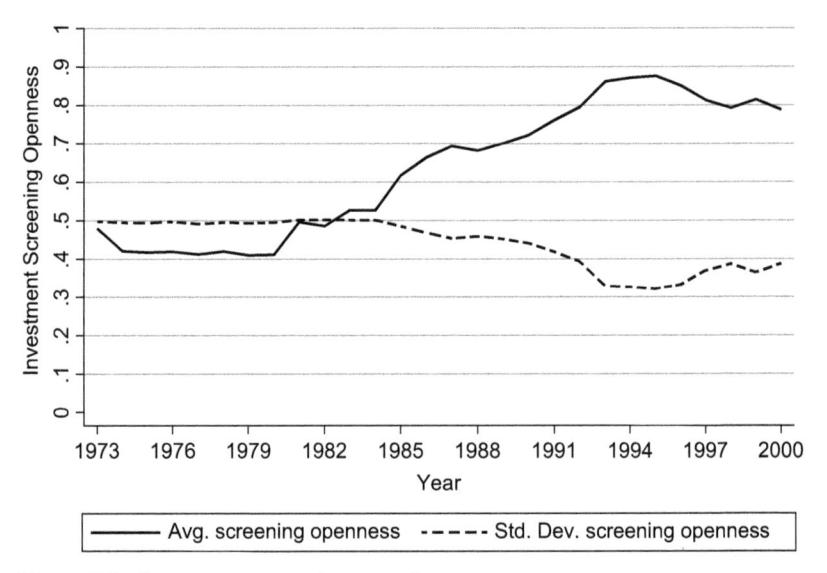

Figure 2.2 Investment screening over time

[40] Golub (2009), United Nations Conference on Trade and Development (2013b).
[41] United Nations Conference on Trade and Development (2013b), 93.
[42] Taylor (2000), United Nations Conference on Trade and Development (2013b), 98.

through the early 1990s but experienced a reversal in the second half of the decade.[43]

Since 2000 and especially since the Global Recession of 2008, many governments have further tightened investment approval requirements. UNCTAD estimates 30 percent of all cross-border mergers and acquisitions (M&As) withdrawn after announcement in 2010 were due to restrictive investment policies.[44] The total value of M&As withdrawn for regulatory reasons between 2008 and 2012 approximated $265 billion, or about 10 percent of cross-border deals concluded over the same time period.[45] A recent analysis of G20 policy and trends toward trade and investment found that G20 governments implemented almost 350 measures that harmed foreign investors in the first 8 months of 2016.[46] The same report found that G20 governments have implemented almost as many restrictive policies toward FDI since 2008 as liberalizing ones.[47] While global FDI as a percentage of world GDP grew from approximately 1 to 4 percent from 1990 to 2000, its role in the global economy declined after 2007 and is now around 2 percent of world GDP.[48] According to UNCTAD, while 85 percent of all investment-related policy changes in 2015 were liberalizing, a significant subset of regulatory measures were restrictive.[49] Of these, almost all relate to entry and establishment, and developed countries account for a disproportionate share of these restrictions, most related to strategic industries such as agriculture, real estate, and infrastructure.

In sum, government regulations over foreign direct investors is generally much more liberalized today than it was in 1970, but important variations persist. In particular, while developing and developed countries alike embrace the importance of foreign investment for economic growth both rhetorically and in practice, discontent over the distribution of benefits to such investment has grown since the 2000s.

---

[43] Pandya (2013).
[44] United Nations Conference on Trade and Development (2013b), 97.
[45] United Nations Conference on Trade and Development (2013b), 8, 97.
[46] Evenett and Fritz (2016), 7.
[47] Ibid.
[48] Ibid., 9.
[49] United Nations Conference on Trade and Development (2016c), 93.

Governments increasingly view their role in regulating multinationals as active managers – encouraging investment in priority sectors and erecting barriers to entry in areas for which FDI is considered unnecessary or detrimental to national economic policy objectives. Indeed, the recurring theme at the fourteenth convention of UNCTAD in June 2016 was a call from high-level governmental officials to preserve states' "right to regulate" foreign investment in the service of broader public policy goals.[50] In other words, investment policies globally remain varied, complex, and bidirectional.

Regulating FDI

One of the challenges of studying FDI regulations is their complexity. Because multinational participation in local ownership markets intersects with multiple regulatory issues such as business licensing, trade, labor, finance, intellectual property protections, and infrastructure, no one regulatory agency can completely "own" policies toward foreign direct investment. This makes the regulatory environment over FDI complex, confusing, sometimes contradictory, and often a space of inadequate coordination among partner ministries or agencies.[51] Scholars interested in rigorously comparing investment regimes across countries and through time have responded to the challenge of measuring FDI policies in a systematic way by paying careful attention to both the policy bodies and texts through which regulations emerge and by categorizing FDI regulation by what component of the investment life cycle it affects.

Of first concern to those interested in the politics that undergird national FDI policy decision-making is the location of regulator authority over foreign investors within the government. For the most part, investment policy stems first from the national legal code, which is promulgated through a government's legislative body. Investment or company laws, therefore, provide the legal basis on which a government's regulatory authority rests. However, these laws often reserve a great deal of policy autonomy and flexibility for regulatory agencies in the executive branch. Sometimes, these laws create investment boards, which are regulatory bodies tasked with reviewing and approving

---

[50] Author observation, Nairobi, Kenya, July 17–22, 2016.
[51] Interview, World Bank official, January 17, 2017.

foreign entry as well as providing guidance on entry and operation procedures to multinational firms. Other times, these laws vest regulatory authority in preexisting and related agencies such Japan's powerful Ministry of International Trade and Industry (later, the Ministry of Economy, Trade, and Industry), which can coordinate FDI regulation with other macroeconomic policy objectives of the agency. The broader point, however, is that, while investment law provides the rough contours of FDI regulation, executive branch agencies often retain a great deal of authority in interpreting, reviewing, and adjusting finer details. This means many of the most consequential decisions regarding investment regulation happen within the bureaucracy and with little legislative oversight.

It is important to note that federal systems further complicate the question of where regulatory authority lies, particularly over investment promotion policies. For the purposes of this study, however, I restrict analysis to national-level regulations. This is defensible for several reasons. First, most countries are unitary systems. Second, measurement limitations make it difficult to obtain measures of FDI regulation at the local level across time and space. Third, the theory that I present in Chapter 3 could easily apply to subnational political dynamics as well. That is, I have no reason to expect that investment policies set at the local level should follow a different political logic. Finally, while local governments in federal systems can modify policies toward multinational firms at the margins, national policies still set the baseline for how FDI is treated.

In the remainder of this section, I briefly describe the development of investment and company law since the 1970s and then outline the categories of investment-related policy measures that are typically viewed as most relevant for understanding the local investment policy environment.

Investment/Company Law

Many countries, particularly developing ones, have enacted investment or company laws in recent decades. Some of these laws, particularly older ones, are *foreign* investment laws; that is, they establish through the legal code a set of rules regarding the regulation of foreign investors that is separate and distinct from domestic investors. In more recent years, however, and with the guidance of international development organizations such as UNCTAD, countries have increasingly moved toward investment laws that combine regulation of domestic and foreign investors. According to UNCTAD, at least 108 countries currently have an investment law in place.[52] However, in my own review of all investment laws made available in UNCTAD's Investment Laws of the World series, which catalogues all available investment laws globally from 1973 to the present, I found a total of 288 laws. Many countries have had multiple laws, with each new one replacing the last.

While each law varies in its regulatory effect and in the degree to which the law establishes a liberal or protectionist environment toward foreign investors, most of these laws share several key characteristics. First, these laws tend to provide regulations over entry with respect to industry-specific caps on foreign equity, minimum capital requirements for foreign investment, and regulations over foreign access to land and real estate. These laws also establish procedures for the authorization and administration of investments, usually through a specific lead agency. Second, these laws provide a series of measures regarding treatment and operation. These include investor rights and guarantees around national treatment, compensation in the event of expropriation, and the right to transfer capital across borders. Many laws also include provisions related to the obligations of investors, particularly around compliance with local laws, corporate disclosure, and protection of labor rights. Finally, many but not the majority of such laws include provisions related to investment promotion and facilitation, particularly with respect to investment promotion agencies, investment incentives, and investment facilitation tools such as "one-stop shops" for assisting foreign investors with registration requirements.

Figure 2.3 uses data I collected on all investment laws from 1973 to 2013 to illustrate the frequency with which governments promulgated investment laws during the time period.[53] We see a good deal of activity, with most years recording at least five new investment laws globally. The decade between 1990 and 2000 shows the highest frequency of investment law promulgation, with 1991 recording the most new laws in a single year. This is unsurprising because newly formed countries in the aftermath of the collapse of the Soviet system now needed laws and regulations over their economies.

[52] United Nations Conference on Trade and Development (2016b).
[53] UNCTAD's Investment Laws of the World (2013).

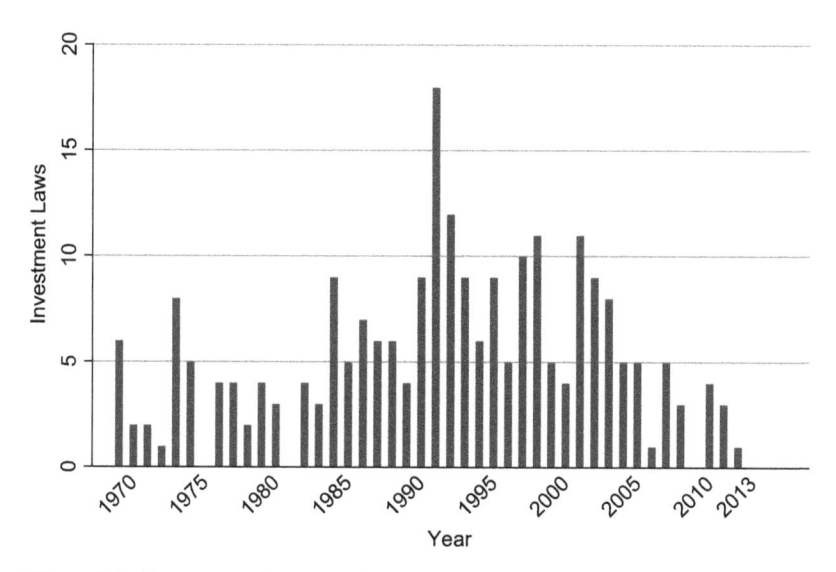

Figure 2.3   Investment law over time

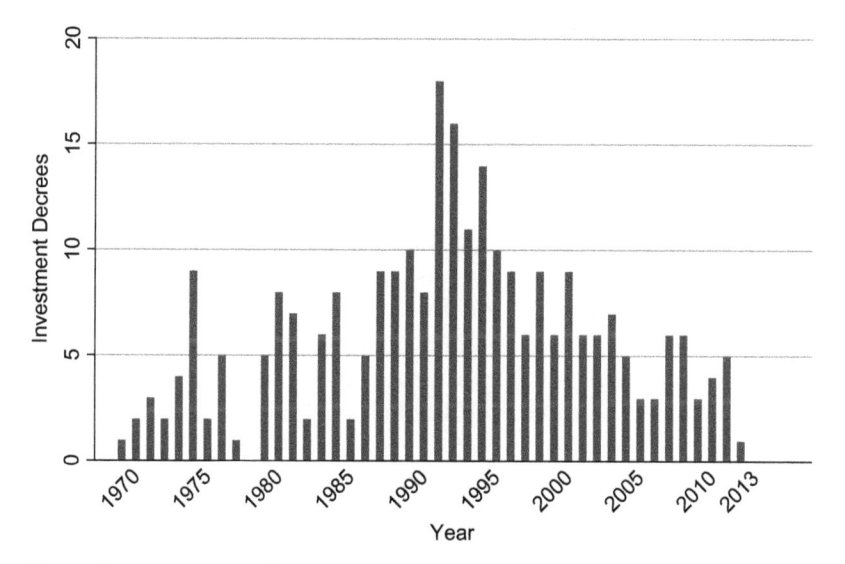

Figure 2.4   Investment decrees over time

As mentioned above, while investment laws often form the basis of the FDI regulation regime, most countries imbue a considerable degree of authority over investment regulatory decision making in the executive. Figure 2.4 shows the prevalence of investment policy decrees made during this time period.[54] We can immediately see that executive decrees have been issued more frequently than have investment laws and that the peak of decrees lasted slightly longer in the early 1990s.

Right of Entry

Regulations defining right of entry entail measures related to the requirements and restrictions associated with establishing a foreign-owned subsidiary in a local jurisdiction. According to UNCTAD's Investment Policy Monitor, countries have implemented a total of 403 regulations related to right of entry from January 2010 to May 2017 alone.[55] These types of regulations are most critical to defining a country's policy stance toward FDI because entry requirements function as the gate through which any foreign investment must enter. These rules are often established through investment laws that codify the process through which foreign investment may enter the country and any limitations on foreign ownership or acquisition of domestic assets. At the same time, many investment laws provide the executive branch with the authority to update regularly a list of industries for which foreign ownership is restricted.[56]

Along with equity restrictions on foreign investors' ability to own and control local investments, right of entry regulations also include policies related to foreigners' access to land and whether there exist any screening requirements through which investment must be authorized. Many countries, particularly postcolonial ones, have constitutionally mandated restrictions on foreign ownership of domestic land. In these circumstances, laws and regulations related to landownership and long-term leases can create significant barriers to foreign investors' ability to enter a local economy. While most countries have ended or curtailed their use of screening procedures in recent years, in some sectors and in some economies, all potential foreign investment, or investments of sufficient size, must be approved by the central

---

[54] Ibid.

[55] UNCTAD (2017).

[56] This is called a negative list. Previously, most countries maintained a positive list, meaning FDI was restricted from all sectors unless the positive list explicitly allowed it. Most countries have switched to negative lists in which foreign equity holdings are allowed unless the list provides an industry-specific carve out.

government before proceeding. These sorts of requirements are not just relevant in developing countries. Many advanced industrial economies such as Canada, the United Kingdom, and the United States have some amount of governmental review of large foreign investment projects, particularly for M&A. In March 2016, Australia increased its regulatory authority to screen large infrastructure investments, even for projects that are not owned by foreign enterprises.[57]

Treatment

Regulations regarding treatment have to do with measures that affect the ability of multinationals to operate freely in a jurisdiction once established and to do so in a way that discriminates against foreign firms in favor of domestic enterprises. These sorts of regulations therefore relate to the extent to which the host government retains the regulatory space to make operations more difficult for foreign firms. Measures in this category include whether a country has agreed to policies of nondiscrimination on the basis of owners' country of origin, policies toward nationalizations and expropriations, capital transfers and access to foreign exchange, operational conditions, and access to dispute settlement. Those familiar with the proliferation of bilateral investment treaties (BITs) and preferential trade agreements (PTAs) with investment chapters through the 1990s and early 2000s will recognize substantial overlap between the types of investor rights guaranteed through such international investment agreements (IIAs) and domestic policies related to treatment. This overlap is substantially different from that between entry rights and IIAs because most BITs do not cover preestablishment rights.[58] While changes to treatment measures were more common during the 1990s,[59] reforms in these areas

---

[57] The Treasury of Australian Government, *Critical Asset Sales to Fall within Foreign Review Net*, March 18, 2016.

[58] Historically, the United States is the only country that has insisted that BITs cover preestablishment. The U.S. BIT regime is very small compared to the universe of treaties, with just 46 as of May 2017 compared to 2,960 globally. Even for these treaties, signatory states have included a negative list for preentry rights exclusions. In recent years, Canada and Japan have also begun to include preestablishment provisions in their model BITs, but for the most part, BITs rarely commit signatories to liberalizing commitments around right of entry and establishment.

[59] Kobrin (2005).

have decreased. From 2010 to May 2017, 138 measures related to treatment of foreign investors were implemented globally.[60]

Promotion

Regulations regarding promotion concern measures governments take to facilitate investment in particular priority sectors or in specific geographic locations. These regulations include the establishment of investment promotion agencies tasked with facilitating investment, tax incentives available to qualified investment projects, and the creation and maintenance of special economic zones that provide special treatment to foreign firms. Incentives and promotion have become a focal point for much of investment policy because there is a growing desire on the part of governments to manage their investment policies so that they attract investment projects that each government deems beneficial to broader policy objectives while discouraging or denying entry to projects that are considered harmful for one reason or another. According to UNCTAD's Investment Policy Monitor, countries have implemented a total of 239 new regulations related to promotion from January 2010 to May 2017. As with the other forms of investment policy, the authority to set and implement promotion measures is split between the legislative branch, which authorizes incentive programs through laws on investment promotion, and the bureaucracy, which often retains the authority and flexibility to modify tax incentives and other facilitation strategies to align with broader government development policy objectives.

Patterns of Investment Policy Implementation

Figure 2.5 uses UNCTAD data on investment measures from 2000 to 2015 to illustrate the frequency with which measures related to each of the categories listed above have been implemented worldwide. We see first that investment policies are far from static. In most years, countries collectively institute more than 100 new measures related to foreign investment. We also see that most of these changes to investment law are liberalizing but that the percentage of measures that have restrictive effects has risen in recent years, particularly following the global financial crisis.

[60] UNCTAD Investment Policy Monitor, accessed May 10, 2017.

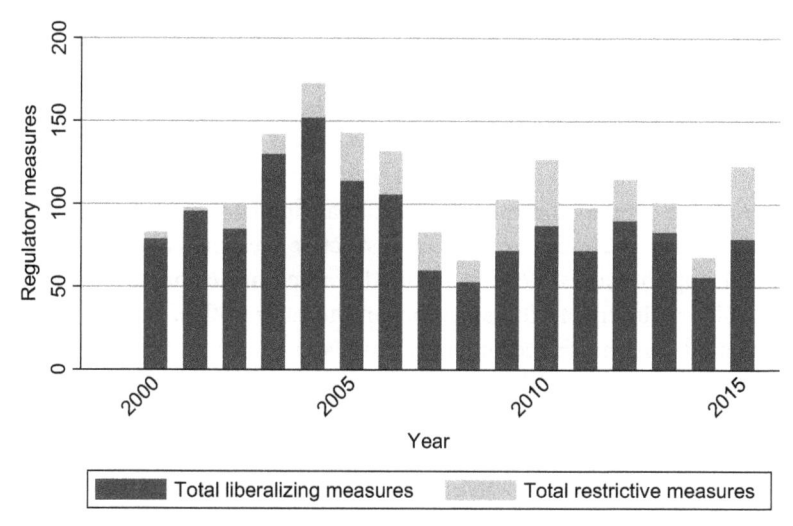

Figure 2.5 Total FDI regulatory measures, 2000–2015
Source: UNCTAD Investment Policy Monitor

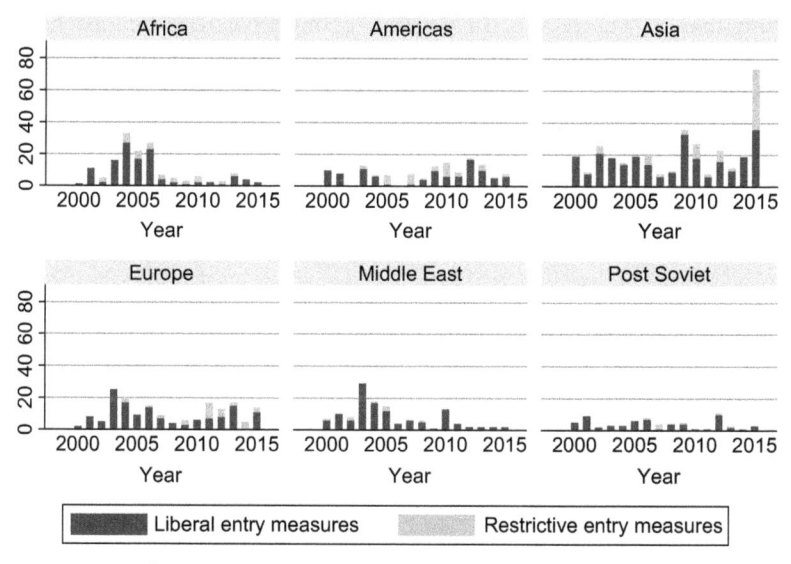

Figure 2.6 Changes to entry regulation, 2000–2015
Source: UNCTAD Investment Policy Monitor

As mentioned above, we can disaggregate FDI regulation into three distinct categories: entry, treatment, and promotion. To what extent can we find patterns in regulatory changes both within these categories and across space? Figure 2.6 looks at changes to entry requirements across six world regions, as defined by the UN: Africa, the Americas, Asia, Europe, the Middle East, and post-Soviet Union countries. We can quickly see that Asian economies have experienced the most change in entry regulation over this time period. Most of these changes have be liberalizing, except that restrictive measures began to rise in importance around the time of the global financial crisis and spiked precipitously in 2015. In that year, restrictive measures about equaled liberalizing measures. Beyond Asia, African countries pursued a spate of equity requirement liberalizations in the early 2000s, but this trend dissipated and more recent years have seen a larger proportion of restrictive measures. Other regions have seen relatively fewer changes to equity regulation, particularly post-Soviet Union countries. The Americas and Europe both display a similar pattern to Asia and Africa in that the ratio of restrictive to liberalizing measures has increased since about 2010.

Figure 2.7 looks at trends in changes to regulation over treatment of foreign firms. First, note that the scale in this figure is different from that in Figure 2.6. In general, countries across regions have implemented comparatively fewer treatment measures during this time period than measures related to entry. However, the ratio of restrictive

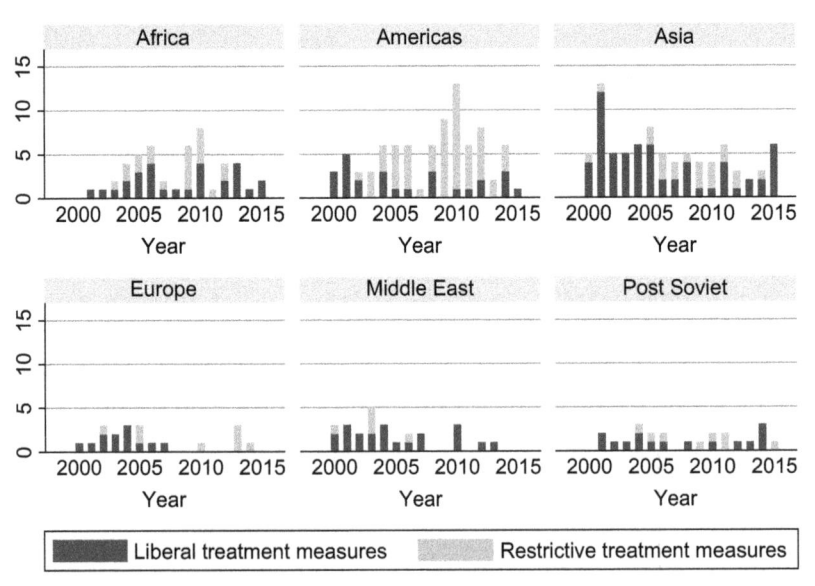

Figure 2.7 Changes to treatment regulation, 2000–2015
Source: UNCTAD Investment Policy Monitor

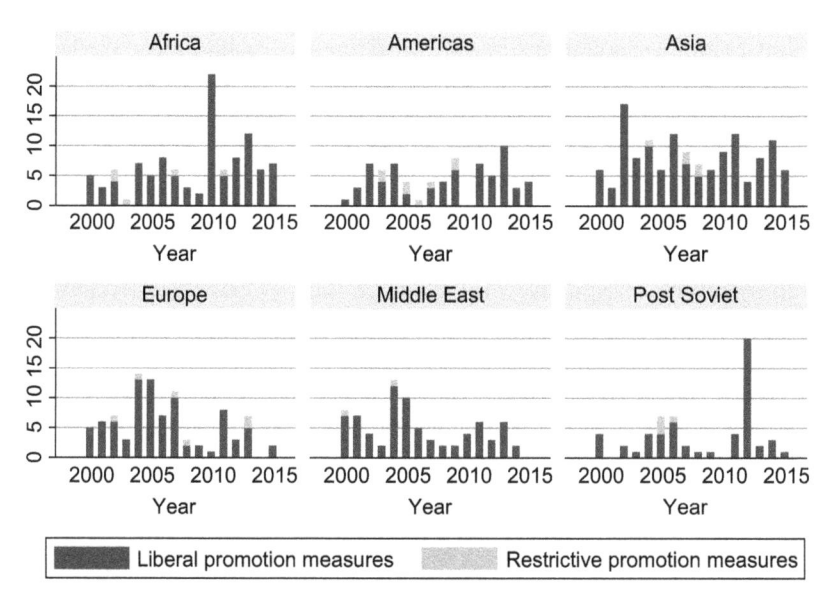

Figure 2.8 Changes to promotion regulation, 2000–2015
Source: UNCTAD Investment Policy Monitor

to liberalizing measures appears to be higher for treatment measures, particularly in the Americas and Africa. Since 2010, Europe has only passed restrictive measures. Figure 2.8 shows a stronger commitment to liberalizing promotion measures across regions. Asia and Africa (after 2009) are the most active regions in this category of investment regulation. It is unsurprising that promotion policies are mostly liberalizing in nature because these policies are usually designed to target particular kinds of investment that are seen as most beneficial to the local economy.

Comparing Broad Measures of Investment Climate

Given the complexity of investment regulation, it is perhaps unsurprising that several measures of national investment climates exist. Most of these measures rely on a combination of governmental and supranational official documents to chronicle the extent of preestablishment and treatment regulations in measured countries over time. One compiles expert surveys to determine qualitatively the extent to which foreign investors are impeded from local operations through regulatory measures. Many of these measures use indexing techniques that combine regulations in various domains – such as entry restrictions and restrictions on overseas worker visas – into a single measure. While these measures have the benefit of a more inclusive conception of what constitutes FDI openness and restrictiveness, they also make it difficult to isolate the specific categories of FDI regulation that change within a country over time. All measures attempt to focus only on components of investment regulation that discriminate between domestic and foreign investors. That is, countries may have regulations that impede business formation and operations, such as onerous and lengthly business registration requirements, that negatively affect local and foreign investors equally. Measures of FDI policy, however, are concerned only with components of the regulatory regime that apply disproportionately toward foreign firms.

At least four widely known measures of FDI regulation have some time-series component.[61] First, the Fraser Institute's annual *Economic Freedom of the World* report has a question on foreign ownership and investment restrictions since 1995. The index covers up to 158 countries, but earlier dates in the dataset tend to have more missing data. This measure uses expert surveys from the World Economic Forum's *Global Competitiveness Report* to generate a score based on Likert-type scale responses to two questions: "How prevalent is foreign ownership of companies in your country?" and "How restrictive are regulations in your country relating to international capital flows?"[62] While this measure may be useful for measuring investor sentiment regarding the local investment climate, it does not measure the specifics of investment regulation and policy. Some might also question the validity of the measure because it is administered by a libertarian think tank.

Figure 2.9 provides the regional average for the index across seven regions from 1995 to 2014.[63] Visual inspection illustrates some of the problems with this measure. First, for most regions, the average index value starts at relatively high levels and declines substantially directly

---

[61] In addition, the World Bank developed several measures of FDI restrictions through its Investing Across Borders Initiative. This project made data available for 87 economies in 2010. Unfortunately, the dataset will not be developed into a time series due to some complaints by powerful bank members (Interview with Bank Official, January 2017).

[62] Gwartney et al. (2016), 280.

[63] Fraser (2015).

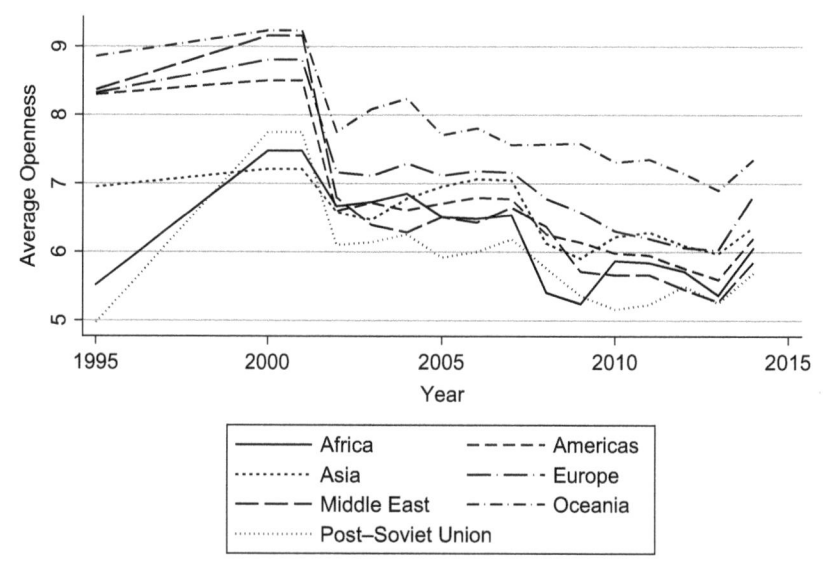

Figure 2.9 Fraser investment freedom index by region, 1995–2014

after 2000. This is largely driven by patterns of data missing in earlier years of the index. Countries included in 2000 and before tend to be wealthier countries with a longer history of economic openness. This skews the data substantially. In addition, the downward trend from 2001 onward for all regions is suspect. The fact that this index relies on expert surveys leaves the measure vulnerable to general negative sentiment over the state of the global economy and shifting expectations of what "liberal" and "restrictive" policies look like.

Second, the Heritage Foundation, another libertarian think tank, includes a measure of investment freedom in its annual *Index of Economic Freedom* that covers up to 186 countries from 1995 to 2017, but in practice many developing countries have missing data early in the temporal coverage.[64] This measure, in contrast to the Fraser Institute's index, is rooted in the regulatory environment. Specifically, the measure creates a point scale in which higher values indicate more openness for six areas: national treatment of the foreign investment, the foreign investment code, restrictions on landownership, sectoral investment restrictions, foreign exchange controls, and capital controls. These data are obtained from a variety of sources including

[64] Heritage Foundation (2017).

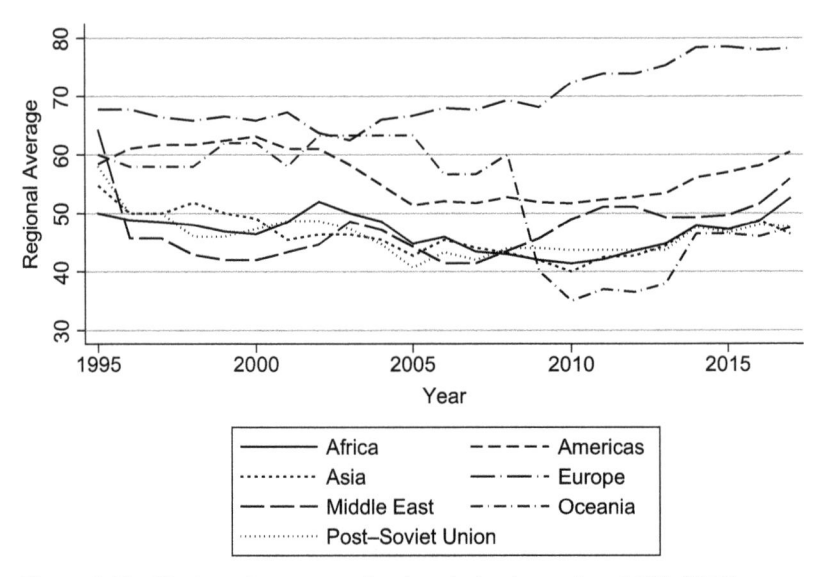

Figure 2.10 Heritage investment freedom index by region, 1995–2017

official government publications, the Economist Intelligence Unit's country commerce reports, Office of the U.S. Trade Representative, and the U.S. Department of Commerce's Country Commercial Guides.

Figure 2.10 provides regional averages for this index from 1995 to 2017. We can see that this measure has far more stability than the Fraser Index. Only Europe has a relatively uninterupted increase in investment openness over the time sample. Most other regions experienced a dip through the early 2000s and then an increase back to 1995 levels by 2017. Oceania experienced a rather rapid decrease in openness just before 2010 and is less open today than in 1995. This is due in large part to a series of restrictions Australia has imposed on foreign investment in recent years.

Third, the Organization for Economic Cooperation and Development (OECD) FDI Regulatory Restrictiveness Index measure covers all OECD countries and a growing number of non-OECD economies that are G-20 members and/or adherents to the Declaration on International Investment and Multinational Enterprises for the years 1997, 2003, 2006, and 2010 to 2016.[65] This index measure four categories

---

[65] Kalinova et al. (2010), OECD (2017).

of restrictions: foreign equity limitations, screening and approval, restrictions on employment of foreigners, and operational restrictions. The main benefit of the OECD measure is that it disaggregates its index by 22 industries. OECD documents such as the country reservation list of the OECD Code of Liberalization of Capital Movements form the basis of the data that underlie the index. However, it is the measure with the least country and temporal coverage.

Figure 2.11 shows regional averages of the composite measure of FDI restrictiveness over the sample period, while Figure 2.12 illustrates trends in the underlying components of the index. Because this index is confined to OECD countries and a few other relatively large economies (mostly in Asia), there is far less variation in these data. We see that all regions experienced some degree of liberalization over the time period. Asia restricts FDI much more than other regions represented in the sample, but even Asia has experienced large-scale liberalization over the time period. The personnel component of the index has changed the least over the sample time period, while "other" restrictions that have to do mainly with treatment demonstrate the most variation among the index subcomponents.

Sonal Pandya's measure of equity restrictions covers 91 countries from 1970 to 2000 and calculates the percentage of industries

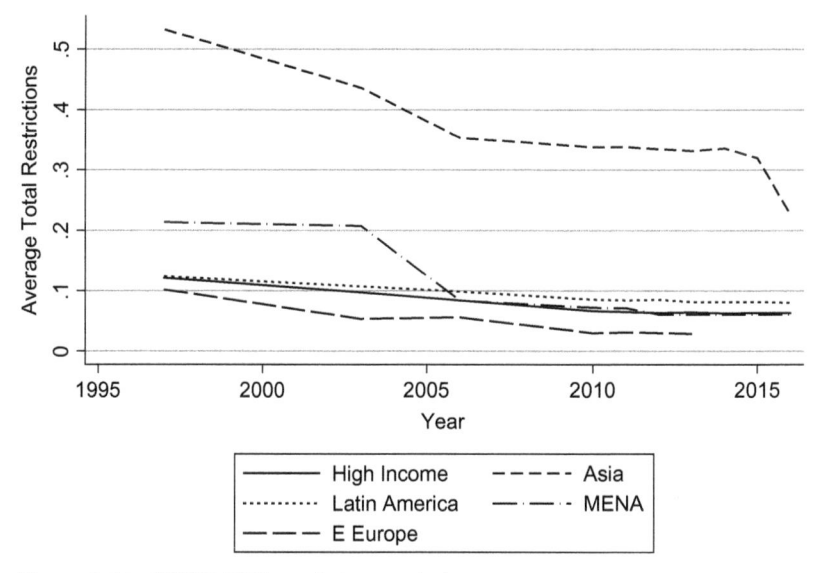

Figure 2.11   OECD FDI restrictiveness index

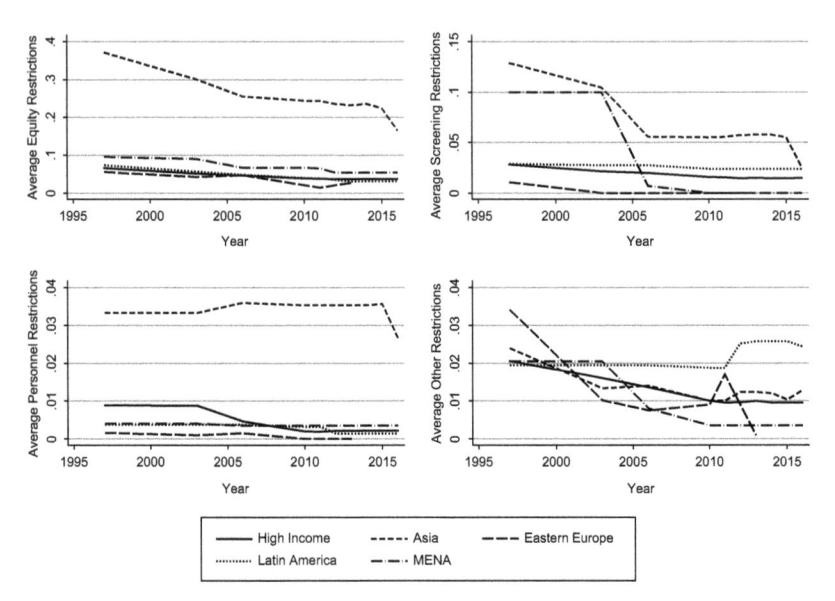

Figure 2.12 OECD FDI restrictiveness index, components

for which the national government maintains foreign equity restrictions such that multinationals cannot hold above a 49 percent stake in a domestically operating firm.[66] This formulation follows standard measurement practices in the trade literature that also create aggregated measures, often expressed as averages, from product-specific tariffs.[67] Pandya's dataset also provides a second variable that calculates the percentage of industries for which the national government maintains screening requirements before approving foreign investment projects.

Pandya uses U.S. Country Commerce Guides, which are authored by the U.S. Department of Commerce and the U.S. Department of State, and which detail statutory restrictions on foreign investment. Because she relies on U.S. data sources, Pandya's variable measures restrictions on U.S. firms. This raises the question of whether U.S. firms are subject to different equity rules than are firms headquartered in other home states. For instance, does Mexico allow U.S. firms to take on larger equity participation stakes in Mexican-based

---

[66] Pandya (2013).
[67] See Milner (1999) and Goldstein (2017) for discussions of average tariffs.

companies than European or Brazilian firms? In short, such discrimination in equity requirements rarely occurs. National investment laws that prescribe equity restrictions do so unilaterally – that is, restrictions are made against any foreign investor. One legal avenue through which equity restrictions may discriminate between source countries is through international investment agreements like BITs and investment chapters in PTAs because, unlike European countries, the United States has generally drafted its BITs to apply to right of establishment. By 2000, the United States had 30 BITs in force. However, in treaty annexes, countries are able to make exceptions to national treatment. For example, the U.S.-Ukraine BIT carves out various mining, media, shipping, and sensitive equipment manufacture for domestic Ukrainian firms.[68] The U.S.-Turkey BIT restricts U.S. firms from a wide array of business activities, including tobacco and retailing.[69] While the North American Free Trade Agreement (NAFTA) provided U.S. firms with certain treatment-related benefits such as access to investor-state dispute settlements that not all foreign firms were entitled to, it did not create a separate equity restrictions schedule for U.S. and Canadian firms relative to other other countries. The relatively high correlation between Pandya's Equity Restrictions measure and the OECD's FDI Restrictiveness Index discussed below provides further evidence that using the Pandya measure as a proxy for equity restrictions on all foreign firms is reasonable.

Figure 2.13 provides regional averages for entry restrictions from 1970 to 2000; Figure 2.14 provides the same information for screening requirements. We can immediately see much more variation across and within these regions over time. With respect to entry restrictions, several regions see increases in restrictions over the sample before returning around 2000 to a regulatory environment roughly equal to what it was in 1970. This includes Europe, the Americas, and Oceania. Africa actually ended the sample with slightly higher restrictions than it had at the beginning of the sample. Asia experienced the largest drop in restrictions over the time period, while the Middle East experienced

[68] Treaty between the United States of America and Ukraine Concerning the Reciprocal Encouragement and Protection of Investments, U.S.A. – Ukraine, November 16, 1996.

[69] Treaty between the United States of America and the Republic of Turkey Concerning the Reciprocal Encouragement and Protection of Investments, U.S.A. – Turkey, May 18, 1990.

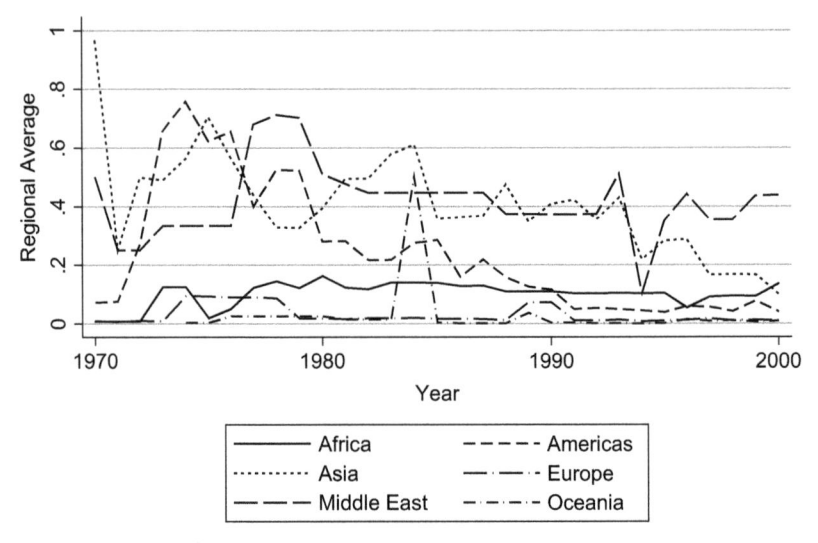

Figure 2.13 Pandya measure of FDI entry restrictions
Source: Pandya (2013)

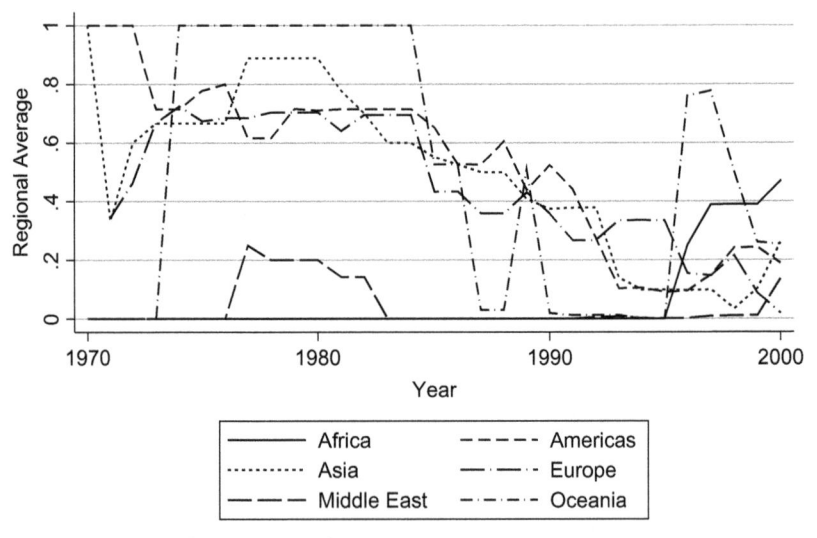

Figure 2.14 Pandya measure of FDI screening requirements
Source: Pandya (2013)

a great deal of variation over the time period before settling in the position of the region with the most restrictions in 2000.

Trends in screening requirements are a bit more chaotic. Africa and Oceania had more screening requirements in place in 2000 than they

Table 2.1. *Correlations among FDI regulation measures*

	Heritage	Fraser	OECD	Pandya Entry
Heritage	1			
Fraser	0.5569 (1,831)	1		
OECD	−0.5406 (422)	−0.0682 (295)	1	
Pandya Entry	−0.4052 (550)	−0.1699 (100)	0.5518 (32)	1
Pandya screening	0.0213 (380)	−0.0609 (88)	−0.0757 (30)	0.1342 (1,376)

N in parentheses.
Note: OECD and Pandya indices measure restrictions while others measure freedoms.

did in 1970. Oceania in particular has a frenetic history with screening regulations. Other regions display a clearer downward push toward fewer restrictions, although it is worth noting that both Europe and Asia experienced a marked increase in screening requirements through the 1970s before embarking on two decades of rather steady decreases in screening regulations.

As variations in regional averages for each of these indices attests, the measures outlined here all emphasize slightly different components of investment regulation. In addition, these measures all document substantial variation in regulatory regimes across time and space. Measures with longer temporal coverage also show the bidirectionality of investment regulation: many regions have experienced wild swings in the degree to which countries restrict or welcome FDI. Table 2.1 provides a correlation matrix for each measure. We can see from the table that the Heritage Index is most closely correlated with each of the other measures except for Pandya's screening measure. The Fraser Index seems to be measuring something very different from the OECD and Panyda measures. The OECD and the Pandya Entry measure are highly correlated. In fact, the correlation between the Pandya Entry and the subcomponent of the OECD measure that only measures equity restrictions is even higher.[70] This suggest first that the OECD measure is driven primarily by regulations on entry, and second that it provides additional confidence that the OECD and Pandya entry measures are valid. Pandya's screening measure is mostly uncorrelated

[70] Correlation = 0.6101, with an N of 32.

with other measures of restrictions. This may be because some countries, such as Canada, have *de jure* screening requirements but very rarely reject an investment application.

For the bulk of my statistical analyses presented in this book, my preferred measure of FDI policy is the Pandya measure of equity restrictions. This measure is particularly useful for assessing changes in investment regulation for several reasons. First, this measure has the broadest country and temporal coverage of any of its competitors. In particular, it covers the time frame during which most of the dramatic changes to FDI policy occurred. Second, it covers a wide range of both developed and developing countries, and has broader coverage in Africa than most other measures. Third, it confines its measurement to just one, but arguably the most critical, component of FDI policy: right of establishment. By measuring only equity restrictions, the measure allows us to understand more precisely what movements in the measure mean. In contrast, other indexes that combine multiple domains of investment policy may change for multiple reasons. If we believe changes to entry, treatment, and promotion regulations might have differential effects on interest groups, and therefore generate distinct political dynamics, we should want to measure FDI policy in ways that allow us to differentiate between these facets of the investment climate.

The Pandya measure also has several important downsides. First, country coverage is driven by the availability of U.S. Country Commerce Guides, which means that U.S. interest in countries as potential investment opportunities in some ways drives the sample. The regional coverage of the measure suggests there is substantially broad representativeness in the sample, but countries with very contentious diplomatic relations with the United States are less likely to be covered. Second, coverage stops in 2000. In some ways, this makes sense because the largest wave of changes to investment policies were made from 1980 to 2000. Still, it is useful to have measures that extend into the twenty-first century to have some sense of trends over the last 15 years. Other measures have more coverage in the contemporary time period, and I leverage their better recent coverage to overcome this weakness of the Pandya measure. Third, the Pandya measure is very conservative. Pandya creates just one threshold in the data: when foreign firms are restricted to minority share or less, or allowed at least a majority share. In practice, more equity thresholds matter.

Historically, some governments have excluded foreign ownership in some sectors altogether. In addition, many governments maintain restrictions on foreign investors such that they may take majority share in locally operating businesses, but they are still required to reserve some ownership for a local partner. Pandya's measure does not capture these nuances of regulatory policy.

Conclusion

This chapter provides important contextual and descriptive knowledge about the FDI policy environment. I explain why FDI policy deserves analytic treatment apart from theories of the politics of capital account liberalization more generally. The primary mechanisms the political economy literature ascribe to capital account liberalization are less useful as explanations of FDI reform. The policy-making process over FDI is qualitatively different from that regarding the short-term capital account. This is clear from the relatively low correlation between FDI regulations and other regulations that apply to short-term flows. I also provide a brief history of regulations over FDI to provide the reader with some context to what caused the movement toward protectionism in the middle part of the twentieth century and to demonstrate that FDI policies display some evidence of conforming to cyclical patterns of both liberalizing and restricting movements. From there, I explicate the ways in which FDI is regulated in domestic economies and how the authority over investment policy tends to be split between the legislative branch and the bureaucracy.

I review existing measures of the FDI policy environment and describe their strengths and weaknesses. These measures display a relatively low level of pairwise correlation, which is most likely the product of two issues. First, FDI policy is complex, and each measure emphasizes a different component of regulation. Second, each measure differs in both country and temporal coverage in ways that may make some measures biased toward finding greater levels of openness and others toward finding more instances of more highly regulated policy environments. It is clear that constructing a comprehensive measure of FDI restrictions is challenging and perhaps also counterproductive. However, by triangulating measures in analysis, it is possible to expand our analysis of cases to include a very broad set of countries over a long period of time. Because these measures are only weakly correlated, finding consistent effects across a broad range of these measures can increase our confidence in the results of the statistical models I present in Chapters 4 and 5.

With this contextual and descriptive background established, I turn in the next chapter to building a theory of FDI liberalization that places large, well-connected firms and their changing access to subsidized finance as central to explaining the conditions under which local firms will support openness toward foreign ones.

3 | *Financing Constraints and Liberalized Entry*

Today, most countries have relatively open policy environments toward foreign direct investment (FDI) that include relaxed equity restrictions, guarantees of national treatment, legal protections through international treaties, and investment incentives.[1] The tenor of these policies stand in stark contrast to dominant opinions of FDI just 30 or 40 years ago, when most developing countries remained largely statutorily closed to FDI. The extent of anti-FDI rhetoric at that time is best illustrated by the push by developing countries in the 1970s to adopt a new international economic order (NIEO) that would establish states' rights to nationalize and expropriate investment of multinational enterprises. While FDI was previously viewed as exploitative of developing countries, today such investment flows are considered vital components of economic development and poverty reduction strategies.[2]

However, while very few countries still impose outright bans on FDI, the freedom to invest directly in foreign jurisdictions is far from complete. Limitations on foreign equity participation remain common, particularly for investments in natural resources and services

---

[1] United Nations Conference on Trade and Development (2012), Elkins et al. (2006).

[2] *Dependencias* argued FDI perpetuated underdevelopment by exploiting natural resources in the periphery, preventing the development of local industry, and repatriating profits to the core, which worsened the investment gap in developing countries. See Evans (1979) for a review. With the development of export platform FDI strategies and a growing intellectual focus on agglomeration effects, development economists in the 1990s emphasized the positive externalities associated with FDI inflows. The Asian financial crisis solidified this stance because the experiences of countries in crises underscored the fragilities associated with securing portfolio investment from overseas while FDI remained robust to crisis and even displayed corrective countercyclical tendencies Prasad et al. (2003). Empirical evidence that FDI is associated with growth further bolstered arguments to liberalize FDI (Borensztein et al. 1998). However, skeptical interpretations of FDI remain. See Rodrik (2008).

that display noncompetitive market structures.[3] Many states maintain screening authority over larger investment proposals and require such projects to demonstrate their positive economic effects on employment, local business, and the national account in order to gain entry. Most governments have maintained the authority to block incoming FDI for national security concerns, and regulatory trends indicate countries are taking increasingly expansive views on what constitutes a threat to national security.[4] FDI policies are subject to protectionist reversion. In the wake of the 2008 global recession, G20 countries have increasingly turned to a variety of measures that protect local firms from foreign investors.[5] Thus, while most countries are at least nominally open domestic economies to FDI, the degree of openness remains varied.

Previous research has argued increased openness to FDI can be explained either by changes in the nature of foreign investment that make FDI more likely to positively affect economic growth[6] or democratization, which provides more political power to labor groups who benefit from increased openness to FDI.[7] Partisanship may also drive FDI liberalization because left governments may be more willing to encourage labor-intensive investment projects.[8] Others more casually argue FDI liberalization reflects a larger trend of neoliberal reform and is therefore best understood as the result of large-scale reorientations to market mechanisms after decades of statist development interventions.[9]

The argument I develop and test in this book is quite different. Like trade, FDI policy is driven by interest group politics. Interest groups, rather than mass politics, drive investment policies for at least two reasons. First, collective action dynamics make it easier for business interests to assert influence on policies toward foreign firms while impeding political action by members of political movements. Second, policies toward FDI are complex and difficult to follow, which prevents

---

[3] United Nations Conference on Trade and Development (2012), 79.
[4] United Nations Conference on Trade and Development (2012), 79–80.
[5] Evenett and Fritz (2016).
[6] Kobrin (2005).
[7] Dorobantu (2010); Pandya (2014).
[8] Pinto (2013); Pinto and Pinto (2008).
[9] See, for example, Willliamson (2000); Noorbakhsh et al. (2001); Kobrin (2005).

them from becoming highly salient to the public and also makes it more likely that politicians and bureaucrats will defer to interest groups with specialized knowledge of investment policy. Thus, changes to invest-ment policies are often driven by elite politics rather than the shifting political power of capital and labor or the extent to which interna-tional financial institutions can force reforms on governments that would otherwise continue to shut out foreign investors.

I argue increased openness toward FDI occurs when conditions at the global and local levels reduce domestic firms' privileged access to alternative sources of finance. As the availability of other sources of investment declines and the costs of such capital increases, powerful business elites will be more willing to open the local economy to for-eign owners. They will do so in order to spur capital formation and therefore economic growth generally, and also to gain greater access to foreign firms' investment financing. In other words, FDI may bring many benefits to local economies – technology, know-how, training, exports – but because foreign firms also threaten domestic enterprises, governments often restrict FDI inflows until domestic firms need capi-tal. Decisions to open domestic economies to FDI occur when domestic business interests try to harness the capital of foreign firms, and they are more likely to do so when they face increasingly costly financing constraints. If this is true, we should expect alternative financing con-straints to be associated with FDI liberalization, while access to other forms of investment will impede reform. Below, I develop expectations for how the presence of, and variations in, formal institutions of finan-cial privilege (state-directed credit), informal mechanisms of financial privilege (industry-finance conglomerates and connected lending), and structural conditions (global credit environment, attraction of short-term foreign investment flows) condition domestic firms' preferences over regulating foreign firms.

The core theoretical argument is that transformations in elite prefer-ences, caused by disruptions to access to capital, rather than changes in political institutions that shift political power toward labor often explain alterations in policies toward FDI. While access to cheap alter-native sources of capital make elites less likely to support reform, policy developments that limit short-term investment and debt financ-ing will cause elites to reevaluate the costs and benefits of openness. In particular, banking sector liberalization reorients powerful societal and state interests from restricting to encouraging foreign entry.

My theory contributes to the literatures of FDI and macroeconomic reform sequencing in the following ways. First, I explain change in policy outcomes as primarily the result of shifting interests rather than changes in domestic political institutions. This approach contrasts sharply with arguments that regime type explains differences in policies toward FDI and complements arguments that institutions in transition are unable to act as constraints on politicians and are therefore improbable sources of major changes in policy outcomes.[10] It also complements explanations of regulatory change developed by scholars working in the comparative historical institutions tradition, who have increasingly looked to incremental changes in interest group preferences, often attributed to shifting economic conditions, to explain changes in legal and regulatory structures.[11]

Second, by emphasizing the role of financing conditions in influencing firms' preferences over FDI, I contribute both to the developing literature on firm heterogeneity[12] and to a more established literature that has emerged from both the varieties of capitalism[13] and the finance-law-growth (FLG) literatures. Scholars working in these traditions increasingly have explored the relevance of financing mechanisms in shaping firms' business and political strategies.[14] More specifically, I combine theory on the tools that firms have to exercise managerial control and raise investment and working capital with insights into how the capacity to employ such tools effectively varies across key firm-level characteristics.

Finally, my theory draws upon renewed interest in the ways in which business groups influence policy outcomes through quiet consultation rather than through highly visible clashes with other societal interest

---

[10] See Pepinsky (2013b) for a critique of the authoritarian institutions literature on the grounds that institutions are often tools rather than constraints in authoritarian contexts. The same is true for institutions in transition. Institutions in the process of formation cannot be constraints on elite behavior when the rules are still being negotiated.

[11] O'Sullivan (2003); Thelen (2011); Ross Schneider (2013).

[12] The development of new-new trade theory (NNTT) attributed most directly to Melitz's 2003 trade model, with heterogeneous firm (rather than industry) preferences, has led to the development of increasingly sophisticated understanding of firm-level variations in preferences and behavior in the political economy literature. See Melitz (2003).

[13] See, for example, Hall and Soskice (2001).

[14] See Claessens (2006) and Pagano and Volpin (2005) for a review.

groups.[15] In doing so, I challenge political economists to be slower to assume economic policy and macro-management choices are the product of particular ways in which political institutions aggregate a diverse set of preferences. In many areas of economic political decision making, publics are simply not in the negotiating room.

In the sections that follow, I first explain why FDI restrictions are puzzling, particularly when viewed in relation to short-term capital account policies. I then briefly review the existing literature on FDI liberalization, and explain why existing theory remains unsatisfying. Next, I explain why it is appropriate to explain FDI regulation through an interest group politics frame. I then establish the preferences over FDI openness of key societal interest groups when global and local conditions render short-term investment and debt finance easily attainable. Fifth, I detail how policies such as domestic banking sector reforms that make borrowing more expensive for politically connected firms change the policy preferences of industrial capitalists, render financial capitalists less influential, and encourage the state to pursue more open FDI policy environments. The sixth and final section briefly discusses the research design strategies I employ in subsequent chapters of the book to test the observable implications that arise from my theory.

FDI Restrictions as a Puzzle

When foreign firms invest directly in an economy, they create both welfare and distributional effects. Standard trade theory, which has often been applied to global finance, predicts FDI has a positive welfare effect by decreasing financing costs and allocating capital more efficiently.[16] Econometric evidences demonstrates FDI inflows are positively correlated with economic growth, though the extent to which this relationship is causal, the direction of this causality, and the extent to which these effects are mediated by the initial economic conditions of particular host countries remains contested.[17]

What is clear, however, is that FDI does not bring with it many of the potentially destabilizing characteristics that does portfolio investment. Because bond and equity markets create opportunities for speculative

[15] Culpepper (2011).
[16] Alt and Gilligan (1994).
[17] Borensztein et al. (1998); Alfaro et al. (2004); Carkovic and Levine (2005).

behavior, openness to short-term capital flows can expose governments to volatile and destabilizing sharp movements in the capital account.[18] Capital account liberalization has been blamed for instigating or exacerbating balance of payment crises. For example Thailand's experience with liberalizing short-term flows proved disastrous in 1997, sparking speculative attacks on the baht, and transmitting crises across the region.[19]

The costs of short-term capital account openness feature prominently in most theoretical explanations of liberalization. Opening the capital account, particularly in times of balance of payment stress, may signal to investors a hard commitment to investor protections.[20] Capital account liberalization may also allow right-leaning governments to lock the political left into fiscal conservatism.[21]

The high costs of liberalization may also explain why capital account policies diffuse across regions. States might prefer to maintain capital controls precisely because of the dangers of an open account but are forced to relax restrictions to compete with their geographic neighbors and their economic peers.[22] Governments are more likely to follow liberalizations of countries with similar export profiles, indicating that global competitive pressures compel states to open their capital accounts. When openness entails uncertain rewards but high risks of triggering an economic crisis, policymakers may take cues from the liberalization experiences of countries with similar historical economic and political legacies.[23]

Given these dynamics, we might expect governments to be more willing to liberalize polices toward FDI than policies toward portfolio flows. This expectation is particularly plausible because FDI liberalization and short-term capital account openness may be functional substitutes because both provide the domestic economy access to investment either through lending or equity. A prominent policy recommendation stemming from the literature on macroeconomic reform sequencing is that short-term capital flows should be essentially the last

---

[18] Eichengreen (2001); Eichengreen and Leblang (2003); Quinn and Inclan (1997); Rodrik (1998).
[19] Johnston et al. (1997).
[20] Haggard and Maxfield (1996).
[21] Brooks (2007).
[22] Simmons and Elkins (2004).
[23] Brooks and Kurtz (2012).

stage of neoliberal reform after current account and domestic financial system liberalizations.[24] International Monetary Fund (IMF) policy papers extoll the virtues of opening economies to FDI inflows early in the reform process before extending liberalization to more volatile short-term flows.[25] FDI seems to provide all of the growth opportunity of other forms of investment flows with little of the risks or technocratic complexity.

Despite the clear policy guidance to sequence FDI and short-term financial liberalization, a 2012 IMF policy review found that about half of all states that have pursued capital account reform liberalized short-term flows before they did long-term.[26] Of course, decisions to liberalize are political because they have distributive implications. And those who benefit from FDI inflows may not be the same as those who benefit from short-term capital flows. Portfolio investment provides increased access to debt financing, which can benefit smaller firms that have difficulty obtaining credit in constrained markets.[27] At the same time, portfolio investment paired with heavy restrictions on foreign ownership of banks can mute credit constraints while still allowing the state to use regulatory authority and close connections with large domestic banks to control credit allocation decisions.[28] FDI inflows create substantial pressures in domestic product and factor markets that make small and less efficient firms unlikely to survive.[29] FDI may also break down tight political connections between domestic capital and the state, which can threaten traditional repertoires of building and maintaining ruling coalitions.[30]

For these reasons, reform experiences may not reflect technocratically "correct" sequences. While many countries pursued early limited FDI reforms, these policies often opened the domestic economy to foreign firms in a very limited sense. Most countries maintained extensive negative lists of industries closed to foreign investment, often required

---

[24] Edwards (1984); Frenkel (1982); McKinnon (1973). But see Little et al. (1970); Michaely (1986); Krueger (1984) for arguments that the current and capital account should be liberalized simultaneously.

[25] Eichengreen and Mussa (1998); Johnston (1998); Kawai and Takagi (2008).

[26] International Monetary Fund (2012), 23.

[27] Rajan and Zingales (2003).

[28] Pepinsky (2013a).

[29] Alfaro and Chen (2018).

[30] Teichman (1995, 2001).

indigenous firm participation in FDI projects,[31] and gave a central screening body the authority to approve projects based on their ability to fulfill a variety of performance requirements such as employment creation and local procurement.

For instance, Vietnam's 1987 Law on Foreign Investment permitted foreigners to invest directly but only under a set of strict conditions. The central government retained a great deal of control over inflows by requiring screening and authorization from central government officials until 1996, when screening was devolved to local officials.[32] The screening process allowed the Vietnamese government to permit FDI selectively and to condition entry on joint venture and local content requirements.[33]

Similarly, Mexico's 1973 Law to Promote Mexican Investment and to Regulate Foreign Investment reserved the petrochemical and utility sectors for the state and set a 49 percent equity limit on foreign investment in most other sectors.[34] Even the 1993 amendment to foreign investment laws, which were deemed North American Free Trade Agreement (NAFTA)-compliant, retained several sectoral exceptions such as minority ownership in banks and outright bans on foreign investors in several other service sectors, for example, ground transportation, cable broadcasting, and retail petro sale.[35]

Indeed, prominent development models have often relied on restricting foreign equity ownership in order to strengthen domestic industry. Many East Asian countries that pursued export-oriented industrialization placed numerous restrictions on FDI, such as limiting foreign equity to minority shares in joint ventures with domestic enterprises. At the same time, these countries pursued a good deal of short-term capital account openness to support exporting and to obtain external sources of investment finance. The Republic of Korea is perhaps the most prominent example of this model.[36]

---

[31] Or, more restrictively, short positive lists detailing the only sectors for which foreign equity participation was authorized.
[32] Malesky (2008); Mai (2004).
[33] Moran (2005).
[34] Graham and Wada (2000).
[35] Ibid.
[36] Cho (2001).

However, selective liberalization of FDI is quite different from allowing FDI inflows regardless of mode of entry (i.e. joint venture or wholly owned subsidiary) or sector or without screening requirements to reject politically sensitive projects.[37] Maintaining restrictions allows governments the opportunity to find investment funding from abroad but also enables them to keep out investment that would be politically costly and makes it possible to pad the pockets of large local firms by requiring incoming foreign investors to join equity sharing agreements with indigenous businesses. At the same time, such restrictions are generally viewed as impediments to market mechanisms for efficient asset allocation.[38] Both firm surveys and analysis of FDI flows provide evidence at the micro and macro levels that firms are often repelled by such restrictions.[39] Therefore, retaining partial FDI liberalization policies is costly; states would receive more FDI inflows in their absence.

Despite these costs, even today FDI policies are frequently far from fully liberalized. The 2014 Annual Report on Exchange Arrangements and Exchange Restrictions (AREAER) dataset lists 151 countries as having some degree of limitations on FDI.[40] In the aftermath of the 2007–2008 global financial crisis many countries, including the United States, Germany, France, China, and Russia, have either passed or debated legislation aimed at further restricting FDI.[41] In the wake of the United Kingdom's successful referendum to exit the European Union (EU), Theresa May's government has indicated it will take

---

[37] Screening requirements are not relegated to developing countries. In the United States, the Committee on Foreign Investment in the United States (CFIUS) is an interagency committee housed in the executive branch that retains limited screening authority over inward FDI, particularly investments considered to have a national security interest. In recent years, the US Congress has more vocally and publicly demanded increased use of executive screening provisions to block high-profile takeovers in certain industries and by investors of particular national origin in the name of national security. See Jackson (2014) for a full review. CFIUS screening has become an increasingly contentious site of FDI oversight as Chinese firms, often with substantial state ownership, continue to establish operations overseas, especially through strategic acquisitions.

[38] Miller et al. (2013).

[39] Adler and Hufbauer (2008); Golub (2003); Gastanaga et al. (1998).

[40] International Monetary Fund (2014), 80.

[41] Marchick and Slaughter (2008).

steps to increase screening and oversight of foreign takeovers.[42] The anti-FDI sentiment arose despite a lack of a similar broad movement for increases in short-term capital controls.

What explains this puzzling empirical reality that FDI liberalization has varied greatly despite its more straightforward positive welfare effects and its lower potential for macroeconomic destabilization than other forms of financial openness? I argue the distributional politics of FDI hinge crucially on the level of domestic financial openness more generally. Because FDI represents one of many ways to raise corporate financing, the costs and benefits of openness to direct foreign equity participation to different key interest groups depend on how restricted are other forms of financing.

Existing Explanations of Investment Policy Liberalization

The dominant explanation of FDI liberalization, and economic liberalization more broadly, in contemporary political economy is one of elite disempowerment. Political economy accounts of economic liberalization have long emphasized the role of vested interests in perpetuating protectionist policies that function to distribute rents to local and politically connected capital. Existing explanations of FDI liberalization follow this tradition. In this framework, small, well-resourced groups are better able to overcome collective action problems in order to lobby for their preferred outcome.[43] Because gains from openness are diffuse, but costs are concentrated, incumbents will work to block economic reform in order to protect their autarkic rents.[44]

In this framework, because domestic firms benefit from competition-reducing policies of economic repression, foreign entry deregulation must occur when some shock disrupts special interests' ability to block reform. Punctuated equilibrium can come from two primary developments. The first is external and accrues through economic shocks. The second, democratization, is the result of an internal process of institutional reconfiguration.

---

[42] Massoudi, Arash, and Jamie Smyth (October 10, 2016), "How Other Countries Tackle May's Foreign Investment Balancing Act," *The Financial Times*, www.ft.com/content/ff76b7de-8e22-11e6-8df8-d3778b55a923.

[43] Olson (1965).

[44] Krusell and Ríos-Rull (1996); Parente and Presott (1999); Grossman and Helpman (1994).

Economic crisis can reduce the bargaining power of governments and local firms vis-à-vis reform-oriented international financial institutions and cash-rich multinational enterprises. As domestic economies becoming increasingly dependent on foreign direct capital, they become more sensitive to peers' investment policies and begin to compete with similar economies for mobile capital. In response, governments must reduce remaining restriction as well as streamline investment approval and provide generous tax and legal incentives to multinationals.

Theories of economic-crisis-induced FDI liberalization are incomplete for several reasons. It may indeed be the case that economic crises may render domestic firms more receptive to FDI inflows due to adverse credit shocks.[45] However, a direct relationship between crisis and FDI liberalization remains elusive. Simple bivariate analysis reveals that FDI policy changes and economic crisis episodes display no discernible relationship.[46] This is not particularly surprising for two reasons. First, crisis response policies matter. As we will see in Chapters 6 and 7, Indonesia and Malaysia followed distinct adjustment paths that had differential effects on local credit constraints. Crisis might create credit market pressures, but whether these pressures ultimately lead to policy change is conditional on how governments choose to manage immediate crisis response.

Second, the politics and processes of FDI policy makes it less likely that governments will focus specifically on regulations over these long-term flows in the middle of a crisis. While banking and short-term capital account reforms are frequently undertaken in the wake of balance of payment crises,[47] these classes of policies have different characteristics and effects than do policies toward FDI. Policy changes in the banking and short-term capital account are meant to quickly ameliorate severe liquidity and solvency concerns in an economy's financial system, and therefore the policy process takes place within the chaotic context of crisis politics in which the preferences of large firms are often temporarily subjugated by an overwhelming need to stabilize the financial sector. The process of reforming investment law

---

[45] Aizenman (2005).
[46] Currency, debt, and banking crises are weakly but negatively associated with liberalizing FDI policies in the following year (author's own calculations).
[47] Abiad and Mody (2005); Haggard and Maxfield (1996).

is quite different, primarily because, unlike other types of cross-border capital flows, FDI is not quickly deployed but often takes multiple years between the start of an MNE's plan for overseas expansion and the actual outlay of investment. "Fire-sale FDI" may be deployed more quickly during substantial drops in host-country exchange rates,[48] but changing laws governing foreign equity are far less integral to crisis stabilization than are regulations of banks and short-term capital flows.

Finally, it is unlikely that pressure from international financial institutions such as the IMF holds much explanatory power over FDI policy reforms. First, there is little evidence that the IMF actually commands the coercive power to compel borrower states to follow through on many of their conditionality requirements.[49] Even if borrower countries fastidiously adhered to IMF conditionality requirements, there is little reason to believe agency officials would emphasize FDI liberalization. A thorough review of IMF structural adjustment programs reveals such programs only rarely explicitly include the lifting of foreign equity restrictions as conditions for future loan disbursements.[50] Thus, crises may create local credit conditions conducive to reform, but they certainly do not operate as a blunt instrument of a totalizing neoliberal project.

Democratization could also disrupt blocking coalitions. Changes in domestic political institutions that empower workers over capital may make economic blocking more difficult as voters demand higher economic growth, better jobs, and higher wages. Under such conditions, local firms have less leverage to extract regulatory rents, and electoral pressures will lead governments to liberalize foreign investment inflows. From this theoretical insight, many scholars have argued democracies, and especially democracies without "elite-bias" components such as bans on left-wing parties or appointed senators, are more likely to enact policies that ostensibly help poor people. Prominent examples include the connection between democracy and trade,[51] FDI,[52] and financial reform.[53]

---

[48] Krugman (2000).
[49] Stone (2011); Pop-Eleches (2009).
[50] Stone (2008), 601.
[51] Milner and Kubota (2005).
[52] Pandya (2014, 2010).
[53] Menaldo and Yoo (2015).

However, explanations that argue democratization, and shifting political power from firms to labor interests, drives FDI policy liberalization are unsatisfying for several reasons. First, it is difficult to assign causality of massive changes in macroeconomic management policies to the expansion of free and fair elections. Government policies toward FDI underwent dramatic changes through the 1980s and 1990s at the same time states adopted packages of other economic reforms such as privatization of state industry, trade liberalization, and short-term capital account openness. These reorientations toward the market occur concurrent to the third wave of democratization, which generated new democratic governments in Latin America, East Asia, Africa, and Central and East Europe. The co-occurrence of these seismic shifts in the organization of economic and political life makes it challenging to ascribe causality of one trend to another. When you look more closely at reform sequencing, you find that governments often liberalized foreign firm entry before they transitioned to democracy. For example, Mexico passed an FDI reform bill in 1993 but did not become a democracy until 2000. Malaysia passed a comprehensive foreign investment reform in 2009 but is still categorized as a single-party regime.[54]

Second, there are several reasons to be wary of explanations of FDI liberalization that emphasize reform pressures from labor groups. First, entry restrictions follow familiar dynamics of other protectionist policies in that the benefits to openness are diffusely shared while the costs are concentrated. Furthermore, the societal groups that are most negatively affected by openness are groups that usually have the capacity and capability to organize successfully against policies of openness. Therefore, even if citizens view foreign investment favorably, collective action dynamics make it unlikely they can lobby successfully for openness. In this respect, the politics of FDI mirrors the interest group politics of trade.[55] Second, the political power and cohesiveness of labor is highly variable across countries. This is not just about the inclusivity of political institutions (i.e. democracy), but also the structure of industrial relations and the prevalence of labor unions. The degree of variability across countries makes it difficult

---

[54] In May 2018, the ruling party lost elections in a surprising upset. Malaysia may be transitioning to democracy if elections continue to offer real opportunities for publics to vote in new political leaders

[55] See Grossman and Helpman (1994), Kono (2008), Ehrlich (2011).

to reach generalizable explanations of labor's influence on FDI policy. Third, even though labor benefits from increased wages, FDI inflows create countervailing concerns for labor groups. In particular, the increase in capital mobility that FDI represents reduces the bargaining power of labor groups because mobile capital has a more credible threat of exit.[56] Labor organization is associated with decreased FDI inflows, and FDI inflows are associated with greater incidence of labor protest.[57]

Though foreign investment policy is rarely a highly salient issue, when FDI does become more visible, it is often within the context of labor and mass groups protesting multinational enterprises (MNEs). In other words, the groups most empowered by democratization are also likely to protest against FDI. This is largely because citizens often interpret foreign investment through the lens of economic globalization and frame their understanding of the implications of investment through a debate about foreign pressures on national interests.[58] Labor in developed countries tends to lump FDI with increased globalization more generally, which they view as bad for workers in developed countries. To the extent that FDI is associated with privatization and moves toward economic liberalism more generally, labor in developing countries may also view FDI with suspicion because it may herald less government support in labor markets.

For example, infrastructure privatization through foreign firms became highly contentious in the early 2000s in Latin America.[59] Indian small shopkeepers, farmers, and citizen groups have reliably protested against Walmart's entry into its market, arguing the retail giant will displace millions of small vendors and suppliers.[60] Protestors against free-trade agreements in South Korea,[61] Australia,[62] Europe,

---

[56] Owen (2015).
[57] Robertson and Teitelbaum (2011).
[58] Bandelj (2008), 672.
[59] See Woodhouse (2003) for a treatment of Bolivia's "water war" in Cochabamba. See Arce (2008) for a narrative on the Arequipazo in Peru.
[60] Opposition to Walmart has become a perennial protest issue in India. See, for example, Rhitu Chatterjee, "Indian Shopkeepers Greet Wal-Mart Expansion Plans with Protests," *NPR*, November 20, 2015.
[61] Tree, Oliver, "U.S.- South Korea Free Trade Agreement Begins Amid Protest," *International Business Times*, March 15, 2012.
[62] See Tienhaara and Ranald (2011) for a review of Australia's eventual rejection of investor-state dispute settlement provisions in the US-Australia treaty.

and the United States all focus their ire against investment chapters and articulate dire warnings about how multinational firms exploit and undermine local economies.

Finally, democracy-driven explanations of FDI policy have trouble explaining the degree of variation in the treatment of multinational investment within democracies, within nondemocracies, and over time. While the policy environment toward foreign investors is clearly more liberal today than it was in the 1970s, there is still quite a bit of remaining variation in regulation of entry, treatment of investors, and incentive programs. As discussed in the previous section, we have seen an increase in restrictive regulation of foreign investors in recent years, especially in developed countries.

In particular, many advanced industrial countries have recently decided to scrutinize foreign entry and acquisitions more closely. Australia and France have especially active screening programs for foreign firms over a certain size, and the UK government has signaled its interest in increasing screening authority over large investments. In the wake of the 2008 financial crisis, the United Nations Conference on Trade and Development's (UNCTAD) Investment Policy Monitor recorded a substantial uptick in the number of restrictive investment policy changes.[63] In other words, at the level of implementation, investment regulation is dynamic, and theories over its drivers should be able to explain variations that persist within and among countries with similar domestic political institutions.

The "Quiet Politics" of Investment Policy

Undoubtedly, economic crisis as well as domestic institutional change can create powerful catalysts for reform. While policy change often occurs despite insider protest to it, policy change does not always occur due to shocks that dislodge vested interests. It may be that policies sometimes change because structural conditions shift in ways that induce incumbents to alter strategies. In such circumstances, incumbents may stand to benefit from, and will therefore support, policy change. If incumbents determine the status quo is unsustainable, setting the agenda for reforms is preferable to quixotic attempts to resist

---

[63] United Nations Conference on Trade and Development (2009).

policy change. Consequently, insiders can decrease rent erosion or even increase their share of the distributive pie.

Insider-driven reform has important distributive implications: if incumbent firms support particular articulations of reforms, then liberalization may not transform power structures as much as existing models suggest. Whether reforms are the product of creative destruction or of elite realignment has implications for the promise that liberalization will empower out-groups or primarily benefit incumbents with the political capital to shape the rules of financial integration in their favor.

Accordingly, I apply analytic focus to the conditions under which firms will support and advocate for changes in investment law. I do so for a number of reasons. First, as discussed in the previous section, citizens may have a difficult time formulating coherent policy preferences over FDI regulation. Even if they do develop clear preferences, investment policy may not be a high-priority issue compared to other concerns such as worker benefits, taxes, and good governance concerns. Therefore, organizing to influence political outcomes in this issue area is very challenging for citizen interest groups. The relatively low salience of regulation coupled with high issue complexity over industry-level equity ceilings; screening review processes; rules over repatriating profits and accessing foreign exchange; and various targeted incentives and regulations over land use, procurement policies, and export balancing render the politics of investment policies firmly in the realm of what Pepper Culpepper calls "quiet politics."[64]

Why Firms

When issues are marked by low salience and high technical complexity, related political battles do not often occur through public debate and citizen group pressure on elected or responsive government officials. Instead, the consequential details of policy are determined through bureaucratic and legislative committees. Domestic firms, particularly large firms with close connections to government officials, have a great deal of influence over policy outcomes in these instances for three reasons.

---

[64] Culpepper (2011).

First, firms are a source of technocratic knowledge. Government bureaucrats may have little understanding of how regulatory choices affect firms' strategic decision making and day-to-day operating environment. Business leaders can provide consultation to government officials who want to understand the likely consequences of any changes to the complex policies that regulate foreign investment. For example, government officials may be unsure how competitive domestic firms would be if foreign firms entered a particular industry space. Officials may also have less information about the financing and human capital needs of domestic enterprises and of particular industries. Firms can provide guidance over the needs of local business, the likely competition effects of liberalizing particular aspects of investment policy, and ways to best incentivize "desirable" foreign investment while limiting other types of FDI that are deemed less useful.

Second, business groups are often well integrated into structures of government and therefore can translate their informational advantages into policy influence. In many nondemocracies, ruling coalitions must co-opt domestic industrial interests into their ranks.[65] In countries characterized by weak formal economic institutions, hierarchical capitalism gives rise to powerful diversified business groups with close ties to political leaders and their families.[66] In developed democracies, business groups are well organized and routinely consulted on economic and technical matters either through informal processes and lobbying efforts common among liberal market economies or through formalized tripartite negotiation principles common among coordinated market economies.[67]

Third, firms often have relatively easy access to bureaucrats and legislative bodies where policy is made. This access comes in part from institutions and practices that formalize business group consultation over economic policy, such as policy working groups that provide forums for policymakers and business interests to develop shared beliefs and expectations over national investment policy

---

[65] See, for example, Gandhi and Przeworski (2006) and Wright (2008).

[66] Ross Schneider (2013).

[67] These distinctions draw on conceptualizations and theoretical frames developed in the influential literature on the varieties of capitalism. See Hall and Soskice (2001) for further discussion. The concept of hierarchical capitalism, developed by Ben Ross Schneider (2013), extends the logic of the varieties of capitalism framework to developing economies.

priorities. Access also comes from coordinated lobbying efforts to influence political leaders' opinions of and willingness to support policy proposals. Perhaps more important than formal channels of influence, however, are the shared norms and ideational commitments that develop as individuals who reach the highest levels of leadership in politics and business frequently come from similar social and academic backgrounds. Repeated consultative interactions between business leaders and policymakers reinforce these shared belief structures, as does the tendency for high-level officials to rotate between positions of official policymaking and advising and business leadership.

For these reasons, it is appropriate to focus on the sources of, and changes in, domestic firms' policy preferences. While governments can rarely make policy over foreign investment with no regard to popular opinion, the opacity of investment regulation to average citizens, coupled with the difficulty of attributing specific aspects of investment policy to the economic outcomes citizens most care about, such as jobs, wages, growth, and consumer prices, give governments room to maneuver most details of investment policy. Firms offer technical expertise and industry knowledge that policymakers value. They also have formal and informal channels of influence over the policymaking process in most countries. And they have access to and epistemic affinity with the individuals in government who design and implement regulatory governance structures. Thus, explanations of government choices over whether and how to regulate foreign investment benefit from first considering the determinants of domestic firms' preferences over FDI policies.

Quiet Politics and Distributive Politics

A focus on firms does not deny that FDI policy has distributive implications. Disproportionate costs and benefits of inward FDI to firms and also workers is a central assumption in the theory that follows. Rather, a quiet politics approach directs analytic attention away from a factor-based explanation of policy fights and toward a model that considers sources of distributive conflict among firms. This theoretic lens reflects a growing interest among scholars of international political economy (IPE) in focusing more on firms as political actors with heterogeneous preference.[68] It also calls into question the assumption that policy outcomes reflect the preferences of average voters, even in well-established democracies. A growing empirical record suggests the interests of workers are often crowded out by those of business elites, even in democratic contexts.[69]

However, it is still useful to consider the preferences of labor groups and the conditions under which they may become more decisive in policy conflicts. Labor groups will support policies that they perceive will create jobs and protect wages. As long as FDI creates employment and leads to rising wages, labor will benefit from FDI. However, as discussed in greater detail below, FDI typically benefits skilled workers more than unskilled workers, which may generate conflict within labor coalitions. Foreign firms also have a more credible exit option than their domestic counterparts, and this may reduce labor's ability to engage in effective collective bargaining. Individuals may view foreign firms as a manifestation of neoliberalism; support for or opposition to FDI may well be tied to individuals' beliefs about the costs and benefits of globalization and their values about equity and competition. In other words, even if formal theory and empirical analysis demonstrates that inward FDI benefits labor, it is not necessarily the case that workers will interpret their interests accordingly.

These countervailing benefits and costs of FDI to labor suggest such groups will have a difficult time generating overarching preferences over foreign entry and instead will focus on regulating FDI postestablishment. However, there may be particular conditions under which FDI policy achieves momentary salience. For instance, publics may become more interested in policies toward foreign firms after governments announce an intention to alter investment law or when economic distress invokes a broader and more public argument about the most appropriate policy tools for generating economic growth and employment. Note that both of these mechanisms for increasing the salience of FDI policy are ultimately elite-driven. Labor groups may react to elite decisions to reevaluate the wisdom of status quo policies, but they rarely act as catalysts for changes to policy.

---

[68] Osgood (2017); Osgood et al. (2017); Kim (2017).
[69] Bartels (2016); Culpepper (2011); Giger and Kluver (2016); Gilens and Page (2014); Hacker and Pierson (2014); Walker and Rea (2014).

If FDI becomes salient to publics, then a question remains about how easily labor groups develop cohesive policy preferences over MNE entry, and if they do, in what direction. Previous research on public opinion in Latin American and transition economies suggests investment is a valence issue, with most individuals holding positive views toward FDI.[70] But other public opinion data suggest individuals are likely to hold negative opinions around MNEs during times of economic crisis, reform, and transition, precisely the periods in which FDI policy is likely to become more salient.[71] This is largely because individuals often view foreign investors as unaccountable elite outsiders who will exploit local communities.[72] National context matters for the extent to which labor holds united preferences over economic policies. For example, Denisova et al. find skilled and unskilled labor express increasing disparate economic policy preferences as democracy and quality of governance increases.[73] These microfoundational findings suggest that labor may hold generally positive opinions of FDI when investment policy is of low salience but increasingly negative opinions when policies toward MNEs become more salient. This suggests that, when labor does become an important factor in policy formation, it often agitates to heavily regulate MNE entry.

Quiet Politics versus Bureaucratic Politics

Some may argue, in contrast, that reformist attitudes arise from state bureaucrats themselves, and therefore domestic business interests are superfluous to policy reforms. Scholars of the politics of economic adjustment often characterize reform coalitions as fragile in the face of better organized beneficiaries of illiberal economic policies. These scholars often emphasize the need to insulate reform-oriented politicians and bureaucrats from anti-reform sentiments. In other words, economic adjustment happens "from above;" state capacity to resist rent seeking from incumbent economic elites explains successful reform efforts.[74]

---

[70] Pandya (2010, 2014); PAIZ (2006); European Bank for Reconstruction and Development (2005).
[71] Rohrscheider and Whitefield (2004).
[72] Bandelj (2008); Sinn (1997).
[73] Denisova et al. (2009).
[74] See Haggard (1990); Stacey (2009); Haggard and Kaufman (1995).

The problem with these sorts of explanations is their inability to articulate where state preferences for reform come from. Some suggest epistemic communities, particularly among government economists trained in neoliberal institutions, can generate ideational support for reforms.[75] Others emphasize governments' desire to develop reputations for sound policy in order to prevent capital flight.[76] However, governments are constrained by the preferences of societal groups from where they draw their authority. The process of economic liberalization, of which FDI policy is one component, often creates opportunities for incumbent economic elites to structure policy change to their advantage.[77] Trade, capital account, exchange rate, and privatization reforms create both threats and opportunities for politically influential firms, and economic liberalization can often function to consolidate the economic and political power of large domestic conglomerates rather than unseat incumbents.[78] Therefore, a theory of FDI policy that takes seriously the interests of domestic firms is better able to address questions of where "state" preferences originate, and the conditions under which local business interests might shift their orientation toward global markets.

Domestic Firms and Threats and Opportunities of FDI

Like other policies of economic openness, allowing foreign firms to invest domestically has distributional implications that create political conflict over policy decisions. The distributional effects of FDI are more challenging to identify than their net welfare effects because foreign firms invest directly for multiple reasons, each of which affect domestic firms differently. For instance, multinationals can invest to better compete in local markets, to exploit natural resources, to take advantage of inexpensive labor to produce goods for export, or to establish export platforms close to key product markets.[79]

---

[75] Chwieroth (2010).

[76] Haggard and Maxfield (1996).

[77] Schamis (1999).

[78] Schamis (1999) outlines the reform experiences of Chile, Mexico, and Argentina and demonstrates how constellations and sequencing of liberalizing reforms further cemented powerful coalitions between political elites and large diversified conglomerates.

[79] Dunning (1988, 2009).

Explanations of preference formation imported from the trade literature emphasize cleavages either along factor lines, with capital in developing countries losing from FDI inflows, or sector lines, with import-competing firms preferring protection from foreign entrants. But these microfoundations of FDI policy preference are incomplete and perhaps misleading because, as the large literature on FDI spillovers suggests, the ways in which foreign firms influence domestic markets are complex. The preferences of different groups over FDI are largely contingent upon the broader policy context, particularly with respect to the financial sector, because the opportunity costs associated with FDI depend on access to and cost of alternative sources of finance. For these reasons, incumbent firms face identifiable and universal costs but uncertain and firm-specific benefits to multinational entry. FDI inflows entail clear, economy-wide costs to indigenous firms by placing upward pressure on wages. Foreign entry also creates large-scale productivity pressures that erode incumbent firms' rents. In this section, I outline the sources of these threats and opportunities and then discuss the ways in which changes to the domestic financing environment can alter the cost-benefit calculations of domestic industries, especially the largest and most politically connected.

Threats from Openness

There are many reasons why local firms may view FDI as disadvantageous. Standard international economic models provide simple factor-proportion-based assessments of the short- and long-term effects of capital inflows on incumbent rents. In the short term, the specific factors model demonstrates that investment will flow into industries for which increased capital can raise the marginal product of labor.[80]

---

[80] For an excellent and accessible formal treatment see Feenstra and Taylor (2014, 144–147). In the long run, FDI has no effect on wage or investment rents. This is because over time capital-intensive industries increase output while output in labor-intensive industries declines. As capital and labor are allocated to where they are most efficient, the capital-labor ratio remains the same as it was pre-investment. The long-term welfare effects, therefore, are due to increased output in host countries and increased rental income in the home country. Long-term factor-price insensitivity is important to determining the overall distribution of gains from investment liberalization. However, politics occur mostly in the short term, and therefore I restrict most of my analysis of the anticipated and realized distributive effects of FDI inflows to those that emerge from a specific-factors model.

Consequently, employment and wages will increase in industries that attract FDI. In contrast, industries that do not attract investment will lose workers but will still have to pay a higher equilibrium wage. Increased wage costs mean capital rents decline, and this is true both in industries that attract investment and those that do not. In the short-term, formal economic theory shows capitalists lose relative to labor from capital inflows. From this, we would expect domestic firms to oppose foreign entry and to be quite united in their opposition. Capital should not face industry-level divisions because FDI decreases rents in all industries through the wage channel.

We see substantial empirical validation of some of the core findings of the specific-factors model's expectations over the distributive effects of FDI inflows. There is robust evidence that foreign-owned firms pay higher wages than their domestic-owned counterparts.[81] This is true in both developed and developing countries, and studies typically find a wage premium of around 10 to 30 percent. Some of this differential can be attributed to characteristics of the types of firms that engage in FDI. Direct investment is often concentrated in high-wage industries and tends to be employed by large firms that are comparatively more capital-intensive and therefore require more highly skilled labor. However, even after controlling for these characteristics, foreign firms' wage premium persists.

There is also evidence that these wage effects permeate the broader economy. Foreign ownership has a positive effect on wages in domestically owned firms in nonmanufacturing sectors in the United States.[82] A study of aggregate wage growth in South Carolina suggests wage spillovers from foreign entry are large and extend to manufacturing.[83] Replication efforts for wage effects in other developed countries generally suggest similar spillovers exist. However, the size of such effects is conditioned on skill levels and is often regionally contained.[84] The sensitivity of wage spillover findings may be evidence in support

---

[81] See Lipsey (2004) for a comprehensive review.
[82] Feliciano and Lipsey (2006).
[83] Figlio and Blonigen (2000).
[84] See Driffield and Firma (2003) for UK data. Girma et al. (2001) find limited evidence of wage spillovers that depend on the productivity gap and import penetration.

of factor price insensitivity over the long run, consistent with the Rybcznyski theorem.[85]

Empirical studies of wage spillovers in developing countries find more consistent evidence that FDI inflows lead to increased wages across the local economy. Aitken, Harrison, and Lipsey demonstrate foreign-owned plant establishment in Mexico and Venezuela leads to industry-wide wage increases.[86] Similarly designed studies show maquiladora activity in Mexico increased wages of skilled labor.[87] Lipsey and Sjöholm calculated wage spillovers with consideration for industry-specific and location-wide effects in Indonesia. They find significant spillovers to wages in domestic-owned firms and that these spillovers increase with skill level.[88]

In sum, the empirical record shows foreign firms pay wage premiums in local labor markets and contribute to broad-based wage increases. For this reason, we may expect domestic firms to support policies that restrict foreign investment – particularly firms in labor-intensive industries – and to advocate for liberalization of FDI entry. Indeed, previous research on the political economy of FDI policy conforms to this theoretical framework.[89]

The factor-proportion models that emphasize short-term positive wage effects from FDI inflows rest upon several simplifying assumptions: market clearing conditions, full employment, and constant returns to scale. What happens when we begin to relax these assumptions? A growing emphasis on industry- and firm-level heterogeneity, especially with respect to imperfectly competitive industry structures, and differential productivity increases expectations that many domestic firms will be disadvantaged by inward FDI. Because of entry costs associated with establishing a foreign subsidiary, FDI usually occurs in monopolistically competitive industries that are characterized by increasing returns to scale.[90]

[85] Rybczynski (1955).
[86] Aitken et al. (1996).
[87] Feenstra and Hanson (1997).
[88] Lipsey and Sjöholm (2003).
[89] See Pandya (2010, 2014); Pinto (2013).
[90] Keller and Yeaple (2009); Markusen and Venables (1998).

The superior access to finance and technological sophistication that characterize MNEs make them better able to overcome natural entry barriers in concentrated markets and to significantly reduce incumbents' market share. Firms that choose to engage in FDI have higher productivity than other firms in both their home and host countries.[91] This productivity gap is more pronounced when multinationals locate in previously protected industries because rents accrued from protection reduce the propensity to invest in productivity-enhancing technology.[92]

Multinational entry, by increasing competition in host country product and labor markets, also forces less efficient domestic firms to exit.[93] For these reasons, inefficient domestic firms will view FDI as a threat to their survival. This will be especially true of small and medium-size firms who typically have higher labor costs, lower capital investments, lower productivity, and lower access to investment financing. A prominent example of this displacement effect is the widespread concern that large retailers such as Walmart can easily run family-owned retail shops out of business since smaller shops cannot compete with the extensive distribution networks and volume-driven discounts of larger retailers.

Opportunities from Openness

FDI is routinely viewed as positive for host country development because countries largely open to multinational production display higher average productivity and more rapid economic growth. This finding is widely established at both the macro and firm levels.[94] Many studies exploring the mechanisms through which foreign affiliate presence may generate positive spillovers in host economies have examined the wage and productivity effects of FDI inflows. Central to these findings is, though the wage effects of FDI are clearly positive, the spillover effects to domestic industry are conditional on many firm, industry, and state characteristics. Therefore, domestic firms will view FDI with

---

[91] Helpman (2006).
[92] Schwab and Werker (2018).
[93] Alfaro and Chen (2018).
[94] Alfaro et al. (2004); Borensztein et al. (1998); Kose et al. (2011); Prasad et al. (2003).

caution because ex ante the costs of foreign entry are mostly known but the potential benefits are less easily identified. More plainly, domestic firms know that foreign entry will place upward pressure on wages, particularly of skilled labor, but they are less able to anticipate positive spillovers that may accrue to their particular firm.

A local firm is most likely to profit from FDI inflows when it joins a multinational in a joint venture or merger.[95] Local participants benefit from capital injections, risk sharing, procurement contracts with parents, and technology and knowledge spillovers. Research on FDI externalities consistently finds vertical integration through foreign-domestic equity partnerships that develop backward linkages with multinational parents is most likely to increase local firms' productivity and profits of local firms.[96] Conversely, competition effects disadvantage domestic enterprises when foreign investors establish wholly owned subsidiaries. Indeed, there is stronger evidence for the existence of vertical spillovers through such backward linkages than for positive horizontal spillovers.[97] Backward linkages are more likely under conditions of trade openness and are more likely in the manufacturing sector than in services.

Local firms may wish to restrict FDI to minority shares in order to ensure that FDI inflows will benefit them. However, such restrictions often reduce foreign firms' willingness to engage in joint venture activity and impede technology transfer and industrial upgrading in the joint ventures that foreign firms do establish.[98] Foreign investors view minority stakes as particularly problematic when corporate

---

[95] Entry through mergers and acquisitions (M&As) dominate FDI flows. While the composition of flows to developing countries tends to tilt toward greenfield investment, it is erroneous to conclude that most FDI in developing countries occurs through the establishment of wholly owned subsidiaries of foreign firms. A large percentage of these flows counted as greenfield investment actually come from retained earnings of already established enterprises. In 2010, for example, 40 percent of FDI income was retained and reinvested in host countries.

[96] Irsova and Havranek (2013).

[97] Blalock and Gertler (2005); Havranek and Irsova (2011); Javorcik and Spatareanu (2005). Another potential vertical spillover could occur from forward linkages, where domestic upstream firms purchase inputs from foreign affiliates. However, there is much greater evidence that productivity spillovers from FDI are more likely to occur through backward linkage than any other. See Havranek and Irsova (2011).

[98] Moran (2005); Qui and Wang (2013).

governance structures privilege majority owners and make corporate oversight challenging.[99] Investors with noncontrolling interests in firms owned by conglomerates are particularly vulnerable to tunneling as parents can strip value from subsidiary joint ventures and transfer assets to other subsidiaries to which the foreign investors have no claim.[100] Therefore, attracting substantial FDI inflows often requires governments to allow foreign firms to own majority stakes in local enterprises.[101]

Uncertainty and Status Quo Bias

While obtaining supplier status may generate substantial pecuniary externalities for individual firms, domestic enterprises face large uncertainties ex ante about whether they will win such procurement contracts if a multinational was granted entry. Thus, foreign entry projects known costs through upward pressure on wages and increased competition in product markets that decrease producer surplus. The potential benefits to individual firms from foreign entry are difficult to identify, however, because firms do not know if they will secure lucrative downstream supply or upstream distribution contracts with foreign firms. Accordingly, industrial incumbents will view unrestricted FDI with caution and instead prefer foreign entry be restricted entirely or to joint ventures. This status quo bias creates a strong resistance to

---

[99] Corporate laws characterized by weak minority shareholder protections are common among both developed and developing countries. Strong protections for minority owners are in many ways unique to the United States and the United Kingdom. See Claessens (2006), Claessens et al. (2002), and La Porta et al. (2000).

[100] For example, a March 14, 1998, article from *The Economist* emphasized the chilling effect equity restrictions had on joint venture FDI in South Korea. Restrictions limiting foreign ownership to minority stakes "allowed South Korea's Chaebol (conglomerates), which like to use strong subsidiaries to prop up weak ones, to plunder joint ventures' coffers ... The safest course for an outsider is to buy a majority stake." See Johnson et al. (2000).

[101] The experience of India is illustrative. While a collection of business organizations called the "Bombay Club" lobbied for continued protection against FDI, other family-owned business groups seized the opportunity to become domestic partners of foreign entities (Chair and Gupta, 2008; Kochanek, 1996a; 1996b; Tripathi, 2004). The Tata and Birla groups were proponents of reform and were partners in 45 of the 625 MNE joint ventures formed in the wake of the regulatory reform (Chair and Gupta, 2008, 637).

reform.[102] A protectionist bias will be especially powerful among small and medium-size firms who typically have higher labor costs, lower capital investments, lower productivity, and lower access to investment financing.[103] Such firms are most in danger of failing to remain competitive in a sector with foreign firms and also, due to their size, capacity constraints, and low productivity, are least likely to benefit from lucrative procurement contracts.[104]

As mentioned above, industrial incumbents will oppose unrestricted foreign entry but may support a partial easing of foreign ownership restrictions to allow multinationals to enter into joint ventures with local firms. Such policies provide domestic incumbents with access to capital while restricting intra-industry competition and ensuring domestic firms retain managerial control. Larger industrialists may be particularly interested in policies that allow foreigners the opportunity to take minority stake in incumbent firms because they are likely the most attractive potential merger partners. They tend to have higher productivity than their Small and Medium Enterprises (SME) counterparts, and, perhaps most important, large incumbents typically have political connections and bureaucratic access points that foreign entrants value.[105] Smaller domestic firms, however, will be less likely to benefit from potential partial acquisitions and will be hurt by the productivity and investment gains large incumbents will make through such equity deals with foreign firms.

Endogenizing Firm Financing Constraints

From the discussion above, it is clear that domestic firms often have reasons to view foreign entry with suspicion. What then might shift incumbent strategies toward regulation? I consider how financial constraints influence local firms' preferences over admitting foreign firms into their economies. In doing so, I place firms' financing environments in the center of understanding their interests. Other scholars operating from the varieties of capitalism (VoC) tradition and scholars of

---

[102] Fernández and Rodrik (1991); Roland (2000).
[103] Rajan and Zingales (2003).
[104] Brown (2002); Crespo and Fontoura (2006); Damijan et al. (2013); Helpman (2006).
[105] Desbordes and Vauday (2007); Evans (1979); Teichman (2001); Vitalis (1995).

the FLG nexus consider how businesses' financing requirements influence their behavior in industrial relations and corporate governance. I expand on some of these insights, particularly from FLG, to show how firms' attitudes toward foreign investors will shift as their needs for raising equity increase.

A rich tradition in the FLG literature considers the ways in which the legal environment surrounding company law both structures firm strategies and is shaped by political processes.[106] This literature emphasizes the problem of agency costs that arise when insiders (entrepreneurs or managing owners) seek financing from outsiders (financiers or minority shareholders). Firms develop strategies over how they structure finance and ownership based on the laws that govern protection of creditors and minority shareholders. Simultaneously, firms use their political influence to push for investor protection laws that maximize the utility of controlling owners.

Most of this literature emphasizes the complementarities and trade-offs between investor protections and the private benefits that accrue to owner-managers. Standard models consider how shifts in minority investor protections influence the amount of equity entrepreneurs decide to issue.[107] Access to debt finance is either ignored or treated as a constant. However, insights from these models have bearing on the decision to finance firms' capital needs through debt or equity, which in turn depends on the relative cost of different financing options. Local firms' policy preferences toward foreign direct investors rest fundamentally on this decision.

As economic agents, local business owners seek to maximize wealth. More specifically, they maximize the value of their ownership stake in their company – which is the market value of the firm multiplied by their equity stake – plus any resources they are able to divert for personal use. For simplicity, I treat local owners as unitary actors. While in reality management is often comprised of multiple individuals, this simplification is justified for several reasons. First, the firm can agree upon arrangements to distribute private benefits among managers. Second, concentrated ownership patterns are far more prevalent globally than diffuse ownership structures typical of Anglo-American firms[108]

---

[106] See especially Haber and Perotti (2007); Pagano and Volpin (2005).
[107] Pagano and Volpin (2006).
[108] La Porta et al. (2000).

and are often associated with family control.[109] It is more plausible that firms owned by a single family or firms owned by groups that are highly interconnected will be able to reach agreements about how to distribute private benefits across individuals. Third, in treating local owners as unitary, I follow a large formal literature in the law and finance literature.[110]

The value of local firms depends on a complex set of factors ranging from macroeconomic consideration, such as local economic growth prospects and exchange rates, to firm-specific assets such as technology and managerial acuity. However, all firms' values rely fundamentally on their ability to raise external finance such that operations and investment activities can exceed the wealth of owner-managers. Firms can raise finance through debt or equity. Equity investment can be raised through portfolio or direct investment. The distinction between these types is that portfolio equity investment is merely a claim on future cash flow, while direct investment also entails some amount of managerial control. Thus, portfolio investors are by definition "outsiders" while direct investors become "insiders."

The value of private benefits of control depends upon the local legal environment. Where there exist high levels of minority stockholder protection, private benefits are lower because the probability that managing owners will be detected and prosecuted for asset stripping is higher. This assumption is robustly supported empirically. Investors routinely discount their valuation of firms located in countries with poor minority investor protections.[111] Investors value controlling bloc shares more highly in countries with poor minority investor protections, as measured by the price premium afforded to controlling shares.[112] It may be conceptually clarifying to consider briefly a formal treatment of an owner's utility function, which we can represent as:

$$U_e = \beta_e V + D \qquad\qquad (3.1)$$

where β_e is the owner's equity stake in the firm; V is the value of the firm, which is a function of sales minus expenses, some of which include cost of any debt financing; and D is the value of private benefits of control.

---

[109] Pagano and Volpin (2005).
[110] Haber and Perotti (2007).
[111] Doidge et al. (2004).
[112] Dyck and Zingales (2004).

This simple equation helps highlight the way in which financing affects a local firm's maximization problem. First, debt-financing costs decrease profits. This indicates that as firms' borrowing costs cross some threshold, they will begin to view equity financing more favorably. A substantial literature on corporate governance reforms establishes theoretically and empirically that firms often must strengthen minority shareholder protections in order to raise adequate capital. Without such protections, equity valuations are low and therefore owner-managers must relinquish more cash flow rights in order to raise substantial funds. Strengthening corporate governance decreases D because such protections make owner-managers more accountable to minority investors. Firms could also raise equity through direct investment. Direct investors may not require stronger minority shareholder protections because they will take a management stake. However, owner-managers will need to share in D with direct investors.

Thus, firms face trade-offs with regard to financing decisions. They can borrow, which allows them to raise capital without relinquishing future cash flow rights or the private benefits of control, but at the expense of firm value because borrowing comes at a cost. They can raise equity diffusely through stock offerings, which does not decrease V, but does decrease insiders' ownership stake and will probably also require some decrease in D in order to attract potential investors.

In other words, as the cost of borrowing increase, domestic firms will increasingly view inward FDI as a potential solution to their financing constraints. This will be especially true in countries with weak corporate governance laws, for large and politically important firms that previously had privileged access to finance, and for firms in industries that are capital intensive and therefore more sensitive to changes in the cost of finance.

There are several channels, both direct and indirect, through which foreign firm presence can ameliorate local firms' financing constraints. The first is through MNE choice of entry. FDI often, particularly at moments of initial openness, enters new markets through mergers and acquisitions (M&As) in which foreign firms acquire management stakes in local companies. When foreign businesses engage in green-field investing, they frequently do so with local partners and integrated local suppliers. Accordingly, FDI done through M&A and joint venture deals provide direct channels of equity finance to local firms. Vertically integrated FDI also decreases financing constraints for integrated suppliers.[113] These cash injections can be used to finance both operations and expansion activities. They also do so without requiring local partners to be subjected to short-term discipline mechanisms through equity markets.

Second, foreign entry can alleviate financing constraints of local firms without foreign participation in at least two ways. First, local firms who become suppliers to MNEs achieve lucrative boosts in sales and also often benefit from financing arrangements that multinationals employ to assist their local suppliers in weathering cash flow cycles. For example, multinationals may choose to pay their local suppliers before delivery, so that local firms can more easily finance production. They may also choose to provide low interest loans to their suppliers for production costs, which are then settled at time of sale.[114] Second, when multinationals invest locally, this can generate more business lending capacity on the part of local banks because acquired and partnered firms can now rely on foreign parents rather than local capital markets for finance. Consequently, local banks have more capacity to lend to other local firms.[115]

Finally, FDI is a particularly important source of investment finance during times of economic distress. While patterns of foreign portfolio investment flows follow business cycles, inward FDI flows tend to be countercyclical.[116] Foreign firms increase their local acquisitions when local economies face negative liquidity shocks.[117] MNEs can also draw on self-financing and financing from home country capital markets when local conditions are tight.[118] Access to finance during times of financial crisis lead foreign-owned firms to perform better than locally owned counterparts during local recessions.[119]

Mechanisms of Financing Environment Changes

What, then, can shift firm borrowing costs enough that they will be more willing to support openness to FDI? In previous work, Aizenman

---

[113] Kersting and Görg (2017).
[114] Javorcik and Spatareanu (2009).
[115] Harrison et al. (2004).
[116] Forbes and Warnock (2012).
[117] Aguiar and Gopinath (2005).
[118] Desai et al. (2008).
[119] Alfaro and Chen (2018).

shows formally that financial shocks induce investment reform because domestic firms will be more welcoming of foreign investors when $i_d > i_w$.[120] However, changes in foreign entry restrictions are not associated with banking, currency, or debt crises for two reasons. First, responses to financial crises depend on the capacity of local banking systems to absorb shocks. Financial repression serves to insulate favored firms against insurmountable liquidity shocks in the wake of financial crises. Reformed banking systems do not have that cushion and therefore have to turn to foreign equity. The second is that investment policy takes time to enact and is a response to long-term needs rather than immediate liquidity crises. In times of a liquidity crisis, searching for FDI is not a principal priority because deployment times are long. Quick capital injections, usually through lending and short-term finance, are more important. That is, the mechanisms that generate local support for reform must create relatively long-term upward shifts in the cost of capital. I identify four such channels.

First, local capacity to finance business activity should influence domestic firms' policy preferences over foreign investment. When the domestic banking sector is so small that it cannot generate enough low-cost credit for the state, firms may perceive that the benefits of regulated FDI outweigh complete restriction. African experiences with FDI follow this pattern, with many governments pursuing partial openness to foreign investment early in their postcolonial histories.[121]

Second, local access to and cost of international sources of credit can mute local financing constraints as domestic banks can channel large volumes of investment debt finance to local firms.[122] Loosening of capital controls on portfolio flows, therefore, may decrease pressures for FDI openness because local firms will have increased access to debt finance as domestic banks use foreign investment flows to expand loan portfolios. This is especially true when global credit conditions

---

[120] Aizenman (2005).

[121] United Nations Conference on Trade and Development (2005a).

[122] This argument suggests that some success at attracting foreign investment may function to reduce elites' financing constraints and therefore prevent further FDI liberalization. These expectations run counter to claims that liberalization of capital flows are complementary (Haggard and Maxfield, 1996) and claims that FDI inflows give foreign firms a foothold in which they can pressure the government to enact further liberalization. See also Desbordes and Vauday (2007); Hewko (2002); Malesky (2009).

are loose because the cost of borrowing is low. Under such conditions local elite will be better able to generate investment financing through international debt markets and therefore will be less likely to press for FDI openness. However, as global conditions reduce the supply of debt financing, local firms will become more credit constrained and therefore more likely to support openness to foreign investors.

Third, regulations over connected lending also affect firms' borrowing costs and therefore their preferences for FDI. In many countries, closely held and interconnected business groups dominate enterprise. These related firms, often held together through bloc shareholding and interlocking directorates, can form powerful diversified conglomerates. These firms can lend to their related partners at below-market rates, often with less collateral requirements. Firms in countries with stricter regulations over financial-industrial conglomeration and related lending will face higher borrowing costs than those in countries that allow or even encourage such arrangements. Thus, stricter regulation of connected lending should increase local firms' willingness to open to foreign firms.

Fourth, the extent to which governments use domestic banking regulation to intercede in credit markets should influence indigenous firms' preferences for FDI. When financial markets are thin and characterized by state repression, powerful firms benefit from unequal access to debt finance at subsidized terms. Under these conditions, they can easily finance expansion without selling cash-flow rights or relinquishing managerial control. As the banking sector is liberalized and prominent firms no longer have preferential access to debt finance, the costs associated with limiting foreign invested partners increases. Prominent firms will become more willing to support liberalization of foreign equity restrictions.

Finally, even in generally financially constrained environments, firms should face heterogeneous preferences over FDI liberalization. First, as discussed above, large firms are more likely to view FDI as an opportunity than are small and medium-size firms. This is because large firms are more likely to be attractive acquisition targets and suppliers in the eyes of foreign firms and because large, politically powerful firms are most likely to benefit from directed credit schemes under financial repression, which means their cost of borrowing increases the most when domestic banking undergoes reform. Second, we should expect variation in policy preferences at the industry level. If the mechanism that drives firms' willingness to support FDI openness is access to finance, firms in capital-intensive industries should respond to changes in the financing environment more strongly than firms in labor-intensive industries.[123]

Financial Repression and FDI Preferences

Above, I articulate multiple channels through which firms' borrowing costs may shift substantially so that politically powerful firms may desire more openness to foreign investors. In this section, I focus on one of these channels – changes to state control of credit markets. I do so because whether or not the state exerts control over the domestic banking sector to channel capital to favored industries and firms substantially affects both the cost of credit for large domestic firms and the political coalitions that support incumbent governments. Tracing the co-movement of banking and FDI policies over time provides a useful schematic for illustrating the causal logic underpinning a financing constraints theory of FDI liberalization. And, in the following empirical chapters, I use a variety of data at multiple levels of analysis to examine the connection between changes to banking sector regulations and foreign investment policies.

Anti-FDI Coalitions under Financial Repression

In a previous section I outlined the reasons why domestic firms prefer to limit foreign firms' ability to invest directly in local markets. Foreign entry pushes up wage costs, forces local firms to sacrifice rents for increases in productivity, and is generally disruptive to existing market structures. Therefore, domestic firms will support restrictive policies toward FDI as long as their access to operations and investment financing is sufficient. Under the terms of financial repression, large and politically important firms can easily finance operation and expansion

---

[123] Substantial empirical work demonstrates that firms in industries that are more dependent on external finance (that is, external to the firm) are more negatively affected by banking sector shocks than are other industries, which is closely related to capital intensity. See Chor and Manova (2012); Campello et al. (2010); Dell'Ariccia et al. (2008); Kroszner et al. (2007); Rajan and Zingales (1998).

through subsidized debt. They will support policies that restrict foreign entry outright or to minority joint ventures. This allows them to maintain ownership and control as well as protect rents. While repressed financial systems ration credit, the losers of financial repression – small, weakly organized firms – are poorly situated to pressure governments to reform.[124] Such firms are the least likely to benefit from FDI liberalization because foreign entry typically increases dropout rates among small and inefficient firms.[125] Because financial repression channels cheap credit to politically powerful firms, such systems also tend to consolidate industries into large and closely held industrial-financial conglomerates. Conglomeration intensifies market distortions in credit markets because the financial arm of these groups loan to connected corporations at below-market rates.[126] The rise of powerful conglomerates thus further entrenches local firms' capacity to use domestically intermediated sources of finance.

Local capital can build large anti-FDI coalitions under conditions of financial repression. Where labor is well organized, capitalists can buy off union support for restrictions on FDI through sharing rents.[127] Directed credit to labor-intensive industries creates an alliance between firms and the state because these investments create jobs and economic growth that help maintain popular support for the ruling government. Politico-bureaucrats benefit from expanded jurisdiction, power, and control over investment project proposals. This allows them to use their influence over credit allocation to develop patronage networks to construct ruling coalitions, reward supporters, and punish detractors.[128] Public and private banking interests benefit from restricting foreign firm entry because multinationals impinge on local banks' privileged position of mediating between international capital and local borrowers. In sum, FDI openness threatens the material and political profits of many influential domestic actors, while the benefits of openness to other groups are too small to encourage mobilization efforts for reform.

---

[124] Rajan and Zingales (2003).
[125] Alfaro and Chen (2018).
[126] Akerlof and Romer (1993); La Porta et al. (2000).
[127] Teichman (1995, 2001).
[128] Bueno de Mesquita et al. (2003); Haggard et al. (1993); Pepinsky (2013a).

Pro-FDI Coalitions under Financial Reform

As explained above, under conditions of financial repression, governments will place high restrictions on FDI by either banning foreign equity outright or by limiting FDI to joint ventures with local firms, usually as minority partners, and by maintaining screening requirements. When governments undertake banking sector reforms, often in response to financial crises, the coalitions supporting such policies can weaken significantly.[129]

One may ask why politically connected firms have the political power to shape FDI policies to their liking, but are unable to prevent the banking sector reforms that ultimately lead to FDI liberalization. Differential time horizons and the distinction between "crisis politics" and "normal politics" is important here. Banking sector reforms are usually unanticipated by domestic firms that might otherwise oppose them. Abiad and Mody find balance of payment crises significantly raise the probability of such reforms.[130] This is because banking reforms generally occur due to liquidity shocks that demand some kind of adjustment. In such situations, normal policy processes are often suspended because political leaders must attend to very urgent crises. FDI policies, however, are generated and modified through normal political processes. Because FDI is less liquid, it is not a rapid solution to a financial crisis. Thus, by the time that FDI policy reforms are considered, the short-term thinking and chaos that characterizes banking reforms has subsided and interest group politics has become more relevant again. This is why powerful firms can be unable to stop banking reforms but then be instrumental in the FDI policy reform process.

Banking sector reforms, by eliminating subsidized credit schemes, encourage incumbent firms to consolidate and increase productivity. Successful firms, therefore, are better poised to have increasingly international orientations. These firms are likely to develop their own ability to invest abroad and therefore will support further openness to FDI to encourage reciprocity. They are also best poised to benefit from FDI inflows because they have the capacity and productivity

---

[129] Banking sector reforms are usually unanticipated by domestic firms that might otherwise oppose them. Abiad and Mody (2005) find balance of payment crises significantly raise the probability of such reforms, although banking crises make financial sector reform more difficult.

[130] Abiad and Mody (2005).

that make them attractive partners, acquisition targets, and sources of inputs. The high cost of credit encourages them to seek FDI as a less costly financing option. Because they are highly productive, these firms are also less likely to become uncompetitive in markets that include foreign investors.

Banking sector reforms also erode the power of other societal groups that might continue to support FDI restrictions. First, banking reform decreases the political power of domestic financial interests that may prefer to continue to restrict FDI as a means of maintaining their privileged position intermediating between foreign investors and local firms.[131] Banking sector reforms entail privatizing state-owned banks and severing the close connections between government bureaucrats and bankers. This makes the financial sector a weaker political actor less capable of successfully lobbying for protective policies. Second, such reforms soften governments' antipathy for FDI because financial repression is no longer a viable strategy for industrial expansion. When the government liberalizes banking, it no longer retains the ability to control credit allocation for political purposes. Therefore, it cannot rely on cheaply obtained credit to finance development projects and needs to cultivate new sources of investment to drive economic growth. Thus, banking sector reforms erode the power of societal groups that are most opposed to FDI openness and create new capital interests that are more internationally focused. As the banking sector liberalizes, therefore, states will be more likely to pursue greater openness to FDI to accommodate these new interests.

Liberal Economic Backsliding?

One important question follows: is the theory put forth here symmetrical? That is, if banking deregulation leads firms to lobby for more openness toward FDI, does increased banking regulation or other changes that make the domestic financing environment more favorable lead firms to prefer more restrictions on foreign entry? One answer, perhaps, is that a move toward state control of the banking sector in the early twentieth century did make domestic firms advocates of restricting MNE entry and operations. This interpretation is in line with a large, established literature on the developmental state and its

---

[131] Pepinsky (2013a).

stance toward global capital.[132] It is less clear, however, if an increased availability of cheap credit today would encourage firms to lobby for increased restrictions on foreign firms, largely because the proliferation of global value chains has rendered the distinction between local and foreign firms increasingly murky. This is a question that I explore at greater length in the concluding chapter.

Implications and Research Design

I explained above why local firms should be wary of foreign entry due to competitive pressures but be more willing to support policies of openness and even promotion when local financing conditions are constraining. I also identify sources of heterogeneous preferences among firms; firms in capital-intensive industries should be more sensitive to financing cost changes as should large firms that benefit from privileged access to subsidized loans when governments intervene in domestic credit markets. This theoretical framework suggests a series of observable implications that inform the remainder of this book.

First, liberalization of FDI policies should occur when financing constraints make other sources of debt and equity financing untenable for large local firms. Chapter 4 presents a series of quantitative tests of the effect of financing constraints on changes in foreign equity restrictions at the national level.

Second, if firm preferences have a substantial influence over policy, we should also see these liberalizing shifts occur more frequently when domestic political institutions favor business interests, but only when the local financing environment is constrained. Again in Chapter 4, I use country-level data on domestic political institutions to probe whether institutions that privilege elites are associated with greater FDI liberalization after the domestic banking sector has undergone reforms.

Third, domestic firms should be less finance constrained in countries characterized by liberal FDI environments than in countries with sizable restrictions on foreign entry. This should be especially true of firms that have some degree of foreign equity participation, large firms, and firms in capital-intensive industries. In Chapter 5, I use World Bank Enterprise Surveys to explore how the foreign investment

---

[132] See especially Frieden (1981), Lipson (1985), and the section in Chapter 2 entitled *"Investment Policies in Historical Perspective."*

regulatory environment affects firms' perceptions of their ability to obtain sufficient finance.

Fourth, if local firm preferences drive movements toward more liberal foreign investment regulations, we should see variations in industry-level investment policies related to the capital intensity of the industry and the relative political strength of key firms within the industry. In Chapter 5, I also use industry-level data on investment policy changes to determine the relationship between capital intensity and the propensity to enact liberalizing policy change. In particular, I test three observable implications of the financing constraints theory. First, industries characterized by high levels of capital intensity should be more likely to experience liberalizing changes when local banking regulations reduce governments' ability to channel subsidized credit to influential firms. Second, capital-intensive industries should be less likely to undergo policy liberalization where political leaders retain tools to intercede in credit markets. Finally, banking sector reforms should be associated with increases in policy liberalizations related to entry restrictions but not to other more ancillary policy tools such as regulations over treatment or investment promotion.

In Chapters 6 and 7, I supplement quantitative analysis with qualitative process tracing. I use the comparative cases of Malaysia and Indonesia to trace changes to banking and FDI laws in both countries from 1965 to 2013, paying particular attention to the aftermath of the 1997 Asian financial crisis.

Together, these empirical exercises provide substantial evidence in support of a financing constraints theory of investment policy liberalization. Examination of firm-, industry-, and country-level outcomes of interest, combined with case studies that more fully explore causal processes, suggest domestic firms can be powerful actors in reformist coalitions. This finding challenges dominant narratives in the political economy of economic reform that view liberalization processes as empowering outsiders at the expense of incumbents. However, insiders are not as flatfooted as such explanations suggest. Influential firms are powerful in part because their political connections and economic resources provide them with multiple tools and strategies of adaptation. Therefore, they can use these resources to shape reform agendas in their interests and further entrench their advantage vis-à-vis domestic entrants.

4 | *Quantitative Tests: Financing Constraints and Liberalization*

In Chapter 3, I present several hypotheses linking decisions to liberalize foreign direct investment (FDI) inflows to the local financing environment. The first two relate to how characteristics of domestic banking regulations and access to finance condition local firms' policy preferences over foreign investment regulation. Banking sector reforms that reduce government control over credit allocation processes will be associated with increasingly liberal FDI policy environments. In contrast, high levels of domestic credit availability should be negatively associated with liberalizing changes to FDI policy because domestic firms face less burdensome financing constraints. The remaining hypotheses relate to the mechanisms that tie domestic firms' financing concerns to changes in national policies toward FDI. These include expectations that governments with more access points for elite control will be more likely to liberalize FDI policies as financing constraints for large firms increase, that firm-level reports of financial constraints should depend on both domestic banking regulations and openness toward FDI, and that industries characterized by higher capital intensities will be more likely to liberalize foreign entry in the wake of changes to the domestic banking environment.

In this chapter, I present statistical analysis that assesses hypotheses that operate at the country-year unit of analysis. These include the expectation that domestic banking regulations and access to finance condition openness to foreign investment and the expectation that domestic political institutions that favor business interests will make investment liberalization more likely as credit allocation processes become more market, rather than politically, driven. I use a variety of data, with different temporal and cross-sectional coverage, to test these hypotheses. Because my theory most directly challenges Pandya's democracy-driven liberalization theory,[1] I begin by using her data.

---

[1] Pandya (2013).

When combined with my preferred measure of banking sector reforms, this creates a sample of approximately 70 developed and developing countries from 1973 to 2000, which represents the time period in which policies toward FDI exhibited the most change. However, we may also be curious about the relationship between the banking sector and FDI policy since 2000, especially given the global financial crisis of 2007–2008. I explore these more recent trends using data on FDI policy changes globally from 2000 to 2015.[2] Readers may be concerned that pooling across developed and developing countries may be inappropriate due to causal heterogeneity. However, because countries at all levels of development underwent banking sector reforms during the period studied, I expect my theory to apply broadly. In several models, however, I constrain analysis to only developing countries and find that my central results hold.

The results from the models I present in this chapter provide robust support for the contention that changes in local financial environments influence governments' policies toward FDI. Countries that undergo changes to banking rules that decrease politically driven credit allocation processes are more likely to subsequently decrease restrictions on foreign ownership of locally incorporated enterprise. This relationship is robust to the inclusion of a variety measures that serve as proxies for prominent alternative explanations of what might drive changes to the treatment of foreign firms. Multiple techniques to ensure results are not driven by endogenous processes confirm that this relationship is not a statistical artifact. In models restricted to only developing countries, the relationship between changes in the domestic financing environment and FDI liberalization is even more pronounced. Countries with high levels of domestic sources of finance are less likely to undergo liberalizing changes to FDI policy, although this finding is more dependent on modeling specification.

I also find substantial evidence that it is business interests, rather than other societal groups or technocrats, who push for these liberalizing changes. If firms guide liberalizing coalitions, we should see increasing openness to foreign investment when domestic conditions augment business interests' ability to influence policy. If, instead, democracies liberalize FDI because workers demand it, domestic institutions that privilege labor over capital should be more closely

---

[2] United Nations Conference on Trade and Development (2016a).

associated with liberalization. Using measures from the Database of Political Institutions (DPI) and the International Country Risk Guide (ICRG), I explore how several measures of firm influence affect FDI liberalization: executive and legislative partisanship, corruption, and bureaucratic quality. I also leverage data on election cycles to determine whether political leaders liberalize in advance of elections – a pattern that would be consistent with liberalizing to appease voters – or whether they liberalize in election off years – a pattern more consistent with elite-driven policy change coalitions. I find that the relationship between banking sector reforms and FDI liberalization is stronger under right-leaning executives, in more corrupt political environments, and when bureaucracies are weak and underprofessionalized. I also find some evidence that liberalizing changes to FDI policies are less likely, while restrictive changes are more likely, during election years. Beyond probing causal mechanisms, these tests also provide evidence in direct opposition to a democracy-driven explanation of FDI policy reform because if FDI liberalization occurred due to the increased political power of labor, we should expect that political institutions that favor firms would provide insulation against reforms rather than make liberalization more likely.

Historical Analysis, 1973–2000

I begin by examining the relationship between banking sector reforms and FDI policy openness during the last half of the twentieth century. I do so in part because this historical period is particularly important to explain given the substantial transformation in many countries' investment policies that occurred during this time frame. I also begin with this historical analysis in order to evaluate my theory using the same data and time frame that Pandya uses to establish her democracy-driven liberalization theory.

Variables, Measurement, and Methodology

As discussed in greater detail in Chapter 2, policies toward FDI are multifaceted and encompass a diverse set of rules regarding equity restrictions, screening requirements, licensing laws, and legal provisions regarding profit repatriation, export balancing requirements, nationalization, and legal recourse for aggrieved firms. The complexity of FDI policy has been a contributing factor to the lack of study of this topic, and measurement remains a challenge to researchers. For these historical tests, I primarily measure FDI regulation using Pandya's dataset of *Equity Restrictions* for 94 countries from 1970 to 2000.[3] For detail about this measure's construction, as well as its strengths and weaknesses, I refer interested readers to Chapter 2, "Comparing Broad Measures of Investment Climate."

One substantial drawback of the *Equity Restrictions* measure is that the data end in 2000. Given my interest in this section of assessing the historical patterns of FDI liberalization, I believe the time period of the 1970s through 2000 to be most appropriate for my analysis. After all, as discussed at length in Chapter 2, this time period exhibited the largest shifts in policies toward foreign investment since the abrupt closure of local markets from foreign investors that marked the decolonization period.

As a check that my results are robust to other measurement approaches, I also perform analysis using the Organisation for Economic Co-operation and Development's (OECD) FDI Regulatory Restrictiveness index, the Fraser Institute's measure of Investment Freedom, the Heritage Foundation's similar Investment Freedom Index, and Pandya's alternative measure of Investment Screening Requirements. Inclusion of these measures allows me to analyze determinants of FDI policy through 2012. The disadvantage of these measures is they have more limited country and temporal coverage. They generally place less emphasis on right to entry in favor of assessing postestablishment treatment. These variables' limited cross sectional and temporal coverage restricts my ability to run analyses to only more simple models with few control variables. Despite these limitations, my central findings hold.

Measuring the Domestic Financing Environment

Hypothesis 1 anticipates that governments will loosen foreign equity restrictions as large, politically important firms lose their privileged access to finance. As discussed at greater length in the previous chapter, this will occur as banking sector liberalization reduces the ability

---

[3] Pandya (2013).

of the government to channel subsidized credit to favored industries and firms. To measure *Banking Reform*, I use a modified version of Abiad et al.'s index of financial sector reforms.[4] This measure has broad temporal and cross-sectional coverage, including 103 countries from 1973 to 2005. The index compiles qualitative judgments over liberalization in five aspects of banking sector policy: credit controls and excessively high reserve requirements, interest rate controls, state ownership in the banking sector, prudential regulations and supervision of the banking sector, and securities market policies. Countries score higher in each component of the index when government intervention declines. The notable exception is the prudential regulation component; higher scores for this component correspond with the implementation of regulatory oversight generally seen as preventing excessive risk taking such as Basel compliant reserve requirements.[5]

Case Coverage and Estimation Diagnostics

Compiling these data, I obtain a dataset of 68 countries from 1973 to 2000 for which measures of both FDI and banking sector policies exist. Table 4.1 lists the countries included in analysis; most regions are well covered, but transition economies are underrepresented. These data exhibit several features that complicate statistical inference. First, *Equity Restrictions* and *Banking Reform* are nonstationary series. Diagnostics indicate each displays a first-order integration. Second, the data structure is such that groups (countries) exceed panel length (time periods). Such data can produce artificially small standard errors due to contemporaneous correlation and panel heteroskedasticity. Third, diagnostics confirm these data display both unit and time fixed effects.

To correct adequately for potential bias and inconsistency, I use several techniques to ensure my results are insensitive to modeling choice. First, following Beck and Katz, I model panel dynamics by including

---

[4] Abiad et al. (2010).
[5] The original index also included component scores for restrictions on foreign bank ownership and capital account openness. I deleted these elements from the index to be sure that the variable does not conflate banking sector reforms with FDI liberalization.

Table 4.1. *Countries included in historical models*

Algeria	Denmark	Indonesia	Nicaragua	Switzerland
Argentina	Dominican Rep.	Israel	Nigeria	Tanzania
Australia	Ecuador	Italy	Norway	Thailand
Austria	Egypt	Japan	Pakistan	Tunisia
Belgium	El Salvador	Jordan	Paraguay	Turkey
Bolivia	Ethiopia	Kazakhstan	Peru	Uganda
Brazil	Finland	Kenya	Philippines	United Kingdom
Cameroon	France	Madagascar	Portugal	Uruguay
Canada	Germany	Malaysia	Singapore	Uzbekistan
Chile	Ghana	Mexico	South Africa	Venezuela
China	Greece	Morocco	South Korea	Zimbabwe
Colombia	Guatemala	Mozambique	Spain	
Costa Rica	Hong Kong	Netherlands	Sri Lanka	
Cote d'Ivoire	India	New Zealand	Sweden	

a lagged dependent variable.[6] Second, I approach problems associated with standard error estimation by including fixed country effects, year dummies, and standard errors clustered by country.[7] I prefer to report Fixed Effects models because panel corrected standard errors (PCSE) techniques can report artificially small standard errors if unit heterogeneity and serial correlation are not adequately corrected (Wilson and Butler, 2007). However, my main results are largely robust across both specifications, and I provide model output for other specifications in the chapter appendix.[8] All variables exhibiting left-hand skew are log transformed. To aid in interpreting relative substantive effects, I standardize all non-indicator variables. Table 4.2 provides descriptive statistics for the variables used in my main models; I include a correlation matrix in the chapter appendix.

---

[6] Beck and Katz (2011).

[7] Hausman tests indicate random effects are inappropriate for xtreg time series models. For all models with country and year dummies, I confirm their inclusion is warranted with block F tests.

[8] To save space, I only report alternate estimations for my main models (Models 8 and 9), but the results of all models are robust to estimation technique.

Table 4.2. *Descriptive statistics, historical models*

Variable	Mean	Std. Dev.	N
Equity Restrictions	0.178	0.353	1394
Screening Requirements	0.347	0.464	1115
Banking Reform	6.997	4.310	1394
ln(GDP Per Capita)	8.399	1.552	1394
ln(inflation)	3.747	0.601	1394
ln(Trade)	3.921	0.571	1383
ln(Tertiary Enrollment)	3.944	0.565	1383
ln(Domestic Credit)	50.851	37.232	1366
Fixed Exchange Rate	0.304	0.46	1394
Democracy	0.589	0.492	1394
Crisis	0.095	0.293	1394
Under IMF	0.325	0.469	1390
Regional Equity Restrictions	0.174	0.204	1393

Analysis

I begin by estimating baseline models of the relationship between FDI restrictiveness and banking sector openness.[9] Model 1 in Table 4.3 reports the result of the most basic model, which includes a lagged dependent variable, a 1-year lag of *Banking Reforms*, and the natural log of *GDP Per Capita*,[10] which captures the level of development, also lagged by 1 year. The model returns a negative and statistically significant relationship; as a country experiences a one standard deviation increase in banking sector openness, it experiences a decrease in equity restrictions equal to 7.2 percent of a standard deviation. Models 2 and 3 provide further confirmation for this relationship by disaggregating components of the *Banking Reforms* index; *Interest Rate Controls* has a negative and statistically significant relationship with *Equity Restrictions*, while the coefficient estimate for *Bank Privatization* is negative but not statistically significant. These findings corroborate a

---

[9] Assessing spare models is especially important to guard against the possibility that increasing covariates can actually induce statistical significance of key explanatory variables. See Lenz and Sahn (2019).

[10] All control variables, unless otherwise specified, are taken from the World Development Indicators.

Table 4.3. *Banking reforms and FDI policy*

	Model 1	Model 2	Model 3
Equity Restrictions$_{(t-1)}$	0.611***	0.605***	0.614***
	(0.04)	(0.04)	(0.04)
Banking Reform$_{(t-1)}$	−0.072*		
	(0.03)		
Interest Rate Controls$_{(t-1)}$		−0.073*	
		(0.02)	
Bank Privatization$_{(t-1)}$			−0.011
			(0.03)
Ln GDP Per Capita$_{(t-1)}$	−0.065	−0.093	−0.050
	(0.30)	(0.29)	(0.30)
Observations	1394	1394	1394
Countries	67	67	67
R^2	0.457	0.459	0.456

Fixed effects estimated with year dummies and country-clustered standard errors. Constant not reported. Std Error in parentheses. *$p < 0.05$, ** $p < 0.01$, ***$p < 0.001$

relationship between the dismantling of subsidized credit and FDI liberalization. At the same time, the lack of a statistically significant correlation between *Bank Privatization* and *Equity Restrictions* suggests the relationship between banking reforms and FDI policy is driven by credit concerns and not by broad programmatic embrace of neoliberal deregulation.

Next, I consider whether these baseline models are robust to alternative measures of FDI openness, and particularly to measures that extend to more recent years. Table 4.4 reports results that replicate Model 1 but use four different measures of FDI restrictions and openness.[11] *Screening* also comes from Pandya's data and is constructed in a similar fashion to *Equity Restrictions* except that it measures the percentage industries for which FDI requires government approval for each country-year. The *OECD Restrictiveness Index* has much less coverage, and because the *Banking Reform* measure stops in 2005, I can only run this analysis using values for the year 2006. The *Heritage*

---

[11] See Chapter 2, "Comparing Broad Measures of Investment Climate," for detailed information on these measures.

Table 4.4. *Banking reforms and alternate FDI policy measures*

	Model 4 Screening	Model 5 OECD	Model 6 Heritage	Model 7 Fraser
Lagged DV$_{(t-1)}$	0.744** (0.029)			
Banking Reform$_{(t-1)}$	−0.083 (0.053)	−0.092 (0.066)	3.209* (1.333)	0.824** (0.192)
Ln GDP Per Capita$_{(t-1)}$	−0.275 (0.179)	−0.064 (0.057)	6.136** (0.883)	0.540** (0.136)
Estimation Technique	Fixed Effects	Pooled	Pooled	Pooled
Observations	1147	32	442	142
Countries	55			
R^2	0.6531	0.3921	0.2741	0.4222

Fixed effects estimated with year dummies and country-clustered standard errors. Pooled Regressions exclude lagged dependent variables due to limited data availability.
Standard errors in parentheses. * $p < 0.05$, ** $p < 0.01$, *** $p < 0.001$

Index and the *Fraser Index* both use expert surveys and desk review to measure "investment freedom," in which higher values indicate more open policy environments. These variables have greater cross-sectional but limited temporal coverage when restricted to country-years. in which *Banking Reform* is also available. As Table 4.4 reports, despite small numbers of observations both cross-sectionally and temporally, there is evidence that *Banking Reform* is associated with FDI policy liberalization across almost all available measures of the investment climate. Models that measure investment policy through *Screening* and *OECD* do not obtain traditional levels of statistical significance but are signed as expected and approach significance.

To what extent is the relationship between investment restrictions and banking sector reforms robust to other variables that may affect policies toward FDI? In the next set of models, I include a variety of other measures to account for complementary and alternative explanations of FDI liberalization. First, as anticipated by hypothesis 2, if countries are more likely to liberalize FDI when financing constraints tighten, higher levels of domestic credit should dampen proclivities toward liberalization. Therefore, I include a measure of *Private Domestic Credit* scaled by gross domestic product (GDP), which is a standard measure of credit market deepness in the financial growth literature.[12] Second, following a specific factors model of preference formation, labor may be more supportive of FDI than domestic capital, and therefore democratic countries may be more permissive of investment inflows than autocratic regimes.[13] I measure democracy through an indicator variable that takes a value of 1 if a country's score on the Polity scale is greater than or equal to 6 and 0 otherwise.[14]

Other explanations of FDI reform have emphasized economic crises as catalysts for investment reform either in direct response to a need for capital inflows or indirectly through international financial institutions that demand neoliberal reforms in exchange for crisis assistance.[15] I include indicators for *Crisis* and *Under IMF Program* to capture these external pressures for reform. *Crisis* equals one for any year in which a country experienced a currency, banking, and/or sovereign debt crisis. In the chapter appendix, I provide models that measure each of these crises separately; substantive effects do not change. *Under IMF Program* equals one for any year in which a country is subject to a conditionality clause associated with an International Monetary Fund (IMF) loan. To account for generally poor macroeconomic conditions, I include a measure of *Inflation*. I also control for *Fixed Exchange Rates* because countries with fixed currencies may be less willing to liberalize foreign equity ownership due to upward pressure on local currencies from large capital inflows.[16]

In the reform sequencing literature, FDI policy is often assumed to follow real sector reforms.[17] Therefore, I include a measure of de facto *Trade Openness*. Arguments that subscribe to an "opportunities cost of closure" explanation of investment policy suggest governments will be more accepting of inward FDI when their economies are poised to attract investment projects that demand highly skilled

---

[12] See Cihak et al. (2012).

[13] Pandya (2014).

[14] Marshall et al. (2017).

[15] This argument is most prevalent among scholars studying short-term capital account liberalization. See, for example, Brooks (2004), Mukherjee and Singer (2010). For a counterargument, see Pepinsky (2012).

[16] Levy-Yeyati and Sturzenegger (2005).

[17] Johnston et al. (1997).

labor.[18] Accordingly, I include a measure of *Tertiary Enrollment* to account for the domestic level of human capital.[19]

Finally, because many policy liberalizations exhibit wave-like patterns of implementation, it may be the case that decisions to liberalize FDI follow mechanisms of policy diffusion across peer groups.[20] I control for the FDI policies for regional peers by constructing *Regional Restrictions*, which measures the average equity liberalization score in each country-year for a country's regional peers.[21] In robustness checks, I also control for the FDI policies of income peers by constructing *Income Restrictions*, which measures the average equity liberalization score in each country-year for countries in the same World Bank income category as the referent country. I report these results in the chapter appendix, and my results are robust to the inclusion of this additional variable.[22]

In Table 4.5, Models 8 and 9 report results for these more inclusive models. Both *Banking Reforms* and *Interest Rate Controls* retain statistical significance.[23] A one standard deviation increase in *Banking Reform* (*Interest Rate Controls*) is associated with a decrease in *Entry Restrictions* equal to 7.5 (6.7) percent of a standard deviation. As anticipated by hypothesis 2, higher levels of private domestic credit

---

[18] Kobrin (2005).

[19] Some readers may prefer a more comprehensive set of control variables including *Current Account/GDP*, *Exports/GDP*, and *Manufacturing/GDP*. In robustness checks across all models presented in this chapter, I include these additional controls. My main substantive effects hold for the most part. In some models that include *Manufacturing/GDP*, the statistical significance of banking reforms slips out of traditional bounds of significance, but it is still signed correctly. Measures of model fit suggest inclusion of this variable generates substantial noise in the residuals. I report models of these controls in the chapter appendix.

[20] Simmons and Elkins (2004).

[21] Regional categories include: Advanced Economies, Emerging Asia, Latin America, Sub-Saharan Africa, Transition Economies, and Middle East/North Africa.

[22] Income categories include: High Income OECD, High Income Non-OECD, Middle-High Income, Middle-Low Income, and Low Income.

[23] Data availability issues prevent me from performing more robust analysis using alternative measures of FDI openness such as the OECD FDI Restrictiveness Index, the Heritage Index, and the Fraser Index. However, I am able to run additional analysis on Pandya's Screening Requirements measure. Models explaining Screening Requirements consistently return negative coefficient estimates for Banking Reforms, but the *p*-value on these estimates ranges from 0.08 to 0.19.

Table 4.5. *Banking reforms, FDI policy, and alternative mechanisms*

	Model 8	Model 9	Model 10	Model 11
Equity Restrictions$_{(t-1)}$	0.585**	0.581**	0.565**	0.5658**
	(0.042)	(0.042)	(0.050)	(0.048)
Banking Reforms$_{(t-1)}$	−0.075*		−0.144*	
	(0.038)		(0.062)	
Interest Rate Controls$_{(t-1)}$		−0.067*		−0.086
		(0.031)		(0.052)
Ln GDP Per Capita$_{(t-1)}$	−0.100	−0.108	−0.414	−0.335
	(0.273)	(0.266)	(0.298)	(0.290)
Ln Inflation$_{(t-1)}$	0.005	0.011	0.010	0.020
	(0.025)	(0.024)	(0.028)	(0.027)
Ln Trade/GDP$_{(t-1)}$	0.223	0.228	0.244	0.238
	(0.165)	(0.158)	(0.171)	(0.168)
Ln Tertiary Enroll$_{(t-1)}$	−0.297	−0.295	−0.291	−0.278
	(0.187)	(0.181)	(0.203)	(0.203)
Democracy$_{(t-1)}$	0.113*	0.115*	0.150*	0.154*
	(0.052)	(0.052)	(0.062)	(0.062)
Crisis$_{(t-1)}$	−0.010	−0.005	−0.008	0.005
	(0.052)	(0.049)	(0.061)	(0.060)
Under IMF$_{(t-1)}$	0.016	0.019	0.023	0.026
	(0.052)	(0.053)	(0.064)	(0.063)
Ln Private Dom Credit$_{(t-1)}$	0.067+	0.065+	0.060	0.055
	(0.039)	(0.037)	(0.068)	(0.063)
Fixed Exchange Rate$_{(t-1)}$	0.084*	0.078+	0.091	0.091*
	(0.042)	(0.043)	(0.070)	(0.036)
Avg Regional Restrict$_{(t-1)}$	0.094**	0.092**	0.088*	0.091*
	(0.032)	(0.031)	(0.034)	(0.036)
BITs$_{(t-1)}$			0.022+	0.015
			(0.012)	(0.012)
Ln Resource Rents$_{(t-1)}$			0.012	0.014
			(0.106)	(0.112)
Observations	1342	1342	812	812
Countries	65	65	44	44
R^2	0.6782	0.6823	0.6096	0.6394

Fixed effects estimated with year dummies and country-clustered standard errors. Standard errors in parentheses. $+p < 0.1$, $*p < 0.05$, $**p < 0.01$, $***p < 0.001$

are associated with higher levels of entry restrictions.[24] The models also suggest regional patterns matter; the more restrictions a country's peers erect, the more likely that country is to maintain barriers of its own.[25] Perhaps surprisingly, *Democracy* is statistically significantly and positively associated with increased restrictions on foreign equity ownership. Other variables such as *GDP Per Capita*, *Inflation*, *Crisis*, and *Under IMF* are not statistically significant predictors of *Equity Restrictions*. I interpret this as evidence against brute economic determinism; macroeconomic conditions may create pressures on governments to respond, but governments retain a degree of agency over how precisely they will choose to manage these constraints.

Two additional features of the domestic environment may also affect the propensity to liberalize. First, it may be the case that international treaty agreements drive FDI policy reform. Second, countries endowed with substantial natural resources may have greater capacity to generate foreign exchange and therefore be less likely to encourage FDI into nonresource sectors. In models 10 and 11, I include a measure for *Natural Resource Rents* and a count of the bilateral investment treaties (*BITs*) to which a host country is party. Because such treaties are typically signed between a developed and developing country with the understanding that bilateral FDI flows will overwhelming travel from developed to developing economy, it is generally assumed that these treaties are more binding to developing country co-signers than developed country initiators. Therefore, these models only include

---

[24] One may worry that banking reform and private domestic credit are too collinear to include in the same equation, and so it may be preferable to use the change in private domestic credit rather than the level. I report models using levels for two reasons. First, the pairwise correlation coefficient between *Banking Reform* and *Private Domestic Credit* is 0.49, which is relatively high but not approaching levels that are typically considered problematic. Second, I am theoretically interested in the level of private credit availability, not the change. Changes may be temporary, and the relationship between changes in credit availability and FDI policy should take place over a longer temporal span. Therefore, *Change in Private Domestic Credit* is not an appropriate measure of the availability of local credit. However, I report models in the chapter appendix that uses the difference in *Private Domestic Credit* rather than its level. I find that my central results hold (i.e. *Banking Reform*) but that the coefficient estimate for *Change in Private Domestic Credit* is not statistically significant.

[25] I also reestimate these models dropping one region at a time to ensure a particular region, notably East Asia, does not drive results.

developing countries and lose substantial observations due to data missingness. Nonetheless, the basic findings hold. Although *Interest Rate Controls* slips just over standard significance levels, the coefficient estimate on *Banking Reforms* increases in precision and in substantive effect. A one standard deviation increase in *Banking Reforms* is associated with a decrease of 14.4 percent of a standard deviation of *Equity Restrictions*. Neither *Natural Resource Rents* nor *BITs* seem to influence entry restrictions. These findings are consistent with arguments that natural resources place countervailing pressures on investment law because resource-rich countries often have balance of payment cushions but resource extraction is capital- and technology-intensive and that BITs do more to establish legal certainty postestablishment than to liberalize right of entry.[26]

Endogeneity Concerns

Next, I address the potential that banking sector reforms are endogenous to FDI policy liberalization. The main concern is that economic liberalizations are often structured around comprehensive reform packages, and therefore the statistical relationship between banking sector and foreign equity liberalization may be driven by simultaneity.

From the perspective of policy elites, technocratic reports on reform sequencing tend to associate FDI liberalization with real sector reforms, such as tariff reductions, and banking sector reforms with policies toward portfolio investment.[27] Therefore, the experience of policy elites suggests governments do not routinely consider banking policy to be technocratically tied to FDI policy in any particular way. While a substantial literature around the optimal sequencing of financial sector liberalization arose in the 1980s and early 1990s, there are few reasons to believe this literature substantially influenced policy around equity restrictions for at least two reasons. First, this literature was primarily concerned with the relationship between the domestic banking sector and liberalizing portfolio flows. The central writings in this debate at the time rarely mentioned FDI specifically, and only

---

[26] In recent years, US, Canadian, and Japanese BITs have generally required more commitment to loosing establishment restrictions, but the majority of BITs have traditionally applied only to postestablishment treatment.

[27] Johnston et al. (1997).

in passing when they did so.[28] Second, if one piece of shared technocratic understanding regarding FDI policy emerged at the time, it was that it was technically preferable to liberalize the long-term capital account – meaning, FDI (before the short-term capital account) – portfolio flows. This advice was both silent on the relationship between banking reforms and FDI restrictions and routinely ignored; an IMF study found that governments chose to liberalize portfolio investment before direct investment around half of the time.[29]

While a review of technocratic writing and thought at the time suggests policymakers rarely saw technocratic rationale for sequencing banking and FDI reforms,[30] I also employ two modeling techniques to establish statistically the temporal ordering of banking and FDI reforms, and to rule out concerns that all neoliberal reforms simply lump together. These results are reported in the chapter appendix. First, I use error correction models to differentiate between the short- and long-term effects of banking reforms on FDI policy. I find banking sector reforms are associated with long-term changes in FDI policies but not short-term changes. Second, I use Granger causality tests to demonstrate banking sector reforms precede FDI policy liberalization, but not the reverse, and that banking sector reforms do not "Granger cause" other liberalization reforms such as short-term capital account openness or trade liberalization. Jointly, these tests provide increased certainty that the relationship between banking sector reforms and FDI liberalization are neither endogenous nor spurious.

Domestic Credit Environments and FDI Policy, 2000–2015

The analysis above provides substantial evidence that FDI policy liberalizations from 1973 to 2000 were driven by changes in domestic banking regulation that reduced governments' control over credit allocation. But to what extent does this relationship adhere in the more recent time period? In this section, I leverage data from 2000 onward to answer this question.

---

[28] See, for example, Johnston and Sundararajan (1999) and McKinnon (1991).
[29] International Monetary Fund (2012).
[30] In fact, the IMF's advice of "FDI before debt" specifically suggested inward FDI be the first step in reform sequencing and did not require prior banking reform. See IMF (2012), especially Figure 2 on page 14.

Variables, Measurement, and Methodology

To measure FDI policy since 2000, I turn to the United Nations Conference on Trade and Development's (UNCTAD) database of all changes to national government investment policies made globally from 2000 to 2015.[31] This dataset catalogs changes to investment law and implementation and categorizes investment policy changes both by their effects – that is, if they are liberalizing or restrictive of foreign investment – and by their type – that is, if they affect FDI through changes to entry, treatment, or promotion policies. I use a series of dependent variables, each of which count the number of relevant FDI policy changes in a given country-year and are coded "0" otherwise. I estimate separate models for each of the following dependent variables. *Liberal* counts the number of any liberalizing FDI policy change, regardless of type. *Lib Entry* identifies liberalizing FDI policy changes that are specific to entry requirements. This includes changes to foreign equity ceilings, screening procedures, and other forms of regulation that place barriers to foreign firm establishment such as ability to lease land. *Lib Treatment* counts liberalizing changes that relate to the treatment of foreign investors after establishment. Policies in this category include regulations over capital transfers and access to foreign exchange, regulations over operational conditions, access to dispute settlement procedures, investor protections in the case of expropriation, and other changes to legal codes that influence standards of nondiscrimination. *Lib Promote* identifies measures increase the use of tax incentives, expenditures to aid in investment facilitation, and the creation or expansion of special economic zones. Finally, *Restrict* counts any changes to FDI policy that are restrictive in nature.[32]

This dataset has several important advantages. First, it covers the universe of all investment policy changes across all countries globally. UNCTAD gathers this information from communications with governments and other official sources. Therefore, it has the broadest coverage of any measure of FDI policy. Second, its coverage begins

---

[31] United Nations Conference on Trade and Development (2016a).
[32] Due to separation issues, I am unable to model different types of restrictive FDI policy measures separately.

in 2000, when Pandya's *Equity Restrictions* coverage ends.[33] By using these data, then, I extend my analysis forward by 15 years. This allows me to ascertain whether the dynamics between banking sector reforms and FDI policy have continued into the new century. It also functions as an out-of-sample test because it includes a completely new set of observations to analyze. Finally, its granularity provides important variation over which to leverage analysis. The UNCTAD data allow me to differentiate between different types of investment policy changes that each vary in how likely they are to affect firm financing. Therefore, these data allow me to test whether banking sector policies have a differential effect across distinct classes of investment policies.

Measuring the Domestic Financing Environment

Because Abiad et al.'s measure of banking sector reforms ends in 2005, I need a different proxy for the domestic financing environment. Following the World Bank's framework for measuring global financial development, I use *Net Interest Margin* to measure the efficiency of the domestic banking sector.[34] This variable is the accounting value of a country's aggregated banks' net interest revenue as a share of its average interest-bearing assets, the raw values of which are sourced from the Bankscope database.[35] Recall that I am interested in measuring the degree to which credit allocation decisions are market-or politically driven. In repressed banking systems, credit allocation is inefficient because the government drives banks' decisions about to which industries and firms to lend.[36] In such systems, overall lending is expensive while politically important firms receive subsidized credit. While a measure of regulation, such as the existence of directed credit requirements, would be preferable to an outcome measure, *Net Interest Margin* is available across my sample and time period and is widely used as a proxy for banking sector efficiency, with higher margins indicating less efficient systems.[37] Inspection of the variable shows that countries that score low on *Banking Sector Reform* in

---

[33] The full dataset can extend back to 1992, but substantial changes in the way data were collected and coded in 2000 introduce a structural break in the series.

[34] Cihak et al. (2012).

[35] World Bank (2017).

[36] McKinnon (1973).

[37] See Cihak et al. (2012, 9).

2005 have, on average, higher values of *Net Interest Margin* (around 5 percent) than do countries that measured highly reformed on the *Banking Sector Reform* measure in 2005. These countries had average *Net Interest Margin* values of around 2 percent. In addition, visual inspection of individual countries' *Net Interest Margin* over time suggests the variable did not react in a systematic way to the global financial crisis.

Case Coverage and Estimation Diagnostics

Compiling these data, I obtain an unbalanced dataset of 166 countries. Table 4.6 lists the countries included in the analysis; asterisks denote the 138 countries for which all control variables are available. Because I model counts of investment policy changes in a given country-year, I use a negative binomial regression.[38] Because most of the variation in my explanatory variables occurs across, rather than within, countries, I do not include country fixed effects. Included fixed effects would drop any country from my model that did not enact a policy change over the time period analyzed. I do include year fixed effects, which model the influence of global market conditions on the propensity to liberalize. Because governments react to changing conditions over time, I lag all explanatory variables. All nonindicator variables are standardized to ease interpretation. Table 4.7 provides descriptive statistics; a correlation matrix is included in the chapter appendix.

Analysis

As before, I begin by estimating spare baseline models of the relationship between the efficiency of the banking sector and the propensity to enact liberalizing and restrictive investment policies. In Table 4.8 we see that *Net Interest Margin* is statistically significantly associated with a decreased propensity to enact any liberalizing policy, a liberalizing entry policy, and a liberalizing promotion policy. In contrast, the efficiency of the banking sector is not statistically significantly associated with liberalizing policies related to treatment or the propensity to enact restrictive policies. This makes sense because treatment policies deal with the way foreign firms are treated postestablishment and

---

[38] Model diagnostics indicate outcome variables are characterized by overdispersion, so a poisson link function is inappropriate.

are not directly related to entry. On the other hand, policies related to entry and promotion are more closely tied to allowing and enticing foreign firms to establish local operations. It is interesting that *Net Interest Margin* does not have an effect on the probability of enacting a restrictive change. We might expect less efficient banking sectors to encourage local firms to lobby to restrict investment. However, we do not see evidence of that in these data. I discuss interpretation of this finding in greater detail in a future section.

The size of the effect of *Net Interest Margin* on liberalization is rather large. Remember, higher values of *Net Interest Margin* indicate a less efficient banking sector in which well-connected firms receive subsidized credit. Model 12 calculates a one-standard-deviation increase in this variable above the mean decreases the propensity to enact any liberalizing change by 20.6 percent. Model 13 finds that the same increase in *Net Interest Margin* decreases the probability of enacting a liberalizing change to entry requirements by 22.1 percent. And Model 15 finds a similar effect for the likelihood of promulgating a liberalizing policy related to investment promotion (17.5 percent).

Next, I explore whether these findings are robust to inclusion of other variables that may influence investment policy changes. Table 4.9 reports results of these expanded models for outcome variables for which *Net Interest Margin* was statistically significant in spare models: *Liberal*, *Lib Entry*, and *Lib Promote*. I use the same control variables as I did in the previous section, with a couple of slight modifications. First, I cannot include *Private Credit/GDP* because it is highly (negatively) correlated with *Net Interest Margin*. Second, I create average regulation liberalization variables for each outcome variable in the same manner that I did in the previous section. Third, while I used the Levy-Yeyati and Sturzenegger de facto exchange rate regime dataset in the historical models, these data end in 2000.[39] Therefore, I use Shambaugh's *Peg* variable, which also uses a de facto coding rule to determine exchange rate regime.[40] As with models in Table 4.5, in robustness checks I include additional controls: current account balance as a percentage of GDP, exports over GDP, manufacturing as a share of GDP, and average liberalization by income group. My results remain largely unchanged, although the statistical significance for *Net*

[39] Levy-Yeyati and Sturzenegger (2005).
[40] Shambaugh (2004).

Table 4.6. Countries included in policy change models

Afghanistan*	Chile*	Guinea-Bissau	Malta	Slovenia*
Albania*	China*	Guyana*	Mauritania*	Solomon Islands
Algeria*	Colombia*	Haiti	Mauritius*	South Africa*
Angola*	Congo*	Honduras*	Mexico*	South Korea*
Argentina*	Costa Rica*	Hong Kong	Moldova*	Spain*
Armenia*	Cote d'Ivoire*	Hungary*	Mongolia*	Sri Lanka*
Australia*	Croatia*	Iceland	Morocco*	Sudan*
Austria*	Cuba	India*	Mozambique*	Suriname*
Azerbaijan*	Cyprus*	Indonesia*	Myanmar*	Swaziland*
Bahamas	Czech Rep*	Iraq*	Namibia*	Sweden*
Bahrain*	Dem Rep Congo*	Ireland*	Nepal*	Switzerland*
Bangladesh*	Denmark*	Israel*	Netherlands*	Syria
Barbados	Djibouti*	Italy*	New Zealand*	Taiwan
Belarus*	Dominican Rep*	Jamaica*	Nicaragua*	Tajikistan*
Belgium*	Ecuador	Japan*	Niger*	Tanzania
Belize	Egypt*	Jordan*	Nigeria*	Thailand*
Benin*	El Salvador*	Kazakhstan*	Norway*	Togo*
Bhutan*	Equatorial Guinea	Kenya*	Oman*	Trinidad*
Bolivia*	Eritrea	Kuwait*	Pakistan*	Tunisia*

Bosnia and Herzegovina
Botswana*
Brazil*
Brunei
Bulgaria*
Burkina Faso*
Burundi*
Cambodia
Cameroon*
Canada*
Cape Verde*
Central African Republic
Chad*

Estonia*
Ethiopia*
Fiji
Finland*
France*
Gabon*
Gambia*
Georgia*
Germany*
Ghana*
Greece*
Guatemala*
Guinea*

Kyrgyz Rep*
Laos*
Latvia*
Lebanon*
Lesotho
Liberia*
Libya*
Lithuania*
Luxembourg*
Macedonia*
Madagascar*
Malawi*
Malaysia*
Maldives
Mali*

Panama*
Papua New Guinea*
Paraguay*
Peru*
Philippines*
Poland*
Portugal*
Qatar*
Romania*
Rwanda*
Saudi Arabia*
Senegal*
Sierra Leone*
Singapore
Slovak Rep*

Turkey*
Turkmenistan
Uganda*
Ukraine*
United Arab Emirates
United Kingdom*
United States*
Uruguay*
Uzbekistan
Venezuela*
Vietnam*
Yemen*
Frm Yugoslav Rep
Zambia*
Zimbabwe

Table 4.7. *Descriptive statistics, policy change models*

Variable	Mean	Std. Dev.	N
Yearly Liberal	0.4774	1.3063	2962
Yearly Lib Entry	0.2741	0.9587	2962
Yearly Lib Treatment	0.0557	0.3276	2962
Yearly Lib Promotion	0.1735	0.6114	2962
Yearly Restrict	0.1060	0.4927	2962
Net Interest Margin	4.9166	3.3006	2426
GDP Per Capita	12662.81	18258.71	2789
Inflation	17.0945	474.8725	2652
Trade	89.9159	55.5461	2737
Tertiary Enrollment	34.6875	26.0072	1864
Democracy	0.5445	0.4981	2755
Fixed Exchange Rate	0.4976	0.5001	2532
Crisis	0.0117	0.1175	2894
Under IMF	0.6546	0.4756	2894
Regional Lib	0.4801	0.4014	2945
Regional Lib Entry	0.2757	0.2885	2945
Regional Lib Treatment	0.0560	0.0700	2945
Regional Lib Promotion	0.1745	0.1659	2945
Regional Restrictions	0.1066	0.1482	2945

Table 4.8. *Policy change and banking efficiency*

	Model 12 Liberal	Model 13 Lib Entry	Model 14 Lib Treat	Model 15 Lib Promote	Model 16 Restrict
Net Interest	-0.231***	-0.250***	-0.202	-0.192***	-0.059
Margin$_{(t-1)}$	(0.05)	(0.06)	(0.11)	(0.07)	(0.10)
AIC	4619.169	3219.452	1132.536	2526.409	1707.251
BIC	4723.453	3323.737	1236.821	2630.694	1811.536
N	2425	2425	2425	2425	2425

Standard errors in parentheses. Constant and year fixed effects not reported.
* $p < 0.05$, ** $p < 0.01$, *** $p < 0.001$

Table 4.9. *Policy change, banking efficiency, and alternative mechanisms*

	Model 17 Liberal	Model 18 Lib Entry	Model 19 Lib Promote
Net Interest Margin$_{(t-1)}$	−0.323***	−0.362***	−0.205
	(0.08)	(0.10)	(0.11)
Ln GDP Per Capita$_{(t-1)}$	−0.024	−0.003	0.070
	(0.13)	(0.16)	(0.18)
Ln Inflation$_{(t-1)}$	1.823	2.620	1.310
	(2.28)	(2.91)	(3.31)
Ln Trade/GDP$_{(t-1)}$	−0.308***	−0.298**	−0.232**
	(0.08)	(0.10)	(0.09)
Ln Tertiary Enroll$_{(t-1)}$	0.481***	0.317*	0.784***
	(0.10)	(0.13)	(0.15)
Democracy$_{(t-1)}$	−0.352**	−0.242	−0.405*
	(0.13)	(0.17)	(0.19)
Crisis$_{(t-1)}$	−0.267	0.143	−2.034
	(0.49)	(0.60)	(1.16)
Under IMF$_{(t-1)}$	0.734***	0.709**	0.875***
	(0.19)	(0.25)	(0.26)
Fixed Exchange Rate$_{(t-1)}$	−0.266*	−0.219	−0.385*
	(0.12)	(0.16)	(0.16)
Avg Reg Liberalization$_{(t-1)}$	0.626***	0.907***	0.480
	(0.16)	(0.27)	(0.46)
AIC	3087.709	2187.894	1692.851
BIC	3231.470	2331.655	1836.613
N	1517	1517	1517

Standard errors in parentheses. Year fixed effects and constant not reported.
* $p < 0.05$, ** $p < 0.01$, *** $p < 0.001$

Interest Margin on *Lib Entry* slips just over the 95 percent confidence interval to a *p*-value of 0.062. These results are reported in the chapter appendix.

I find *Net Interest Margin* retains significance for models of all liberalizing changes and for changes related to entry regulation, and the inclusion of control variables actually increases the association of banking sector efficiency with increased liberalization. However, Model 19 shows that the relationship between banking efficiency and promotion policies is not robust to these control variables. This is in line with the expectation that firms motivated to embrace FDI to solve financing constraints should be most concerned with regulations on entry. Some additional findings bear mentioning. In general, more control variables are statistically significant in these models than in those in the historical analysis. High levels of trade reduce the propensity of enacting more liberalizing policies across each model. High levels of human capital, proxied by tertiary enrollment, increase the likelihood of a liberalizing change. Neighbors' policies have a positive effect on *Liberal* and *Lib Entry*, but not *Lib Promote*. In contrast to the historical models, countries under IMF programs are more likely to liberalize. These findings suggest economic distress has become more likely to lead to liberalizations of FDI policies in recent years. However, these findings are largely consistent with a financing constraints logic to investment liberalization.

Probusiness Institutions and FDI Policy

Above, I find substantial evidence that financing constraints lead to liberalization of investment policies, particularly those related to entry restrictions and investment promotion. This is consistent with the theory that large domestic firms lobby for openness when they lose access to subsidized credit, but we could imagine other explanations for the patterns in the data. In particular, it may be that technocrats increasingly view openness to FDI as essential for economic development and growth, particularly in the wake of economic distress. Despite my controlling for regime type in the models above, some readers may also be concerned that the statistical association between banking sector reforms and FDI liberalization is an artifact of the relationship between banking sector reforms and regime type. Both of these alternative explanations generate measurably distinct expectations about the characteristics of domestic politics that should be more likely to lead to more open FDI policy environments. A firm-driven liberalization process suggests political institutions that empower business interests such as right parties, politicized bureaucracies, and endemic corruption should be associated with FDI liberalization when the banking sector is reformed. In contrast, an association between bureaucratic autonomy and FDI liberalization would be indicative of a technocratic-driven liberalization process. Similarly, if labor generates demand for liberalization in democracy, left parties and elections should be more associated with liberal policies. To probe whether domestic political institutions that empower business interests condition FDI liberalization, I reestimate the models reported above, this time sequentially adding measures of both electoral and bureaucratic institutions. Because I am most interested in within-country variation, I focus my attention on historical analysis from 1973 to 2000, but I use the UNCTAD policy change data to examine the relationship between policy changes and elections.

Partisanship and FDI Policy

First, I consider whether partisanship of the executive and the legislature influence FDI liberalization. To do so, I turn again to the Database of Political Institutions (DPI). *Executive Partisanship* and *Legislative Partisanship* each measure the economic policy orientation of the party of the chief executive and the largest party in government, respectively. Right parties (1) include "conservative, Christian democratic, or right-wing parties," as determined by party names and/or handbooks with further information on party platforms.[41] Center parties (2) include parties that advocate for a more robust private sector within a social-liberal framework. Left parties (3) are those characterized as "communist, socialist, social democrat, or left-wing."[42] Parties that do not follow a particular economic program are coded as zero.

If governments face pressures from business interests to liberalize FDI policy when banking reforms disrupt their privileged access to finance, we should expect lobbying pressure from these groups to be particularly successful when the party in power is closely aligned with capital. Thus, governments run by right parties should be more likely to liberalize regulations for FDI when the domestic banking sector has deregulated the credit allocation process. As discussed at length in Chapter 2, changes to investment law are often promulgated through the executive branch. This suggests the party of the executive should be more critical for the direction of FDI policy than the economic orientation of the party in control of the legislature. Models 20 and 21 in Table 4.10 report results. Remember that these models use the Pandya measure of *Equity Restrictions*, which is coded so that decreases in the measure's value indicates a reduction in restrictions on foreign entry.

[41] Cruz et al. (2016), p. 9.
[42] Ibid.

Table 4.10. *FDI policy and domestic political institutions*

	Model 20	Model 21	Model 22	Model 23
Entry Restrictions$_{(t-1)}$	0.538***	0.541***	0.478***	0.473***
	(0.06)	(0.06)	(0.08)	(0.08)
Bank Reform$_{(t-1)}$	−0.113	−0.104	−0.197	−0.237*
	(0.07)	(0.07)	(0.14)	(0.10)
Executive Partisanship$_{(t-1)}$	−0.028			
	(0.03)			
Legislative Partisanship$_{(t-1)}$		−0.007		
		(0.04)		
Corruption$_{(t-1)}$			−0.007	
			(0.04)	
Bureaucratic Quality$_{(t-1)}$				−0.062
				(0.05)
Interaction	0.011	0.000	0.039	0.074*
	(0.03)	(0.03)	(0.03)	(0.03)
GDP Per Capita$_{(t-1)}$	0.146	−0.001	−0.439	−0.463
	(0.33)	(0.32)	(0.37)	(0.36)
Inflation$_{(t-1)}$	0.006	0.002	−0.000	−0.008
	(0.02)	(0.02)	(0.02)	(0.02)
Trade$_{(t-1)}$	0.129	0.012	−0.037	0.064
	(0.24)	(0.25)	(0.15)	(0.15)
Human Capital$_{(t-1)}$	−0.189	−0.113	−0.157	−0.232
	(0.29)	(0.27)	(0.18)	(0.16)
Crisis$_{(t-1)}$	0.003	0.005	−0.039	−0.029
	(0.07)	(0.07)	(0.06)	(0.06)
Under IMF$_{(t-1)}$	0.068	0.013	0.048	0.051
	(0.06)	(0.07)	(0.06)	(0.06)
Domestic Credit$_{(t-1)}$	0.061	0.113*	0.079	0.065
	(0.03)	(0.05)	(0.06)	(0.06)
Fixed Exchange Rate$_{(t-1)}$	0.054	0.051	0.062	0.070
	(0.04)	(0.04)	(0.04)	(0.04)
Regional Restriction$_{(t-1)}$	0.090*	0.066	−0.020	−0.027
	(0.04)	(0.04)	(0.05)	(0.05)
R^2	0.417	0.409	0.332	0.337
BIC	1277.000	1320.920	1201.543	1194.886
N	897	941	895	895

Fixed effects estimated with year dummies and country-clustered standard errors.
Standard errors in parentheses. * $p < 0.05$, ** $p < 0.01$, *** $p < 0.001$

Table 4.11. *Marginal effects of bank reform by partisanship*

	Executive Partisanship		
	Marginal Effect	Standard Error	*p* Value
Right	−0.0946[+]	0.0568	0.096
Center	−0.0843	0.0526	0.110
Left	−0.0740	0.0574	0.198
	Government Partisanship		
	Marginal Effect	Standard Error	*p* Value
Right	−0.0512	0.0552	0.354
Center	−0.0498	0.0507	0.326
Left	−0.0484	0.0556	0.384

[+]$p < 0.1$

The models show some support for the contention that the effect of *Bank Reform* on *Entry Restrictions* is conditioned on *Executive Partisanship*. *Legislative Partisanship*, however, does not display a statistically significant conditioning effect. In both Models 20 and 21, the coefficient estimate for *Bank Reform* is negative but just over traditional thresholds of statistical significance. Because these models include an interaction between *Bank Reform* and the respective partisanship measure, however, these point estimates are not particularly informative on their own. Table 4.11 reports marginal effects. We see that *Entry Restrictions* are more likely to decline under right executives, and that this relationship is significant at the 90 percent confidence interval. No other executive party is associated with statistically significant changes to investment regulation. There is no evidence that the party of the legislature conditions the relationship between the banking environment and restrictiveness toward foreign firm entry. Together, these estimations provide continued, though somewhat limited, support for the contention that firm preferences drive FDI liberalization processes. Certainly, the results run counter to arguments that left parties embrace FDI to generate employment opportunities for constituents.[43]

---

[43] Pinto (2013), Pinto and Pinto (2008).

Informal Influence Channels and FDI Policy

Government partisanship can help ascertain how much formal representation business interests have through the elevation of ideologically sympathetic individuals and groups to positions of political power. However, a "quiet politics" approach suggests that firms' political influence may also occur through more informal channels. To consider how exercise of informal influence may condition the effects of *Bank Reform* on *Equity Restriction*, I turn again to International Country Risk Guide (ICRG) measures of *Corruption* and *Bureaucratic Quality*. These data are compiled through expert assessment of ICRG staff, and while ICRG publishes the general conceptualization of each of its measures, it does not publish a detailed coding handbook.[44] *Corruption* is measured on a six-point scale in which higher values indicate a better institutional environment, that is, one characterized by less corruption. ICRG characterizes corruption as "excessive patronage, nepotism, job reservations, 'favor-for-favors,' secret party funding, and suspiciously close ties between politics and business."[45] While *Corruption* accounts for system-wide tendencies to blend political and business interests in non-transparent ways, *Bureaucratic Quality* measures the extent to which a country's bureaucracy is professionalized in ways that allow it to be relatively autonomous from ruling political parties and figures. This four-point scale, with higher values indicating a more autonomous bureaucracy, considers attributes such as formal mechanisms for recruitment and personnel training that allow government bureaucrats to maintain consistency from one government to the next.[46]

One potential alternative explanation for the relationship between banking regulation and FDI policy presented above is that technocrats within government bureaucracies push for investment reforms when banking reforms limit their ability to funnel credit to priority sectors of the economy. If this is the case, the relationship between banking and FDI regulations may be due to technical constraints and "best practices" among bureaucrats tasked with managing the domestic economy. If this alternative explanation is correct, we should expect

---

[44] ICRG is a for-profit risk assessment firm and therefore views this information as proprietary.

[45] Howell (n.d., 4–5).

[46] Howell (n.d., 7).

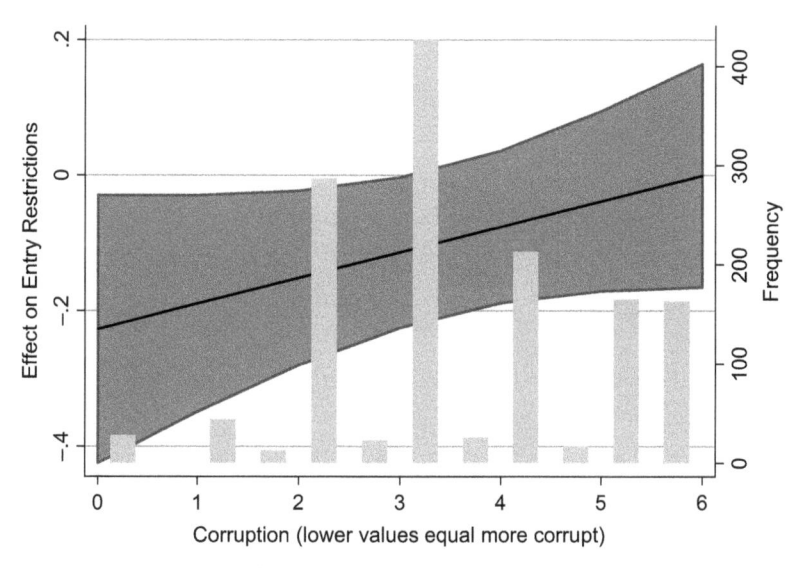

Figure 4.1 Marginal effects of bank reform by corruption, 95% confidence interval

that political institutions characterized by less corruption and by more professionalized bureaucracies that are effectively shielded from interest group pressures to be more likely to liberalize FDI restrictions after the banking sector undergoes reforms. If, instead, business interests rather than technocratic bureaucrats press governments to liberalize, we should see the opposite. That is, banking sector reforms should be more associated with subsequent FDI liberalization when corruption is high and bureaucratic quality is low because business interests are more influential under these circumstances.

Models 22 and 23 in Table 4.10 report the results of these models. The inclusion of an interaction term makes interpretation easier through marginal effects plots. Figure 4.1 illustrates the effect of *Bank Reform* on *Equity Restrictions* conditional on the level of domestic *Corruption*. The upward sloping line indicates *Bank Reform* predicts reduction in *Equity Restrictions* in countries characterized by high levels of corruption but not in countries with lower levels of corruption. The shaded area around the line indicates 95 percent confidence intervals; after countries cross the middle of the corruption scale, the statistical significance of the relationship between *Bank Reform* and *Entry Restrictions* ceases.

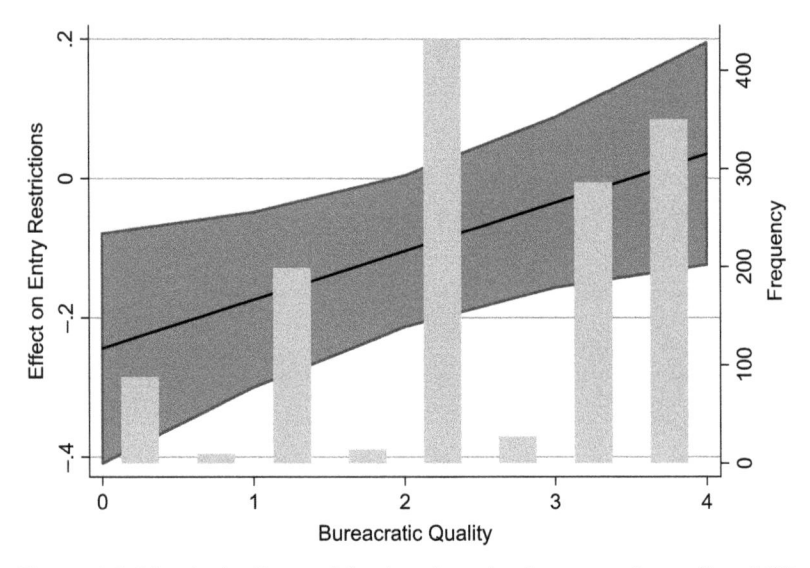

Figure 4.2 Marginal effects of bank reform by bureaucratic quality, 95% confidence interval

Figure 4.2 provides a visual representation of the effect of *Bank Reform* on *Equity Restrictions* conditioned on the quality of the domestic bureaucracy. Here we see a similar, but more pronounced, relationship. At low levels of *Bureaucratic Quality*, *Entry Restrictions* has a negative and statistically significant effect on *Entry Restrictions*, while in countries characterized by high levels of bureaucratic autonomy, this relationship goes away. The size of the effect can be rather large. At a rating of "1" on the *Bureaucratic Quality* measure, a standard deviation increase in *Banking Reform* is associated with a decrease in *Equity Restrictions* equivalent to 20 percent of a standard deviation.

Elections and the Timing of Policy Change

The models presented in Table 4.10 provide additional evidence that influential firms are active in pushing for policies of increasing openness toward FDI when banking sector is reformed. In particular, FDI policy is more likely to be liberalized after banking reforms when under right executives – that is when the chief executive is programmatically disposed to advance the interests of domestic capital. Furthermore, countries that have institutional structures that allow firms greater informal access to policymakers – that is, countries that tolerate and rely on corrupt practices and politicized bureaucracies – are more likely to liberalize equity restrictions under similar conditions. These findings help to discredit alternative explanations of FDI policy liberalization that rest on technocratic "good governance" arguments or those that emphasize the interests of labor groups.

One final consideration of domestic political institutions and FDI policy change concerns elections. Because the UNCTAD data on investment regulation from 2000 onward collects discrete policy changes in the year of their enactment, I can examine whether governments are more or less likely to promulgate different types of investment policies in election years. Therefore, I reestimate models from Table 4.9, this time including indicators for whether there was a legislative or executive election, respectively, in the year in which a policy change was made. If governments' enact FDI liberalization due to popular pressure, we should expect incumbent politicians to enact policy changes more frequently in election years in a bid to generate electoral support. If, on the other hand, increasing openness to FDI more often reflects the adaptive policy preferences of firms rather than publics, we should see governments delaying liberalizing regulatory changes during election years.

Table 4.12 reports results for legislative elections, and Table 4.13 provides results for models that estimate the effects of executive elections. In general, these estimations provide evidence that liberalizing regulatory changes are less likely in election years, especially policies unrelated to promotion. Legislative elections are associated with reduced occurrence of liberalization of entry and treatment. Executive elections make any liberalization, entry liberalization, and promotion activities less likely. For both legislative and executive elections, the sign on the coefficient for restrictive changes is positive, although not statistically significant.

Jointly, these models demonstrate that FDI liberalization episodes tend to occur in electoral "off seasons." This finding suggests that popular pressures to reform are likely not driving FDI liberalization processes.

Table 4.12. *FDI policy changes and legislative elections*

	Model 24 Liberal	Model 25 Lib Entry	Model 26 Lib Treat	Model 27 Lib Promote	Model 28 Restrict
Legislative Election	−0.232	−0.369*	−0.697*	0.001	0.141
	(0.13)	(0.17)	(0.34)	(0.17)	(0.21)
Net Interest Margin$_{(t-1)}$	−0.328***	−0.378***	−0.352*	−0.203	−0.126
	(0.08)	(0.10)	(0.17)	(0.11)	(0.14)
Ln GDP Per Capita$_{(t-1)}$	−0.036	0.000	0.052	0.028	0.291
	(0.13)	(0.16)	(0.29)	(0.17)	(0.23)
Ln Inflation$_{(t-1)}$	1.996	3.105	2.592	1.542	6.900
	(2.18)	(2.80)	(3.95)	(3.21)	(3.69)
Ln Trade/GDP$_{(t-1)}$	−0.303***	−0.294**	−0.289	−0.232**	−0.393**
	(0.07)	(0.10)	(0.15)	(0.09)	(0.13)
Ln Tertiary Enroll$_{(t-1)}$	0.491***	0.333*	0.678**	0.777***	0.592**
	(0.10)	(0.13)	(0.24)	(0.15)	(0.19)
Democracy$_{(t-1)}$	−0.349**	−0.227	−1.102***	−0.414*	−0.328
	(0.13)	(0.17)	(0.30)	(0.19)	(0.24)

	(1)	(2)	(3)	(4)	(5)
Crisis$_{(t-1)}$	-0.265	0.137	-0.809	-2.039	0.323
	(0.49)	(0.59)	(1.37)	(1.17)	(0.79)
Under IMF$_{(t-1)}$	0.716***	0.717**	1.657***	0.800**	1.187***
	(0.19)	(0.25)	(0.45)	(0.25)	(0.36)
Fixed Exchange Rate$_{(t-1)}$	-0.271*	-0.239	-0.201	-0.362*	0.156
	(0.12)	(0.16)	(0.27)	(0.16)	(0.20)
Average Regulatory Policy Change$_{(t-1)}$	0.593***	0.831***	1.221	0.505	0.727
	(0.16)	(0.27)	(0.00)	(1.87)	(0.83)
AIC	3131.083	2212.430	762.191	1725.800	1175.344
BIC	3280.608	2361.955	911.716	1875.325	1324.869
N	1541	1541	1541	1541	1541

Year fixed effects and constant not reported. Standard errors in parentheses.

* $p < 0.05$, ** $p < 0.01$, *** $p < 0.001$

Table 4.13. *FDI policy changes and executive elections*

	Model 29 Liberal	Model 30 Lib Entry	Model 31 Lib Treat	Model 32 Lib Promote	Model 33 Restrict
Executive	−0.491**	−0.531*	−0.417	−0.504*	0.169
Election	(0.18)	(0.24)	(0.42)	(0.24)	(0.29)
Net Interest	−0.314***	−0.360***	−0.337*	−0.193	−0.129
Margin$_{(t-1)}$	(0.08)	(0.10)	(0.16)	(0.11)	(0.14)
Ln GDP Per	−0.072	−0.027	0.027	−0.019	0.309
Capita$_{(t-1)}$	(0.13)	(0.16)	(0.29)	(0.17)	(0.23)
Ln Inflation$_{(t-1)}$	1.877	2.584	2.922	1.559	6.982
	(2.13)	(2.68)	(3.85)	(3.18)	(3.69)
Ln Trade/	−0.302***	−0.294**	−0.286	−0.230**	−0.396**
GDP$_{(t-1)}$	(0.07)	(0.10)	(0.15)	(0.09)	(0.13)
Ln Tertiary	0.499***	0.332*	0.660**	0.805***	0.591**
Enroll$_{(t-1)}$	(0.10)	(0.13)	(0.24)	(0.15)	(0.19)
Democracy$_{(t-1)}$	−0.347**	−0.230	−1.116***	−0.405*	−0.325
	(0.13)	(0.17)	(0.30)	(0.19)	(0.24)
Crisis$_{(t-1)}$	−0.217	0.209	−0.826	−2.019	0.288
	(0.49)	(0.59)	(1.36)	(1.18)	(0.80)
Under IMF$_{(t-1)}$	0.681***	0.692**	1.633***	0.764**	1.204***
	(0.19)	(0.25)	(0.45)	(0.25)	(0.36)
Fixed Exchange	−0.261*	−0.220	−0.179	−0.369*	0.157
Rate$_{(t-1)}$	(0.12)	(0.16)	(0.27)	(0.16)	(0.20)
Average Regional	0.616***	0.877**	1.534	0.564	0.696
Policy	(0.16)	(0.27)	(0.00)	(1.87)	(0.83)
Change$_{(t-1)}$					
AIC	3126.740	2211.919	765.699	1721.267	1175.431
BIC	3276.265	2361.444	915.225	1870.792	1324.956
N	1541	1541	1541	1541	1541

Year fixed effects and constant not reported. Standard errors in parentheses.
* $p < 0.05$, ** $p < 0.01$, *** $p < 0.001$

Conclusion

In the statistical analyses presented in this chapter I demonstrate robust support for the contention that changes to the domestic credit environment influence governments' policies toward FDI. Of the hypotheses I generated in Chapter 3, hypothesis 1 – which anticipates domestic banking sector reforms will lead to decreases in foreign equity restrictions – is most central to my theoretical argument. In the analyses presented above, I show that a substantively important and robust relationship exists between banking sector reforms and foreign equity restrictions. Across a wide range of specifications, using a variety of measures of FDI policy environments, and including a broad range of control variables, I show that the statistical relationship between banking reforms and FDI policy is quite stable. Statistical techniques designed to guard against endogeneity provide additional assurances that the relationship between banking sector reforms and subsequent liberalization of FDI policies is neither an endogenous process nor is it an artifact of general propensities toward neoliberal reforms. I find additional evidence in support of a financing constraints–driven mechanism for FDI policy reforms. Countries with deeper private credit markets have better cushions for domestic financing options for local firms and therefore demonstrate less propensity to liberalize rules against foreign equity ownership.

Finally, I use country-level data on both measures of openness toward FDI and discrete changes to FDI regulation to examine the relationship between domestic political institutions and policy outcomes. If regulatory changes reflect the policy preferences of domestic economic elites rather than other actors, we should expect liberalization to be associated with institutional configurations that favor business interests over labor or technocrats. I find that the relationship between banking sector reforms and FDI liberalization is stronger under right-leaning executives, in more corrupt political environments, and when bureaucracies are weak and underprofessionalized. I also find some evidence that liberalizing changes to FDI policies are less likely, while restrictive changes are more likely, during election years. Collectively, these data provide evidence that the relationship between disruption to elites' privileged access to credit markets and FDI policy is conditional on a variety of domestic political institutions that strengthen the influence of business interests, that the presence of strong technocrats makes this relationship weaker, and that executives and legislatures do not liberalize investment policies to generate popular support during election seasons.

These findings suggest the process of FDI liberalization should be understood as arising from broader changes to the local financing environment that can alter domestic firms' interpretations of the opportunities and threats that FDI entry entails. As local credit allocation processes become more market-based rather than politically driven, well-connected firms begin to lose their privileged access to finance and start to view multinational enterprises (MNEs) as important sources of investment and operational finance through joint ventures, mergers, acquisitions, and supplier/procurer trade finance structures. In turn, pathways toward FDI policy liberalization can be instigated and managed by domestic firms best poised to benefit from MNE entry into the local economy. This possibility challenges scholars and policymakers to rethink assumptions that the promise of jobs is the primary driver of support for policies aimed at fostering MNE investment in local economies. It also suggests that a more nuanced view of the distributional effects of FDI liberalization is warranted.

Despite the strong evidence of a relationship between banking sector regulations and FDI policies reforms, however, it is important to be clear about the limitations of the modeling exercises presented in this chapter. The analyses shown here provide strong evidence of a connection between banking sector reforms and liberalizing policies toward FDI. However, like all statistical analyses, they cannot confirm causality. They do not explicitly test each step in the causal chain through which we may expect domestic financing constraints to lead to FDI policy reforms. To make the case for the causal connection more convincingly, we must do more to break down the proposed causal pathway and isolate testable observable implications of the theoretical expectation that domestic firms' preferences for FDI policy is rooted in changes to their financing constraints.

In the next chapter, I do precisely that by leveraging several different firm-level and industry-level data sources to probe more carefully the causal mechanisms that may lead from changes to domestic credit allocation process to FDI policy reforms. Specifically, I explore two questions. First, I consider how firm-level characteristics and country-level variations in banking sector and FDI policies influences firms' perceptions of financing constraints. Second, I use industry-level data on policy reforms to explore whether and how the capital intensity of industries affects the propensity to liberalize FDI policy. Jointly, these additional tests help to disentangle the mechanisms that tie banking sector reforms to subsequent FDI policy changes.

APPENDIX

Endogenity Tests

Error Correction Models

The estimations in Tables 4.3–4.5 assume panel dynamics are adequately modeled through a 1-year lag. My theory argues banking sector reform creates a policy environment more conducive to foreign direct investment (FDI) liberalization. Because interest realignment takes time to transfer into policy change, the causal process may move more slowly. To address this possibility, I augment my analysis by estimating a series of single-equation error-correction models (SECMs). Such models are useful for several reasons. First, SECMs are particularly suited for integrated time series; diagnostics confirm that both measures of FDI openness as well as banking sector reform conform to a first-order integration. Second, unlike estimation models that include each explanatory variable lagged by a predetermined amount, SECMs remain agnostic to the length of time it takes for the effect of explanatory variables to transfer fully into outcomes of interest. SECMs estimate three qualitatively important quantities of interest – the average instantaneous change in Y as a result of x, the average long-term effect of x on Y, and the rate at which the long-term effects of x change Y. Third, SECMs accommodate many problems typical when running dynamic models. These models can handle both integrated and stationary explanatory variables within the same equation,[47] and they also are robust to weak endogeneity.[48]

My estimation equation is as follows:

$$\Delta(FDI\ Policy)_{(i,t)}$$
$$= \alpha_0 + \alpha_1(FDI\ Policy)_{(i,t-1)} + \beta_0\Delta(Banking\ Reform)_{(i,t)}$$
$$+\beta_1(Banking\ Reform)_{(i,t-1)}+\beta_2\Delta X_{(i,t)}+\beta_3 X_{(i,t-1)}+\gamma_{(i,t)}+\varepsilon_{(i,t)}$$

---

[47] Engle and Granger (1987); Keele and DeBoef (2008).
[48] DeBoef (2001).

where β_0 and β_1 are the main coefficients of interest and represent the short-term and long-term effects of *Banking Reform on FDI Policy* respectively, $\Delta X_{(i,t)}$ and $X_{(i,t-1)}$ consist of differenced and lagged country-level controls; $\gamma_{(i,t)}$ are fixed country effects; and $\varepsilon_{(i,t)}$ are errors clustered by country to account for serial correlation.

Table A.1 reports the results of SECMs for *Equity Restrictions*; these are SECM replications of Models 8–11 (Table 4.5). Recall that all nonindicator variables are standardized to aid in interpreting relative effects. These models jointly demonstrate the core findings explicated above continue to hold even when employing this more conservative statistical estimation technique.

Interpreting SECMs requires separating the short-term effects of explanatory variables from the long-term effects, which transfer into the data through an equilibrating process. The intuition behind error-correction models is if two or more time series are cointegrated, they should share a stochastic trend that moderates toward an equilibrium relationship. First, note that for all models, the coefficient estimate for the lagged dependent variable is negative and statistically significant. This finding provides evidence that an error-correction model is indeed appropriate for the data; the differenced level of FDI openness is stationary and trends back toward an equilibrium value. Interpreting the short-term effects of the explanatory variables is straightforward; the coefficient estimate of the differenced value of an explanatory variable represents the average instantaneous change in FDI openness. Interpretation of long-term effects requires dividing the coefficient estimate for the lagged explanatory variable by the coefficient estimate for the lagged dependent variable. Because all variables have been standardized, the resulting coefficient estimate represents the average total effect of a standard deviation change in the explanatory variable; the coefficient estimate for the lagged dependent variable provides an indication for how quickly the total long-term effect transfers into the data.

What becomes immediately clear is financial reform has no instantaneous effect on FDI liberalization, but instead influences openness to foreign investment through a longer temporal process. This finding establishes that the correlation between FDI and financial sector liberalization is not driven by contemporaneous reforms in both policy areas. The substantive long-term effect of financial sector reform on liberalization of equity restrictions is quite large. Overall, Model 12 predicts that a standard deviation change in banking sector liberalization leads to an average increase in FDI openness equal to 18.75 percent of its standard deviation. Model 14, which is restricted to just developing countries, predicts a standard deviation in *Banking Reform*, on average, is associated with a 33.65 percent decrease in *Equity Restrictions*. Models 13 and 15 find similar effects for decreases in *Interest Rate Controls* on *Equity Restrictions*. They find that a standard deviation loosening of *Interest Rate Controls* corresponds to a 17.86 and a 23.08 percent average decrease, respectively, in *Equity Restrictions*.

Among the various control variables, only two are consistently statistically significant across all models. First, the lagged value of *Democracy* is consistently positively and statistically significantly related to *Equity Restrictions*. The sign for democracy is particularly interesting because it contradicts previous findings that democracy drives FDI openness.[49] In a large cross-sectional analysis, it is not clear whether this negative association is due to democracies blocking reform or because countries are typically open to FDI before they transition to democracy. Regardless, the results do call into question theories of FDI reform that emphasize democratic transition. Second, and unsurprisingly, both differenced and lagged values of *Regional Entry Restrictions* are positive and statistically significant. This confirms that FDI policies do exhibit patterns consistent with regional diffusion.

Granger Causality Analysis

Next, to further deal with identification issues stemming from endogeneity, I run a series of Granger causality tests to ascertain the extent to which lagged values of banking sector reforms predict levels of FDI openness in time t, and vice versa. I establish that *Banking Reforms* Granger-cause reductions in *Equity Restrictions*, but *Equity Restrictions* do not Granger-cause *Banking Reforms*. A related concern is that the relationship between reforms in the banking sector and investment law may reflect a latent propensity on the part of governments to pursue neoliberal reforms more generally. If my findings are driven by a latent neoliberal bias of governments, reforms in the banking sector should be dynamically associated with other types of neoliberal

---

[49] Pandya (2014); Dorobantu (2010).

Table A.1. *Historical models, error correction estimations*

	Model 12	Model 13	Model 14	Model 15
Equity	−0.416***	−0.420***	−0.428***	−0.429***
Restrictions$_{(t-1)}$	(0.00)	(0.00)	(0.00)	(0.00)
Banking	−0.078*		−0.144*	
Reforms$_{(t-1)}$	(0.04)		(0.03)	
Δ Banking	0.020		0.072	
Reforms	(0.78)		(0.45)	
Interest Rate		−0.075**		−0.099*
Controls$_{(t-1)}$		(0.01)		(0.01)
Δ Interest Rate		−0.028		−0.014
Controls		(0.34)		(0.71)
Ln GDP	0.061	0.030	−0.117	−0.103
Per Capita$_{(t-1)}$	(0.79)	(0.88)	(0.66)	(0.68)
Δ Ln	0.426	0.353	0.399	0.248
GDP Per Capita	(0.65)	(0.70)	(0.72)	(0.81)
Ln Inflation$_{(t-1)}$	−0.016	−0.006	−0.016	−0.002
	(0.49)	(0.78)	(0.51)	(0.92)
Δ Ln Inflation	−0.055	−0.053	−0.061	−0.059
	(0.22)	(0.23)	(0.17)	(0.19)
Ln Trade/GDP$_{(t-1)}$	0.275	0.285*	0.308	0.322
	(0.06)	(0.05)	(0.09)	(0.07)
Δ Ln Trade/GDP	0.417	0.418	0.451	0.458
	(0.31)	(0.28)	(0.30)	(0.27)
Ln Tertiary	−0.365*	−0.367*	−0.390	−0.390
Enroll$_{(t-1)}$	(0.02)	(0.02)	(0.06)	(0.07)
Δ Ln Tertiary	−0.478	−0.484	−0.516	−0.520
Enroll	(0.28)	(0.25)	(0.27)	(0.24)
Democracy$_{(t-1)}$	0.165**	0.164**	0.197**	0.197**
	(0.00)	(0.00)	(0.00)	(0.00)
Δ Democracy	0.060	0.057	0.073	0.067
	(0.54)	(0.54)	(0.51)	(0.52)
Crisis$_{(t-1)}$	0.053	0.058	0.120	0.123
	(0.57)	(0.54)	(0.23)	(0.23)
Δ Crisis$_{(t-1)}$	0.017	0.021	0.070	0.071
	(0.79)	(0.73)	(0.27)	(0.26)
Under IMF$_{(t-1)}$	0.041	0.046	0.047	0.055
	(0.56)	(0.52)	(0.56)	(0.49)
Δ Under IMF$_{(t-1)}$	0.009	0.012	−0.003	0.004
	(0.91)	(0.88)	(0.97)	(0.97)

Ln Private Dom	0.065	0.059	0.059	0.054
Credit$_{(t-1)}$	(0.06)	(0.05)	(0.35)	(0.35)
Δ Ln Private Dom	0.013	0.013	0.050	0.051
Credit	(0.79)	(0.78)	(0.56)	(0.55)
Fixed Exchange	0.079	0.068	0.106	0.098
Rate$_{(t-1)}$	(0.20)	(0.27)	(0.28)	(0.31)
Δ Fixed Exchange	0.014	0.009	0.044	0.037
Rate	(0.79)	(0.86)	(0.53)	(0.59)
Average Regional	0.139***	0.136***	0.140***	0.142***
Restrict$_{(t-1)}$	(0.00)	(0.00)	(0.00)	(0.00)
Δ Average Regional	0.190***	0.187***	0.191***	0.191***
Restrict	(0.00)	(0.00)	(0.00)	(0.00)
BITs$_{(t-1)}$			0.021	0.012
			(0.11)	(0.31)
Δ BITs			−0.006	−0.012
			(0.77)	(0.51)
Ln Resource			−0.001	−0.000
Rents$_{(t-1)}$			(0.90)	(0.97)
Δ Ln Resource			0.004	0.005
Rents			(0.57)	(0.53)
Observations	1333	1333	830	830
Countries	65	65	45	45
R^2	0.241	0.243	0.253	0.253

Nonindicator variables standardized. Fixed effects estimated with year dummies and country-clustered standard errors. Standard errors in parentheses.
$+p < 0.1$, $*p < 0.05$, $**p < 0.01$, $***p < 0.001$

reform. Granger causality tests reveal no relationship between *Banking Reforms* and *Trade Liberalization* or between *Banking Reforms* and *Short-Term Capital Account Openness*.

The idea behind Granger causality is that temporal ordering implies a causal sequence.[50] Therefore, if lags of x jointly explain y after controlling for an equal number of lags of y, we can say that x Granger-causes y. To test for this, I run block F tests on the lags of x. A statistically significant p value indicates the lags of x jointly improve model fit. Choosing the correct lag structure for Granger causality tests is somewhat controversial due to issues of sensitivity and overfitting.[51]

[50] Granger (1969).
[51] Thornton and Batten (1985).

Table A.2. *Granger causality – banking reform and equity restrictions*

Equity Restrictions $=$ Equity Restrictions$_{(t-1)}$ + Bank Reform$_{(t-1)}$				
Number of Lags	AIC	BIC	Test Statistic	p Value
1	−758.672	−748.142	12.8	0.0006
2	−729.322	−708.458	6.22	0.0033
5	−747.582	−716.594	8.33	0.0396
Bank Reform $=$ Bank Reform$_{(t-1)}$ + Equity Restrictions$_{(t-1)}$				
Number of Lags	AIC	BIC	Test Statistic	p Value
1	3713.333	3739.660	1.78	0.1884
2	3552.408	3588.920	2.98	0.2249
5	−747.5821	3440.955	5.34	0.1484

Power loss from long lags becomes particularly problematic in unbalanced panels. I err on the side of a shorter lag structure in order to increase model power and to include the largest group of countries possible given the limitations of the data. Following the convention of choosing lag structure through measures of model fit, I begin with one lag and then increase the number of lags sequentially until model fit decreases. Based on AIC and BIC scoring, a two- to five-lag model emerges as the best fit for the data.

First, I run analysis to test the temporal ordering of the relationship between *Bank Reforms* and *Equity Restrictions*. Table A.2 shows *Bank Reform* Granger-causes *Equity Restrictions*, but *Equity Restrictions* does not Granger-cause *Bank Reforms*, as indicated by the statistically significant p values for models with *Equity Restrictions* as the dependent variable and the statistically insignificant p values for models with *Bank Reforms* as the dependent variable.

Next, I consider whether *Bank Reforms* is really just a proxy for a latent propensity to pursue neoliberal reforms broadly defined. Table A.3 demonstrates no evidence that *Bank Reforms* Granger-cause *Trade Liberalization*, as measured by applied tariff rates, or short-term *Capital Account Openness*, as measured by the widely used Chinn and Ito variable of capital account restrictions.

Table A.3. *Granger causality – banking reform, tariff levels, and capital account (KA) open*

Tariff Levels $=$ Tariff Levels$_{(t-1)}$ $+$ Bank Reform$_{(t-1)}$				
Number of Lags	AIC	BIC	Test Statistic	p Value
1	−419.699	−363.002	1.49	0.2259
2	−306.177	−249.681	1.64	0.2003
5	−198.900	−146.306	0.94	0.4642
KA Open $=$ KA Open$_{(t-1)}$ $+$ Bank Reform$_{(t-1)}$				
Number of Lags	AIC	BIC	Test Statistic	p Value
1	−1196.759	−1179.925	0.13	0.7213
2	−1132.683	−1104.885	1.23	0.2926
5	−1092.028	−1032.689	0.75	0.5884

Table A.4. *Historical models, alternate estimations*

	Entry Restrictions	Entry Restrictions	Entry Restrictions	Entry Restrictions
Lagged DV	0.2148 (0.0098)**		0.2133 (0.0091)**	
Banking Reform$_{(t-1)}$	−0.0275 (0.0146)+	−0.0399 (0.207)+		−0.0437 (0.0117)**
Interest Rate Controls$_{(t-1)}$			−0.0245 (0.0068)**	
Ln GDP Per Capita$_{(t-1)}$	−0.0368 (0.0704)	0.0567 (0.1157)	−0.0396 (0.0679)	0.0773 (0.1154)
Ln Inflation$_{(t-1)}$	0.0018 (0.0075)	−0.0027 (0.0090)	0.0041 (0.0064)	−0.0003 (0.0088)
Ln Trade/GDP$_{(t-1)}$	0.0819 (0.182)**	0.0808 (0.0853)	0.0839 (0.1831)**	0.0773 (0.0850)
Ln Tertiary Enrollment$_{(t-1)}$	−0.1091 (0.0115)**	−0.0766 (0.0878)	−0.1083 (0.0105)**	−0.0731 (0.0876)
Democracy$_{(t-1)}$	0.0415 (0.0184)*	−0.0109 (0.0316)	0.0423 (0.0182)*	−0.0081 (0.0314)
Crisis$_{(t-1)}$	−0.0037 (0.0203)	0.0144 (0.0154)	−0.0017 (0.0203)	0.0141 (0.0154)
Under IMF$_{(t-1)}$	0.0058 (0.0131)	−0.0030 (0.0176)	0.0071 (0.0123)	−0.0001 (0.0176)
Ln Private Domestic Credit$_{(t-1)}$	0.0246 (0.0171)	0.0474 (0.0186)**	0.0238 (0.0171)	0.0439 (0.0184)*
Fixed Exchange Rate$_{(t-1)}$	0.0308 (0.0163)+	0.0325 (0.0150)*	0.0286 (0.0163)+	0.0316 (0.0149)*
Average Regional Restriction$_{(t-1)}$	0.0346 (0.0084)**	0.0566 (0.0094)**	0.0339 (0.0086)**	0.0552 (0.0093)**
Estimation Technique	PCSE	FGLS	PCSE	FGLS
Observations	1342	1341	1342	1341
Countries	65	64	65	64
R^2	0.7399		0.7407	

Nonindicator variables standardized. Fixed effects estimated with year dummies and country-clustered standard errors. Standard errors in parentheses. ** $p < 0.01$, * $p < 0.05$, + $p < 0.1$; two-tailed tests

Table A.5. *Historical models, disaggregated crises*

	Entry Restrictions
Lagged DV	0.5850 (0.0423)**
Banking Reform$_{(t-1)}$	−0.0766 (0.0373)*
Ln GDP Per Capita$_{(t-1)}$	−0.1010 (0.2720)
Ln Inflation$_{(t-1)}$	0.0035 (0.0231)
Ln Trade/GDP$_{(t-1)}$	0.2292 (0.1622)
Ln Tertiary Enrollment$_{(t-1)}$	−0.3028 (0.1860)
Democracy$_{(t-1)}$	0.1121 (0.0532)*
Bank Crisis$_{(t-1)}$	0.0283 (0.1150)
Currency Crisis$_{(t-1)}$	−0.0060 (0.0449)
Debt Crisis $_{(t-1)}$	−0.0591 (0.0829)
Under IMF$_{(t-1)}$	0.0144 (0.0534)
Ln Private Domestic Credit$_{(t-1)}$	0.0660 (0.0389)+
Fixed Exchange Rate$_{(t-1)}$	0.0835 (0.0405)*
Average Regional Restriction$_{(t-1)}$	0.0946 (0.0405)*
Observations	1342
Countries	65
R^2	0.6782

*$p < 0.05$, **$p < 0.01$, ***$p < 0.001$

Table A.6. *Historical models mostly robust to additional controls*

Equity Restrictions$_{(t-1)}$	0.560***	0.560***	0.552***	0.546***
	(0.00)	(0.00)	(0.00)	(0.00)
Banking Reforms$_{(t-1)}$	−0.099	−0.100*	−0.169*	−0.164*
	(0.12)	(0.04)	(0.04)	(0.04)
Ln GDP Per Capita$_{(t-1)}$	−0.149	−0.193	−0.435	−0.473
	(0.67)	(0.55)	(0.26)	(0.20)
Ln Trade/GDP$_{(t-1)}$	0.500*	0.219	0.590*	0.249
	(0.03)	(0.23)	(0.01)	(0.21)
Ln Inflation$_{(t-1)}$	0.017	0.005	0.026	0.015
	(0.62)	(0.84)	(0.47)	(0.61)
Ln Tertiary Enroll$_{(t-1)}$	−0.512*	−0.237	−0.607**	−0.256
	(0.02)	(0.26)	(0.00)	(0.29)
Democracy$_{(t-1)}$	0.088	0.117	0.106	0.155*
	(0.19)	(0.05)	(0.13)	(0.02)
Crisis$_{(t-1)}$	−0.003	−0.001	−0.028	−0.011
	(0.96)	(0.98)	(0.68)	(0.87)
Under IMF$_{(t-1)}$	0.058	0.037	0.054	0.052
	(0.30)	(0.49)	(0.35)	(0.41)
Δ Ln Private Domestic	0.077	0.066	0.071	0.080
Credit$_{(t-1)}$	(0.30)	(0.22)	(0.55)	(0.39)
Fixed Exchange Rate$_{(t-1)}$	0.048	0.082	0.033	0.091
	(0.36)	(0.12)	(0.65)	(0.28)
Ln Current Account/GDP$_{(t-1)}$	−0.095	−0.073	−0.096	−0.080
	(0.20)	(0.28)	(0.31)	(0.35)
Ln Exports/GDP$_{(t-1)}$	−0.207*	−0.133	−0.229	−0.156
	(0.03)	(0.14)	(0.12)	(0.26)
Ln Manufacturing/GDP$_{(t-1)}$	0.022		0.033	
	(0.76)		(0.69)	
Average Regional Restriction$_{(t-1)}$	0.065*	0.074*	0.070*	0.070*
	(0.04)	(0.02)	(0.04)	(0.04)
Average Income Restriction$_{(t-1)}$	0.042	0.033	0.087	0.059
	(0.40)	(0.49)	(0.26)	(0.41)
BITs$_{(t-1)}$			0.037*	0.031*
			(0.02)	(0.05)
Ln Resource Rents$_{(t-1)}$			0.087	0.096
			(0.48)	(0.42)
R^2	0.462	0.447	0.482	0.469
BIC	1543.258	1807.509	1283.917	1458.833
N	871	1101	641	700.

Fixed effects estimated with year dummies and country-clustered standard errors.
Standard errors in parentheses. *$p < 0.05$, **$p < 0.01$, ***$p < 0.001$

Table A.7. *Policy change models, additional controls*

	Liberal	Lib Entry	Lib Promote
Net Interest Margin$_{(t-1)}$	−0.184*	−0.209	−0.151
	(0.09)	(0.11)	(0.12)
Ln GDP Per Capita$_{(t-1)}$	0.023	−0.117	0.295
	(0.15)	(0.20)	(0.21)
Ln Inflation$_{(t-1)}$	1.315	3.208	0.007
	(2.60)	(3.73)	(3.43)
Ln Tertiary Enroll$_{(t-1)}$	0.378**	0.287	0.514**
	(0.13)	(0.16)	(0.17)
Fixed Exchange Rate$_{(t-1)}$	−0.226	−0.176	−0.393*
	(0.13)	(0.17)	(0.16)
Democracy$_{(t-1)}$	−0.285	−0.065	−0.557**
	(0.15)	(0.19)	(0.20)
Crisis$_{(t-1)}$	−0.071	0.253	−1.688
	(0.51)	(0.64)	(1.15)
Ln Current Account/GDP$_{(t-1)}$	0.230*	0.431**	−0.244
	(0.10)	(0.14)	(0.13)
Ln Trade/GDP$_{(t-1)}$	−0.025	0.020	−0.166
	(0.15)	(0.18)	(0.17)
Ln Exports GDP$_{(t-1)}$	−0.429*	−0.504*	−0.191
	(0.19)	(0.23)	(0.22)
Ln Manufacturing/GDP$_{(t-1)}$	0.419***	0.378***	0.469***
	(0.06)	(0.08)	(0.09)
Under IMF$_{(t-1)}$	0.565**	0.449	0.715**
	(0.22)	(0.29)	(0.26)
Average Regulatory Policy Change$_{(t-1)}$	0.456**	0.625	0.446
	(0.17)	(0.32)	(0.47)
Average Income Policy Change$_{(t-1)}$	−0.506	−0.646	−0.566
	(0.31)	(0.67)	(0.73)
AIC	2681.858	1876.633	1533.105
BIC	2842.792	2037.567	1694.040
N	1328	1328	1328

Standard errors in parentheses. Year fixed effects and constant not reported
*$p < 0.05$, **$p < 0.01$, ***$p < 0.001$

5 | Quantitative Tests: Firm- and Industry-Level Evidence

In Chapter 4, I established the macro relationship between the local financing environment and foreign direct investment (FDI) policy liberalization. Using data from 1973 to 2015, I show states that underwent substantial banking sector reforms that disrupted elite firms' privileged access to finance were much more likely to loosen foreign equity restrictions in subsequent periods. This relationship is robust to a variety of alternative explanations and multiple statistical techniques designed to overcome concerns of simultaneity. I also find that banking sector reforms are more likely to lead to FDI policy liberalization when domestic political institutions advantage elite business interests. The analyses presented in Chapter 4 jointly provide compelling evidence in support of a financing constraints theory of investment policy liberalization.

Country-level analysis suggests firms drive liberalizing coalitions under reformed banking sectors, but cannot isolate why they do so. This chapter uses a combination of firm-level and industry-level data to explore the connection between the FDI policy environment and firm financing constraints, and by doing so, more fully probes the mechanisms through which changing domestic financing environments lead to innovations in FDI policy. I proceed in two steps.

First, I leverage firm survey data to establish the microfoundations of a firm-driven push to pursue more open policy environments toward foreign investors. These data allow me to determine what types of firms are most likely to attempt to influence government regulatory policy. I then use survey questions on firms' perceptions of financing constraints to determine the effect of the FDI policy environment on the financing position of firms that are most likely to lobby governments about regulatory policy. This allows me to move beyond conceptualizing business interests as a homogenous block and to figure out instead the sources of heterogeneous preferences over multinational entry.

Second, I use industry-level data on investment policy changes to determine the relationship between capital intensity and the propensity to enact liberalizing policy change. If business interests press for increased openness toward foreign investors in order to overcome financing constraints, we should see three patterns at the industry level. First, industries characterized by high levels of capital intensity should be more likely to experience liberalizing changes when local banking regulations reduce governments' ability to channel subsidized credit to influential firms. Second, capital-intensive industries should be less likely to undergo policy liberalization where political leaders retain tools to intercede in credit markets because influential firms in these environments face less constraining financing options. Third, if FDI liberalization occurs because powerful firms push for greater access to multinational enterprise (MNE) liquidity channels, we should expect banking sector reforms to be associated with increases in policy liberalizations related to entry restrictions but not to other more ancillary policy tools such as regulations over treatment or investment promotion.

In sum, the data and analyses presented in this chapter allow me to explore more fully the mechanisms through which banking reforms may induce highly connected economic elites to embrace a more open policy stance on foreign firms. By leveraging data across multiple levels of analysis and from different time periods, I further subject my central hypotheses to rigorous testing. Overall, my analysis provides further support for the following: large, well-connected firms benefit from the liquidity that MNEs can provide; and industries that are capital intensive are more likely to liberalize, particularly policies related to entry, in reformed domestic banking environments. These findings complement the analysis presented in Chapter 4, and further support my central contention that FDI liberalization can be driven, rather than blocked, by domestic business interests.

Does FDI Liberalization Affect Firm Financing Constraints?

To explore the mechanisms that connect financing constraints and FDI liberalization, I use firm-level survey data to ask two related questions. First, which firms are most likely to lobby domestic governments for their preferred policies? Second, do more liberalized FDI environments ameliorate financing constraints among firms that are most likely to engage in lobbying? If business interests push governments to liberalize FDI to lessen financing constraints, firms – and especially firms with foreign ownership – should report fewer concerns over financing when FDI policy is more open. Moreover, firms that are less finance constrained in more open FDI policy environments should be more likely to lobby governments than businesses that receive fewer liquidity benefits from FDI inflows.

To answer these questions, I turn to the World Bank Enterprise Survey, which uses a uniform, stratified, random sampling technique to survey owners and managers of private firms in manufacturing and service sector activities in 135 developing and middle-income economies. These surveys record several demographic characteristics of represented firms, including size, ownership structure, and balance sheets. They also ask questions designed to uncover firm-level perceptions of the local business environment across several dimensions, including the regulatory environment, trade openness, crime, corruption, and the financing environment.

I analyze World Bank Enterprise data from its first round of surveys, which were implemented between 2002 and 2005. While the World Bank envisions this survey to eventually include long panels for time series analysis, most countries have only undergone the survey twice. The second round of surveys were implemented around 2007–2010, which coincided with a substantial global financial crisis and economic recession that created credit rationing in many areas of the global economy. A third round of surveys was completed in 2017. However, a key question on lobbying was only present in the first round of surveys. Consequently, I choose to focus on these data.

Who Lobbies?

The first question I ask is: what firm characteristics are associated with lobbying activity? This question is important because firms have heterogeneous preferences. Therefore, to establish which voices are most likely to be heard, it is useful to consider which firms frequently engage in the costly act of trying to influence government officials. To explore this, I use firm answers to the following yes or no question:

Table 5.1. *Lobbying activities by ownership structure*

Lobby	Ownership Structure			
	Domestic	Min Foreign	Maj Foreign	Total
Yes	3,608	160	751	4,519
	14%	25%	21%	15%
No	21,581	472	2,780	24,833
	86%	75%	79%	85%
	25,189	632	3,531	29,352

Pearson $\chi^2(2) = 163.4808$, $Pr = 0.000$, Cramér's $V = 0.0746$

Did your firm seek to lobby government or otherwise influence the content of laws or regulations affecting it? As mentioned previously, this question was only asked in the first round of the Enterprise Survey.[1]

Using simple cross tabulations and difference in means tests, I explore whether and how five characteristics of firms influence their propensity to lobby government. First, I consider whether ownership structure affects lobbying behavior. Table 5.1 shows that domestically owned firms lobby government less than do firms with at least 10 percent foreign ownership. Entities for which foreigners hold a minority stake lobby the most. These differences are statistically significant.[2] Table 5.2 considers whether firms that have been privatized lobby more than those that have never been owned by the state. The answer is yes.[3]

I also consider how other firm characteristics such as size, export status, and sales patterns affect lobbying behavior. Table 5.3 examines how firm size, measured by number of employees, affects lobbying activities. Following standard categorizations, small firms include

---

[1] It is possible that nonresponse drove the decision to drop this question from subsequent surveys. The variable is close to 59 percent missing. However, using difference of means tests, I find that nonresponse is not related to ownership structure or export status. Medium-size firms, however, are slightly more likely than large or small firms to refrain from answering the question. Overall, there is little about missingness patterns to create concern about bias in my analysis.

[2] Domestic = Min Foreign: Prob > F = 0.0000. Domestic = Maj Foreign: Prob > F = 0.0000. Min Foreign = Maj Foreign: Prob > F = 0.0092.

[3] Prob > F = 0.0000.

Table 5.2. *Lobbying activities by previous state-owned enterprise (SOE) status*

	Previously SOE?		
Lobby	Yes	No	Total
Yes	589	2,138	2,727
	24%	12%	14%
No	1,848	15,378	17,226
	76%	88%	86%
Total	2,437	17,516	19,953

Pearson $\chi^2(1) = 259.4866$, Pr $= 0.000$, Cramér's $V = 0.1140$

Table 5.3. *Lobbying activities by size*

	Size			
Lobby	Small	Medium	Large	Total
Yes	1,299	1,407	1,813	4,519
	9%	17%	26%	15%
No	12,611	7,029	5,193	24,833
	91%	83%	74%	85%
Total	13,910	8,436	7,006	29,352

Pearson $\chi^2(2) = 993.4328$, Pr $= 0.000$, Cramér's $V = 0.1840$

those with fewer than 20 employees. Medium firms employ between 20 and 100 people. Companies that employ over 100 people are considered large. Clearly, the larger the firm, the more likely it is to lobby government. Difference in means tests confirm that these variations are statistically significant.[4] As Table 5.4 indicates, firms that export at least 10 percent of their goods and services are more likely to lobby government.[5] Finally, I consider firm lobbying behavior by the origin(s) of their sales. As Table 5.5 demonstrates, entities that sell over 50 percent of their goods or services to the government or to foreign firms or within an integrated supply chain lobby government at the same rate,

---

[4] Small = Medium: Prob $> F = 0.0000$. Small = Large: Prob $> F = 0.0000$. Medium = Large: Prob $> F = 0.0000$.
[5] No vs. yes: Prob $> F = 0.0000$.

Table 5.4. *Lobbying activities by export status*

	Exporter		
Lobby	Yes	No	Total
Yes	3,147	1,319	4,466
	13%	23%	15%
No	20,212	4,413	24,625
	87%	77%	85%
Total	23,359	5,732	29,091

Pearson $\chi^2(1) = 322.2667$, Pr $= 0.000$, Cramér's $V = -0.1053$

Table 5.5. *Lobbying activities by majority sales*

	Maj Dom Sales			
Lobby	Govt/SOE	Domestic	Foreign	Total
Yes	570	2,691	802	4,063
	21%	14%	21%	15%
No	2,165	17,195	2,974	22,334
	79%	86%	79%	85%
Total	2,735	19,886	3,776	26,397

Pearson $\chi^2(2) = 214.3184$, Pr $= 0.000$, Cramér's $V = 0.0901$

while firms that sell primarily to the domestic private market are less likely to lobby.[6]

These simple exercises jointly establish the following. Firms that have foreign ownership, particularly minority foreign ownership, and firms that were previously state owned are more likely to lobby government than are other companies. Larger firms that export and sell primarily to government or multinational firms are also more likely to lobby for their policy preferences. None of these characteristics of high-propensity lobbying is particularly surprising. However, this analysis does establish that large, well-connected firms are most likely to use their influence to affect policy. This insight provides important

---

[6] Govt = Domestic: Prob > F = 0.0000. Govt = MNE: Prob > F = 0.6588. Domestic = MNE: Prob > F = 0.0000.

support for an underlying assumption of the theory presented in Chapter 3. Mainly, to understand the influence of firms on FDI policy, it is important to focus on the preferences of large, politically connected firms that are best poised to capitalize on joint ventures and mergers with MNEs and best able to integrate into global supply chains.

Does FDI Policy Influence Financial Constraints?

Next, I turn my attention to the following question: do more liberalized FDI environments ameliorate financing constraints among firms that are most likely to engage in lobbying? I answer this question by examining how firms' perceptions of financing constraints differ across FDI policy contexts. I connect my analysis of financing perceptions to lobbying behavior by examining particularly the influence of the FDI policy environment on firms that, given their characteristics, are more likely to lobby governments. Overall, I find considerable evidence that firms that are more likely to attempt to guide policy are also more likely to face less constrained financing environments when FDI policy is more open. That is, larger firms with at least some degree of foreign equity participation are more likely to report lower perceptions of financing constraints. This holds regardless of export status. However, an important caveat is that state-owned enterprises (SOEs) seem prone to financing disadvantages in policy environments that are more permissive of foreign investment.

To consider the relationship between the FDI policy environment and firms' beliefs about their ability to obtain financing, I focus on one instrument from the World Bank Enterprise Survey designed to capture firms' perceptions of the overall financing environment: *Please tell us if cost of financing is a problem for the operation and growth of your business.* Respondents can answer: *no obstacle, minor obstacle, moderate obstacle, major obstacle, or very severe obstacle.*

I begin by inspecting frequency tables of firms' perceptions of financing constraints, dividing the sample between countries that score above and below the mean on the Fraser Index's measure for Investment Freedom in 2003. I do this because, of all available measures of FDI policy, the Fraser Index has the most coverage for 2003, the year the first round of Enterprise Surveys began implementation. For ease of comparison, I collapse firm responses from the original five-point

Table 5.6. *Financial constraints by FDI policy environment*

	FDI Policy		
Financial Constraints	Restrictive	Open	Total
No Obstacle	6,150	9,346	15,496
	21%	22%	22%
Moderate Obstacle	7,808	10,370	18,178
	26%	25%	25%
Major Obstacle	15,824	21,890	37,714
	53%	53%	53%
Total	29,782	41,606	71,388

Pearson $\chi^2(2) = 38.5683$, Pr $= 0.000$, Cramér's $V = 0.0232$

scale to three: *No Constraints, Some Constraints, Severe Constraints.* Table 5.6 reports results. Firms in countries with policies more open to FDI are more likely to report no financing constraints than firms in countries with more restrictions on FDI. Firms in more restrictive environments are more likely than others to report both moderate and severe financing constraints. However, while these differences are statistically significant,[7] they are substantively small. It may be that the FDI policy environment has heterogeneous effects on firm financing.

To what extent do perceptions of constraints apply to domestic and foreign-owned firms alike? Table 5.7 reports the frequency of response regarding financing constraints across domestically owned firms, firms with a minority foreign ownership stake, and firms that are majority foreign-owned, segmented by FDI openness. Overall, majority foreign-owned firms face more financing constraints in restrictive FDI environments than do minority foreign-owned firms. Domestic firms face the most financial constraints. In more permissive FDI environments, all firms report fewer financial constraints, but majority foreign-owned firms are more likely to report fewer obstacles to obtaining finance.

These findings suggest the following. First, increasingly open FDI policy environments have limited effects on the liquidity constraints of wholly domestically owned firms. Second, firms with minority foreign ownership seem to occupy a privileged space in restrictive

[7] Restrictive = Open: Prob > F = 0.0001.

Table 5.7. *Financial constraints, firm ownership, and FDI policy*

| | Restrictive FDI Environment | | | |
| | Ownership Structure | | | |
Lobby	Domestic	Min Foreign	Maj Foreign	Total
No Obstacle	5,040	223	887	6,150
	20%	28%	23%	21%
Moderate Obstacle	6,591	217	1,000	7,808
	26%	27%	26%	26%
Major Obstacle	13,467	370	1,987	15,824
	54%	46%	51%	53%
Total	25,098	810	3,874	29,782

Pearson $\chi^2(2) = 44.5748$, Pr $= 0.000$, Cramér's $V = 0.0274$

| | Permissive FDI Environment | | | |
| | Ownership Structure | | | |
Lobby	Domestic	Min Foreign	Maj Foreign	Total
No Obstacle	7,719	171	1,456	9,346
	21%	24%	30%	22%
Moderate Obstacle	8,941	205	1224	10,370
	25%	29%	25%	25%
Major Obstacle	19,429	330	2,131	21,890
	54%	47%	44%	53%
Total	36,089	706	4,811	41,606

Pearson $\chi^2(2) = 233.6455$, Pr $= 0.000$, Cramér's $V = 0.0530$

FDI policy environments. They appear to be uniquely positioned in such environments to raise capital, which suggests some degree of privileged access to finance exists for this group. Finally, majority foreign-owned firms see a large improvement in access to finance in policy environments more permissive to FDI.

Lack of time series data here precludes me from exploring whether ownership patterns change after governments undertake major FDI liberalizations, but previous research suggests both that less productive domestic firms exit the market[8] and that foreign

---

[8] Alfaro and Chen (2018, 2012).

owners increase their holdings in existing and new enterprises to majority-owned stakes.[9] These findings, then, support the hypothesis that firms overall are less financially constrained in economies characterized by increased openness to FDI and that firms with foreign ownership are disproportionately and positively affected.

Of course, the obvious next question is this: do these relationships hold in multivariate regression analysis? Table 5.8 reports results of several regression estimations that test the expectation that firms with some degree of foreign ownership will be less constrained with regard to financing than domestically owned firms in countries with liberalized laws on foreign ownership. The models presented in Table 5.8 use multilevel ordered logit to estimate the effect of FDI regulations on firms' perceptions of financial constraints, controlling for firm ownership status, exporter status, and size. *Financial Constraints* is measured by the Enterprise Survey's original five-point scale, where values equal to zero indicate that firms do not view financing as a constraint on their operations and values equal to four indicate firms believe financial access is a major constraint on their ability to function.

I measure FDI openness in three ways. In Model 1, I use the 2003 value of the *Fraser Index*'s investment freedom measure, standardized. I use the 2003 value because that is the first year for which the first round of Enterprise Surveys began. This measure has the broadest coverage for countries for which Enterprise Surveys exist and is therefore my preferred measure. In Model 2, I use the *Pandya Index* of equity restrictions. I use the 2000 value of this measure because it is the last year for which data exist. To aid in comparability and interpretation, I invert the metric so that higher values equal more open policy environments. I also standardize this variable. Notice that observations drop by approximately 37 percent; this is because the Pandya measure covers less developed and middle-income countries than does the Fraser Index. In Model 3, I employ the Heritage Foundation's Index of Investment Freedoms in 2003. Like the other two measures, higher values along the *Heritage Index* indicate more open policy environments. To ease comparison, this measure is also standardized.

My additional explanatory variables are as follows. *Domestic Owned* is an indicator variable that equals one when foreign investors own less that 10 percent of the firms' value. *Exporter* is coded one

---

[9] Kersting and Görg (2017).

Table 5.8. *Firm financing and FDI policy*

	Model 1	Model 2	Model 3
Fraser Index	-0.108^{+}		
	(0.06)		
Pandya Index		0.157	
		(0.12)	
Heritage Index			-0.143
			(0.11)
Domestic Owned	0.463***	0.452***	0.402***
	(0.03)	(0.04)	(0.05)
Domestic Owned × FDI Openness	0.082**	0.016	0.224***
	(0.03)	(0.03)	(0.06)
Exporter	0.034	0.064*	0.092*
	(0.02)	(0.03)	(0.04)
Medium	0.111***	0.083**	0.071
	(0.03)	(0.03)	(0.04)
Small	-0.011	-0.058	0.002
	(0.03)	(0.03)	(0.04)
cut1	-0.509^{***}	-0.372^{***}	-0.179
	(0.08)	(0.10)	(0.12)
cut2	0.243**	0.299**	0.478***
	(0.08)	(0.10)	(0.12)
cut3	1.249***	1.190***	1.342***
	(0.08)	(0.10)	(0.12)
cut4	2.764***	2.410***	2.545***
	(0.08)	(0.10)	(0.13)
var(FDI Open)	0.729***	1.288**	1.194**
	(0.15)	(0.41)	(0.38)
var(Country)	1.250***	1.854***	1.893**
	(0.22)	(0.46)	(0.58)
AIC	121000.00	74733.444	44990.167
BIC	121000.00	74831.583	45082.373
N	41740	26323	16057

Standard errors in parentheses.
$^{+}p < 0.1$, $^{*}p < 0.05$, $^{**}p < 0.01$, $^{***}p < 0.001$

when at least 10 percent of firm sales are exports. *Medium* equals one when the firm employs between 20 and 100 workers. *Small* equals one when the firm employs fewer workers. Because I am interested in the financing needs of private business, I exclude firms with over 10 percent state ownership. Therefore, my referent category is a large firm with at least 10 percent foreign ownership that produces mostly for domestic markets.

Because the model has an interaction term between *Domestic Owned* and each model's measure of *FDI Openness*, we can interpret the coefficient estimate for the FDI policy environment as the estimated effect of a one standard deviation increase in FDI openness on the probability that firms perceive finance to be a serious constraint on their business. The coefficient estimate for *Domestic Owned* indicates the propensity of domestically owned firms to report high levels of financial constraints in the context of an economy closed to FDI. The summation of the coefficient estimate for *Domestic Owned* and the coefficient estimate for the interaction term *Domestic Owned* × *FDI Openness* reveals the point estimate for the effect of a one standard deviation increase in *FDI Openness* on domestic firms' perceptions of financing constraints.

Model 1 estimates that the odds of a firm with some amount of foreign participation reporting it has any amount of financing constraint is about 10 percent lower in a country with a level of FDI openness one standard deviation above the mean versus a country with an in-sample average level of openness. However, domestically owned firms are 58.9 percent more likely than firms with some amount of foreign participation to report some amount of financing constraint. The positive and statistically significant interaction term indicates that domestic firms are even more likely to experience worse finance constraints compared to firms with at least 10 percent foreign ownership under more open FDI policy environments. Domestic firms are, on average, 68 percent more likely to report substantial financing constraints than are firms with some amount of foreign ownership when FDI liberalization increases by one standard deviation.

Models 2 and 3 use alternative measures of FDI policy, and provide mixed results. Model 2 does not show a statistically significant relationship between changes to the *Pandya Index* and firm financing constraints, but it does demonstrate that domestic firms are more financing constrained than those with some foreign equity. Model 3 uses the *Heritage Index* to measure FDI openness, and, like Model 1, finds that domestic firms face higher financial constraints when FDI policy is open. In this model, domestic firms are 75 percent more likely, on average, to face substantial financing constraints than are firms with some amount of foreign ownership as the liberalness of the FDI policy environment increases by one standard deviation.

These models provide qualified support for the contention that the FDI policy environment influences firms' access to finance. The strongest evidence is that wholly domestic firms face a financing penalty relative to firms with some degree of foreign ownership when FDI is liberalized. Model 2 shows this is not robust to the Pandya measure. However, the distribution of that index becomes compressed in 2000 because most of the variation in the measure occurs earlier in the time series. There is also limited evidence that a liberal FDI environment makes foreign firms less financially constrained; this only approaches statistical significance in Model 1. In general, however, we do see that domestically owned firms have incentives to pursue mergers with foreign-owned firms when they face financial constraints; across all models, domestic firms always are statistically significantly more likely to report substantial financial constraints in comparison to foreign entities.

A few other findings should be noted. *Medium Firms* are more likely to report financial constraints than large firms in most models, while *Small Firms* seem unaffected. This may be driven by the lower financing needs of firms with less than 20 employees. *Exporters* seem to face more financing constraints than do firms that produce for domestic markets, which may reflect greater trade financing needs.

Overall, analysis of firm-level data on lobbying behavior as well as perceptions regarding financing indicate the following. First, the types of firms that are most likely to lobby governments are large firms, firms with some degree of foreign equity participation, those that export, those that sell primarily to either global markets or the government, and those that were privatized. Second, for the most part, these firms are more likely than their peers to feel less finance-constrained when local policy is permissive of foreign investment. Together, this suggests that the firms most likely to influence policy have an interest in pressing for FDI liberalization when local conditions exacerbate financing constraints. These findings mostly hold across a variety of measures of FDI policy, increasing our confidence in their veracity. While these data alone cannot directly isolate whether firms are lobbying in support of increased openness to foreign investment, they certainly provide stronger evidence that it is in the interest of groups of typically politically powerful firms to do so.

Do Capital-Intensive Industries Tend to Liberalize More?

The previous section established that more liberalized policies toward FDI are associated with reduced financing constraints among large firms, and especially firms with some degree of foreign participation. In this section, I consider another observable implication of a financing-constraints-driven theory of FDI reform. Specifically, if business interests drive investment liberalization as a way to increase access to finance, then to the extent that FDI policy is set at the industry level, liberalization of entry requirements should occur more often for capital-intensive industries because such industries have the greatest financing needs. We should expect this relationship to be especially strong in economies that have undergone banking sector reform because large firms in those environments lose their privileged access to credit markets. This expectation is precisely the opposite of what we would anticipate if FDI liberalization were driven by labor demands for jobs. If the primary societal pressure undergirding FDI policy reform came from worker groups, we would expect labor-intensive industries to be most likely to liberalize because such industries are best poised to generate employment. Thus, testing how industry-level capital intensity affects the propensity to liberalize FDI policy can adjudicate between my theory of policy liberalization and the most prominent alternative explanation in the literature.

To test this hypothesis, I turn to the United Nations Conference on Trade and Development's (UNCTAD) database of all changes to national government investment policies made globally from 2000 to 2015. This dataset codes the industry or industries affected by each investment policy change. It also categorizes investment policy changes by their effects – that is, if they are liberalizing or restrictive of foreign investment – and by their type – that is, if they affect FDI through changes to entry, treatment, or promotion policies. I described this dataset and its advantages in Chapter 4, where I used these data, aggregated to the country level, to explore the relationship between the banking sector and investment policy change.

FDI Policy Liberalization, Banking Regulation, and Capital Intensity

I start by estimating a series of simple discrete variable equations that model the propensity for a government to enact an FDI policy change for a particular industry at time t. I use a series of dependent variables, all from UNCTAD's Investment Policy Monitor, and all coded "1" for every industry-country-year for which a relevant FDI policy change exists and "0" otherwise. As in Chapter 4, I estimate separate models for *Liberal*, *Lib Entry*, *Lib Promote*, and *Restrict*.[10] Note that the Investment Policy Monitor data also include policy changes that are not specific to industry; I exclude these from the following analysis because they cannot be assigned a capital intensity value.

I include two explanatory variables – *Capital Intensity* and *Banking Reform* – as well as an interaction between the two variables. I measure *Capital Intensity* in the following way. Following convention in the economics literature,[11] I construct a measure of capital intensity that subtracts the cost of labor inputs from the value of production divided by the value of production for each industry on a yearly basis. This measure can be thought of as the ratio of capital inputs over the total cost of production. Because these data are rarely available at the country level, especially in developing countries, I use the United States as my baseline.[12] I calculate this measure from the US Bureau of Labor Statistics data on multifactor productivity at the industry level. These data are available at the North American Industry Classification System (NAICS) three-digit industry level from 1987 to 2014. However, the UNCTAD Investment Policy Monitor classifies investment policies through the Standard Industrial Classification (SIC) two-digit system. Therefore, I match the NAICS data to the appropriate SIC code. This creates a unique capital intensity measure for 37 industries, which are reported in Table 5.9, along with the 2005 value of the capital intensity measure during the sample period for each industry. To aid in interpretation, I standardize *Capital Intensity*.

---

[10] See Chapter 4 for more measurement details.
[11] See, for example, Acemoglu and Guerrieri (2008).
[12] Benchmarking from the United States is a standard approach. See, for example, Gupta (2005).

Table 5.9. *Capital intensity measures, by industry*

Manufacture of:	Agriculture (0.813)	Public Admin (0.395)
Chemicals (0.848)	Extraction (0.870)	Media (0.726)
Clothing (0.729)	Administration (0.395)	Research and Development (0.469)
Electronics (0.658)	Arts (0.679)	Real Estate (0.920)
Fabricated Metals (0.694)	Construction (0.593)	Telecom (0.853)
Food products (0.855)	Education (0.786)	Trade (0.537)
Publishing (0.659)	Electric (0.853)	Transport (0.600)
Metals (0.813)	Finance (0.694)	Water (0.395)
Other (0.682)	Health (0.768)	
Petrol (0.969)	Hospitality (0.642)	
Pharmaceuticals (0.848)	Information Technology (0.447)	
Plastics (0.782)	Legal Services (0.363)	
Transport Equipment (0.776)	Professional Services (0.379)	
Wood Products (0.760)	Other Services (0.503)	

I measure the banking environment in three ways. First, I use the Abiad et al. measure of *Banking Reform* that was used in the previous chapter. This measure has broad temporal and cross-sectional coverage, including 103 countries from 1973 to 2005. Because my analysis covers 2000–2015, I use countries' scores from 2005 for the remaining 10 years of the sample. Second, as in the previous chapter, I use the *Interest Rate Controls* component of the index to better isolate the mechanism through which banking reforms reduce well-connected firms' privileged access to finance. As the banking sector reduces controls on interest rates, governments have less ability to direct credit to politically important firms at subsidized rates. Finally, because the Abiad et al. measure ends in 2005, I also run a series of models that instead measure the banking environment through *Net Interest Margin*, taken from the World Bank's Global Financial Development Database.[13] I direct readers to Chapter 4 for more detail about this measure.

---

[13] Cihak et al. (2012).

Table 5.10. *FDI Policy changes, banking regulation, and capital intensity*

	Model 8 Liberal	Model 9 Lib Entry	Model 10 Lib Treat	Model 11 Lib Promote	Model 12 Restrict
Capital	0.131	0.052	−0.287	0.859	1.608
Intensity	(0.35)	(0.32)	(0.39)	(0.57)	(0.83)
Banking	−0.132*	−0.127	−0.253*	−0.156*	0.042
Reform	(0.07)	(0.07)	(0.12)	(0.08)	(0.06)
Interaction	0.027	0.037	0.076	−0.044	−0.051
	(0.03)	(0.03)	(0.05)	(0.05)	(0.07)
Constant	−3.509***	−3.766***	−5.813***	−5.283***	−8.927***
	(0.79)	(0.82)	(1.26)	(0.98)	(1.29)
AIC	5383.362	4271.498	506.661	1442.553	2056.665
BIC	5551.718	4439.854	625.468	1610.908	2214.982
N	52095	52095	35819	52095	48795

Year fixed effects not reported. Standard errors in parentheses.
$^*p < 0.05$, $^{**}p < 0.01$, $^{***}p < 0.001$

Table 5.10 presents results of each of these models, which are estimated with logit link functions and fixed-year effects. I am unable to perform analysis with country and industry fixed effects for two reasons. First, country fixed effects drop all countries that had no changes in investment policy over the time period. Second, industry fixed effects become collinear with the *Capital Intensity* measure. Along with *Capital Intensity* and *Banking Reform*, I include an interaction of these two explanatory variables. It is computationally challenging to perform multilevel analysis for these models because of separation issues. Instead, I cluster standard errors by country. To review, I expect that more capital-intensive industries will be more likely to enact liberalizing changes, but only when the banking sector is sufficiently reformed so that well-connected firms lose their access to privileged finance. I expect this relationship will hold most strongly for liberalizing changes to entry regulations than for changes to treatment or promotion.

In general, model results conform to my expectations. Model 8 estimates the propensity to enact any liberalizing policy change. *Capital Intensity* is positive in all models except promotion, but it is insignificant on its own. *Banking Reform* is actually negative and statistically significant in most models, but the coefficient estimate is not particularly informative here because it represents the effect of *Banking Reform* on the propensity to liberalize when *Capital Intensity* equals zero – a case that does not exist in reality. Instead, what matters here is the interaction term, which must be plotted over a range of values to ascertain their substantive effects and statistical significance because regression output alone cannot communicate this.[14] Marginal effects plots provide an intuitive way to visualize the effect of *Capital Intensity* at various levels of *Banking Reform*. The top left graph in Figure 5.1 illustrates this relationship. At low levels of domestic banking reform – stated slightly differently, in economies characterized by continued government intervention into credit markets – *Capital Intensity* has no statistically significant effect on the propensity to liberalize. However, as the banking sector begins to reform, industries with higher capital intensities do become more likely to undergo reforms. The slightly downward sloping estimated effect suggests that the influence

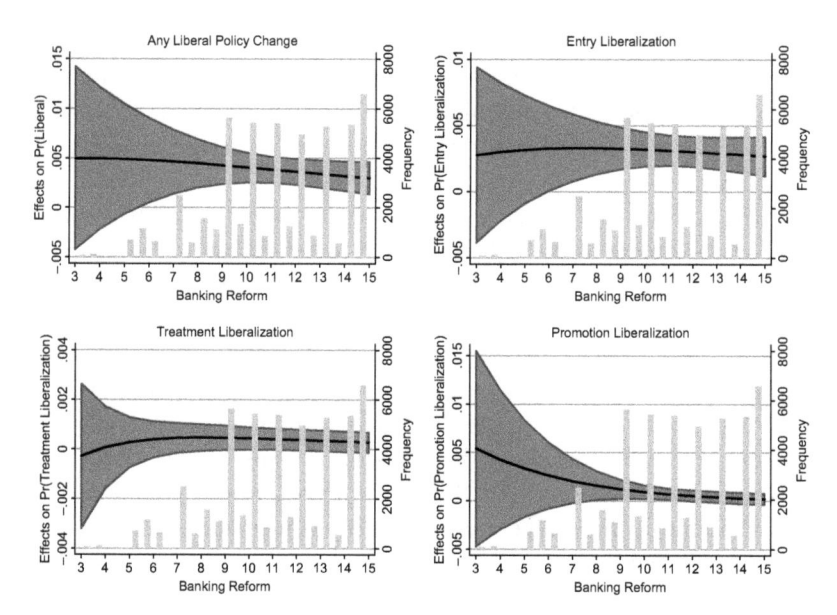

Figure 5.1 Marginal effects of capital intensity at different levels of banking reform, 95% confidence intervals

---

[14] Brambor et al. (2006).

of capital intensity on FDI reforms is strongest in credit environments that are transitioning from heavy state intervention to more market-driven dynamics. The top right graph in Figure 5.1 reveals that this relationship persists when we restrict analysis solely to liberalizing changes to entry regulations. This makes sense because if domestic firms demand openness to foreign investment in a quest to overcome financing constraints, we should see this dynamic most clearly among regulations that set limits on the extent to which foreign investors can acquire equity positions in local firms.

The relationship between FDI measures that regulate treatment and promotion and *Capital Intensity*, however, is quite different. The bottom two graphs in Figure 5.1 demonstrate this contrast. *Capital Intensity* has no affect on the propensity to enact liberalizing measures around foreign treatment. There is some indication that promotion may occur more frequently among highly capital-intensive industries when the banking system is more politically captured. This finding is consistent with a financing constraints theory of FDI liberalization because we might imagine that governments that privilege certain industries and firms may not liberalize entry requirements but may offer tax incentives to targeted investors in order to induce them to partner with particularly influential local firms. However, this relationship is not statistically significant at standard levels of confidence.

There is also some evidence that industries characterized by capital intensity are more likely to be subjected to restrictive FDI regulatory changes when the banking sector is less market-driven. Figure 5.2 depicts the marginal effects plot of Model 12. We see that the curve is downward sloping, meaning that the effect of *Capital Intensity* on the propensity to enact restrictive policy changes declines as the banking sector becomes more liberalized, although the effect always remains somewhat positive. The 95 percent confidence intervals are quite wide at lower levels of *Banking Reform*, so our confidence in this relationship should be more subdued. Nonetheless, these results do suggest that industries with higher levels of *Capital Intensity* are both more likely to experience liberalizing FDI regulation in economies characterized by more open banking systems and more likely to increase restrictions on foreign investment when the banking system is structured to channel subsidized credit to key firms and industries.

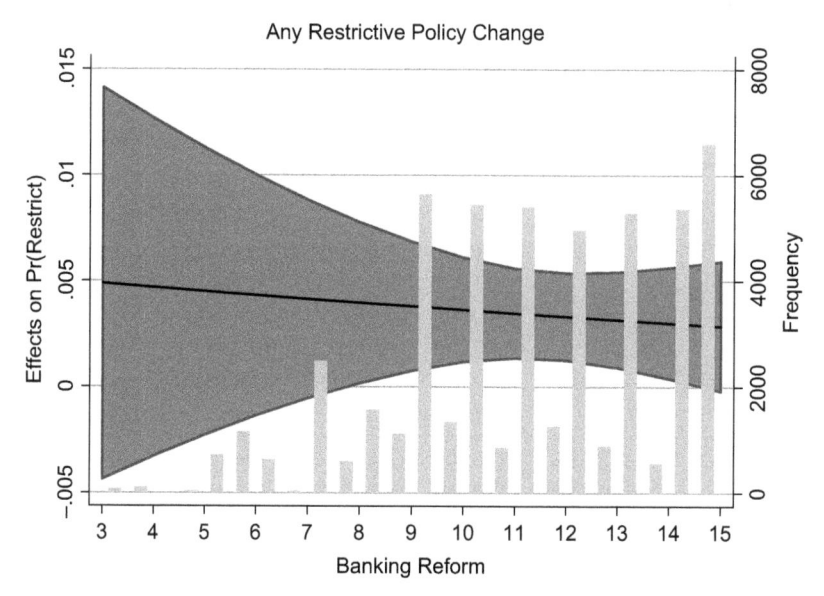

Figure 5.2 Marginal effects of capital intensity on restrictive changes, 95% confidence intervals

FDI Policy Liberalization, Interest Rate Controls, and Capital Intensity

To further probe the relationship between capital intensity, banking reforms, and FDI policy liberalization, I reestimate the models above, this time using only the component of the Abiad et al. measure of *Banking Reform* that measures the degree to which *Interest Rate Regulations* have been liberalized. Recall from the previous chapter that this measure exists along a support of zero to three, with higher values indicating a banking sector with less government intervention in commercial interest rates. Table 5.11 reports results of these estimations, and Figure 5.3 provides marginal effects plots.[15]

---

[15] I do not include histograms on these plots because the high rate of "3" in the sample makes it difficult to see the incidence of "0s" and "1s" in the sample. It is true that by 2000, most countries have liberalized their interest rate policies. However, because the unit of analysis is the industry-country-year, there are over 2000 observations less than or equal to 1 in the sample. Thus, I am confident that the larger standard errors at low levels of *Interest Rate Regulations* are not driven by statistical power concerns.

Table 5.11. *FDI policy changes, interest rates, and capital intensity*

	Model 13 Liberal	Model 14 Lib Entry	Model 15 Lib Treat	Model 16 Lib Promote	Model 17 Restrict
Capital	0.055	0.066	−0.169	0.489	2.205***
Intensity	(0.18)	(0.19)	(0.16)	(0.35)	(0.63)
Interest	−0.444*	−0.425*	−0.806*	−0.551**	0.174
Rate Regs	(0.21)	(0.21)	(0.36)	(0.21)	(0.24)
Interaction	0.144*	0.148*	0.282*	−0.033	−0.441
	(0.07)	(0.07)	(0.12)	(0.14)	(0.22)
Constant	−3.680***	−3.932***	−6.268***	−5.385***	−8.949***
	(0.65)	(0.67)	(1.20)	(0.80)	(1.14)
AIC	5382.298	4270.788	502.517	1441.168	2046.437
BIC	5550.654	4439.144	621.325	1609.524	2204.754
N	52095	52095	35819	52095	48795

Year fixed effects not reported. Standard errors in parentheses.
*$p < 0.05$, **$p < 0.01$, ***$p < 0.001$

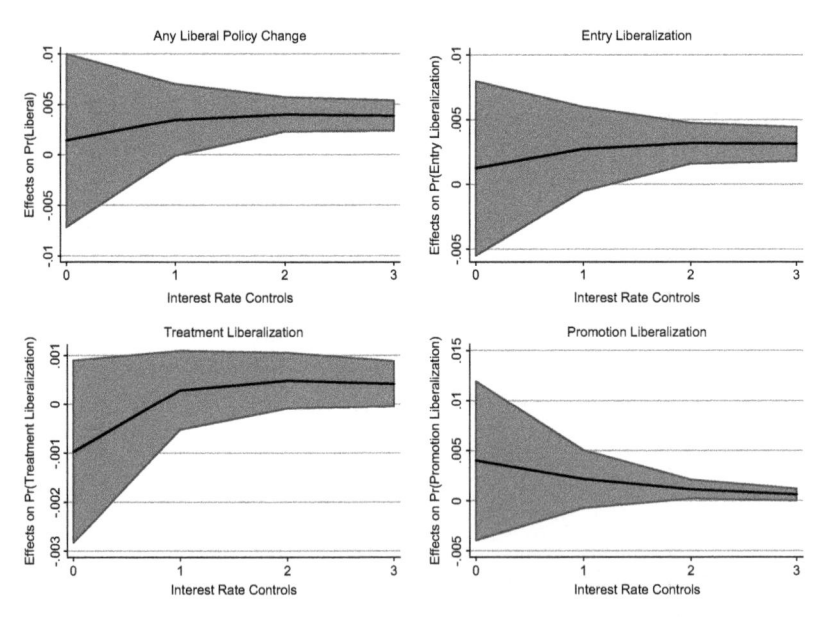

Figure 5.3 Marginal effects of capital intensity at different levels of interest rates reform, 95% confidence intervals

The results of these statistical tests largely reinforce the findings of models that employ the full *Banking Reform* index. Across these estimations, we uncover a similar pattern to that explained above. Liberalizing reforms, and particularly reforms related to entry, increase with the *Capital Intensity* of a given industry, but only when interest rates have been largely liberalized such that either deposit or lending interest rates are fully determined by market rates or when both deposit and lending rates are allowed to float within a prescribed band. On the other hand, when rates are set by the government or subject to prescribed ceilings or floors, *Capital Intensity* provides no predictive value to the propensity to liberalize.

Some context here is useful to better interpret substantive effects. Belarus, Cameroon, China, El Salvador, and Portugal are all classified as having fully or partially repressed interest rates for at least part of the time period under analysis. India transitioned to partially liberalized interest rates in 1998, just before the time period included in these analyses. Further out of sample, several Western European countries underwent a transition to liberalized interest rates in the 1980s and 1990s. For example, France underwent substantial interest rate reforms from 1984 to 1987. Japan underwent a similar process in the 1980s as well. In contrast, *Capital Intensity* does not predict industry-level liberalization of measures related to treatment or promotion at any level of interest rate regulation.

FDI Policy Liberalization, Banking Sector Efficiency, and Capital Intensity

Finally, in Models 18–22, I use *Net Interest Margin* to proxy for the efficiency of the banking sector. Recall that this measure is available across all years in my sample. The results reported in Table 5.12 suggest the relationship between banking sector regulations and FDI policy may have shifted in recent years. As with the analyses above that used *Banking Reform* and *Interest Rate Regulation*, *Net Interest Margin* conditions the effect of *Capital Intensity* on the propensity to enact any liberalizing change and entry liberalization specifically, but it demonstrates no effect on treatment or promotion policy changes. However, the relationship between *Net Interest Margin* and *Capital Intensity* is different from my expectations. As Figure 5.4 illustrates, in these models, it seems that more capital-intensive industries are

Table 5.12. *FDI policy changes, banking efficiency, and capital intensity*

	Model 18 Liberal	Model 19 Lib Entry	Model 20 Lib Treat	Model 21 Lib Promote	Model 22 Restrict
Capital	0.478***	0.530***	0.438*	0.360***	1.030***
Intensity	(0.07)	(0.08)	(0.17)	(0.11)	(0.12)
Net Interest	−0.143*	−0.166*	−0.052	0.027	−0.075
Margin	(0.07)	(0.07)	(0.23)	(0.10)	(0.12)
Interaction	0.167***	0.175***	0.249	0.200**	0.314***
Constant	−5.098***	−5.306***	−8.675***	−7.043***	−8.999***
	(0.25)	(0.27)	(1.01)	(0.52)	(0.99)
AIC	7414.929	5919.875	596.825	1933.742	2597.497
BIC	7593.623	6098.569	723.558	2112.436	2765.661
N	89769	89769	63094	89769	84323

Year fixed effects not reported. Standard errors in parentheses.
$*p < 0.05, **p < 0.01, ***p < 0.001$

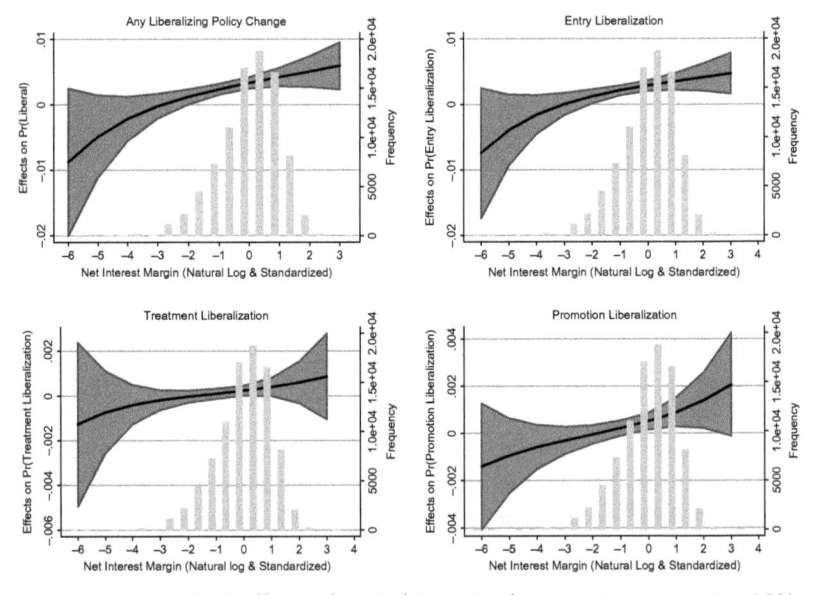

Figure 5.4 Marginal effects of capital intensity by net interest margin, 95% confidence intervals

more likely to undergo reforms when the banking sector is more inefficient. Because more inefficient banking sectors are likely to be more repressed, these findings seem to contradict other analysis.

How should we interpret these findings? First, it is important to note that *Net Interest Margin* was associated with a reduced number of aggregate FDI reforms in Chapter 4. The conflicting results may be driven by the fact that the models presented here drop all reforms that are not specific to an industry. Thus, part of the disparity in results is driven by the fact that countries with more efficient banking sectors also enact more broad-based FDI policy reforms. Second, it does seem that in recent years, economic distress has had an increasing influence on FDI policy. Recall from Chapter 4 that models of country-level policy from 2000 to 2015 found that being under an International Monetary Fund (IMF) program was positively associated with passing liberalizing FDI policy reforms. In robustness presented below, this finding holds in these models as well. Maybe, in recent times, even countries with relatively repressive financial sectors respond to macroeconomic problems by trying to entice foreign investment. Finally, there is evidence that countries with inefficient banking systems are more likely to be active in changing FDI policies, both in a liberalizing as well as a restricting direction. Unlike models that use banking regulatory variables, banking sector inefficiencies seem also to make the passage of restrictive investment policies more likely. Figure 5.5 shows this small positive effect.

Probing Robustness

The models presented above provide collective evidence that capital-intensive industries are more likely to experience liberalization of entry regulations when the local banking system allocates capital through market mechanisms. FDI regulations about postentry treatment and promotion are not correlated, however, with changes in local credit allocation processes. Conversely, industries characterized by high capital intensity are more likely to see the promulgation of increasingly restrictive regulations toward foreign owners when the banking system is structured in ways that facilitate government intervention in credit markets. However, recent developments may make countries with less efficient banking sectors more likely to pursue both liberalizing and restrictive changes to policies related to capital-intensive industries.

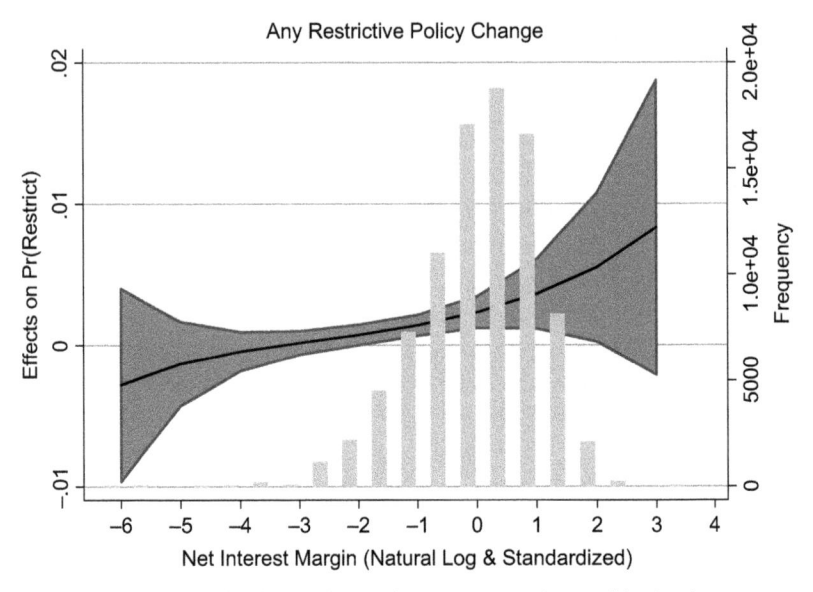

Figure 5.5 Marginal effects of capital intensity conditioned by banking sector efficiency on restrictive changes, 95% confidence intervals

The estimations above, however, are done in spare form. Do their central results hold for the inclusion of a variety of control variables that may also influence patterns of FDI policy change? Below, I reestimate the models presented in Tables 5.10, 5.11, and 5.12 and include measures that account for several alternative explanations for policy change.[16] These controls mirror those introduced in the models estimated in Chapter 4.

Table 5.13 presents the results of estimations that include the full *Banking Reform* index; Table 5.14 presents similarly estimated models that instead use *Interest Rate Regulations* as a measure of the local financing environment. Table 5.15 presents models that proxy the banking environment through *Net Interest Margin*. As with the models reported above, these are estimated with logit link functions and include year fixed effects, with standard errors clustered by country. Generally, these estimations confirm that the patterns described above

---

[16] All control variables are standardized. I do not standardize *Capital Intensity* and *Banking Reforms* because doing so obscures substantive interpretation. Please refer to Chapter 4 for data sources, descriptive statistics, and sample coverage.

Table 5.13. *FDI policy, banking regulations, and capital intensity, controls*

	Model 23 Liberal	Model 24 Lib Entry	Model 25 Lib Treat	Model 26 Lib Promote	Model 27 Restrict
Capital	−0.061	−0.137	−0.189	0.842*	1.060
Intensity	(0.32)	(0.36)	(0.32)	(0.39)	(0.78)
Banking	−0.214**	−0.210**	−0.291**	−0.217***	0.108
Reforms$_{(t-1)}$	(0.07)	(0.07)	(0.10)	(0.07)	(0.09)
Interaction	0.048	0.063	0.044	−0.052	−0.034
	(0.03)	(0.03)	(0.05)	(0.04)	(0.06)
Ln GDP Per	0.246	0.318	−0.464	0.398	−0.173
Capita$_{(t-1)}$	(0.48)	(0.56)	(0.66)	(0.42)	(0.42)
Ln	−0.133	−0.081	−0.499**	0.395	0.097
Inflation$_{(t-1)}$	(0.14)	(0.14)	(0.16)	(0.30)	(0.28)
Ln Trade/	−0.342*	−0.259	−1.577***	−0.259	−0.898***
GDP$_{(t-1)}$	(0.15)	(0.18)	(0.43)	(0.21)	(0.25)
Ln Tertiary	0.259	0.100	2.190***	0.774	1.037*
Enroll$_{(t-1)}$	(0.22)	(0.25)	(0.64)	(0.44)	(0.46)
Democracy$_{(t-1)}$	0.081	0.204	−1.107*	−0.210	−0.477
	(0.48)	(0.52)	(0.49)	(0.47)	(0.51)
Crisis$_{(t-1)}$	0.561	0.602	0.000	0.000	0.174
	(0.37)	(0.37)	(.)	(.)	(1.12)
Under	0.800	0.871	2.239	0.386	1.040*
IMF$_{(t-1)}$	(0.45)	(0.47)	(1.31)	(0.53)	(0.51)
Fixed	−0.284	−0.329	1.230	−0.620	0.532
Exchange	(0.25)	(0.25)	(0.65)	(0.36)	(0.32)
Rate$_{(t-1)}$					
Constant	−3.856***	−4.101***	−7.388***	−2.596**	−10.120***
	(0.83)	(0.85)	(2.13)	(1.01)	(1.64)
AIC	3584.324	2889.053	336.889	887.346	1137.889
BIC	3803.984	3108.713	496.971	1068.403	1347.461
N	34492	34492	22117	27719	32302

Year fixed effects not reported. Standard errors in parentheses.
*$p < 0.05$, **$p < 0.01$, ***$p < 0.001$

Table 5.14. *FDI policy, interest rates, and capital intensity, controls*

	Model 28 Liberal	Model 29 Lib Entry	Model 30 Lib Treat	Model 31 Lib Promote	Model 32 Restrict
Capital	0.062	0.123	−0.032	0.457*	0.341
Intensity	(0.16)	(0.21)	(0.13)	(0.18)	(0.46)
Interest Rate	−0.772***	−0.787***	−0.782**	−0.657***	0.329
Regulation$_{(t-1)}$	(0.20)	(0.23)	(0.26)	(0.19)	(0.27)
Interaction	0.150*	0.154	0.118	−0.056	0.117
	(0.07)	(0.09)	(0.11)	(0.10)	(0.17)
Ln GDP Per	0.235	0.331	−0.606	0.258	−0.109
Capita$_{(t-1)}$	(0.37)	(0.42)	(0.63)	(0.40)	(0.40)
Ln	−0.145	−0.097	−0.504**	0.336	0.103
Inflation$_{(t-1)}$	(0.12)	(0.13)	(0.18)	(0.29)	(0.27)
Ln Trade/	−0.420**	−0.334*	−1.589***	−0.403	−0.863***
GDP$_{(t-1)}$	(0.15)	(0.17)	(0.44)	(0.22)	(0.23)
Ln Tertiary	0.141	−0.026	2.082***	0.611	1.030*
Enroll$_{(t-1)}$	(0.22)	(0.23)	(0.62)	(0.41)	(0.45)
Democracy$_{(t-1)}$	0.445	0.580	−0.665	0.147	−0.599
	(0.53)	(0.62)	(0.53)	(0.43)	(0.51)
Crisis$_{(t-1)}$	0.660	0.693*	0.000	0.000	0.153
	(0.34)	(0.34)	(.)	(.)	(1.13)
Under	1.174**	1.229**	2.567*	0.781	0.868
IMF$_{(t-1)}$	(0.41)	(0.42)	(1.25)	(0.57)	(0.48)
Fixed	−0.461	−0.498	0.878	−0.743*	0.584
Exchange	(0.25)	(0.29)	(0.66)	(0.34)	(0.33)
Rate$_{(t-1)}$					
Constant	−4.645***	−4.804***	−8.857***	−4.598***	−9.627***
	(0.55)	(0.59)	(2.17)	(0.67)	(1.15)
AIC	3554.973	2865.197	335.338	889.079	1137.003
BIC	3774.634	3084.858	495.420	1070.136	1346.575
N	34492	34492	22117	27719	32302

Year fixed effects not reported. Standard errors in parentheses.
*$p < 0.05$, **$p < 0.01$, ***$p < 0.001$

Table 5.15. FDI policy, net interest margin and capital intensity, controls

	Model 33 Liberal	Model 34 Lib Entry	Model 35 Lib Treat	Model 36 Lib Promote	Model 37 Restrict
Capital Intensity	0.500*** (0.08)	0.579*** (0.10)	0.213 (0.15)	0.339** (0.11)	0.725*** (0.14)
Net Interest Margin$_{(t-1)}$	−0.272 (0.18)	−0.261 (0.20)	−0.800** (0.26)	−0.144 (0.20)	−0.206 (0.16)
Interaction	0.174** (0.05)	0.187** (0.07)	0.016 (0.10)	0.241* (0.10)	0.246** (0.09)
Ln GDP Per Capita$_{(t-1)}$	0.132 (0.34)	0.123 (0.39)	−0.369 (0.66)	0.525 (0.32)	0.382 (0.41)
Ln Inflation$_{(t-1)}$	−0.084 (0.16)	−0.061 (0.16)	−0.451* (0.22)	0.509 (0.33)	0.320 (0.30)
Ln Trade/ GDP$_{(t-1)}$	−0.207* (0.09)	−0.210* (0.09)	−0.429** (0.15)	−0.081 (0.11)	−0.192 (0.12)
Ln Tertiary Enroll$_{(t-1)}$	0.280 (0.15)	0.231 (0.15)	1.219*** (0.36)	0.577 (0.45)	0.584 (0.38)
Democracy$_{(t-1)}$	−0.195 (0.51)	−0.101 (0.56)	−1.065 (0.63)	−0.662 (0.38)	−0.120 (0.45)
Crisis$_{(t-1)}$	0.486 (0.35)	0.574 (0.35)	0.000 (.)	0.000 (.)	−0.214 (1.10)
Under IMF$_{(t-1)}$	0.977* (0.45)	0.852 (0.47)	2.783 (1.43)	1.100 (0.59)	1.172* (0.49)
Fixed Exchange Rate$_{(t-1)}$	−0.359 (0.23)	−0.310 (0.24)	0.802 (0.67)	−0.929** (0.36)	0.151 (0.35)
Constant	−5.934*** (0.42)	−6.050*** (0.45)	−10.123*** (1.91)	−5.698*** (0.90)	−8.961*** (0.85)
AIC	4647.998	3767.075	390.798	1128.135	1497.327
BIC	4877.807	3996.885	558.724	1336.723	1716.818
N	50962	50962	32738	43967	48032

Year fixed effects not reported. Standard errors in parentheses.
$^*p < 0.05$, $^{**}p < 0.01$, $^{***}p < 0.001$

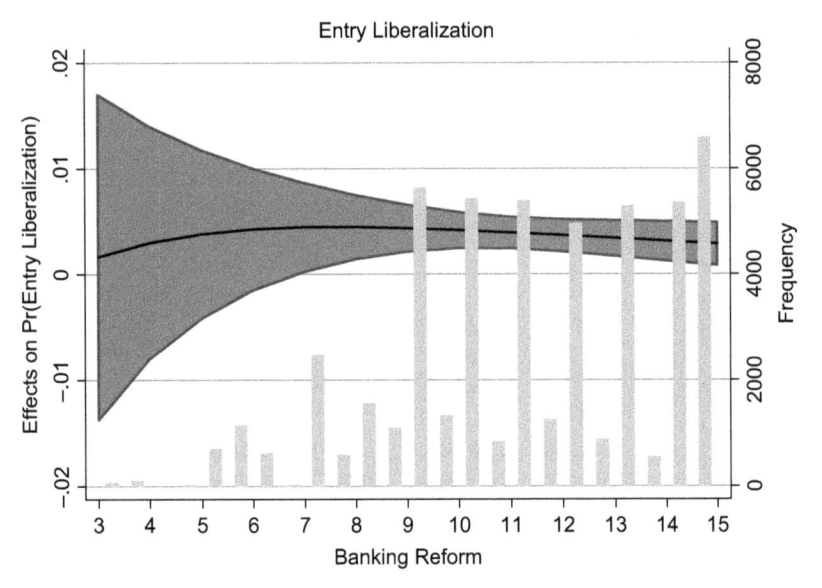

Figure 5.6 Marginal effects of capital intensity, with controls, 95% confidence intervals

are robust to the inclusion of these control variables. For all measures of liberalizing reforms, the interactive effect, when properly plotted, remains statistically significant and in the same direction as reported above. For space considerations, I do not report each of these marginal effects plots, however, Figure 5.6, which plots the marginal effect for Model 24, is instructive. As before, the margin effect of capital intensity on the propensity to enact a liberalizing policy change related to entry only becomes statistically significant as *Banking Reform* crosses a threshold. The inflection point seems to be around a score of seven on the 15-point scale. To give a sense of what types of banking environments score at this critical value, Brazil transitioned to scoring eight on this measure in 2002. Countries as diverse as Bangladesh, China, Costa Rica, Ethiopia, and Uzbekistan all had banking sectors that scored under this threshold for at least part of the time period analyzed.

The estimated effects of a few of the included control variables bear mentioning. First, wealthier countries are no more or less likely to enact liberalizing changes. This stands in contrast to beliefs that poor countries are more likely to be pressured into laxer regulations toward FDI. Across all models, *Trade Openness* is negatively associated with the propensity to liberalize. This may indicate that de facto openness to trade is caused in part by the prevalence of multinational firms in a country rather than the reverse. There is also evidence that high *Inflation* environments are less likely to liberalize at least some kinds of investment regulation, although this is not consistently statistically significant. *Tertiary Enrollment* is not consistently correlated with liberalization efforts. However, countries with more highly educated workforces are actually more likely than others to impose new restrictions on FDI. *Democracy* is not a consistently strong predictor of regulatory change. The *Crisis* indicator is not included in models related to treatment and promotion because of separation issues. However, there is little indication that countries undergoing crisis are more likely to enact changes. This runs counter to others' arguments that emphasize the role of crises in pressuring reform. However, given that openness to FDI does not ameliorate short-term liquidity shocks, this result is unsurprising. *Fixed Exchange Rates* do not seem to have a consistent effect on the propensity to promulgate new investment regulations. Finally, there is evidence that countries that are under an IMF loan are more likely to pursue both liberalizing and restricting investment regulatory changes.

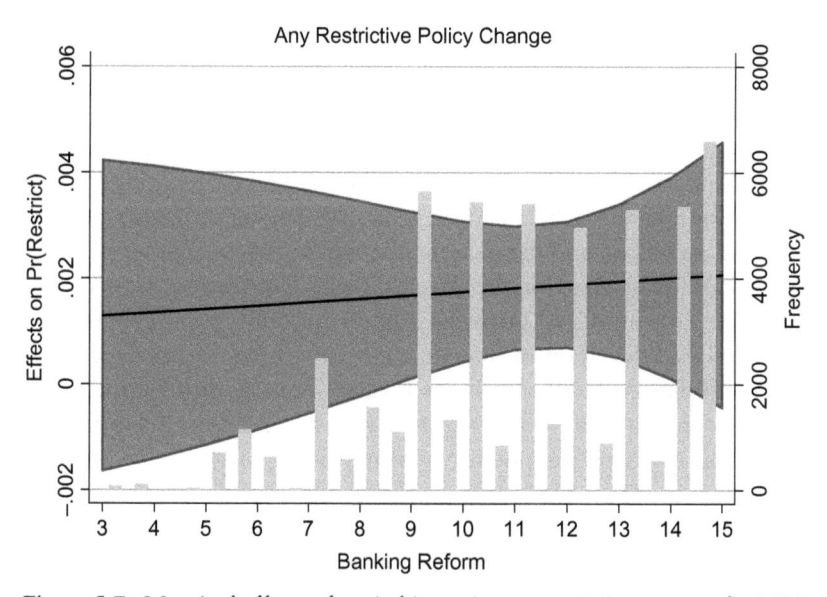

Figure 5.7 Marginal effects of capital intensity on restrictions, controls, 95% confidence intervals

While inclusion of controls only strengthens the main effects in the FDI liberalization models, the models of FDI restrictions that include controls present a different picture. As Figure 5.7 illustrates, the negative relationship between *Capital Intensity* and *Banking Reforms* with respect to the propensity to enact restrictive policy changes is erased by inclusion of control variables. Indeed, these models now show a positive relationship between capital intensity and the propensity to enact restrictive FDI reforms at high levels of banking system openness. These findings are indeed puzzling. However, it is worth noting that the addition of controls constrains my sample significantly – reducing my N by a third. Therefore, I would treat these findings as a caution. It seems that we have far stronger evidence that capital intensity and banking sector reforms influence the propensity to enact liberalizing changes to FDI policy than we have evidence regarding the relationship between these variables and FDI restrictions.

Conclusion

This chapter marshaled a great deal of data at multiple levels of analysis to probe the possible causal mechanisms that link banking sector regulatory reforms to subsequent changes in the foreign investment environment. These exercises are useful because they allow us to examine more closely the pathways through which increasingly credit-constrained economic elites might press for regulatory reform. They also allow us to consider prominent alternative explanations for liberalization, mainly a technocratic consensus among state bureaucrats, external pressures, and democratic institutions. By examining patterns of firm lobbying behavior, the effects of open FDI environments on the financing constraints of firms most likely to lobby governments, and industry-level variation in liberalizing events, I provide evidence that further supports my theory that it is often domestic firms rather than labor, technocrats, or outside actors that push for greater liberalization of the foreign investment policy environment.

First, I use firm-level data on lobbying activity, perceptions of financing constraints, and reported financing patterns to establish microfoundational evidence regarding firm-level preferences over FDI policy. I show that the types of firms that are most likely to lobby governments are large firms, firms with some degree of foreign equity participation, those that export, those that sell primarily to either global markets or the government, and those that were privatized. Second, for the most part, these firms are more likely than their peers to feel less finance-constrained. Together, this suggests that the firms most likely to influence policy have an interest in pressing for FDI liberalization when local conditions exacerbate financing constraints. These findings hold across a variety of, but not all, measures of FDI policy, which increases my confidence in the strength of these relationships.

Second, I use industry-level data on investment policy changes and capital intensity of production to explore whether banking regulation conditions the relationship between capital intensity and the propensity to enact liberalizing changes to a variety of regulations over foreign investment. I demonstrate that industries with higher capital intensity ratios are more likely to experience liberalizing changes to investment regulation, but only once they reach a certain level of banking sector reform. Analysis that limits banking sector reforms solely to changes in interest rate controls illustrates this relationship even more starkly. I find evidence that this relationship holds only for the liberalization of entry restrictions and not for regulations around postestablishment treatment and promotion. This differential effect is consistent with liberalization driven by domestic firms' financing constraints because establishment conditions are most central to bringing in foreign firms that can partner or contract with local enterprises. However, models that use a standard proxy for banking sector efficiency provide some evidence that, in recent years, countries with inefficient banking sectors may be more willing to pursue a range of FDI policy changes to attempt to attract scarce investment.

While none of these data alone can directly isolate whether firms lobby in support of increased openness to foreign investment, collectively they provide substantial evidence in support of this proposition. Firm-level data demonstrate it is in the interest of groups of typically politically powerful firms to liberalize when facing credit constraints. Industry-level variations in changes to investment policies show that the pattern of industry-level liberalization fits with an explanation that emphasizes the financing needs of domestic firms. Analysis in Chapter 4 of the role of domestic political institutions in conditioning policy outcomes also demonstrates increasing liquidity constraints brought on by disruptions to economic elites' privileged access to subsidized finance are most likely to lead to investment liberalization in polities characterized by interest aggregation mechanisms that favor the preferences of business.

In sum, the evidence presented here provides additional support across multiple levels of analysis that the observable implications of a financing-constraints-driven explanation of FDI policy liberalization are consistent with the empirical record.

6 | Comparing Malaysia and Indonesia, 1965–1997

"Foreign Investment should be a supplement to local investment. The investment policy of Indonesia is to decrease the number of foreign direct investments [made annually] in Indonesia." (Mohammad Zuhdi, chair of the East Java Investment Coordinating Board, July 13, 1981)

"[We impose conditions] when you are competing with local producers for local products. We want to make sure that while welcoming foreign investors, we set a target on where exactly they can come in." (Datuk Seri Rafidah Aziz, Minister of International Trade and Industry (Malaysia) March 11, 1997)

The quantitative analysis I provided in Chapters 4 and 5 sequentially tests observable implications of my theory at macro and micro levels, and probes the causal mechanisms that link innovations in banking regulations to subsequent foreign direct investment (FDI) policy changes. However, such tests are limited both by what is measurable and by the difficulty of modeling complex causal processes through statistical inference. In this and the following chapter, I trace the process through which banking and FDI regulation developed in Indonesia and Malaysia from 1965 to 2013. I show how divergent policy responses to banking sector fragility influenced the evolution of investment policy, and tie these regulatory changes to the stated preferences of business elites. I also illustrate how popular pressures often acted to impede, rather than hasten, FDI liberalization.

This chapter focuses on changes to banking and investment policy from 1965 to 1997 while the following chapter focuses on policy reform in the aftermath of the 1997 Asian financial crisis. Because documentation of policymaking processes and business groups' lobbying activities is spotty before 1997, this chapter has less ability to connect policy changes to business elite preferences than the subsequent chapter. Nevertheless, this chapter provides a useful history of banking and investment policy and politics in both countries in the years prior to the 1997 financial crisis. This context serves as a useful corrective to previous beliefs that Indonesia and Malaysia were largely open to FDI. It also exploits intracase temporal variation to show how domestic credit markets influenced the timing and extent of FDI reforms.

Over the time period I cover, Malaysia has more consistently pursued banking sector deepening that has supported gradual liberalization of FDI policies with limited backsliding. In contrast, Indonesia has more often pursued policies designed to maintain substantial control over domestic credit allocation decisions and therefore has less elite support for loosening restrictions on FDI. However, while the level of FDI openness in Indonesia has consistently shown protectionist bias, a period of rapid banking sector deregulation in the 1980s did lead to a period of limited FDI liberalization. These policy developments, along with documentation of elite policy preferences toward FDI policy at the time, provide further evidence that banking sector reforms change firms' interpretation of their policy interests. Subsequent state consolidation of the banking sector in Indonesia has led to reform stagnation and reversal, illustrating that FDI policy can be subject to a partial reform equilibrium as well as increased protectionism even in a global environment of overwhelming economic integration.

The remainder of this chapter is organized as follows. First, I discuss the justification for my selection of cases. I then briefly outline the trajectory for banking and investment policy in both countries from 1965 to 2013. The bulk of the chapter traces the development of these policies in two time periods: 1965–1985 and 1985–1997. The chapter ends with a summary of the development of banking and investment policies in both countries through 1997.

To be clear, this chapter and the chapter that follows are not meant to be definitive tests of my theory, which is fundamentally based on a probabilistic conception of causality. Instead, these chapters provide an opportunity to look more closely at the evolution of banking and investment policies and to probe my argument that the causal link between banking sector reforms and FDI liberalization manifests through shifting elite policy preferences and the diminished political power of domestic banking interests.

Case Selection

Indonesia and Malaysia are ideal for comparison of my theory for several reasons. First, these countries have common political, macroeconomic, and policy characteristics that support a "most similar" case design. They are neighboring island nation-states, and both are spread over noncontiguous territory. Both have a postcolonial history of hegemonic party autocracy with long-tenured executives, though Indonesia under Soeharto also had strong elements of a military dictatorship. Both have crafted development policies within the context of an important political cleavage between poorer indigenous groups and an ethnicly Chinese capitalist class.[1] Both also have substantial natural resource wealth in the form of crude oil and timber; such wealth has often been associated with more restrictive policies toward foreign investment.[2] These shared characteristics provide important controls for potentially relevant factors such as ethnically patterned ownership of key sectors of the economy as well as the role of natural resources in cushioning external financing needs during commodity booms and balance of payment–induced foreign investment needs during periods of low global petroleum prices. Because Indonesia and Malaysia share these characteristics, the cause of any variations in FDI policy between them are unlikely to be driven by ethnic politics or natural resource factors.[3]

Indonesia and Malaysia's economic, political, and geographic proximity allow me to control for a variety of shared external economic pressures. While Malaysia embarked on an export-oriented growth strategy earlier than did Indonesia,[4] by the mid-1980s, both countries had undergone partial FDI liberalization to selectively promote foreign investment in export-oriented activities. Figure 6.1 reports FDI inflows

[1] While this cleavage is dominant in Malaysian politics, the Indonesian case also has important political clashes around nationalist-statist versus Islamic divisions, and a deeper history of a communist/anticommunist political dimension.

[2] See, for example, Kobrin (1987) for an early discussion of how extractive industries face more intractable obsolescing bargaining dynamics vis-à-vis governments.

[3] However, it is important to note that, due to its smaller population and less densely populated islands, Malaysia has always been wealthier than Indonesia.

[4] Malaysia's experience with British colonization helps explain this earlier acceptance of more economically open policies.

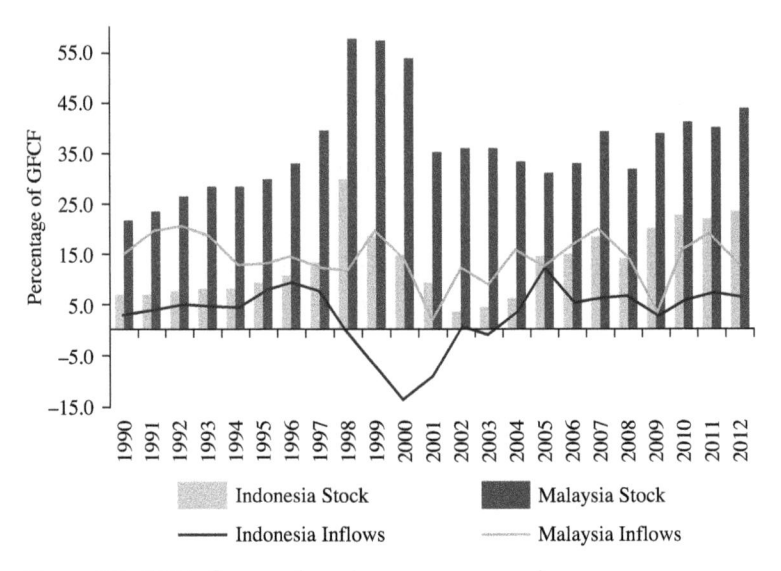

Figure 6.1 FDI inflows and stocks as percentage of gross fixed capital formation (GFCF), 1990–2012

and stocks from 1990 onward for both countries. Indonesia's negative flows in 1998–2002 indicate falling capital stock.

It is important to recognize that many global factors have influenced the rise of development strategies that rely on integrated multinational production chains. Global macroeconomic conditions in the mid- to late 1980s were particularly conducive to foreign-financed, export-oriented strategies in Southeast Asia. Japanese, Korean, and Singaporean firms faced a complex of factors that encouraged off-shoring. Appreciating home currencies, tariff barriers in the Organisation for Economic Co-operation and Development (OECD), and higher local wages encouraged these firms to relocate production. The 1985 Plaza Accord in particular created a Japanese outward investment boon as the yen appreciated. Concurrently, other newly industrialized economies graduated out of preferential market access to the OECD, which also incentivized assembly in countries that still qualified for tariff reductions.[5] Within the context of export-platform production strategies, Malaysia and Indonesia were both attractive

---

[5] These preferential systems included the Generalized System of Preferences (GSP) and the Multi Fibre Arrangement (MFA).

hosts because of their low wages and geographic proximity to firms' preexisting supply chains.[6]

It would be a mistake to conclude, however, that policies toward FDI in Malaysia and Indonesia dramatically liberalized over this time period. These countries selectively allowed specific multinationals entry into domestic export manufacturing through joint ventures and with substantial performance requirements. At the same time, Malaysian and Indonesian banking sectors were dominated by state-owned banks, excluded foreign banking firms, and were used by their respective governments to allocate credit preferentially to politically and developmentally important sectors and firms. These restrictions contributed to increased bank leverage and asset bubbles as loosening of short-term capital account restrictions allowed protected local banks to borrow cheaply internationally and lend domestically at substantial profits.

In Chapter 7 we will see that, in both countries, political leaders made a conscious choice in the wake of financial crisis between protecting either the banking sector or the real sector from foreign ownership. Essentially, policymakers in a constrained financing environment faced a choice: would they encourage short-term inflows to allow banks to continue to finance domestic investment requirements, or would they protect local banks while loosening restrictions on foreign firms' direct investments in the real sector? This trade-off is documented in first-hand accounts of policymaking as well as reporting on interest group lobbying during and after the crisis. When governments chose to protect the banking sector, state technocrats as well as industry leaders pushed for increased liberalization of FDI in the real sector in order to spur domestic capital formation. When governments instead allowed foreign banks to inject capital into ailing banks, they had the financing capacity to retain state-owned banks. Credit allocation continued to be driven by political rather than market relationships and this muted societal pressures for lifting restrictions on FDI into other sectors.

Overview of Policy Periods

Table 6.1 provides an overview of banking sector and FDI policy developments in Indonesia and Malaysia in three time periods: 1965–1985, 1985–1997, 1997–2013. In a postcolonial context, Indonesia's New

---

[6] Association of Southeast Asian Nations (1999).

Table 6.1. *Indonesia and Malaysia banking and FDI policy environments, 1985–2013*

	1965–1985	1985–1997	1997–2013
Indonesia	Military – ethnic Chinese alignment Growth of state-owned banks	Banking deregulation Growth of banking conglomerates	State bank consolidation FDI liberalization imposed by the International Monetary Fund (IMF)
	Highly restrictive FDI policy	Partial FDI liberalization	Subsequent FDI policy backtracking
Malaysia	Bumiputera-driven NEP	Prudential regulation	Bank privatization and restructuring
	Growth of state-owned banks Partial FDI liberalization	Privatization-led stock market boom Little FDI policy change	Prudential regulation Successive FDI liberalization

Order regime fostered close ties between political and military bureaucrats and ethnic Chinese local capitalists. An open capital account combined with a state-dominated banking system allowed the regime to largely self-finance development without relying on FDI. In contrast, a set of political conditions that encouraged Malaysia's dominant political party to pursue an expansive economic affirmative action problem required the government to pursue FDI as a means of limiting the economic power of ethnic Chinese Malaysians.

Negative economic shocks in the 1980s led Malaysia to make comparatively minor changes to banking regulation, while it also developed a relatively large domestic stock market to facilitate privatization of state-owned industry. As a result, Malaysia's FDI policies during the 1980s are best described as maintaining a strategy of partial openness in which the government courted high-value manufacturing FDI while greatly restricting all other forms of direct investment by foreign entities. Indonesia's response to its much more serious economic shocks in the 1980s was to pursue banking sector deregulation, which led to a massive increase in domestically owned private banks and a decrease in the state's control over credit allocation. As a result, the 1980s and early 1990s were characterized by elite-driven selective FDI liberalization, resulting in a more open but fundamentally dualist investment policy position by 1997. In other words, by 1997, Indonesia and Malaysia had similar levels of FDI restrictions, but Indonesia's path to limited FDI openness took longer than did Malaysia's and was largely driven by shifting elite preferences over FDI in the wake of a major deregulation of the Indonesian banking sector. Figure 6.2 illustrates this convergence in FDI policies through the late 1980s and early 1990s.

Divergent crisis response strategies to the 1997 Asian financial crisis led to substantial liberalization of credit allocation in Malaysia, while Indonesia's foreign-bank-led, financial-sector restructuring did little to force fundamental changes in the way banks made debt financing decisions and insulated the state from needing to privatize its extensive state-owned banking system. In fact, state-owned banks in Indonesia were able to consolidate in the aftermath of the crisis and subsequently increase their dominance in domestic credit markets. As a result, Indonesian business interests successfully blocked attempts to implement further large-scale liberalization of FDI beyond the initial policy changes imposed by the International Monetary Fund (IMF) in

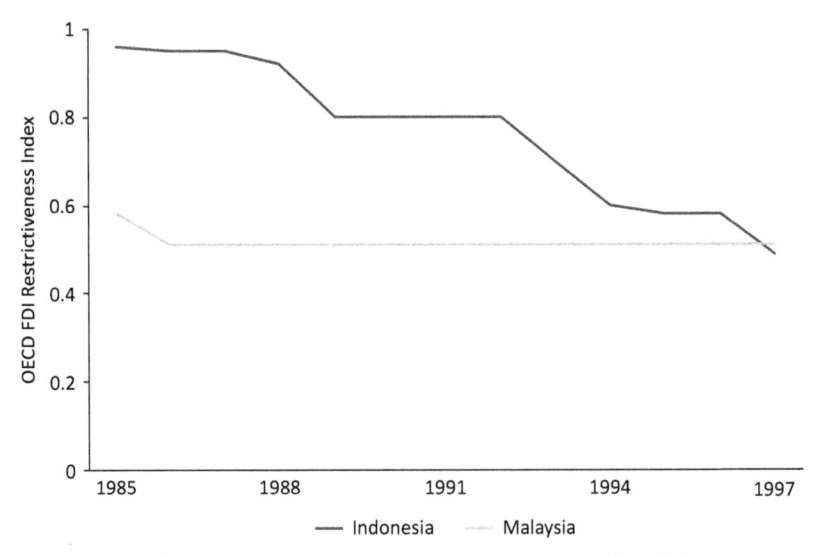

Figure 6.2 Indonesia and Malaysia FDI restrictiveness 1985–1997
Source: OECD FDI Restrictiveness Index; OECD 2013, 56

1998 and 1999. In contrast, the Malaysian business community largely supported, and in many cases drove, more fundamental liberalization of FDI policy.

In the remainder of this chapter, I trace the coevolution of banking and FDI policy from the 1960s to 1997. Studying this time period allows me to provide the context of the initial political and economic conditions that led Malaysia to embrace a limited role for FDI earlier than did Indonesia. It also allows me to use variations across time in banking sector developments in each country to assess the effects of banking policy on the timing of FDI policy change. The developments over this time period provide important context for the policy responses to the 1997 crisis, which are analyzed in Chapter 7, and highlight important within-country variation over the direction and pace of banking sector and FDI policy reforms.

Throughout this analysis, I focus primarily on the ways in which banking sector policy choices affected subsequent reforms of FDI policy. In constructing my case narratives, I use a variety of primary and secondary sources, including central bank reports, first-person accounts of crisis response, newspaper coverage of the politics of reform, reports from key lobbying groups and international economic institutions, as well as other studies of both banking sector and FDI policy reform. First, I use secondary sources on the politics of macroeconomic policy decisions in both countries to construct a time line of relevant banking and investment policy developments over the time period. I begin analysis in 1965, when a failed coup attempt against the postcolonial and largely economic closed government of Sukarno marked the rise of Soeharto and his more globally engaged New Order regime. It also roughly corresponds with the emergence of an independent Malaysian state, which was formed through a series of declarations from 1957 to 1965.[7] I overlay these sources with primary data from the World Bank, the IMF, and United Nations Conference on Trade and Development (UNCTAD) to illustrate the macroeconomic effects of policy choices. To explore lobbying efforts and the process of policy changes, I rely on English language news sources. I find these by running a series of Lexis Nexus keyword searches, both for reports on politics of investment generally and for reporting related to specific laws. To narrow the search, I concentrate on periods leading up to major policy changes and also search on well-known business interest groups such as the Federation of Malaysian Manufacturers. For instance, a search of "Federation of Malaysian Manufactures" and "Foreign Investment" yields 23 articles before 1997 and 70 articles after. In my analysis, I use quotes and news sources that are representative of the coverage I find. While the link between banking and FDI policy has rarely been directly assessed in previous research on these subjects, close analysis of the process of these reform policies reveals just how interrelated these two issue domains are to interest groups and policymakers.

Postcolonial Adjustment and the Oil Boom

In this section, I trace the development of Malaysia and Indonesia's banking and FDI policies from 1965 to 1985, in an era marked by high global liquidity, economic growth, and commodity prices. During this time, the fundamental aspects of both countries' postcolonial political economy crystalized.

---

[7] The Federation of Malay declared independence from the United Kingdom in 1957. A 1963 agreement united Malay, North Borneo, Sarawak, and Singapore. Singapore left the federation in 1965.

After Sukarno, Indonesia's New Order regime guided the country through an investment policy designed to foster party loyalty while also placating ethnic Chinese businesspeople who were an important lending source for the state. As a result, Indonesia adopted an open short-term capital account, a rather restrictive stance on FDI, and a banking system dominated by the state and its politicized credit allocation decisions. High oil prices at the end of the 1970s only increased corruption in state lending decisions and set the stage for later needs to reorganize the banking sector.

Malaysia's hegemonic party regime established a postcolonial policy of racial economic affirmative action, which drove its industrial policy of guiding domestic control over the commanding heights of the economy. Using a combination of state- and domestically owned banks and industrial firms, the government pursued a goal of dividing equity ownership into three roughly equal parts between ethnic Malaysians, ethnic Chinese and Indian Malaysians, and foreign investors. As with Indonesia, the state became heavily involved in financial intermediation processes and promulgated laws designed to attract FDI under very strict guidelines to priority sectors and with the expectation of foreign divestment once sufficient technology transfer was complete.

In both countries, this time period was marked by the political and economic emergence of a narrow set of economic elites who benefitted greatly from protection from foreign firms, especially because their financing needs were easily met by subsidized credit programs. The growth of these protected groups meant anti-FDI elite became firmly entrenched in the political landscape of both countries during this time.

Indonesia: The Expansion of Financial Patronage

In the immediate aftermath of decolonization, Indonesia's banking sector under Sukarno's Guided Democracy government was highly dysfunctional and dependent on the state.[8] By 1965, a series of postcolonial bank nationalizations, mergers, and state directives had created Bank Negara Indonesia (BNI), a massive banking institution that combined all state banks with the central bank (Bank Indonesia [BI]) through which the regime controlled all aspects of domestic credit allocation. Sukarno's government used its control over the banking

---

[8]   Cook (2008).

sector to finance a wide range of expensive development projects, and this ultimately led to high levels of inflation. To combat the ill effects of inflation, BI propped up an overvalued rupiah through a complex web of multiple exchange rates. These policies led to a string of recurring balance of payment crises that fractured an already fragile coalition between the military and the Communist party, resulting in a military coup mounted by Soeharto that collapsed the Sukarno regime.[9] When Soeharto's New Order came to power, it soon identified banking sector reform as essential to attracting and retaining short-term mobile investment.[10] To support needed reforms, Soeharto quickly filled bureaucratic posts with neoliberal policy advisers who pushed for a tight monetary policy and capital account openness to stabilize the economy.[11] The resulting policies were some of the most liberal for the time. Soeharto committed in 1966 to abandon the multiple exchange rate system, devalued the rupiah, and liberalized foreign exchange markets. In 1968, the regime allowed bank deposits and loans denominated in dollars.[12] In 1971, the regime made the currency fully convertible.[13]

With the banking sector stabilized, the New Order regime enacted a series of banking sector reform laws in 1967 and 1968 that were designed to break up BNI into specialized state banks, restore a degree of independence to BI, and create a general banking law that would allow for private banks.[14] These reforms also reopened Indonesia's banking sector to foreign banks in a limited way. By 1969, 11 foreign banks had established operations in Jakarta. However, as the immediacy of the 1965 balance of payment crisis receded, political support for reform softened. Acting in response to domestic state and private banks concerns that foreign banks would undermine state control of credit allocation and drive domestic private banks out of business, the government instituted a set of policies that gave state banks access to increasingly generous credit terms and prevented any additional foreign bank from entry.[15]

---

[9] Haggard and Maxfield (1996); Palmer (1978).
[10] Rosser (2002).
[11] Chwieroth (2010).
[12] Arndt and Suwidjana (1982).
[13] Haggard and Maxfield (1996).
[14] Rosser (2002).
[15] Arndt (1971).

Soeharto's military regime found natural allies in the ethnic Chinese capital class, who were eager to support the New Order regime because they were otherwise politically vulnerable. The ethnic Chinese had mobile assets, so capital account openness provided a signal to them that their investments were safe and they would be able to move funds overseas if economic conditions deteriorated.[16] Capital account openness provided both the regime and the ethnic Chinese financiers access to abundant, cheap international capital. The financiers used their privileged position to extract rents from the mismatch in interest rates on international capital and domestic interest rates. Meanwhile, state banks also benefited from access to cheap credit and funded politically driven development projects.[17] The regime was able to construct an expansive patronage network by fostering tight links between public and domestic finance.[18] Public investment banks channeled easy credit to loyal regime supporters, and private banks used their inexpensive sources of capital to partner with military leaders and private entrepreneurs in industrial expansion.[19]

This alliance was possible because the regime retained highly restrictive measures on foreign entry into the financial sector.[20] In addition to limits on ownership and branching of foreign bank subsidiaries, the regime placed highly restrictive limits on foreign ownership of stock exchange assets while providing preferential credit conditions to domestic banks. While the reforms of the late 1960s and early 1970s eased some restrictions on foreign banks, foreign banks were not allowed to branch outside of the capital, Jakarta. This policy allowed state deposit banks to maintain monopoly control on deposit banking throughout most of the country, especially in rural areas where credit allocation decisions drove patron-client networks.[21]

Capital account openness paired with policies designed to retain the regime's hold on investment allocation decisions provided politically connected firms with access to development financing without needing to find foreign equity partners. The state banks' ability to channel investment into development projects meant the state could

---

[16] Haggard and Maxfield (1996).
[17] Pepinsky (2009); Sharma (2001); Soesastro (1989).
[18] MacIntyre (1993).
[19] MacIntyre (1993); Pepinsky (2009); Winters (1996).
[20] Pepinsky (2009, 2013a); Soesastro (1989).
[21] Haggard and Maxfield (1996); Winters (1996); MacIntyre (1993).

industrialize indigenously. Popular support for indigenous, or *pribumi*, industrial ownership was particularly salient given interethnic dynamics of the majority *pribumi* population, which was relatively rural and poor in comparison with the ethnic Chinese business class. The state managed these intergroup tensions through a vast preferential credit system that provided subsidized credit to state-owned enterprises and indigenous entrepreneurs while granting political bureaucrats wide authority in granting loans for political purposes and often in exchange for bribes.[22] As the credit allocation process became increasingly relationship-based, the ethnic Chinese capitalists with ties to political officials received preferential loans from state banks either directly[23] or through indigenous intermediaries, who profited handsomely from such arrangements.[24] Bad debts, which were estimated to exceed 30 percent of loans outstanding in the late 1970s, were easily written off given Indonesia's petrodollar glut.

Within the context of state-controlled credit allocation, the government enacted the 1967 Law on Foreign Investment, which complemented policies of capital account openness by establishing foreign firms' ability to remit profits and dividends and to repatriate capital.[25] Some observers viewed this law as an indication that Indonesia was relatively open to FDI at this early date. However, while the law opened several sectors to foreign investment conditionally, it concurrently maintained a large list of restricted sectors as well as policies requiring divestiture over time and imposed restrictive licensing requirements.[26] Several sectors including natural resource extraction, manufacturing, and finance were also subject to sector-specific laws and screening at the ministerial level.[27] Most FDI entering Indonesia through the 1970s was in the primary sector, concentrated in oil and natural gas extraction.

Growing foreign exchange revenue throughout the 1970s from high oil prices around the world led to subsequent increased restrictions

[22] Rosser (2002), 56.
[23] MacIntyre (1993), 151.
[24] *Far Eastern Economic Review*, March 27, 1981.
[25] Haggard and Maxfield (1996).
[26] Rajenthran (2002); Tambunan (2011).
[27] Rajenthran (2002).

on FDI.[28] The Indonesian Investment Coordinating Board (Badan Koordinasi Peranman Modal [BKPM]) was established in 1973 to administer the foreign investment law, including investment screening, licensing and permits, and granting of incentives. To gain BKPM approval, prospective investors needed to demonstrate that they would provide capital, technology, or management expertise that domestic firms could not.[29] Shortly after, the government enacted new rules that mandated joint ventures and required foreign firms operating in Indonesia prior to 1974 to divest to a minority stake by 1983.[30] Government officials emphasized their interest in obtaining the benefits that multinational enterprises (MNEs) could provide without needing to relinquish domestic equity. The chair of a regional branch of BKPM said, "The type of economic cooperation between this country and others need not be only joint ventures and other forms of direct investment. Technical assistance, technology transfers, licensing, and franchising are all things which do not involve an equity position."[31]

Malaysia: Financial Repression and Ethnic Quotas

Central to Malaysia's policies for equity control of financial and industrial assets was the National Economic Plan (NEP), which was inspired by widespread riots in 1969 and announced in 1971. The NEP sought to counterbalance the relative poverty of indigenous groups (*bumiputera*) by mandating that foreign investors and ethnic Chinese and Indian capitalists transfer assets to *bumiputera* interests so that, by 1991, *bumiputera* ownership over Malaysian capital assets would increase from 2.4 to 30 percent, foreign investment would decline from 60 to 30 percent, and ethnic Chinese and Indian interests could control the remainder. This affirmative action program thus sought to facilitate massive redistribution of assets to a large, politically

---

[28] Organisation for Economic Co-operation and Development (2010); Rajenthran (2002); Tambunan (2011).
[29] John S. McClenahen, "Indonesia Extends a Guarded Welcome," *Industry Week* July 13, 1981.
[30] Ibid.
[31] Ibid.

important, and economically disadvantaged group. At the same time, the program was careful to provide assurances of nonexpropriation to non-*bumiputera* Malaysians, who have traditionally been powerful local industrial and financial capitalists and important supporters of Malaysia's long-standing ruling party.

The NEP had implications for equity restrictions both in the financial and real sectors. Through the formation of state-run banks and tight control over banking licenses, the share of *bumiputera* ownership of bank equity rose from essentially zero in 1965 to 77 percent of local banks by 1982.[32] The Malaysian government formed Bank *Bumiputra* in 1966 to provide state-supported financial services for the *bumiputera* community. In quick succession, the financial sector saw state maneuvers designed to transform the equity structure of Malaysian banking. In 1966, citing prudential regulatory problems, the Malaysian central bank (Bank Negara Malaysia [BNM]) took control over Malayan Bank, the largest and fastest growing local bank that also happened to be owned by ethnic Chinese investors.

At the same time, the government of Malaysia pursued bank licensing and equity ceiling strategies to encourage the growth of *bumiputera* banks and limit foreign competition.[33] The Bank of Nova Scotia received a license for a new bank branch in 1972, after which the government informally froze foreign bank licenses. Incumbent foreign banks were also prevented from expanding, as they were not granted new branch licenses. The Banking Act of 1973 gave the Malaysian Ministry of Finance the authority to withdraw licenses of banks controlled by foreign countries. This led to the localization of foreign banks that were nationalized in their home countries, including Perwira Habib Bank (Pakistan), Banque de L'Indochine et de Suez (France), and three Indian banks that merged and localized into the United Asian Bank.[34] In addition, the Foreign Investment Committee (FIC), tasked with screening all potential FDI, categorized banking

---

[32] Hara (1991). Prior to independence in 1957, foreign banks had an even larger stake in the financial system, holding over 90 percent of bank assets in the country. See Detragiache and Gupta (2004).

[33] This section draws especially from Cook (2008), who meticulously catalogs changes to the Malaysian banking system from 1965 to postcrisis.

[34] Cook (2008), 72.

as a strategic sector and penalized banks that violated a 30 percent ceiling on foreign equity. In the spirit of the NEP, BNM encouraged incumbent foreign and locally owned banks to divest ownership to *bumiputera* interests in line with the 30 percent equity target. While no legislation mandated this restructuring, banks believed failure to do so would deteriorate their relationship with BNM.[35]

As a result of these interventions, the equity structure of the Malaysian banking sector changed dramatically. In 1970, foreign banks accounted for 60 percent of outstanding deposits and loans. By the mid-1980s, foreign banks' market share dropped to 25 percent. Over the same time, the number of foreign banks in Malaysia fell from 22 to 16. Throughout the first 15 years of the NEP, the banking sector experienced an extended period of consolidation that favored *bumiputeras*. In 1965, all locally owned large banks in Malaysia were controlled by ethnic Chinese investors. In 1990, only one of Malaysia's largest 10 banks was predominately owned by ethnic Chinese investors.[36]

It is important to note the strict limitations on concentrated bank ownership that differentiates the Malaysian financial sector from others. The 1973 Banking Act, under Article 23B, capped limits on individuals to a maximum of 10 percent equity stake in a particular bank and corporate entities to a ceiling of 20 percent ownership. This means Malaysian banks have a diluted ownership structure that encourages consortia, and can facilitate the NEP's goal of shared equity ownership between *bumiputeras*, nonindigenous Malaysians, and foreign investors. However, the minister of finance retained authority to waive Article 23B restrictions and displayed a pattern of doing so when the result was equity consolidation of *bumiputera* interests at the expense of ethnic Chinese and Indian investors.[37]

The NEP also guided policies toward foreign ownership in the real economy. The government formed the FIC in 1974, which was tasked with screening all incoming FDI to ensure the central objective of

---

[35] Cook (2008).
[36] Searle (1999).
[37] Cook (2008).

the NEP that *bumiputeras*, nonindigenousi Malaysians, and foreigners hold 30, 40, and 30 percent of equity assets in Malaysia, respectively.[38] The FIC was comprised of senior-level bureaucrats in the Economic Planning Unit and was chaired by the prime minister. It reviewed all proposed mergers and acquisitions by foreign interests. The FIC applied a standard set of guidelines to all proposed foreign investments that required approved projects to advance the equity goals of the NEP and to transfer technology and knowledge to *bumiputera* interests. The FIC requirements reflected not just the NEP's affirmative action policies but also the government's commitment to an import-substituting industrialization strategy in the postcolonial era.

Indigenization of both the real and financial sectors involved heavy government involvement in economic guidance. In particular, the government used directed credit requirements and foreign firm financing restrictions to channel investment into preferred sectors and help develop local banks. In 1975, the government implemented a number of these programs, including a requirement that 50 percent of all bank lending had to benefit *bumiputera* businesses, a requirement that was reduced to 20 percent in subsequent years.[39] The same year, the government also passed rules that set minimum lending requirements to priority sectors including agriculture, manufacturing, and small and medium-size enterprises (SMEs). These policies made it easier for the government to retain limits on foreign investment because they reduced the cost of debt financing to large and politically connected indigenous firms. Largely due to these programs, lending to

---

[38] Some argue Malaysia has held a liberal stance toward FDI since colonial times. See Narayanan (1996). This claim is largely predicated on the governments' willingness to promote some types of FDI, especially in the wake of the NEP. Indeed FDI became a more important source of fixed capital formation with the passage of the NEP because ethnic Chinese domestic entrepreneurs were largely disadvantaged by the ethnically based redistribution scheme. However, FDI was always heavily regulated in Malaysia, as strict equity ceilings and centralized screening indicate. The Malaysian experience with FDI is a reminder that domestic capitalists can often benefit from foreign equity participation, especially if FDI enters through minority partnerships. Evans's (1979) study of capital-government relations in Brazil makes a similar point by emphasizing the role of the state (and the financing capacity of the state) in forging alliances between local and foreign capital.

[39] Ang (2009), 50.

the *bumiputera* community rose from 4 percent of total loans in 1968 to 28 percent in 1985.[40]

The success of the NEP in developing a large and prosperous "*Bumiputera* Commercial and Industrial Community" was in large part dependent on the development of state- and *bumiputera*-owned banks that would be willing to extend substantial capital to indigenous industrial and commercial interests. To facilitate the maturation of an indigenous banking sector, the government required all foreign firms operating in Malaysia to obtain at least 50 percent of local finance needs from Malaysian banks. This requirement may have crowded out credit needs of local firms, but it also allowed locally owned banks to compete with foreign-controlled financial firms for the most lucrative clients while also helping indigenous firms grow technical and human resources capacity to service the most sophisticated customers.[41]

Crisis, Deregulation, and Credit Booms: 1985–1997

Through the 1970s, riding high on a global commodity price boom, both Indonesia and Malaysia consolidated economic policies designed to benefit politically important domestic constituents. In Indonesia, this manifested through the tight link between the military, bureaucrats, and ethnic Chinese capitalists in urban areas and the party and *pribumi* planter interests in rural settings. In Malaysia, the ruling party cultivated a rising *bumiputera* industrial class while carefully constructing industrial policy to allow ethnic Chinese entrepreneurs and foreign investors to contribute to fixed capital accumulation. In both countries, these strategies required state control over credit allocation decisions, mainly through large state banks, and strict limits on FDI.

The global economic environment that funded such state-directed economic strategies in the 1970s changed drastically in the early 1980s with a US-instigated global recession that rippled throughout international credit and commodity markets. With mounting structural pressures, both Indonesia and Malaysia struggled to maintain political control over credit allocation. Each responded to their balance of payment fragilities and economic recessions by addressing weaknesses

---

[40] Jesudason (1989).
[41] Cook (2008), 72.

in their banking sectors and in their exclusionary FDI policies. However, while Indonesia pursued banking deregulation that ultimately shifted market power from the state to politically important domestic conglomerates, Malaysia responded with a series of prudential regulations designed to limit bank leverage and consolidate the increasingly unwieldy sector. It also raised revenue through a series of real-sector privatizations through public offerings that transferred wealth to the politically influential *bumiputera* class that led subsequently to an equity market boom.

As a result of balance of payment pressures and crisis-induced banking reforms, both countries relaxed equity restrictions on export-oriented FDI projects, particularly those located in export processing and bonded zones. However, while Malaysia entered this time period with a more liberal FDI policy stance than Indonesia, the mid-1980s until the 1997 financial crisis marked a period of sustained opening of Indonesia's investment climate such that it was slightly more open to FDI than was Malaysia on the eve of the Asian financial crisis.

Indonesia's liberalizing trend during this time was driven by shifting policy preferences of the country's rapidly growing and politically connected conglomerates. Banking deregulation during this time period shifted credit allocation decision making from state banks toward private domestic banks run by conglomerates owned by military officials and ethnic Chinese capitalists close to the Soeharto regime. Deregulation also limited the government's ability to use directed credit schemes to generate economic growth. As a result, conglomerates and small *pribumi* industrialists lobbied for targeted relaxation of foreign equity restrictions. As a whole, the Indonesian government pursued a degree of liberalization in subsectors that conglomerates wanted opened to foreign investors and maintained a restrictive stance in areas of the economy in which conglomerates preferred continued protection while smaller indigenous firms preferred increased openness.

Malaysia's FDI policy during this same time period underwent far less change. This is unsurprising given that it responded to banking sector weakness by reasserting state control over lending procedures and pursued, albeit with limited success, policies designed to consolidate the banking sector rather than expand the number of domestic operating banks. Thus, over this time period, the Malaysian government continued to view foreign capital as important in limiting the economic and political influence of the ethnic Chinese and Indian minorities.

It also implemented a new foreign investment law designed to attract FDI in highly skilled, export-oriented manufacturing. However, by implementing relaxation of equity restrictions only in export processing zones, limiting foreign ownership even in export-generating activity to 80 percent, and refusing to open additional subsectors to FDI, Malaysia's investment policy during this time is best described as status quo maintenance rather than as a period of substantial liberalization.

Indonesia: Banking Deregulation and Partial Investment Liberalization

In the context of high oil prices, the Indonesian economy grew quite rapidly through the early 1980s, as Table 6.2 records. A series of balance of payment fragilities began to emerge intermittently in the mid-1980s. When world oil prices began to drop, balance of payment pressures devolved into capital flight at the end of 1986 and again in 1987.[42] In response to the crisis, technocrats and political elites focused on the need to liberalize the financial sector.[43] Deregulation would change the credit allocation landscape in Indonesia considerably and in ways that would benefit large conglomerates at the expense of small indigenous firms dependent on access to subsidized loans from state banks. Liberalization of banking licenses would allow conglomerates to establish new banks to provide easy financing to linked entities, while removal of credit ceilings and interest rate controls would allow these private banks to expand their loan portfolio and compete with state-owned banks for business. Local business interests, especially large conglomerates with close ties to the regime, were vocal proponents of such deregulatory policies.[44]

With overwhelming support of politically connected conglomerates and the political bureaucrats tied to these large firms, the government pushed through a series of two deregulatory banking reforms in 1983 and 1988. The 1983 reforms removed credit ceilings and interest rate controls and substantially limited central bank lending through direct

[42] Haggard and Maxfield (1996).
[43] Rosser (2002).
[44] *Tempo*, April 23, 1998; Joseph P. Manguno, "Indonesia Loosens Credit, Interest Rates in Hope of Boosting Domestic Investment," *Asian Wall Street Journal*, June 6, 1983.

Table 6.2. *International investment flows, 1970–2012*

	1970–4	1975–9	1980–4	1985–9	1990–4	1995–9	2000–4	2005–9	2010–2
Malaysia									
FDI inflows	2.86	3.07	4.05	2.31	7.1	4.56	2.75	3.1	4.27
Total external debt	14.23	23.36	44.58	61.36	36.65	47.39	43.93	33.37	33.71
Portfolio equity							1.59	−0.92	
GDP growth	8.79	7.22	6.87	4.88	9.31	5.19	5.47	4.11	6.06
Indonesia									
FDI inflows			0.24	2.69	1.17	1.09	−0.81	1.72	2.15
Total external debt	28.14	34.49	29.99	56.85	60.74	89.71	65.86	37.06	27.94
Portfolio equity					1.11	−1.18	0.28	0.3	0.15
GDP growth	8.21	7.42	6.72	6.04	7.99	1.68	4.76	5.64	6.31

Source: World Development Indicators; averages authors own calculation; all flows as percentage of gross domestic product (GDP).

channels and liquidity credits.[45] The October 1988 reforms (Pakto 88) contained financial reforms that deregulated the domestic financial sector while simultaneously maintaining an environment highly restrictive of foreign banks. The measure abolished Bank Indonesia's role in approving foreign loans, removed ceilings on funds it could raise overseas, and eliminated several ownership restrictions including stock market participation.[46] Local business elites, including ethnically Chinese business owners, largely supported these reforms because deregulation allowed large conglomerates to establish small private banks to serve as a primary source of cheap credit for their affiliated businesses.[47] In response to the reforms, a manager of one large private domestic bank said, "This is the freest we've ever been."[48] Industry groups such as the Indonesian Private Bankers Association, Perbanas, were similarly jubilant at the news of reform.[49] The number of small private banks ballooned under the new regulations, expanding from 111 in 1988 to 240 in 1995.[50] Under liberalization, financial sector growth averaged 12.1 percent for most of the decade.[51]

Despite these reforms and a clear rhetorical commitment to increase financial openness, Pakto 88 retained the New Order regime's largely exclusionary stance toward direct entry of foreign financial firms.[52] Even though the reforms allowed increased branching capabilities of foreign banks, licensing laws prohibited entry of new foreign banks so only foreign financial firms already operating in Indonesia benefited from this reform. The extent of closure is evident from ownership figures of banks in 1996. While 160 private domestic banks operated in Indonesia in 1996, only 34 joint ventures between domestic and foreign banks and 10 majority-owned foreign banks existed.[53] More telling, foreign and joint venture banks lost market share: from 10 percent of deposits in 1982 to 6 percent in 1996.[54] Over this same

---

[45] Rosser (2002), 61.
[46] Haggard and Maxfield (1996); Pepinsky (2013a); Soesastro (1989).
[47] Rosser (2002).
[48] Joseph P. Manguno, "Indonesia Loosens Credit, Interest Rates in Hope of Boosting Domestic Investment," *Asian Wall Street Journal*, June 6, 1983.
[49] Ibid.
[50] Enoch et al. (2003).
[51] Cook (2008).
[52] Pepinsky (2009); Sharma (2001); Winters (1996); Soesastro (1989).
[53] Sharma (2001), 86.
[54] Rosser (2002), 63.

time frame, state banks lost considerable market share, dropping from 71 to 32 percent.[55] The clear winner of reforms were private domestic banks, often connected to industrial conglomerates. They increased market share of deposits from 14 percent in 1982 to 59 percent in 1996.[56]

The enthusiasm that local political and economic elites displayed over banking deregulation did not extend to prudential regulatory reform. Bureaucrats and indigenous groups lobbied to maintain preferential credit programs, while conglomerates fought to preserve their discretionary authority over raising funds overseas and lending to their affiliates without substantial regulatory oversight.[57] Because no politically important societal group supported prudential regulatory reform, the late 1980s through the mid-1990s saw rapid expansion of credit as conglomerates run by ethnic Chinese used their privileged position to lend cheaply to their affiliates, and the state perpetuated preferential credit schemes in priority sectors such as agriculture to mute interethnic tension and underlying social unrest.[58]

The New Order had always worked to balance its tight political and economic alliance with the ethnic Chinese business community with a need to address *pribumi* concerns, especially in rural areas. Banking deregulation threatened social cohesion because lifting credit controls effectively priced indigenous firms out of the lending market while benefiting larger ethnically Chinese businesses.[59] Therefore, the government continued to provide preferential credit to high-priority sectors such as agriculture, cooperatives, and manufacturing exports even as deregulatory pressures forced it to cut credit programs in trade manufacturing, construction, and services. To further offset *pribumi* concerns, the government maintained its medium-term investment program (KIB), which was available only to indigenous Indonesians and had been implemented in 1974 in response to violent ethnic riots.[60]

However, continued downward pressure on oil prices limited the government's ability to continue such programs. In 1990, it further limited preferential credit to agriculture, subsidized food distribution,

---

[55] Ibid.
[56] Ibid.
[57] Rosser (2002).
[58] Habir (1984), 130; Rosser (2002), 63.
[59] Rosser (2002).
[60] Cook (2008); Habir (1984).

cooperatives, and medium-term investment credit. To offset these cuts, the government required private banks to direct 20 percent or more of their loan portfolios to small *pribumi* commercial interests.[61] Even with pressure from declining revenue and technocrats in BI, senior government officials and the conglomerates whose continued support the New Order regime relied upon were able to maintain access to a more limited preferential credit program that facilitated the continuance of patrimonial ties.[62] In other words, the contraction of preferential credit squeezed *pribumi* interests from the benefits of the program but did not fundamentally alter the regime's ability to control credit allocation processes to favor political allies.

As with the politics of preferential credit programs, there was also near universal domestic opposition to prudential regulatory reforms. Technocrats in BI wanted to pair the banking deregulations of 1983 and 1988 with a series of prudential requirements that would regulate lending limits, capital adequacy requirements, loan-to-deposit ceilings, and lending decision processes in state banks.[63] The de jure prudential requirements in these packages were very weak by international standards. Capital adequacy ratios were set below Basel I standards, legal lending limits were set high enough to allow banks to lend up to 50 percent of their portfolios to a combination of firms within a single conglomerate, and even these regulations were largely unenforceable due to long compliance periods and regulatory capacity problems associated with the rapid growth in the number of banks.[64] State officials as well as conglomerates also strongly opposed regulatory cleanup of state-owned banks because both groups benefitted from the patrimonial system of access to subsidized credit in exchange for political support and economic favors.[65]

The rapid expansion of ethnic Chinese conglomerates during this period, enabled through largely underregulated lending from affiliated private banks and amplified through increased public offerings on the burgeoning Jakarta stock exchange, led to increased societal tension as *pribumi* populations increasingly resented the economic fortunes of

---

[61] Rosser (2002), 65.
[62] MacIntyre (1993), 159.
[63] Bihandi (1995), 179; Rosser (2002), 66; Wardhana (1994), 80.
[64] Cole and Slade (1999), 91; Rosser (2002), 67; Symons and White (1989), 1974–5.
[65] Rosser (2002), 67–8.

the large and nonindigenous domestic capitalist class.[66] Banking deregulation had made credit more expensive, thereby benefiting the large
firms with deep pockets while freezing smaller indigenous firms out of
lending markets. Large firms were willing to pay the higher costs of
credit in order to limit their competition from smaller firms, consistent
with the theories of support for financial underdevelopment discussed
in Chapter 3.[67] This dynamic was strengthened by continued limits
on foreign bank branching, which meant large conglomerates with
access to international capital intermediated through affiliated banks
had important advantages in an otherwise limited financial system.
Soeharto sought to dull the anticonglomerate rhetoric advanced by
small and medium-size *pribumi* businesses that had pressed the government to limit lending to nonindigenous interests and to find ways
to actively promote the development of indigenous firms.[68] The easiest
way to satisfy these concerns, and indeed the preference of the vocal
pribumi business owners, was to provide these groups increased access
to preferential credit through the state-owned banks and to extend
several procurement contracts to indigenous firms.[69]

In this political climate, banking regulation expanded conglomerates' access to finance, increased private domestic banks' ability to
expand their lending portfolios rapidly through borrowing internationally, and placed additional pressure on the government to combat
interethnic tensions through extending preferential credit to *pribumi*
firms. The inherent instability of such unchecked financial expansion
quickly became clear through a series of near collapse of several banks
through the early 1990s. A stricter banking regulation passed in 1991,
but it included a lengthy compliance schedule and did not provide reg-
ulators with the capacity to enforce lending limits adequately.[70] The
buildup of overleveraged private domestic banks and unserviceable
debts in state banks left the domestic financial sector increasingly vulnerable and set the stage for a severe banking crisis after the 1997
currency crisis. The decade preceding the crisis, then, consisted of substantial banking deregulation that shifted credit allocation power from

---

[66] "Indonesia Big Business 'Affecting Growth of Small Firms,'" *The Straits Times*, December 28, 1993.
[67] Rajan and Zingales (2003).
[68] *Tempo*, July 20, 1991.
[69] Robison (1996), 95.
[70] Rosser (2002), 74.

the state to conglomerates. At the same time, the regime retained a more limited ability to provide targeted preferential credit to favored firms. If FDI policy is driven by financing constraints, we should expect that the loosening of state control over credit allocation would result in a period of policy opening toward FDI as firms would increasingly look to foreign sources of investment, at least in areas that were no longer supported by preferential credit arrangement. Indeed, Indonesian FDI policy during this time conforms to expectations.

Table 6.3 highlights investment policy changes from 1986 to 1996. Indonesia began the 1980s as much more closed to FDI than its geographic and economic neighbors in island Southeast Asia. By the eve of the 1997 financial crisis, it had closed the gap in FDI restrictiveness and had become slightly more open to foreign investment than Malaysia. However, the reforms to FDI policy made during this time are best described as moving the country from an unconditionally closed to a partially open investment environment. A series of laws and decrees opened the economy to FDI in export-generating activities, primarily as a way to generate foreign exchange at a time in which declining oil prices placed greater urgency on the regime to diversify exports.[71] It is important to note that some relaxation of restrictions on export-oriented firms preceded the 1988 banking reforms. However, the 1986 loosening of restrictions on export-oriented FDI were minor compared with the 1989 switch from a positive to a negative list. This change, which occurred in the wake of the 1988 banking reforms, fundamentally altered FDI policy from a system in which foreign entry was allowed only if an industry was explicitly opened to a system in which foreign entry was denied only if the government enacted specific industry-level controls.

Japan was the largest potential source of FDI at the time, and most of the regulatory reforms were drafted in response to Japanese government and business officials who focused on minimum investment and divestment requirements as being the largest impediments to Japanese FDI, which was mainly done by small and medium-size export manufacturers.[72] However, despite a clear commitment to fostering a more welcoming environment for manufacturing exporters, the regime

---

[71] Rosser (2002), 128–9.
[72] *Jakarta Post*, August 28, 1986.

Table 6.3. *Investment policy changes, 1986–1996*

1986	Relaxation of limits of foreign ownership for export-oriented firms
	Opened several sectors previously closed to FDI, including retail trade
1987	Foreign investors allowed on stock exchange
1988	Sixteen-year ban on foreign bank entry removed
	Joint ventures allowed to distribute their products locally
1989	Switch from positive to negative list, with hundreds of sectors opened to foreign investment under certain conditions (e.g. export requirements, co-operation with SMEs)
	Foreigners allowed to purchase 49 percent of shares of listed companies
1994	Minimum capital requirement for foreign investment eliminated
	Nine strategic sectors opened to 95 percent foreign ownership
	Up to 100 percent foreign ownership permitted throughout Indonesia (80 percent previously)
	Divestiture requirement reduced to only a token amount of local equity
	Domestic partnership requirements relaxed
1995	Ten sectors removed from negative list, including motor vehicles

Source: OECD 2010, 45.

maintained tight restrictions on investment in domestic-oriented industries and agriculture that still benefitted from Indonesia's circumscribed directed credit program.[73]

Government-industrial relations over FDI policy reform reflected the shift in economic and political power engendered by banking deregulation. Domestic conglomerates supported these limited reforms because most foreign firms were required to enter joint ventures with local firms, which facilitated the transfer of technology from foreign companies to conglomerate affiliates.[74] These conglomerates were in a stronger negotiating position due to their leadership gains in Indonesia's main chamber of commerce, KADIN, which previously

---

[73] Rosser (2002), 134–42.
[74] United States State Department (1990); Sadli (1993), 43.

had never confirmed nonindigenous businesspeople to the organization.[75] Liberalization of SME FDI reflected the dual reality of a *pribumi* capital class that was severely weakened by a credit environment that favored large, ethnically Chinese conglomerates over small firms and by a subsequent need to finance SME business expansion through joint ventures rather than bank loans.[76] The government also retained extensive screening of all FDI project proposals, and the conglomerates' close political ties meant they could easily lobby investment board officials to block foreign projects that would disadvantage them. A prime example of the conglomerates' power is the government's decision to ban new foreign-funded projects in palm plantations in early 1997 at the urging of ethnic Chinese interests. *Pribumi* SME business owners protested the move, arguing the freeze of "all new foreign investment in palm plantations opens the possibility of monopolies" because only seven ethnic Chinese conglomerates held licenses for palm plantations after the ban was implemented.[77]

Thus, FDI policy changes during the period prior to the 1997 crisis offered tentative openness to export-oriented projects while maintaining heavy state control over individual projects and requiring foreign investors to cooperate substantially with local firms. These changes in FDI policy reflected the policy preferences of business elites. In contrast, *pribumi* labor groups resented the continued economic success of ethnic Chinese and foreign firms in the country, and worker demonstrations and riots were a continual threat, especially in areas outside Jakarta.[78] During this time, an unsanctioned labor union became increasingly militant in North Sumatra; in one case a Chinese factory owner was killed in strikes organized to protest low wages and poor working conditions.[79] These demonstrations failed to translate into

---

[75] Maggie Ford, "Ethnic Chinese Get Senior Indonesian Chamber Posts," *Business Times*, Februrary 5, 1994.

[76] Douglas Wong, "Indonesia Now More Attractive for Investment," *The Straight Times*, January 13, 1995.

[77] Vice chairman of KADIN, Adiwarsita Adinegoro, quoted in "Indonesia Seeks to Limit Foreign-Owned Plantation; Jakarta Hopes to Overtake Malaysia in Palm-Oil Production," *The Nikkei Weekly*, April 14, 1997.

[78] Lee Kim Chew, "Medan Troubles Cast Show on Indonesia," *The Straits Times*, April 25, 1994.

[79] Lee Kim Chew, "Trying Times Ahead for Indonesia's Labour Movement," *The Straits Times*, May 1, 1994.

policy wins, however, because labor groups were largely marginalized from industrial and political relations.

Thus, business interests, rather than labor, drove investment policies. In sectors in which conglomerates benefitted from FDI restrictions, especially agribusiness, the New Order regime was quick to erect barriers to foreign investment. The liberalization of FDI was carefully paired with new SME credit programs designed to decrease *pribumi* anger over the ethnic Chinese conglomerates' outsized benefits from new FDI policies.[80] Investment incentives for foreign companies were revoked in 1984 and only reinstated in 1996 when stressed state-owned bank balance sheets severely reduced the ability of the government to extend preferential credit to priority sectors.[81]

Malaysia: Status Quo Maintenance

Largely due to the success of the NEP in rapidly developing a burgeoning class of *bumiputera* business elites, the Malaysian government's primary NEP policy goal in the 1980s was to divest its extensive holdings in banking and real sector interests to indigenous owners. The realization of this objective was complicated by a recession and debt crisis in 1985 and 1986. As a result of a global recession brought on by US monetary contraction, export commodity prices collapsed in 1985. This put substantial pressure on the current account as export income fell by 6.2 percent in 1986. Public debt, driven by state borrowing to fund expansion of heavy industry, rose from 44 percent of GDP in 1980 to 112 percent in 1986.[82] More than half of this debt was denominated in foreign currency, which became problematic as the yen appreciated as a result of the 1985 Plaza accords. The government's weak fiscal position left it unable to pursue countercyclical fiscal policies in response to weakening aggregate demand, and GDP growth fell sharply into negative territory in 1986, as Table 6.2 indicates. Unemployment doubled to 8 percent in 1986, and the country experienced a banking crisis; nonperforming loans accounted for 30 percent of all loans in 1987 and 1988.

---

[80] "Kadin, Golkar to Form Guarantee Fund New Year," *Business Times*, October 1, 1994.
[81] Organisation for Economic Co-operation and Development (2010).
[82] Athukorala (2010), 3; Doraisami (2014), 7.

As would be the case in 1997, the Malaysian government decided to manage postcrisis adjustment without IMF assistance. IMF loans could lessen fiscal distress, but they would come with conditionality requirements that would severely undercut the NEP. The dominant party, Barisan Nasional (BN), relied on the political support of Malaysia's *bumiputera* majority and therefore was unwilling to pursue structural adjustment policies that would preclude continuance of economic redistribution policies.[83] However, the crisis weakened the government's ability to underwrite development through fiscal expansion and required the state to look elsewhere to generate investment finance. This imperative led to policy changes in three key areas: banking, privatization, and FDI.

The banking sector was substantially weakened due to high levels of nonperforming loans and increased incidence of corporate bankruptcies. In response, the government moved to increase BNM regulatory banking oversight and facilitate local bank consolidation. It did this by temporarily imposing interest rate controls and passing a series of financial sector regulatory reforms. In immediate response to the crisis, the government imposed interest rate controls to limit excessive credit rationing during the crisis. Interest rates had been liberalized since 1978, but the central bank imposed direct controls from 1985 to 1987. In February 1987, BNM implemented a base lending rate method of control until 1991.[84] After 1991, interest rates returned to being determined by competitive market rates. This policy liberalization reflected a return to strong economic growth along with a surge in inward foreign capital flows and increasingly stringent banking regulations.

Most important in these regulatory reforms was the October 1989 Banking and Financial Institution Act (BAFIA), which provided enhanced power for licensed institutions' auditors while increasing BI's authority to bail out ailing banks. Local bankers greeted the reforms warmly, especially after amendments dropped initial language that many believed gave BI sweeping authority in determining when a

---

[83] Narayanan (1996).
[84] Yusof et al. (1994).

bank would be subject to takeover.[85] BAFIA also limited private foreign borrowing to prevent the banking sector, which benefited from an increasingly liberal short-term capital account, from taking on too much short-term foreign debt. This would later help insulate Malaysia from the worst of the 1997 financial crisis; South Korea, Indonesia, and Thailand faced higher bank losses due to the extent to which banks were overleveraged to foreign creditors. However, as will be seen below, BAFIA limited foreign debt issuance, but it did not limit raising capital through equity markets. Thus, domestic intermediation of foreign capital in Malaysia in this period was done primarily through equity markets.[86]

As the banking crisis subsided, the government tried to facilitate local bank consolidation to enhance capitalization, simplify regulatory oversight, and further consolidate bank equity holdings in the hands of well-connected *bumiputeras*. The central bank stopped issuing new banking licenses in 1982, which meant that banks wishing to consolidate had to obtain permission from the minister of finance. As a result, banking sector restructuring in the early 1990s mainly benefitted state- and *bumiputera*-owned firms. Only two of the seven banking mergers that occurred from 1992 to 1994 resulted in non-*bumiputera* ownership.[87]

Through the rest of this period, the state remained committed to protecting its financial sector from foreign ownership. The United States, China, and Australia specifically targeted Malaysia's banking sector during the financial services negotiations of the Uruguay Round. The government of Malaysia, like Indonesia, strongly resisted these pressures by leveraging their leadership in the South East Asian Central Banks Research and Training Centre (SEACEN), the developing G15, and the UNCTAD to prevent meaningful liberalizing commitments. At the same time, the government implemented new regulations to prevent foreign banks from gaining advantages in the local market through technological advances. The growth of automated teller machines (ATMs) threatened to give foreign banks with superior technology systems an advantage vis-à-vis local banks. BNM defined

---

[85] Wong Sulong, "Malaysia to Tighten Banking Laws," *Financial Times*, October 23, 1985.

[86] Pepinsky (2012).

[87] Cook (2008).

off-site ATMs as separate branches, effectively preventing foreign banks from building out their ATM networks.[88]

In addition to its efforts to shore up the banking sector in the wake of the 1985–1986 crisis, the government of Malaysia also pursued a privatization agenda in which state assets were divested primarily to United Malays National Organisation (UMNO)-linked companies. They did so mostly by issuing stock on the Kuala Lumpur Stock Exchange (KLSE). As a result of these offering, KLSE quickly grew into one of the largest stock exchanges in the world relative to GDP, with a market capitalization of $200 billion just before the 1997 crisis.[89] By early 1997, it was the third largest exchange in East Asia, behind Tokyo and Hong Kong.[90]

The quick rise of KLSE is important to understanding the politics of investment policy for two main reasons. The first is that it facilitated rapid expansion in foreign portfolio investment, which accounted for 60 percent of trading volume and 25 percent of ownership in 1997.[91] The increase in portfolio investment meant short-term foreign investment quickly became an important source of inward investment, accounting for 43.3 percent of total inflows in 1995, up from 13.2 percent just the previous year.[92] This inflow of foreign investment provided local banks with an inexpensive and seemingly limitless supply of capital to increase lending capacity.

Banks were particularly willing to leverage themselves in this way due to a two-tiered regulatory system introduced in December 1994 in which more highly capitalized banks could provide foreign exchange accounts of unlimited size. This policy was designed to encourage consolidation, but banks were able to increase market capitalization to gain tier one status without relinquishing managerial control by offering new shares and then borrowing from foreign sources to buy these shares. As long as KLSE continued to climb in value, banks had the collateral necessary to borrow these funds. As a result, only one bank merger occurred between 1994 and 1997 and credit surged.

The 1985–1986 crisis also led the government of Malaysia to modify its restrictive stance toward FDI in order to upgrade its exports

[88] Organisation for Economic Co-operation and Development (2013), 216.
[89] Delhaise (1998).
[90] Cook (2008), 75.
[91] Cook (2008), 75.
[92] Athukorala (2003).

from commodity-driven to higher-tech manufacturing. This change was largely due to the need to generate exports to offset persistent current account deficits made worse by a global recession and a concern that commodity markets were too volatile to count on for generating foreign exchange. FDI was needed to supplement domestic capital due to the government's weak fiscal position, a banking sector unwilling and unable to lend sufficient amounts needed for industrialization immediately following the crisis, and a need for technology transfer to switch rapidly from an export sector dominated by processing primary products like palm oil to one engaged in manufacturing higher-value-added products like electronics.[93]

However, rather than pursuing full liberalization of its FDI regime, the government of Malaysia implemented a modified version of its partially open policy framework by incentivizing export-oriented FDI while maintaining high levels of restrictions in other sectors. The 1986 Promotion of Investment Act (PIA) is illustrative of this strategy. PIA permitted exporters and firms transferring high levels of technology and knowledge to retain greater levels of foreign equity than previously allowed. Firms exporting 80 percent or more of their goods were exempt from joint venture requirements. The government relaxed equity restriction in no other industry subsectors during this time, and the FIC continued to screen all foreign equity acquisitions. The government also retained screening authority over wholly owned foreign affiliates in the export-oriented manufacturing sector through the Malaysian Industrial Development Authority (MIDA), which issued manufacturing licenses and determined investor eligibility for investment incentives. MIDA, in conjunction with the Ministry of International Trade and Industry, increasingly used this authority to approve only those projects that would help the country transition from labor-intensive to high-technology sectors.[94] Domestic business interests remained central to the development of investment rules throughout the period, lobbying for policies that would incentivize technology transfer to local firms while also allowing domestic industry to set the terms of joint ventures with foreign investors.[95] For example, the

---

[93] Ang (2009); Athukorala (2003); Doraisami (2014).
[94] Chen May Yee, "Foreign Investment in Malaysia Falls in 1995," *Agence France Presse*, January 22, 1996.
[95] "Industries Seek More Investment from Abroad," *The Nikkei Weekly*, September 26, 1992.

Federation of Malaysian Manufacturers (FMM) advocated forcefully for policies that would facilitate co-ventures between larger Malaysian firms and foreign small and medium-size enterprises.[96] While domestic firms welcomed high-skill manufacturing FDI, local business groups were concurrently able to push through more equity restrictions on market-oriented FDI such as in the distribution industry.[97] Meanwhile, business lobbying groups such as the Federation of Malaysian Manufacturers (FMM) successfully pushed for public sector support for research and development in order to reduce dependence on foreign firms for technological development.[98]

Thus, at the time of the 1997 financial crisis, the investment climate in Malaysia was characterized by extensive government guidance over credit allocation decisions and foreign investment activity. Interest rates were liberalized, and prudential regulation prevented gross excesses in bank leverage, but a government-driven stock market boom, further fueled by high levels of foreign investment inflows, created a rapid expansion of credit on which well-connected firms were best poised to capitalize. State-owned and *bumiputera* banks remained central to the banking sector. FDI was encouraged in export-oriented activities, but with extensive government oversight. FDI in other subsectors was severely circumscribed. As we will see in Chapter 7, this policy environment drastically changed in the wake of the 1997 crisis. As the government relinquished its control over the banking sector, important voices in commerce and industry lobbied for increased openness for FDI to help finance further economic expansion. Over time, these voices triumphed over poorer *bumiputera* community members who viewed foreign firms with suspicion.

Conclusion

In this chapter, I trace the coevolution of banking sector and FDI policies in Indonesia and Malaysia from 1965 to the eve of the 1997 Asian financial crisis. While Malaysia had initially developed a more liberal,

---

[96] "SMIs to Lead Next Wave of Investment," *New Straits Times*, February 21, 1995.
[97] Esther Tan, "Guidelines on Wholesale, Retail Trade Out Soon," *New Straits Times*, March 5, 1996.
[98] Kartini Abd. Kadir, "Call to Tap Public R and D Potential," *Business Times (Malaysia)*, July 19, 1996.

but fundamentally partially open, stance toward foreign investors in order to limit the economic and political power of ethnic Chinese capitalists, Indonesia experienced a policy shift from a mostly closed to a conditionally open FDI climate through this time period. I show how banking sector deregulation in Indonesia, in response to substantial balance of payment weakness, shifted policies toward conditional openness, and I find some contemporaneous accounts that suggest business elites supported these changes. As credit allocation decisions became increasingly driven by private rather than state-owned banks, and as state financing constraints limited the availability of preferential credit, industrial elite and state bureaucrats became increasingly willing to raise equity ceilings on foreign investors, especially in the manufacturing sector. At the same time, the state retained ultimate authority over foreign investment projects through its centralized screening capacity and showed its willingness to block investment projects that would threaten domestic industrial elites, to the extent that labor groups held strong preferences over FDI, they were largely suspicious.

Malaysia experienced status quo maintenance with respect to its FDI policies through the 1970s and 1980s. This is unsurprising given the fact that it did not undergo substantial changes to its banking sector regulatory regime during this time period. Malaysian officials responded to banking sector weakness in the 1980s with increased prudential regulation, but these steps were mostly supported by domestic capital because the regulations provided the central bank with increased bailout authority and limited the growth of foreign banks by requiring them to incorporate locally. These policy initiatives did little to change the fundamental nature of the domestic credit allocation process and therefore did not generate substantial changes in elite preferences over FDI openness. However, the banking policies of the late 1980s and early 1990s did help insulate the Malaysian banking sector from the very worst of the 1997 crisis. We will see in the next chapter how Malaysia's ability to weather the crisis without IMF assistance actually facilitated major liberalizing changes in the banking and FDI policy spaces.

The processes through which Indonesian and Malaysian banking and FDI policies did or did not change through the 30-year period prior to the Asian financial crisis provide us with important insight into how status quo and reformist pressures are created and sustained. Indeed, these cases provide some insight into how domestic credit conditions and allocation processes narrow the set of policy options related to FDI that governments subsequently face. They also provide clear examples of how shifts in FDI policy correspond with business elites' preferences rather than labor or SME interests. The next chapter illustrates this dynamic more starkly by examining how crisis policy responses modified elite preferences for foreign investment since 1997.

7 Crisis, Reform, and Policy Divergence: Malaysia and Indonesia, 1997–2013

"We need to use foreign investment in a smart way, like China has done. But Indonesia has to decide what it wants to promote and specialize in." (Yuri Sato, economist for Indonesia Chamber of Commerce and Industry [KADIN] November 7, 2009)

"[Malaysia should adopt] a truly liberalised position to foreign equity and ownership not only in the manufacturing sector but also in the services sector ... This is not a time for faint-heartedness but for meeting the immediate challenges with pragmatism, innovation, and fundamental change." (Malaysian International Chamber of Commerce and Industry, April 8, 2002)

In the previous chapter, I traced the coevolution of banking sector and foreign direct investment (FDI) policies in Indonesia and Malaysia from the late 1960s to the eve of the 1997 Asian financial crisis. While regime management of interethnic political cleavages initially led the Malaysian government to cautiously embrace highly regulated foreign investors as a way of limiting the economic dominance of non-*bumiputera* capitalists, Indonesia's tight alliance between the military, ruling party, and ethnic Chinese financiers provided the political logic for largely excluding foreign capital from direct investments in the local economy. The Indonesian government's policy of banking deregulation in the 1980s in response to tight global credit conditions and elite interest in establishing private banks linked to powerful domestic conglomerates, however, created local elite support for limited FDI reforms so that, by 1997, Indonesia's FDI policies were slightly less restrictive than were Malaysia's.

In this chapter, I demonstrate how divergent crisis response strategies to the 1997 Asian financial crisis led to substantial liberalization of credit allocation in Malaysia, while Indonesia's foreign-bank-led financial sector restructuring did little to force fundamental changes in the way banks make debt financing decisions and insulated the state from needing to privatize its extensive state-owned banking system. As a result, Indonesian business interests have successfully blocked attempts to implement large-scale liberalization of FDI beyond the initial policy changed imposed by the International Monetary Fund (IMF) in 1989 and 1999. In contrast, the Malaysian business community has largely supported, and in many cases driven, more fundamental liberalization of FDI policy.

Figure 7.1 shows Indonesia's and Malaysia's level of FDI restrictiveness starting in 1997 onward. In early 1997, Indonesia and Malaysia had similar levels of openness to FDI. Both had centralized screening requirements, often required foreigners to enter joint partnerships with local firms, and heavily targeted export-oriented manufacturing while denying entry to other investors. However, their policies toward FDI have since diverged. Malaysia has experienced sustained movements toward more openness over time and now has an FDI policy that is at the average level of openness for a panel of 52 advanced and emerging economies. Indonesia, in contrast, experienced a small and immediate decrease in its restrictiveness score, followed by a decade without

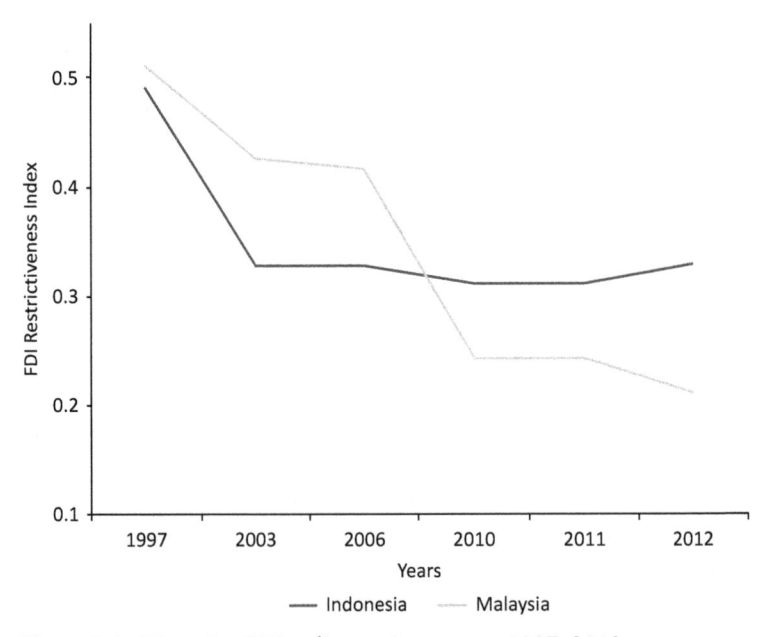

Figure 7.1 Diverging FDI policy environments, 1997–2012

change to its level of openness. Since 2010, Indonesia has actually become slightly more restrictive toward FDI. In 2012, its restrictiveness was one standard deviation above the average level of restrictiveness in 52 advanced and emerging economies. In other words, Indonesia's and Malaysia's level of openness was identical in 1997 and today shows substantial divergence, with Malaysia being much more open than Indonesia.

The timing of this divergence follows a common, arguably exogenous, shock in 1997 when a twin currency and banking crisis originating in Thailand spread throughout Southeast Asia. Subsequently, Malaysia and Indonesia each pursued different crisis response strategies. Indonesia accepted IMF loans and recapitalized ailing private banks by opening the banking sector to foreign ownership. At the same time, the Indonesian government refused to privatize its large state-owned banking sector and used the crisis to consolidate state-owned banking assets. Malaysia eschewed IMF funding and instead used self-financed banking sector recapitalization while also privatizing state-owned banks and pursuing prudential regulatory reform. The difference in crisis response meant that the Indonesian government and powerful domestic industrial-financial conglomerates still retained an important degree of control over domestic credit allocation, while the credit allocation process in Malaysia became more market-based.[1] I argue below how these different outcomes affected key societal groups' preferences over an alternative source of investment finance: FDI.

The postcrisis experience of Indonesia and Malaysia is a hard test of my theory for several reasons. First, Indonesia experienced two political developments commonly associated with FDI liberalization – democratic transition and IMF conditionality – while Malaysia did not. Thus, if existing theories of FDI liberalization have more explanatory power than does my financing opportunity cost theory, we would

---

[1] There is a large and growing literature on comparative financial systems that characterizes domestic systems as "bank-based" or "market-based." See Demirguc-Kunt and Levine (2001), Hardie et al. (2013), and Rajan and Zingales (2003) for reviews. My terminology above should not be construed as building upon this literature. Instead, I merely mean to distinguish between financial systems in which political relationships are important for obtaining credit and financial systems in which market mechanisms influence financing decisions, especially in terms of risk assessment.

expect Indonesia to have liberalized to a greater extent than Malaysia. Because Indonesia recapitalized banks by reducing restrictions on foreign ownership of banks, while Malaysia retained its policies of protecting local banks. Thus, one might expect that Indonesia was more willing to open its economy to foreign investors either due to the political triumph of liberalizing technocrats or simply due to desperation in the midst of crisis. Finally, Indonesia and Malaysia are neighbor states with reasonably similar export potential. Previous research has found cross-border policy diffusion to have statistically significant effects on FDI policy.[2] Therefore, given Indonesia's and Malaysia's geographic proximity and economic similarities, we should expect these countries to hold very similar policies toward FDI.

Below we will see that, in both countries, political leaders made a conscious choice between protecting the banking sector or the real sector from foreign ownership. This trade-off is documented in firsthand accounts of policymaking as well as reporting on interest group lobbying during and after the crisis. When governments chose to protect the banking sector, state technocrats as well as industry leaders pushed for increased liberalization of FDI in the real sector in order to spur domestic capital formation. When governments instead allowed foreign banks to inject capital into ailing banks, they had the financing capability to retain state-owned banks. Credit allocation continued to be driven by political rather than market relationships, and this muted societal pressures for lifting restrictions on FDI into other sectors.

The Asian Financial Crisis and Bank Recapitalization Strategies

As detailed in Chapter 6, the 1980s and early 1990s were a time of rapid economic growth and financial expansion in Indonesia and Malaysia as well as the entire region. The causes and key events of the financial crisis that swept through East Asia in the summer of 1997 are well documented elsewhere, and I will limit my focus here to crisis response strategies in crisis response strategies that Indonesia and Malaysia pursued to stabilize their banking sectors, and how these choices influenced subsequent reforms to FDI policy. Both countries experienced substantial pressure on their currency pegs. Financial

---

[2] Vadlamannati et al. (2014).

sectors highly leveraged in foreign currency quickly transformed currency crises into banking crises as foreign liabilities skyrocketed and banks struggled to remain solvent while their balance sheets quickly deteriorated. As their twin currency and banking crises worsened, the Indonesian and Malaysian governments experienced rapidly building technocratic and political pressures to deal with their collapsing banking sectors while managing popular and elite preferences over how to pay adjustment costs. While Indonesia turned to the IMF, Malaysia managed its crisis response without conditional lending. Counterintuitively, the result was that Malaysia underwent a fundamental change to the way the domestic economy intermediated finance, while Indonesia's embrace of foreign banks actually provided the state space to consolidate and strengthen state-owned banks.

Indonesia: Using IMF Loans to Save State Banks

While the balance of payment crises in the late 1980s led to domestic financial liberalization, the external pressures were small enough and the regime strong enough that the episode did not fundamentally weaken the alliance between the regime and domestic banks. The Asian financial crisis, however, placed much greater external pressure on the government and fatally weakened domestic banks. The crisis began in earnest in August 1997, when the government gave up defending the rupiah's peg and allowed it to float freely. Over the next 2 years, Indonesia experienced a severe economic contraction as the money supply dwindled, the government faced severe fiscal constraints, financial intermediation halted, and negotiations with the IMF for emergency lending led to huge popular protests and social unrest. When the worst of the crisis was over, over 80 million Indonesians or 40 percent of the population had fallen below the poverty line, Soeharto's 32-year rule was over, foreign banks had mostly replaced private domestic institutions, and state-owned banks consolidated their substantial market share over domestic lending activities.

The Asian financial crisis of 1997–1998 decimated the domestic financial sector, which had experienced substantial overheating through the early 1990s due to poor regulations and politically connected lending decisions. At the start of the crisis, the Indonesian banking sector comprised 90 percent of all domestic financial assets,[3] the country had no system of deposit insurance, and local banks had the lowest capital adequacy ratios in the region.[4] Lax regulations on domestic banks' foreign borrowing contributed to the highest foreign debt to foreign reserves ratio in the region, high levels of public debt denominated in foreign currency, and comparatively low levels of foreign reserves.[5] Domestic lending was so concentrated and so politically driven that, as the crisis took hold, the largest 21 debtors were responsible for a third of the value of all nonperforming loans (NPLs) in the banking sector, and all of these large debtors had substantial political and business ties to the Soeharto regime.[6]

When Bank Indonesia (BI) abandoned its commitment to maintain the rupiah's value in August 1997, bank balance sheets quickly deteriorated while the value of foreign-denominated liabilities grew 48 percent in 1997. By the end of the year, NPLs topped 32 percent of outstanding debt.[7] Facing increasing strains on BI resources as local banks drew on central bank overdrafts, the Soeharto regime announced the first of four IMF emergence assistance packages in October 1997. The initial loan package was a result of negotiations in which the IMF conditioned assistance on closing politically connected insolvent banks. When the government closed 16 small local banks that represented less than 3 percent of total domestic bank assets, investors responded with a run on private banks to shift their funds into state banks that were assumed to implicitly guarantee deposits.[8] As a result, the private domestic banks, many of which were affiliated with large conglomerates and tightly connected to the Soeharto regime, bore the brunt of the banking crisis.

One of the banks subjected to closure, Bank Andromeda, was owned by one of Soeharto's sons. In December 1997, the bank was permitted to remain open by purchasing another bank license, which cemented IMF concern that conditions would not be followed and popular opinion that the cause of the crisis was not international financial markets but a deeply corrupt New Order regime that maintained power

---

[3] Dobson and Jacquet (1998).
[4] Sorsa (1997).
[5] Cook (2008).
[6] Asami (2000).
[7] Cook (2008).
[8] Chou (1999).

through its patrimonial control over domestic finance.[9] The status of bank closures remained a constant source of friction between the Soeharto regime and the IMF during bailout negotiations. On March 9, 1998, the IMF refused to release a $3 billion tranche, citing Soeharto's unwillingness to abide by the loan conditions. At the same time, popular protest over rising food prices and IMF demands to end food and fuel subsidies placed additional pressure on the regime. Student protests over IMF conditions on subsidies erupted in January 1998, preceded by a run on food supplies. The ensuing riots led the United States to provide a $70 million food and medical aid package in an attempt to quell unrest. On April 8, 1998, only after the sustained popular protests, Soeharto conceded to IMF pressures and agreed to more bank closures in exchange for the IMF dropping conditions over food and fuel subsidies.

The shift in content in letters of intent between the government of Indonesia and the IMF during this time is particularly instructive. The October 31, 1997, letter emphasizes improving the government's fiscal position by eliminating fuel subsidies, has a section on reducing equity restrictions on FDI, and in its section on social safety nets emphasizes the potential benefits of rupiah depreciation in increasing agricultural exports. Concerns about social spending are relegated to educational and medical spending:

Indonesia has made significant progress in alleviating poverty over the past 30 years. Yet, large numbers of poor still remain, and it is imperative that the adjustment program does not result in a worsening of their economic and social conditions. The depreciation should benefit the rural poor by raising output prices in the export-oriented agricultural sector. Measures necessary to achieve fiscal targets will protect expenditures on health and education.[10]

The April 10, 1998, letter includes a lengthy section on the need to support the food and fuel needs of Indonesia's poor through subsidies. The section on liberalizing foreign investment is replaced with a commitment to supporting the development of small and medium-size enterprises and cooperatives through preferential credit allocation. The social safety net section explicitly states:

---

[9] Milner (2003).
[10] IMF: Indonesia October 31, 1997 Letter of Intent 1.111.3.d.45.

It is imperative that the adjustment program does not result in a worsening of the economic and social conditions of the poor. Our policies stated previously on providing a social safety net will be continued and strengthened. As noted above, budgetary subsidies on food, fuel and electricity have been increased. The Government also is broadening subsidized credit schemes for small- and medium-size enterprises where most of the non-agricultural labor force is employed.[11]

Increased popular pressures, coupled with IMF negotiations that forced the Soeharto regime to choose between popular demands and protecting its allies in the domestic financial sector, proved fatal. Soeharto resigned in May 1998. The domestic banking elite no longer had privileged political access, and many fled the country.[12] Without Soeharto and the financial interests that supported his regime, the new government quickly lifted foreign ownership restrictions in the financial sector. The IMF and technocrats in the newly created Indonesian Bank Restructuring Agency (IBRA) were key actors in implementing this policy.[13]

The IBRA was created in February 1998 as an asset management corporation tasked with socializing bank recapitalization by acquiring NPLs from distressed banks. It quickly acquired close to 500 trillion rupiah in bank assets, gained controlling stakes in 54 banks, and controlled close to 80 percent of bank assets by the end of its acquisitions.[14] In the process, the agency was repeatedly accused of political favoritism, and many believed it bailed out insolvent banks alongside illiquid ones.[15] In May 1999, the Bank of Indonesia issued a directive allowing up to 99 percent foreign ownership of local banks (up from 49 percent).[16] Conditions on foreign branching were eliminated.[17] Foreign banks were not eligible to sell NPLs to IBRA, but they were the primary buyers of previously nationalized local private banks when IBRA initiated sales starting in 2002.

---

[11] IMF: Indonesia April 10, 1998 Letter of Intent p. 4.
[12] Pepinsky (2009).
[13] Sato (2003).
[14] Claessens et al. (2000).
[15] Cook (2008).
[16] The Banking Law No. 7 of 1997, which was amended by Law No. 10 of 1998, began restructuring the banking sector, but it was not until this 1999 decree that foreign equity participation was expanded.
[17] Tambunan (2011).

The decision to liberalize foreign equity ceilings in the banking sector marked an important, but circumscribed, change in domestic banking market structure. The Habibie government was in large part forced to open the banking sector to further foreign participation due to the extent to which private local banks were unable to raise funds necessary to submit tender offers. Financial interests strongly opposed this move but had lost their key ally when Soeharto resigned.[18] At the same time, IMF conditionality made substantial government borrowing to facilitate local control over private banks untenable. Democratization also made it difficult to provide public support of local private banks because public perception painted these banks as corrupt vestiges of Soeharto's patrimonial practices. As a result of IBRA sales of previously nationalized private banks to foreign entities, by the end of 2002, foreign banks controlled more than 30 percent of total banking sector assets.[19] However, ownership structures of banks with foreign participation remained far below legal limits; four banks were sold to foreign owners, but in each of these transactions, the foreign owner acquired just enough equity to confer a majority position (51–52 percent).[20] The government retained centralized control over acquisitions by foreigners; all equity acquisitions over 25 percent required BI authorization.[21]

While the government ceded market share from private local banks to foreign ones, it also used the financial crisis to consolidate its control over state-owned banking institutions. The original IMF lending agreement from October 1997 emphasized a need to consolidate and privatize state-owned banks. In October 1998, the government directed its three weakest state-owned banks to merge into Bank Mandiri, which immediately became the largest bank in Indonesia.[22] However, the government never followed through with a comprehensive bank privatization program and as of 2013, no state-owned banks had sold off controlling shares to local or foreign private interests.[23] In 2003, the government did sell a 40 percent stake in state-owned Bank Rakyat Indonesia to multiple investors, but it did so in a way that

[18] Pepinsky (2013a).
[19] Sato (2005).
[20] Cook (2008).
[21] Robson and Loveless (2013).
[22] Cook (2008).
[23] Robson and Loveless (2013).

ensured continued state control over operating decisions.[24] Announced plans to pursue further bank privatizations, including BI, were permanently put on hold during the 2008 global financial crisis. As a result, the banking sector in Indonesia has a strong state and foreign presence with an absence of significant private domestic bank holdings.

The continued dominance of state-owned banks means that large and well connected domestic firms continue to receive preferential lending terms, while small and medium-size enterprises are largely frozen out of credit markets.[25] The transfer of market share from private domestic to foreign banks has resulted in a decline in local private bank market share from 52 percent in 1996 to 35 percent in 2000,[26] and a banking structure in which one-third of all banks have some amount of foreign equity participation and 10 of the 15 largest banks in the country have significant foreign ownership.[27]

But continued state presence in the sector as well as BI screening over significant foreign banking acquisitions means that the Indonesian banking sector has undergone a far less radical transformation with respect to how credit allocation decisions are made than one might initially assume. The state's continued fundamental control over credit allocation is also highlighted by several recent banking law decisions that make the domestic banking sector less open to foreign equity. A 2012 decision to halt a foreign acquisition of Bank Danamon, along with a new complex banking law that limits individual firms and individuals' bank equity holdings, has made it impossible for a foreign bank to take immediate majority ownership in an Indonesian bank.[28] In other words, Indonesia's banking sector reforms in the wake of the 1997 crisis introduced foreign equity participation in the sector without fundamentally weakening the state's substantial control over credit allocation. Local banks linked to family-owned conglomerates lost their ability to provide cheap leverage to their business partners, but state-owned banks are still large players in the domestic credit market and continue to provide substantial lending services to well-connected firms.

---

[24] Cook (2008).
[25] Asian Development Bank (2005).
[26] Sato (2005).
[27] Robson and Loveless (2013).
[28] Robson and Loveless (2013).

Malaysia: Eschewing IMF Cash, Fundamentally Reforming

Malaysia pursued a different response to its twin banking and currency crisis. Unlike Indonesia, it resisted IMF concessional lending in favor of a heterodox policy response aimed at protecting the domestic banking sector from foreign takeovers and preserving macroeconomic policy autonomy. Malaysia's go-it-alone strategy in large part reflected its relatively strong fiscal position and the fact that its banks were not as deeply distressed as were Indonesia's, primarily because prudential regulation prevented Malaysian banks from amassing the same level of foreign-asset-denominated debt. It also reflected considerably more preference homogeneity among business elites. Most Malaysian firms preferred adjustment through temporary capital controls and a repegged ringgit, primarily because the most politically important business interests had predominately fixed capital assets.[29] Mobile asset holders who were disadvantaged by capital controls were mostly ethnic Chinese Malaysians and largely marginalized from politics.[30]

The politics of rejecting IMF assistance clearly reflected a commitment to the National Economic Plan (NEP). In Prime Minister Mahathir's June 19, 1998, address to the United Malays National Organisation (UMNO) General Assembly, he stated:

[I]f we have to resort to the International Monetary Fund assistance . . ., the conditions imposed by the IMF will require us to open up our economy to foreigners. There will not be any Bumiputera quota as the New Economic Policy is an injustice, and unacceptable to their liberal democracy.[31]

At the same time, the Malaysian government's decision to protect local banks meant it did not have access to foreign bank assets. As a result, while the goals of local equity ownership were deepened in the financial sector, the ensuing credit crunch led to a relaxation of foreign equity restrictions in the real sector.[32] In other words, Malaysia did open its economy to foreign equity as a result of the crisis. However, the process of opening was deliberate and unfolded as credit conditions made Malaysian business groups embrace liberalization.

---

[29] Pepinsky (2012).
[30] Pepinsky (2008, 2012).
[31] Dato' Seri Bin Mohamad Mahathir, Currency Turmoil: Selected Speeches and Articles by Prime Minister of Malaysia (Kuala Lumpur: Lomkokwing Integrated), 60–61.
[32] Cook (2008).

Indonesia chose to recapitalize banks through foreign acquisition. Malaysia, in contrast, used two state-owned special entities to facilitate consolidation and recapitalization. First, through a special act of parliament, the government created *Pengurusan Danaharta Nasional* (Danaharta) in 1998 as a special vehicle owned by the Ministry of Finance and tasked with acquiring NPLs from local banks at a discount. This allowed banks to clean up their balance sheets and unload toxic assets. Danaharta acquired NPLs with a face value of 47.49 billion ringgit, or 43 percent of all NPLs in Malaysia, at an average discount of 40 percent. Bank Negara Malaysia (BNM) subsequently established a special-purpose vehicle, Danamodal, to provide liquidity to local banks. Over the course of the crisis, Danamodal injected close to 8 billion ringgit into 10 of the largest Malaysian banks. Both entities were funded by state-guaranteed local bond issues that were mostly held by state pension and investment funds. In this way, the Malaysian government chose to socialize the cost of bank recapitalization rather than open the banking sector to foreign equity. The total cost of recapitalization reached 60 billion ringgit. Danamodal closed out its mandate in 2003; Danharta followed in 2005.

The government also intervened to guide bank consolidation. However, while Indonesia's crisis response led to an increased importance of both foreign and state banks, consolidation in Malaysia did not fundamentally alter the distribution of bank equity among the state, local, and foreign investors. Instead, Bank Negara Malaysia (BNM) issued a plan in July 1999 in which small local banks would be required to merge quickly with six chosen "anchor" banks. Many banks balked at this plan both because the BNM mandate did not allow banks to negotiate their own mergers and also because the choice of anchors was seen as a way for the new finance minister Diam Zainuddin to punish political allies of the disgraced former finance minister and deputy prime minister Anwar Ibrahim.[33] Subsequently, BNM modified

---

[33] Anwar led a coalition of neoliberal reformers from within the UMNO to challenge Prime Minister Mahathir's response to the financial crisis. Central to his argument was the ruling party manipulated the NEP to further enrich well-connected *bumiputeras* while failing to lift ordinary citizens out of poverty. His orthodox economic preferences gained him vocal allies among foreign business communities and he was removed from his posts in September 1998. That October he was jailed after leading public rallies for reform.

the plan to allow existing banks to choose which of a list of 10 anchor banks they would merge with.

Malaysia's statist approach to banking sector recapitalization and restructuring, along with its continued commitment to preserving high local equity ownership requirements in the sector, have led some to argue the financial crisis amounts to a missed opportunity for banking sector reforms.[34] However, this interpretation is misguided. While Malaysia remained restrictive of foreign entry,[35] crisis response led to greater banking sector reform in two key areas: privatization and prudential regulatory oversight. Both of these reforms led to increased competition and more market-based credit allocation decisions, which are reflected in Malaysia's lower net interest margins compared with Indonesia.

The first area of meaningful banking reform was privatization. Ownership structures of Malaysian banks are typically challenging to assess because banks are primarily owned through publicly listed shares. Therefore, even though state investment vehicles frequently hold shares of banks, they do not hold majority positions. Before the crisis, the government of Malaysia held a significant equity stake in both Bank *Bumiputra* and Sime Bank. Both of these banks were heavily exposed to NPLs, and their size along with their quickly eroding balance sheets led the government to find local buyers for these institutions in 1998, before the creation of Danaharta and Danamodal. Bank of Commerce acquired Bank *Bumiputra* and RHB Bank acquired Sime Bank, each with generous terms from the government, including a guaranteed ability to unload NPLs to Danaharta at face value.[36] These mergers effectively diluted the government's equity share in these banks to the point that the state owned less than 30 percent of each of these merged banks; RHB's acquisition in 1999 by Utama Bank further reduced government's ownership in the banking system.

Some observers have emphasized the state's continued equity stakes in these banks through government-linked investment company (GLIC) holdings in bank parent companies. However, while government ownership of banking assets in 2011 was close to 23 percent

---

[34] Cook (2008).
[35] As will be described in greater detail below, the Malaysian financial sector has subsequently undergone multiple reforms that have reduced, but not eliminated, restrictions to foreign bank entry.
[36] Cook (2008), 88–89.

when measured on an effective interest basis,[37] the state no longer has a majority stake in any domestic bank.[38] Unlike typical models of state-owned banks, government ownership of banks in Malaysia is indirect; GLICs take equity participation through investment vehicles that make them primarily responsible to unit holders investing for profit rather than government officials.[39] Unlike banks owned directly by state entities, banks in Malaysia with GLIC equity participation do not benefit from soft financing constraints.[40] In other words, while the Malaysian government does retain passive equity holdings in several domestic banks through its GLICs, the state relinquished much of its control over banks in response to the 1997 financial crisis. Unlike Indonesia, the Malaysian government does not operate banks, and no banks in Malaysia enjoy an implicit and open-ended funding guarantee from the central government.

Second, the Malaysian government increased prudential regulation after temporarily easing rules on classifying NPLs during the height of the crisis.[41] In 1997, Malaysia already complied with 23 of the 25 core principles of the Bank for International Settlements. However, the government responded to the financial crisis by deepening prudential regulations, particularly by shifting from a compliance-based to a risk-based approach to supervision. The government devised the Financial Sector Master Plan (FSMP) and a series of capital market master plans in consultation with the private sector to develop a plan for strengthening the regulatory framework while deepening access to bank-based and market-based finance and gradually increasing foreign participation in the financial sector.[42] As a result, several programs aimed at increasing regulatory oversight were implemented in the following decade. In 2004, Malaysia adopted Basel II standards. In 2005,

---

[37] Organisation for Economic Co-operation and Development (2013), 32.

[38] Databases that define state ownership as 50 percent or greater record Malaysia as having no state-owned banks. See, for example, Hawkins and Minhaljek (2001).

[39] Organisation for Economic Co-operation and Development (2013).

[40] See Gonzalez-Garcia and Grigoli (2013) for a detailed discussion of soft financing constraints and state-owned banks. See Ramirez and Tan (2004) for econometric evidence that government-linked companies do not have preferential credit access in the Singaporean context.

[41] BNM temporarily allowed banks to extend the arrears window on loans from 3 to 6 month (Cook, 2008).

[42] Organisation for Economic Co-operation and Development (2013).

it created a deposit insurance system: Perbadanan Insurance Deposit Malaysia. The Central Bank Act of 2009 increased BNM's surveillance and supervisory capabilities. In 2010, the Credit Reporting Agencies Act created a centralized bureau for collecting information about creditworthiness. In January 2012, Malaysia became fully compliant with International Financial Reporting Standards.

In particular, increased prudential regulation raised the cost of debt financing relative to equity sources of investment, at least for large firms that had previously benefited from loose regulatory standards.[43] Indeed, we can see the effect that regulatory reforms had on reducing preferential access to finance of large, politically connected industries by the extent to which smaller firms, the traditional losers of financial repression,[44] benefited from reforms. Interest rates for small and medium-size enterprises (SMEs) averaged below 5 percent from 1998 to 2005; as a result, their share of total corporate lending increased from 27 percent in 1998 to 40 percent in 2009.[45]

Finally, under the FSMP, the Malaysian government gradually opened the domestic banking sector to increased foreign competition. In 2003, the government ended its requirement that foreign firms raise 50 percent of their locally required credit from local banks. In 2006, BNM announced foreign banks that already had operations in Malaysia would be eligible for up to four new licenses. In addition to relaxation of foreign equity requirements in Islamic banking, the government also began to issue new foreign bank licenses in 2009. The lifting of foreign bank automated teller machine (ATM) restrictions in 2011 removed a major barrier to foreign banks trying to compete for retail customers.[46]

Postcrisis Banking Sectors Compared

As detailed above, Indonesia and Malaysia pursued different strategies in the wake of the Asian financial crisis, and these strategies affected banking sector structure and competition. Table 7.1 reports key banking sector indicators in Indonesia and Malaysia from 1990 to 2010.

---

[43] See Rosser (2004), Pepinsky (2013b).
[44] See Rajan and Zingales (2003) and Abiad and Mody (2005) for further discussion of why small firms are disadvantaged by financial sector repression.
[45] Organisation for Economic Co-operation and Development (2013).
[46] Ibid.

We see how key measures of banking sector performance have diverged postcrisis. For example, both countries experienced a decline in the percentage of bank assets that are state owned, but in Indonesia the state owns more than half of all banking assets while the government of Malaysia owns less than 1 percent of all banking assets in its country. Data on net interest margin, a common indicator of profitability, is not available before the crisis; however, we see that Indonesia has an average net interest margin twice as large as Malaysia, which indicates the Malaysian banking sector is more competitive than is Indonesia's. Net interest margin in Malaysia is comparable to averages in advanced industrial countries with more highly developed financial sectors.

The indicators in Table 7.1 as a whole suggest the financial sector in Indonesia, although it became less concentrated after 1997, retains several key characteristics of repression. The state directs a large share of credit allocation decisions due its ownership of close to half of all bank assets. Banks are relatively well protected from competition, as indicated by high net interest margin and return on equity. Financial development remains weak, as denoted by a bank credit to deposit ratio around 76 percent and a bank deposit to gross domestic product (GDP) ratio close to 30 percent.

In contrast, Malaysia's banking sector, as a result of its restructuring postcrisis, displays the hallmarks of financial sector development and liberalization. While bank credit to deposits ratio is lower than its 1997 peak of 140 percent, it is close to 90 percent, and the ratio of bank deposits to GDP reached a peak in 2010 at 119 percent. While the percentage of bank assets owned by foreigners has remained steady at 18 percent, the state has largely divested its control of bank assets. While bank concentration has increased since 1997, this has not been through nationalization. As a result of these liberalizing measures, banks in Malaysia face similar levels of competition as do their counterparts in advanced industrial economies. This is illustrated by Malaysian banks' relatively low net interest margin and return on equity averages postcrisis.

Disparate crisis-response policies, therefore, resulted in quite different banking sector structures in Indonesia and Malaysia. The fundamentals of the Indonesian financial sector indicate a repressed system with credit rationing in which large and politically powerful firms receive preferential lending terms, banks are insulated from competition, and smaller and less politically connected firms are denied

Table 7.1. *Indonesia and Malaysia banking sector indicators, 1990–2010*

Indonesia	1990	1995	1997	1998	2000	2005	2010
Bank Credit to Deposits[a]	131	121.6	118.2	95.9	40.4	65.8	75.9
Bank Deposits to GDP[a]	39	39.2	46	48.9	44.7	35.6	31.9
Percentage Bank Assets State Owned[b]	55		72.8		55.1		45.2
Percentage Bank Assets Foreign Owned[c]	4		9		31	32	46
Concentration[a]		72.8	43.4	40.2	64.3	42.9	44.8
Net Interest Margin[a]				-3.86	2.47	5.81	6.64
Return on Equity[a]				408.3	5.59	16.3	20.2
Malaysia							
Bank Credit to Deposits[a]	126.5	120.2	140.5	134	112.3	97.36	89.1
Bank Deposits to GDP[a]	80.6	94.99	102.1	113.1	107.6	105.9	119
Percentage Bank Assets State Owned[b]			13.05			0.45	
Percentage Bank Assets Foreign Owned[c]	24	18	18	18	18	17	18
Concentration[a]			43.95	41.26	50.27	49.56	54.2
Net Interest Margin[a]				3.17	3.37	3.5	2.99
Return on Equity[a]				0.16	12.29	18.77	15.7

[a]IMF Financial Development and Structure Dataset
[b]Cornett et al. (2010); IMF (2012); state owned defined as at least 20% stake.
[c]Claessens and Van Horen (2012); foreign owned defined as at least 50% stake.

debt financing. Malaysia, in contrast, has continued to develop and deepen its financial sector by privatizing and liberalizing the sector. As we will see below, these developments have implications for societal support for liberal FDI policy. The Indonesian government is still able to leverage its financial system to provide preferential credit to key supporters. Access to subsidized debt financing has encouraged the most important business groups in Indonesia to actively lobby to increase foreign equity restrictions; this has substantially stalled and even reversed FDI policy reforms. Debt finance in Malaysia is no longer driven by state preferences and bureaucratic favors. The decoupling of the state and the banking sector has led to increased competition among banks, increased access to debt finance for smaller and less politically powerful firms, and the decline of subsidized credit to politically important corporations and industries. As a result, business groups in Malaysia have substantially changed their lobbying strategy for FDI policy from one advocating regulatory exclusion to one championing liberalization. This strategic shift has motivated the Malaysian government to gradually reduce barriers to FDI even in the face of opposition from *bumiputera* workers who may not be well organized but who form an important base of support for the ruling UMNO.

Investment Policy Politics

In this section I outline the politics of investment policy in Indonesia and Malaysia from 1997 to 2013, paying particular attention to lobbying efforts of business groups. As described below, Indonesia underwent immediate but partial FDI reform following 1997. After IMF pressure to liberalize foreign equity restriction subsided, however, reform efforts stalled and then backtracked significantly starting in 2009. These policy developments reflect the policy preferences of politically important business groups that have consistently lobbied to protect domestic firms from foreign entrants. Indonesian business interests have largely relied on state-led credit allocation to finance investment and industrial expansion while eschewing FDI except in specific circumstances. Malaysia's approach to FDI liberalization has been more gradual but consistent. Following a substantial change to the banking sector after the 1997 financial crisis, business leaders increasingly looked to foreign firms as sources of investment equity.

Malaysia's long history of consulting closely with business groups has led to substantial opening of the economy to foreign entrants, and with increasingly less oversight.

Indonesia: Continued Suspicion of FDI

As Figure 7.1 indicates, Indonesia experienced a rather immediate but partial FDI liberalization following the 1997 crisis, mostly at the instance of the IMF. Afterward, however, reform stalled. A new investment law was passed in 2007, but it did not result in substantial openness; Indonesia's performance on the Organisation for Economic Co-operation and Development (OECD) FDI restrictiveness index did not change as a result of the new law. In recent years Indonesia has seen an increase in FDI restriction, especially with respect to mining, agriculture, and processing raw materials. The Indonesian Chamber of Commerce and Industry (KADIN) has used its influence in Badan Koordinasi Peranman Modal (BKPM) and National Team on Export and Investment Promotion (PEPI) to spearhead this protectionist push. As a result, in 2013, Indonesia had an FDI policy climate that was more liberal than it was in 1997 but substantially more restrictive than most countries for which the OECD monitors investment climate.

Initial postcrisis FDI reform was driven by a decision to liberalize the banking sector and thus recapitalize failing domestic banks and meet the IMF conditionality that demanded decreased foreign equity restrictions in several key subsectors, including retail and wholesale trade and palm oil plantations.[47] The IMF also initially demanded a revision of Indonesia's negative list, which was originally scheduled to be completed by June 30, 1998. However, this condition was subsequently dropped in the October 19 letter of intent (LOI). The decision to eliminate this requirement and focus conditionality on bank restructuring and fiscal discipline was in part due to the more immediate needs of crisis response, but it also reflected targeted push back by Soeharto with respect to FDI liberalization. According to J. Soedradjad Djiwandono, former governor of the Bank of Indonesia, Soeharto explicitly stated in a January 21, 1998, cabinet meeting that he was unprepared to comply with the LOI's condition of eliminating foreign equity restrictions,

---

[47] IMF: Indonesia April 10, 1998 Letter of Intent Appendix, p. 15.

stating, "The national development that was based on the development trilogy as stated in the state guidelines has been securely ingrained in our society."[48]

Unlike foreign equity restrictions in the banking sector, which were quickly eliminated after Soeharto's departure from power, FDI policy toward the real sector was not fundamentally altered following regime change. Instead, the government of Indonesia has continued to pursue an FDI policy that is fundamentally targeted and conditional in nature, meaning it uses an array of fiscal and legal incentives to attract FDI into sectors it wishes to promote while maintaining high levels of restrictions on FDI in sectors it wishes to protect for domestic firms. This guiding policy framework has been implemented through the 2007 Law on Investment, which mostly clarified rather than liberalized FDI policy, and increased efforts to implement targeted investment incentives. Investment policy has become more restrictive since 2009, with the passage of a protectionist mining law and a series of investment regulatory decisions that are widely seen as illiberal.

As Table 7.2 indicates, Indonesia made no major alterations to its FDI law between 1999 and 2007. In 1999, to comply with IMF loan conditions, several sectors were opened to FDI by presidential decree. The next notable change to investment law came in 2007 with the passage of the 2007 Law on Investment, which replaced the 1967 law and unified the investment code for foreign and domestic investors. The government engaged in extensive consultation with business groups as it prepared the law. BKPM held multiple advisory meetings with chambers of commerce and investor groups, both foreign and domestic in origin. As the primary lobbying group for domestic investors, however, KADIN was the most influential business group in prelegislative discussions.[49] The law was applauded mainly for clarifying regulations and procedures that had previously been confusing. In particular, it provided guidance on investment licensing procedures and on restricted sectors. At the same time, it failed to reform land ownership restrictions and has been accused of fostering the impression that foreign equity restrictions are arbitrary and subject to capricious manipulation by bureaucrats.

---

[48] Djiwandono (2005), 163.
[49] Organisation for Economic Co-operation and Development (2010).

Table 7.2. *FDI liberalization in Indonesia, 1997–2010*

1997	Presidential decree removes 49 percent foreign equity limit on purchases of listed shares
1998	Full foreign ownership allowed in banking
1999	BKPM no longer requires presidential signature for approvals Local content program for motor vehicles phased out Fully foreign ownership of holding companies allowed, including through acquisitions Several sectors opened further to FDI, including retail, general importing, palm oil plantations, broadcasting, and downstream operation in the oil sector
2007	Investment law does away with general divestiture requirements New negative list opens some sectors to greater foreign participation
2009	Mining law allows foreign ownership of concessions Electricity law allows for private operators in areas not served by public electrical utility
2010	New negative list opens some sectors to greater foreign participation

Source: OECD 2010, 45.

First, the 2007 investment law clarified and, in some ways, simplified investment licensing procedures. The BKPM is in charge of investment licensing; administering licenses now comprises 70 percent of its operating budget.[50] Unlike in earlier years, the BKPM's screening authority is limited to ensuring that investment proposals comply with current laws, especially foreign equity restrictions. BKPM is not endowed with the power to reject investment applications for any other reason, including vague considerations of the "national interest." The 2007 law provides investors the right to sue if their proposals are rejected on grounds not stipulated in law. However, the investment licensing process is much more complex than the 2007 reform suggests due to the 1999 Regional Autonomy Law (RAL). The RAL granted broad licensing authority to subnational governments, which has led to a fragmented and overlapping licensing and permitting environment.

---

[50] Organisation for Economic Co-operation and Development (2010), 90.

Investment approval from BKPM is just the start of a complex set of licenses and approvals investors must obtain from a variety of central and regional government agencies. Companies are required to obtain several different kinds of onerous permits before participating in government tenders or applying for bank loans. Local governments' regulatory authority means BKPM cannot mandate streamlining of regulatory procedures or require provinces to set up "one-stop shops" for obtaining business licenses. As a result, there is a large regional disparity in ease of doing business; the Jakarta Special Capital Region is generally held as an example of a foreign-investor-friendly regulatory environment, while many more rural provinces rich in natural resources tend to have much more complex and onerous licensing requirements.[51] Foreign investors have repeatedly voiced their frustration with decentralization of business licenses and approval, arguing such policies create legal uncertainty and expose firms to the whims of local leaders.[52] However, KADIN and its affiliates actively lobbied for decentralized licensing and permitting procedures because they view their local political ties as a comparative advantage vis-à-vis foreign firms.[53] Because domestic investors only require local approval, foreign firms complain that the national-level BKMP screening is discriminatory against FDI.[54]

In addition to a complex screening process that discriminates against foreign investment and was promoted by local business interests, the 2007 investment law also included a new and expanded negative list of subsectors in which foreign investors face equity ceilings. The revised negative list included 338 subsectors subject to foreign investment limits, which was a large increase for the 83 subsectors included on the previous negative list.[55] Energy, plantation agriculture, and mobile and fixed-line telecommunications all experienced increased restrictions; fixed-line telecom saw the most substantial closure, from a 95 percent foreign equity cap to a required minority position (49 percent). Mari Pangestu, the trade minister at the time, maintained the new list

[51] Organisation for Economic Co-operation and Development (2010).
[52] Shoeb Kagda, "Jakarata Needs to Engage Provinces; It Must Work with Provinces in Reforming Cumbersome Regulations Imposed by Regional Governments," *The Business Times Singapore*, February 15, 2005.
[53] KADIN (2007).
[54] United States Bureau of Economic and Business Affairs (2013).
[55] Bill Guerin, "Indonesia Blacklists FDI," *Asia Times Online*, July 10, 2007.

was formulated to protect "national interests," while regional news analysts argued the restrictive list reflected the government's need to bolster support among indigenous business groups in the run-up to the 2009 elections.[56] The composition of the negative list reflects the government's long-standing policy of protecting small and medium-size domestic firms from foreign competition, and the 2007 investment reforms also included extensive state-led credit programs aimed at financing local companies.[57] The 2007 investment law places authority over the negative list with the executive and does not require parliamentary approval.

In tandem with the new investment law, the government of Indonesia also introduced a new incentive program. Foreign investment incentives have been contentious in Indonesia. Incentives were first introduced in 1967, canceled in 1984, reinstated in 1996, and again canceled in 2000. The 2007 reintroduction of incentives has several key features, including an expanded role for BKPM. Under the new law, foreign investors wishing to qualify for incentives must apply to the BKPM, which evaluates applications based on a range of factors, including employment creation potential; whether the proposed investment would contribute to infrastructure construction or technology transfer; whether the proposed investment is a priority activity or a pioneer industry; whether the project would be located in a depressed area or promote environmental sustainability; and whether the project will contribute to local business development through research and development, local partnership, or using local content. If BKPM thinks the project deserves fiscal incentives, it forwards a recommendation to the Ministry of Finance. If the Ministry of Finance concurs, it publishes individual decrees to authorize incentives for specific projects.

The framework of incentives and conditions for eligibility are controlled by the PEPI, which was formed in 2003, is chaired by the president, and includes extensive involvement of BKPM and KADIN officials. The targeted nature of these incentives, combined with individual project eligibility screening requirements, further indicates the extent to which Indonesian FDI policy remains fundamentally conditionally open in construction. A 1999 review of Association of

[56] Bill Guerin, "Indonesia Blacklists FDI," *Asia Times Online*, July 10, 2007.
[57] Organisation for Economic Co-operation and Development (2010).

Southeast Asian Nations (ASEAN) FDI policy is particularly negative toward such screening boards:

The screening agency serves a political purpose as well as an economic one. It demonstrates to a local population, which may be hostile to, or suspicious of, foreign investment, that such investments are actively monitored by the government. The principal aim of such an agency, however, is to further the development strategies of the host government. The agency will favour certain sectors on a priority list or those investors that fulfill pre-established criteria, usually related to exports.[58]

KADIN's influence in BKPM, especially since the two signed a memorandum of understanding in 2009, further ensures FDI incentives target projects that benefit local partners.[59]

Despite tentative movements toward openness described above, Indonesia has experienced backtracking with respect to FDI policy since 2009. The 2009 mining law is a prime example of such protectionism. Mining investments had previously been regulated through a 1967 law that had been widely seen as stable and transparent but had become increasingly difficult to sustain after the 1999 RAL. The 2009 law stipulates several conditions that discriminate against foreign investors. For example, foreign operators must transfer 20 percent of project equity to local private or public investors within 9 years of the initial investment. Regional powers have created more uncertainty over foreign ownership, sometimes canceling mining licenses without warning or clear cause.[60] The law also places restrictions on foreign-owned mining services companies, requiring all refining and processing to occur locally, and phases out foreign-owned service companies as local firms develop greater technical capabilities. KADIN officials stated publicly in 2012 they were actively campaigning to further restrict foreign investment in mining through the elimination of profit sharing and long-term mineral rights to foreign entities.[61]

---

[58] Thomsen (1999), 19
[59] Organisation for Economic Co-operation and Development (2010), 89.
[60] Eric Bellman, "Regional Powers Sting Firms in Indonesia," *The Wall Street Journal*, October 8, 2013.
[61] John Berthelsen, "Indonesia Makes Tracks for Economic Nationalism," *The Nation*, June 12, 2012.

The backsliding in foreign mining rights is indicative of a broader pattern of policy slippages in Indonesia due to consistently positive economic performance. KADIN officials have argued Indonesia's strong growth indicates "it may be time to complete Sukarno's 1958 revolution, [and] kick out the foreigners."[62] This anti-FDI sentiment is reflected in Bank Indonesia's blockage of a domestic bank's acquisition by a Singaporean holding company in April 2012, an announcement of new foreign equity restrictions in banking in the same month, and a series of new regulations since October 2011 aimed at protecting the local palm oil refining industry.[63] KADIN had been particularly vocal about increasing FDI restrictions in anticipation of the scheduled 2013 revision to the negative list, which had not been announced as of January 2014. KADIN had successfully lobbied for further protection of domestic retail businesses in previous negative list revisions and petitioned hard for restrictions in the wholesale distribution industry. A KADIN spokesperson Fernando Hutahaean argued for a 30 percent equity cap on foreign investors in the subsector, arguing, "The wholesale distribution business does not need huge capital or high-end technology to be developed. National players already have the skills. Foreign investment should be directed to a sector in which we lack capability."[64] This statement reflects a general sense among KADIN officials that the government of Indonesia should emulate China's FDI policies that limit FDI to priority sectors and then guide domestic acquisition of foreign holdings after sufficient technology transfer has occurred.[65]

Indeed, a close look at Indonesia's FDI policy indicates the government's focus on finding foreign equity partners to finance major infrastructure projects through public-private partnerships (PPPs).[66] Local business leaders support such moves because inadequate roads, electricity, telephony, and internet connectivity are some of the largest

---

[62] John Berthelsen, "Indonesia Makes Tracks for Economic Nationalism," *The Nation*, June 12, 2012.

[63] Ibid.

[64] "Indonesia Commerce Body Urges Government to Restrict Foreign Investment," *BBC Monitoring Asia Pacific*, October 25, 2013.

[65] "Indonesian Economists Discuss Chamber of Commerce's Economic Road Map," *BBC Monitoring Asia Pacific*, November 9, 2009.

[66] "Larger Share of Foreign Ownership in Indonesia's Infrastructure Projects," *Indonesia Investments*, December 27, 2013.

impediments to growth in the country.[67] Infrastructure gaps became even more problematic in the aftermath of the 2004 tsunami, and technological and financing constraints make many of these projects untenable through purely domestic input. Most liberalizing revisions to the negative list have been in infrastructure to accommodate this pressing need, but many in the domestic and foreign business communities view equity limits in these areas to be unstable and that the government will place increasing foreign equity restrictions on infrastructure once a sufficient number of high-priority projects are complete.[68]

As a result of these policy changes, Indonesia's investment climate is best characterized as protectionist and unstable. An Asian Development Bank survey of firms in 2003 found 70 percent of firm indicated policy uncertainty was a major obstacle to business.[69] The 2007 investment law clarified equity restrictions but also increased investor perception that the negative list is unstable and arbitrary.[70] The OECD measure of FDI restrictiveness finds protectionist backsliding since 2010. The restrictive stance of Indonesia's FDI policy seems strange given severe long-term credit rationing. KADIN has identified long-term credit expansion as a primary need of the local business community.[71] According to a 2009 World Bank Enterprise Survey, 47.9 percent of Indonesian firms identify access to finance as the most important constraint on business development.[72] The same survey of 1,044 businesses found financing constraints were most severe for small and medium-size firms with 99 employees or less; large firms were more worried about the regulatory environment and inadequate infrastructure.[73]

This divide between large and small firms is unsurprising; in a repressed financial system, smaller firms experience credit rationing while large and politically powerful firms receive preferential access

---

[67] "Taking a Closer Look into Kadin's Economic Road Map," *The Jakarta Post*, November 7, 2009.

[68] Organisation for Economic Co-operation and Development (2010), 135.

[69] Asian Development Bank (2005).

[70] Laurel Teo, "Indonesia's New Investment Rules Add to Confusion; Chambers Say Many Grey Areas in Caps on Foreign Stakes," *The Business Times Singapore*, July 13, 2007.

[71] "Taking a Closer Look into Kadin's Economic Road Map," *The Jakarta Post*, November 7, 2009.

[72] World Bank (2009).

[73] Ibid., 4.

to credit instruments. However, given the state's dominance in the banking sector, with a 50 percent market share, lobbying efforts from the business community have focused on state-led credit expansion programs rather than further banking sector and FDI liberalization.[74] The government has even pursued increased equity restrictions in the banking sector in recent years. While the lack of sufficient long-term credit and an increasingly hostile policy environment toward FDI seems counter-intuitive, this dynamic is explained well by the overarching theory of this book. When credit allocation decisions are largely driven by the state rather than by the market, the most politically connected firms will receive subsidized credit, while their competitors are left out. Under these conditions, these politically connected firms will prefer to prevent foreign entry in order to capitalize on a larger slice of a smaller pie.

Malaysia: Industry-Led FDI Liberalization

Unlike Indonesia, Malaysia's statutory restrictions on FDI did not change immediately following the financial crisis. This is largely because Malaysia was not subject to IMF conditionality and it did not stabilize the banking sector through foreign acquisitions. However, the tenor of FDI policy did change substantially, if gradually, in the decade following the crisis with no major policy reversals; Table 7.3 outlines some of these changes. Before the crisis, Malaysia's investment policy stance reflected partial openness to foreign investment that encouraged export-oriented investment under very specific conditions while greatly restricting foreign investment in sectors oriented to the domestic market. The government responded ad hoc to the crisis by temporarily lifting equity restrictions in the manufacturing sector in 1998.[75]

Over the next decade, a long process of consultation with local business developed a coalition that supported major liberalizing reforms. These reforms were guided by the New Economic Model, which

---

[74] "Taking a Closer Look into Kadin's Economic Road Map," *The Jakarta Post*, November 7, 2009.

[75] Because these equity restrictions were at first only temporarily repealed, the OECD measure of FDI Restrictions does not measure a change until 2003, when the ability of foreign firms to establish wholly owned subsidiaries in the manufacturing sector became permanent. See Organisation for Economic Co-operation and Development (2013).

Table 7.3. *FDI liberalization in Malaysia, 1998–2012*

1998	Temporary relaxation of foreign ownership and export requirements for manufacturing companies not directly competing with local producers (with certain sectoral exceptions)
	Foreign equity allowed in wholesale and retail companies raised from 30 percent to 51 percent
	Foreign equity allowed in telecommunications companies raised from 30 percent to 49 percent (61 percent on a case-by-case basis in mobile telephony), provided that the investor reduces the share to 30 percent within 5 years
2003	Removal of requirement that foreign-controlled companies obtain 50 percent of their local credit from Malaysian banks
	Relaxation of guidelines for foreign equity participation in local firms which previously stipulated a 30 percent limit on foreign equity
	Indefinite extension of policy permitting 100 percent foreign ownership in new investment and expansion of existing investment in manufacturing and removal of sectoral exceptions
	New guidelines on employment of expatriates in manufacturing: companies with paid-up capital of at least USD 2 million receive automatic approval for up to 10 expatriate posts
2005	Foreign-controlled companies no longer face domestic borrowing requirement or require BNM approval for any amount of ringgit credits
2009	Elimination with immediate effect of foreign equity restrictions in 27 service subsectors (including health and social services, tourism, transport, business and computer services)
	Some relaxation of rules on foreign property ownership: property transactions over RM 500,000 for commercial, industrial, and agricultural land no longer require Foreign Investment Committee (FIC) approval
	One hundred percent foreign equity allowed in some maritime services
	Deregulation of FIC guidelines: the FIC no longer processes any acquisitions, mergers, or takeovers nor imposes equity conditions
	Foreign equity guidelines in air transport to be set by regulator and no longer fixed at 30 percent
2011	Announcement that another 17 service subsectors would be liberalized in 2012

Source: OECD 2013, pp. 58–59.

identified investment as the most important component of Malaysia's strategy to become an OECD country by 2020, and the Industrial Master Plan of 2006–2020, which focused its attention on attracting more FDI to the manufacturing and service industries.[76] A series of partial liberalizations of the financial sector starting in 2003 relaxed, but did not eliminate, equity caps on foreign equity in local banks and insurance firms. In 2009, the government made a major and permanent change to investment policy when it removed Foreign Investment Committee (FIC) screening for all foreign mergers and acquisitions (M&As) except some large real estate transactions. In addition, the FIC was no longer authorized to place equity conditions on M&A activity. The same year, the government opened 27 service subsectors to up to 100 percent foreign ownership. In 2011, the government announced a further round of investment liberalizations in 17 service subsectors and a further opening of the financial sector.

The political process of FDI liberalization demonstrates a marked shift in the policy preferences of both government bureaucrats and industrial capitalists. Prior to the Asian financial crisis, the main policy objective of the government and supportive industrial capitalists was to maintain a regulatory approach of incentivizing targeted export-oriented manufacturing FDI while preventing foreign investors from meaningfully competing in the domestic market. This approach included a combination of equity restrictions on foreign participation in local business as well as a strong centralized investment screening bureaucracy, the FIC, which was chaired by the prime minister. The FIC reviewed all applications for foreign acquisitions and approve or denied projects based on a set of criteria that emphasized contribution to the national interest and "more balanced" distribution of wealth, meaning distributing benefits to *bumiputera*.

Before the financial crisis, local chambers of commerce universally supported this strategy of partial openness. In 1992, the Malaysian government scrapped a proposed liberalization measure due to local firm opposition.[77] At that time, local business owners were particularly resistant to efforts to increase joint ventures between local and foreign firms.[78] As late as November 1995, a coalition of Malaysian chambers

---

[76] Organisation for Economic Co-operation and Development (2013).
[77] "Industries Seek More Investment from Abroad," *The Nikkei Weekly*, September 26, 1992.
[78] Ibid.

of commerce, including the Malaysian Retailers' Association, the National Chamber of Commerce, Industry Malaysia, and the International Chamber of Commerce Malaysian, successfully lobbied the Domestic Trade and Consumer Affairs Ministry to implement new regulations that required wholesale and retail companies with foreign equity to incorporate locally and comply with more onerous performance requirements.[79] These new laws were widely seen as implemented to protect local business owners from foreign competition.[80] In early 1997, Ministry of International Trade and Industry (MITI) head Datuk Seri Rafidah Aziz further clarified the government's prevailing policy of investment dualism in an address at the Malaysia-US Business Council Roundtable meeting, "We want to make sure that while welcoming foreign investors, we set a target on where exactly they can come in."[81]

In the aftermath of the crisis, local business groups along with key bureaucrats began to see investment screening, equity restrictions, and performance requirements as problematic barriers to foreign investors that needed to be removed in order to promote healthy economic growth. Reforming the FIC quickly became a focal point of negotiations around changes to foreign investment laws. The Federation of Malaysian Manufacturers (FMM) began to lobby the minister of finance publicly to review and limit the role of the investment screening body as early as July 1998.[82] In a memorandum prepared for dialogues with the Finance Ministry over the 1999 budget, the most prominent chamber of commerce for local manufacturers emphasized the need to push through a number of measures designed to improve access to credit, including liberalizing reinvestment allowances and extending limits on foreign currency accounts.[83] The FMM pointed to a need to finance expansion of production capacity, particularly since the depreciation of the ringgit provided an opportunity to capitalize

[79] Ester Tan, "New Rules for Wholesale, Retail Trade," *New Straits Times*, November 1, 1995.

[80] Ibid.

[81] "Focus on Do-Able Investment Policies," *New Straits Times*, March 12, 1997.

[82] "FMM Appeals for Better Export Financing Incentives," *New Straits Times*, July 8, 1998.

[83] Ibid.

on cheaper production costs.[84] Foreign affiliates brought with them access to offshore sources of finance, which was crucial to overcoming credit rationing in the aftermath of the banking crisis.[85] [86] To facilitate the manufacturing sector's financing needs, the FMM proposed reducing the investment screening role of the FIC, preferring that it only monitor foreign acquisitions in sectors deemed to be in the national interest, which it defined as utilities such as power generation and distribution, telecommunications, and water treatment; defense; air and seaports; and banking and financial institutions.[87]

The government initially responded to the FMM's demands by temporarily lifting equity restrictions in the manufacturing sector. But this policy concession was not sufficient for local businesses, who saw FDI liberalization, particularly with respect to foreign M&As, as a solution to a financing gap. Chambers of commerce used the MITI's annual dialogues with the business community to lobby jointly for liberalizing changes. In 2002, the Malaysian International Chamber of Commerce and Industry (MICCI), the oldest trade association in the country, and the FMM renewed their repeated calls for eliminating foreign ownership restrictions in both manufacturing and services, limiting the power of the FIC, and reforming immigration rules to allow more skilled workers permanent residency in the country.[88]

Increased support of FDI liberalization was clearly linked to the government's decision to recapitalize the banks without allowing foreign bank takeovers. As one authority on Malaysia's crisis response puts it:

[State intervention] focused on narrowing the NEP in the real economy and deepening it in the banking sector through state-guided consolidation. The Malaysian state used this crisis to discipline the Malaysian economy in some sectors while protecting the NEP and its limits on competition in others.[89]

---

[84] "FMM Appeals for Better Export Financing Incentives," *New Straits Times*, July 8, 1998.

[85] United Nations Conference on Trade and Development (1998).

[86] A 1998 survey of electronic manufacturing foreign affiliates in Malaysia found that the majority financed operations through primarily offshore sources, while less than a sixth operated through self-financing.

[87] Rupa Damodaran, "Lower Energy Cost Tops Manufacturers' Wish List," *New Straits Times*, June 12, 2009.

[88] Eddie Toh, "Businessmen Urge Malaysia to Ease Foreign Equity Cap in Key Sectors; They Also Seek to Mothball Foreign Investment Panel," *The Business Times Singapore*, April 9, 2002.

[89] Cook (2008), 86.

In other words, the government's decision to preserve foreign equity limitations on banks made continued equity ceilings in other sectors untenable. This is because constrained credit made industry look to alternatives over bank-based finance. Government appeals for banks to lend were ineffective as banks worked to clean their balance sheets.[90] Raising foreign equity through stock offerings was unattractive due to both temporary restrictions on the capital account and because portfolio investment flows were considered a major contributor to the asset bubble and collapse in the first place. Unlike Indonesia, the Malaysian government did not directly control any local banks and therefore was unable to directly influence credit allocation decisions because it did not offer banks a soft financing constraint. The result of the government-guided banking sector restructuring actually reduced the government's concentration of equity holdings in any given bank.[91] Under these conditions, FDI emerged as an attractive financing option for the largest and most powerful industry groups.

As business support coalesced around liberalizing FDI and particularly M&A activity, the government announced its intention to remove the FIC approval requirement starting in August 2004.[92] The news was met with substantial approval from local and international chambers of commerce, including the MICCI,[93] the FMM,[94] the American Malaysian Chamber of Commerce,[95] the British Malaysian Chamber of Commerce, and the European Union–Malaysia Chamber of Commerce.[96] However, support was not universal, with local real estate moguls arguing FIC oversight over land sales was important to prevent foreigners from acquiring excessive amounts of real property.[97]

[90] Kasmiah Mustapha, "Daim Repeats Call to Banks: Lend to Productive Sectors," *New Straits Times*, July 9, 1999.
[91] The Abiad et al. (2010) Financial Sector Liberalization dataset codes Malaysia as shifting from a "largely liberalized" to a "fully liberalized" score for the bank privatization component of the index in 1999.
[92] "MICC Welcomes New Investment Regulations," *New Straits Times*, June 27, 2004.
[93] Ibid.
[94] G. Umakanthan. "FIC Still Useful," *New Straits Times*, May 1, 2004.
[95] G. Umakanthan, "Easing Guidelines for Foreign Investment," *New Straits Times Malaysia*, July 24, 2004.
[96] G. Umakanthan, "FIC Still Useful," *New Straits Times*, May 1, 2004.
[97] Ibid.

Despite the strong support from the business community, the FIC screening requirement was not removed until 2009. The delay reflected an interrelated bureaucratic power struggle between the prime minister and the executive cabinet and the political economy of *bumiputera* redistributive policy. As a result of business sector feedback from annual MITI consultations, Prime Minister Tun Abdullah Ahmad Badawi tried multiple times to overhaul the FIC, an action requiring cabinet approval. The cabinet twice rejected this proposal, because of concerns that dismantling the screening power of the FIC would be politically unpopular with *bumiputera* groups and because the senior civil servants comprising the committee were reluctant to relinquish their bureaucratic power.[98] In a December 2007 business awards ceremony, Abdullah told industry groups that stalls to reforms were temporary and a reflection of the political business cycle, saying, "Whatever you hear, it's because the elections are coming. I believe we will come back after the elections with a two-thirds majority."[99] The subtext was clear: *bumiputera* riots combined with an obstructionist cabinet were temporary obstacles reflective of preelection politicking. Changes in the cabinet membership after the election would provide political space for reform.

Indeed, the precise timing of the government's major foreign investment policy overhaul corresponds with key political developments. The 2008 election was the most closely contested race since 1969. The BN lost its two-thirds majority in Parliament and had a particularly poor showing in traditional wealthy urban strongholds, including Kuala Lumpur and Penang. The main opposition parties, the Democratic Action Party (DAP), the Parti Keadilan Rakyat (PKR), and the Pan-Malaysian Islamic Party (PAS), all campaigned on platforms to limit preferential treatment of *bumiputeras*. The poor electoral showing weakened Prime Minister Abdullah; he eventually announced in July 2008 that he would relinquish his leadership position the following year.

Abdullah formally handed power to his Deputy Prime Minister Najib Razak on April 2, 2009. The same month, Razak announced the

---

[98] "Sweeping Changes to FIC, Toll Cut on the Cards," *The Malaysian Insider*, June 29, 2009.

[99] Deborah Loh, "Rules Eased to Woo Foreigners Yet Help Bumis," *New Straits Times*, December 5, 2007.

liberalization of foreign equity restrictions in 27 service sub-sectors.[100] On June 30 in the same year, Razak announced the overhaul of the FIC on the same day he reduced the percentage of equity publicly listed stock reserves for *bumiputera* from 30 percent to 12.5 percent.[101] The timing of these changes reflects changes within the executive cabinet associated with Razak's ascension to prime minister/Razak appointed a smaller cabinet, with 39 fewer members than Abdullah's second cabinet. Investment reformers like Deputy Prime Minister Muhyiddin Yassin, who had formerly served as the head of MITI, were given more prominent positions in the cabinet and therefore were better positioned to lobby successfully for reform. Pressure from the unified opposition also motivated BN leaders to overcome strong *bumiputera* opposition to reform because no viable opposition parties lobbied to continue the affirmative action program unchanged and because failure to reform would only increase opposition support among those prominent in the business community. Even without a strong challenge from a *bumiputera*-focused opposition party, the BN was careful to announce a new *bumiputera* equity holding company program in conjunction with reformation of the FIC in order to counter indigenous complaints that such policies favored foreign investors over small local firms.[102]

The Malaysian reform experience therefore illustrates three key points. First, business groups were quick to change their policy preferences over FDI policy postcrisis. While supporting a heavily regulated, partially liberal investment policy was beneficial when debt finance and portfolio investment were readily available, the Malaysian government's response to its banking crisis led to large changes in credit allocation decisions in which large powerful firms found it increasingly difficult to obtain sweetheart deals for their financing needs. In the absence of subsidized credit, business groups began to lobby for liberalization of FDI policy. These policy demands were not immediately acceded to, however, because the ruling coalition needed to appease

[100] Pauline Ng, "Najib Expected to Trim Investment Panel's Role; Review of FIC Aimed at Boosting Foreign Investment Flows into Country," *The Business Times Singapore*, June 17, 2009.

[101] Hazlin Hassan, "KL Scraps 30% Equity Share for Bumis," *The Strait Times*, July 1, 2009.

[102] "Sweeping Changes to FIC, Toll Cut on the Cards," *The Malaysian Insider*, June 29, 2009.

bumiputera interests, which were traditional sources of electoral support. A history of racially motivated riots in response to policy actions perceived as antithetical to the spirit of the NEP made BN leaders particularly keen to avoid public confrontation that might create negative perceptions of Malaysia's political climate among potential investors.

It is important to note that while increased political contestation within Malaysia's competitive authoritarian electoral system did indeed motivate eventual reforms, interest groups in the country had different policy preference structures than theories that place democratization at the center of FDI liberalization processes assume. *Bumiputera* laborers were among the domestic groups most opposed to liberalization, while domestic business interests continually lobbied for liberalization in order to reap the benefits of easier access to foreign equity participation. The success of opposition parties in 2008 helped catalyze change because these groups gained support among urban capitalists. A labor-driven theory of FDI liberalization is not supported by this case.

A final key point is that policy change lagged shifting policy strategies of industrial capitalists, as found in news reporting and chamber of commerce statements, by a decade. A large reason for this delay was due to pressures from *bumiputera* groups to maintain equity restrictions and government screening authority over foreign acquisitions. Another significant factor, however, was the intransigence of elites on the FIC who were reluctant to cede their power. Successful reform of the screening authority was only achieved after a change in leadership of the ruling coalition and a subsequent cabinet reshuffle. Thus, it is important to note that while domestic business groups shifted their policy preferences for FDI policy after the government instituted important reforms to the banking sector after the 1997 crisis, these changes are best understood as creating a set of conditions conducive to, but not necessarily sufficient for, reform.

Conclusion

This chapter outlined the coevolution of banking and FDI policy in Malaysia and Indonesia from 1997 to 2013, with an emphasis on how disparate policy responses to the Asian financial crisis of 1997 affected credit allocation practices and therefore business groups' preferences for openness to FDI. Starting from a similar level of openness to FDI in

1997, the countries diverged widely in their investment restrictiveness. While Indonesia experienced some investment liberalization directly following the crisis due to IMF conditionality, Malaysia underwent much more substantial and sustained policy liberalization. In 2012, Malaysia's investment policy environment was at the average level of openness for a panel of 52 advanced and emerging economies. Indonesia, in contrast, was one standard deviation above the average level of restrictiveness in this same sample. Indonesia also saw significant policy backtracking from 2010 to 2013, when domestic business groups began a sustained lobbying effort to pursue additional restrictions on FDI.

I argue the divergent experiences with FDI policy in Indonesia and Malaysia after the crisis can be explained by development in each country's bank sector that altered elite strategic assessment of FDI openness. Indonesia's banking sector has become more state-dominated since 1997, while Malaysia privatized its state-owned banks in the aftermath of the crisis and pursued substantial prudential regulatory reform. Indonesian banking regulatory reform has not been as extensive as has Malaysia's, and credit allocation in the country has never fully recovered since the crisis. At the same time, Indonesian banks benefit greatly from repressive policies that push the cost of credit higher and that create strong incentives for the government to use preferential credit as a tool of coalition building. As a result, the most politically important Indonesian firms received preferential access to credit, while remaining firms face substantial financing constraints.

Documentation of prominent domestic business groups' lobbying efforts for FDI policy indicate Malaysian firms experienced a sharp change in policy preferences for FDI in the wake of the crisis when preferential credit was diminished and financing constraints were perceived as the largest impediments to business growth. Indonesian firms, however, became increasingly hostile to foreign direct equity, particularly after the banking sector restabilized after the crisis with a more prominent state-owned banking system. As a result, Indonesian FDI policy reform efforts stagnated and even reversed after an initial round of IMF-instigated liberalizations.

Comparing these two cases offers several interesting conclusions about the process of FDI reform. First, policy reform is most likely to occur when elite policy preferences for foreign investment change.

The Malaysian experience has been that elites have driven the process of FDI reform, while the Indonesian experience indicates elites are powerful blocking mechanisms when they are opposed to foreign equity entry. This finding runs counter to existing arguments about FDI liberalization that places great weight on the role of labor in a democratizing state at pushing reforms. Indeed, the UMNO, under the BN umbrella, has been able to maintain hegemonic party control in Malaysia while also gradually but substantially liberalizing the investment climate. Indonesia, on the other hand, has undergone a democratic transition, but anti-FDI elites have successfully impeded FDI policy reform.

Second, other explanations for FDI liberalization place great emphasis on the capacity of the IMF to be an agent of change. Indeed, we see that Indonesia initially experienced movements toward openness under IMF conditionality. Without elite support, however, reform efforts quickly stalled and eventually were partially reversed. Conversely, Malaysia underwent more gradual but sustained and substantial reform without the external pressure of IMF conditionality. Because elite interests undergird regulatory policies toward FDI, substantial policy liberalization cannot be forced through by external groups. For liberalization to take hold, business groups must believe policy openness will be in their interest.

Thus, the comparison of Malaysian and Indonesian FDI policy reforms after the 1997 crisis corroborates my central argument that FDI policy reform occurs when financing constraints shift dominant firms' preferences for openness. These cases more closely evaluate elite lobbying efforts for FDI policy as domestic credit allocation processes change, and indicate firms are more likely to view FDI positively when the state is less involved in the lending process. In conjunction with the previous chapter, these cases also show that FDI policy liberalization can experience reversal and that changes in the domestic credit allocation process can explain both levels of and changes to openness to FDI.

8 | *Implications of Elite-Driven Integration*

Throughout this book, I have employed mixed methodologies at multiple units of analysis to explore robustly the relationship between privileged firms, their loss of access to subsidized finance, and foreign direct investment (FDI) policy changes. While actual lobbying activity is challenging to uncover in one country, let alone cross-nationally, I use a variety of firm-, industry-, and country-level data to test several observable implications of the contention that large firms are likely to support and actively lobby for policies of openness toward FDI when they lose their privileged access to finance. I find substantial evidence that banking sector reforms precede FDI liberalization, that large firms are more likely to lobby their governments than are smaller firms, and that large firms face less financing constraints when they have some degree of foreign participation. I also find that industries that are more capital intensive are more likely to enact liberalizing policies, particularly around entry, when the banking sector is not able to direct subsidized credit to well-connected firms. The connection between the decline in privileged finance and FDI policy reforms is stronger in countries with domestic political institutions that empower business elites. A comparative case study of Indonesia and Malaysia provides a way to process trace changes to investment policies and demonstrates that business groups in Malaysia were champions of FDI reforms when they became credit constrained, while Indonesian business lobbying groups did not face the same financing shock after 1997 and instead were much more wary of multinational entry. As a whole, these empirical exercises lend considerable support to the claim that business interests often drive liberalization of FDI policy and that they do so to gain access to new sources of finance and business opportunities.

When Elites Manage Reform

What do we learn from a financing-constraints-driven explanation that we miss from other theories of economic integration? Usually, arguments about FDI liberalization narrowly and economic openness more broadly emphasize the power of economic liberalism to disrupt incumbents' rents and to foster more competitive and ultimately fairer economic and political markets. In this view, elites are obstacles to welfare-enhancing reforms. This argument has been made to bolster theories of democratization-driven economic liberalization.[1] In terse form, "innovations often erode political elites' incumbency advantage, increasing the likelihood that they will be replaced. Fearing replacement, political elites are unwilling to initiate economic and institutional change."[2] The presumption that opening markets to foreign investors, capital, and goods dislodges economic elites and fosters new innovation and standards of living permeates the discourse on the political economy of globalization.

This book suggest, however, scholars must rethink our understandings of how and why states adopt more open economic policies and for whose benefit these market reorientations occur. Politically important domestic firms demand privileged access to finance, and when local sources dry up, these firms can use their prominent connections to draw in foreign investment. These entrenched incumbents can generate rents under more open policy environments by promising foreign investors access to local policymakers and assistance navigating complex and unfamiliar commercial environments. By trading one form of privilege for another, these elites can adapt to new economic realities in ways that smaller enterprises, with fewer resources and fewer connections, cannot. In doing so, politically important domestic firms can deepen inequalities of opportunities and competitiveness by capitalizing on the opportunities that foreign firms present – access to finance, technology transfer, workforce skill upgrading, business-to-business (B2B) sales, and supply chain integration – while small and medium-size firms face upward pressure on wages and productivity that may force them into insolvency.

---

[1] Pandya (2016); Pinto (2013); Milner and Kubota (2005).
[2] Acemoglu and Guerrieri (2008), 129.

Stated differently, FDI liberalization can make markets less rather than more competitive. Of course, scholars have long recognized that multinational enterprises (MNEs) are likely to develop in industries with oligopolistic structures, but the general political economy framework for understanding the distributive effects of FDI has often overlooked the ways in which FDI inflows may further market concentration and split domestic capital as a relatively coherent interest bloc. Rather than provide access points to small firms to participate in global value chains, FDI liberalization may encourage industry consolidation and increase the cost of subsequent entry. In doing so, large and politically connected domestic firms may cast their lot with MNEs that can provide them greater access to finance and external markets, while smaller firms, potential start-ups, and entrepreneurs disconnected from ruling coalitions may be largely left out of newly formed networks of global production. This has implications for the immediate distributive effects of MNE entry as well as the more long-term influence of big business on domestic politics.

In the short term, FDI policy liberalization may reduce the viability of small and medium-size firms and reduce the pace of new firm formation. Indeed, there is already ample evidence that MNE entry can crowd out smaller firms.[3] However, much of the literature on the economic effects of FDI inflows focuses analytic attention on wage and productivity spillovers. To the extent that start-ups are essential to economic dynamism, concentration-induced barriers to entry may limit markets' potential over the long run. Because small and medium-size firms are important locations of employment for women and minority groups, consolidation has important negative implications for equity and justice.

That MNEs may impede new firm formation and subsequent innovation is at odds with standard treatments of FDI that emphasize the importance of MNEs in bringing research and development activity to emerging markets.[4] But market concentration in both the United States and around the world has increased markedly in recent years. At the same time, total factory productivity has leveled off. A rash of economics research has recently documented the correlation

---

[3] Alfaro and Chen (2018); de Backer and Sleuwaegen (2003).
[4] Evans (1979); Wellhausen (2013).

between market concentration and increased firm profits, decreased reinvestment, and increased inequality, at least in the United States.[5] These effects are substantively large. Profits in the United States have increased from 2.5 percent to 21 percent of gross domestic product (GDP) from 1984 to 2014.[6] Recent evidence finds that firm mergers do not effect productivity but increase markups by as much as 50 percent.[7] The theory and empirics presented in this book suggest that more liberal policies toward FDI may be at least partially to blame for these global trends.

In the longer term, economic consequences have more time to translate into political problems. As industries concentrate domestically and internationally, the political power of large firms becomes both more potent and more essential for their continued survival. Concentrated industries face fewer obstacles to collective action and also face a fractured and weak opposition. "Superstar" firms are afforded greater access to lawmakers because of their prominence and the weight of their contribution to economic growth. When the regulatory environment is complex, these incumbents have great incentives to push for their preferred policy outcomes, and policymakers are more likely to defer to industry "experts."[8] Political apparatuses become increasingly controlled by the oligarchs, and electoral processes become less likely to provide government accountability to mass publics.[9] These large firms are rewarded for their policy relevance; from 2009 to 2015, stock prices of companies whose CEOs visited the US White House increased by about 1 percent in the subsequent month.[10] Much of the current research on the effect of industry concentration on democratic accountability focuses on the United States; however, these findings echo earlier and emerging work on rent seeking and crony capitalism globally.[11]

---

[5] Autor et al. (2017); Barkai (2016); Baker and Salop (2015); Gutierrez and Pilippon (2017).
[6] Barkai (2016), 21.
[7] Blonigen and Pierce (2016).
[8] Culpepper (2011).
[9] Gilens and Page (2014); Zingales (2017).
[10] Brown and Huang (2017).
[11] See especially Faccio (2006) and Fisman (2001).

Our Current Moment

The analysis presented throughout this book takes a historical approach. The data mainly allow us to estimate the relationship between liberalizing changes to domestic banking sectors and regulations toward FDI. This is because of the global trend toward FDI liberalization that has characterized the 1990s through the early 2000s. These data show that it is the breakdown of financial repression regimes that leads to more open FDI policy environments. One may ask, Is the theory presented here relevant to today? There are at least two ways to approach this question. First, is a financing constraints theory of FDI regulation symmetric? That is, would movements toward more state-directed credit systems lead to greater regulation of FDI? Second, is the theory path dependent; once local firms integrate ownership and supply chains with foreign enterprises, do they still view their interests as distinct from FDI? Or do they align politically with global business? In this section, I briefly address these questions, although much more research is needed to examine these possibilities fully.

It is especially important to ask these questions now. The global political and economic order seems to be at an inflection point where political forces are increasingly agitating against the rules and beliefs that supported the cause of economic integration since the end of World War II. The economic nationalist turn in the United States under the Trump administration is the most prominent manifestation of a growing disillusionment with an open liberal order, but it is not the only example of reorientations toward more managed economic systems. The global financial crisis of 2007–2008 helped spark a backlash against financial capitalism in the West, as embodied by groups like Occupy Wall Street. Right-wing populism became an increasingly powerful political force in Europe. Beyond the West, many viewed the spectacular collapse of the Western financial system as a rebuke against the Washington Consensus view of open markets, open capital accounts, and limited state intervention in market activities.

A Restrictive Turn?

While no country has responded to the current environment by substantially closing its economy to multinational firms, FDI policy has become increasingly mixed in recent years. Reform to investor-state dispute settlement agreements has become a central focal point of a movement to reclaim the regulatory power of the state against state-less multinationals, with governments in emerging and advanced economies alike vowing to rescind or substantially overhaul MNEs' abilities to force states into arbitration. For example, India developed a new model bilateral investment treaty in 2016 that curtailed the amount of compensatory damages that MNEs could obtain through arbitration, required firms to exhaust local courts before turning to arbitration, and narrowed issues for which MNEs could claim mistreatment. Other countries have also sought to excise these arbitration clauses from their trade and investment agreements, including South Africa[12] and Indonesia.[13] The European Union (EU) has also indicated it will stop including such clauses in the trade agreements it negotiates.

Beyond arbitration clauses, the FDI regulatory environment has become more nuanced in other ways as well. The impulse to regulate and manage FDI more actively comes from two distinct sources: (1) a growing desire to use inward FDI strategically as part of a larger industrial policy and (2) concerns about the growing incidence of countries such as China using outward FDI strategically and as part of a broader set of development and security objectives.

The growing use of investment policy as part of a comprehensive industrial policy is an outgrowth of two related developments. First, there is mounting evidence that the development value of FDI is largely dependent on contextual factors such as host country "absorptive capacity," productive connections to local firms, and technology transfer.[14] Second, the 2008 financial crisis led many to view the policy prescriptions associated with the Washington Consensus as largely discredited, particularly in the wake of a steadily rising Chinese economy.

As a result, countries have sought to manage inward FDI more actively. This may be to ensure that domestic firms are likely to benefit from foreign firm activity, to placate labor concerns about access to well-paying and stable jobs, or a combination of the two. To this end,

---

[12] Andrew Misner, "New Dawn for South African Arbitration," *African Law and Business* February 13, 2018.

[13] Ben Bland and Shawn Donnan. "Indonesia to Terminate More Than 60 Bilateral Investment Treaties," *Financial Times* March 26, 2014.

[14] See, for example, Alfaro et al. (2004); Javorcik and Spatareanu (2008); Harding and Javorcik (2012); Irsova and Havranek (2013); Havranek and Irsova (2011).

governments have increasingly used more complex FDI regulations to encourage investment in industries and activities deemed beneficial to broader development objectives while discouraging or even excluding investment in other activities. Often, these measures include minimal restrictions on statutory limits on foreign ownership, but they do entail more stringent screening for investment licenses as well as increased local context requirements for domestically produced goods, either as a mandatory requirement or as a condition for receiving preferential tax treatment. For example, Indonesia simplified its investment licensing process in December 2017, but in that same year also increased mandatory local content requirements for smartphone manufacturers.[15] Angola, Namibia, and Egypt all introduced performance requirements for specific sectors or in order to obtain tax incentives in recent years.[16] Among the 100 country-level industrial policies the United Nations Conference on Trade and Development (UNCTAD) has reviewed, 20 percent of those in developing countries include performance requirements, while 25 percent of least developed countries and 3 percent of developed economies do.[17] Developing and least developed countries have also turned to some restrictions in entry and establishment regulation to support industrial policy, while over 90 percent of countries with industrial policies have enacted targeted incentives programs to encourage the types of investments they deem most beneficial to broader development strategies.[18]

While countries have increasingly turned to more active management of FDI to fulfill development objectives, they have also become more wary of the potential security concerns associated with inward investments. This has been especially concerning in developed economies, who worry that Chinese outward investment functions to transfer critical technologies and market power to firms that are either directly controlled by or indirectly connected to the Communist party. In the United States, a governmental agency called the Committee on Foreign Investment in the United States (CFIUS) reviews proposed cross-border mergers and acquisitions (M&As) that would

[15] United Nations Conference on Trade and Development (2018b), 151, United Nations Conference on Trade and Development (2018a), 15.
[16] United Nations Conference on Trade and Development (2018b), 151.
[17] United Nations Conference on Trade and Development (2018b), 144.
[18] Ibid.

result in the transfer of control of a US business to a foreign individual or enterprise, investigates transactions it deems may have national security concerns, and refers cases it believes problematic to the president for final review. This process has become increasingly contentious. From 2005 to 2007, less than 5 percent of transactions covered by the agency resulted in an investigation. Between 2014 and 2016, over 42 percent of covered transactions produced an investigation.[19] Recent high-profile examples of acquisitions blocked due to national security concerns include Lattice Semiconductors' proposed takeover by Canyon Bridge, a Chinese venture capital fund,[20] and the blocked acquisition of Qualcomm, another chip maker, by Broadcomm, a Singapore-based firm that even attempted to redomicile in the United States in order to complete the deal.[21] Beyond the United States, other countries have moved to exert more review over foreign acquisitions, especially by firms headquartered in emerging markets. The Australian Foreign Investment Review Board (FIRB) has applied increasingly exacting standards on foreign acquisitions, particularly related to real estate and infrastructure in recent years. Starting in 2016, FIRB assesses application fees for individuals and entities wishing to obtain permission for a covered investment; these fees start at AUD $2,000 for majority acquisition of a local business entity, but they can reach AUD $25,300 depending on the value of the business in question.[22] In the 2013–2014 fiscal year, over 74 percent of applications by value were approved without conditions.[23] In the 2016–2017 fiscal year, this rate plummeted to about 25 percent.[24] EU member states currently have authority over inward investment screening, but French and German leaders have recently pushed

---

[19] ww.treasury.gov/resource-center/international/foreign-investment/Documents/CFIUS_Stats_2014-2016.pdf

[20] David McLaughlin, and Jonathan Browning, "Lattice Weighs Seeking Trump's Intervention on China Deal," *Bloomberg Politics*, August 29, 2017. www.bloomberg.com/news/articles/2017-08-29/lattice-said-to-weigh-seeking-trump-intervention-on-china-deal

[21] Huileng Tan, "Here are the real reasons Trump blocked Broadcom's Qualcomm Takeover," *CNBC* March 13, 2018, www.cnbc.com/2018/03/13/trump-blocks-broadcoms-qualcomm-takeover-concerns-about-china-5g.html

[22] http://firb.gov.au/applications/estimator/

[23] Treasury of the Commonwealth of Australia, 2018, 24.

[24] Ibid.

for the development of a centralized investment screening authority. The plan for such a screening mechanism has largely been justified as a response to increased Chinese investment in strategic sectors.[25]

In sum, no country has fundamentally transformed its FDI policy environment from openness to closure in recent years, but we have seen a growing impulse to carve out more policy space for governments to exercise discretion in encouraging inward investment deemed beneficial while repelling MNEs that are seen as problematic from a development or security perspective. These developments have translated into policy in complicated ways. The Organisation for Economic Co-operation and Development (OECD) FDI Regulatory Restrictiveness Index has failed to show a measurable increase in FDI protectionism, largely driven by an emphasis on the absence of increases in statutory equity restrictions.[26] However, UNCTAD's Investment Policy Monitor has tracked a rather substantial uptick in restrictive measures in recent years. There was a significant upward tick in these measures just after the 2007–2008 financial crisis, largely driven by changes to investment measures among developed economies. From 2007 to 2013, about 25 percent of all investment policy measures were restrictive;[27] in contrast, through the 1990s, the share of restrictive regulatory changes never rose above 14 percent and was often less than 5 percent.[28] The first quarter of 2018 saw a sharp rise in restrictive measures, with 29 percent of all policy changes categorized as restrictive.[29]

Domestic Firms' Preferences After Liberalization

Given these developments, we may wish to examine two related issues. First, is a financing constraints theory of FDI regulation symmetrical? That is, if domestic firms drive FDI liberalization, do they also precipitate restrictions on foreign firms? And, if so, do they do so in response to changes in the local financing environment? Historically, it seems plausible that this theory can apply to the enactment of increasingly

[25] Jonathan Stearns, "Amid China M&A Drive, EU Rushes for Investment-Screening Deal," *Bloomberg Business*, 2018. www.bloomberg.com/news/articles/2018-03-04/amid-china-m-a-drive-eu-rushes-for-investment-screening-deal

[26] Thomsen and Mistura (2017).

[27] United Nations Conference on Trade and Development (2018b), 80.

[28] United Nations Conference on Trade and Development (2005b), 22.

[29] United Nations Conference on Trade and Development (2018a), 1.

restrictive policies toward inward direct investment in the middle of the twentieth century. As countries embraced tools of financial repression, domestic business interests often lobbied successfully to impose barriers to FDI. However, a lack of good data on investment restrictions prior to the 1970s makes this claim difficult to test more rigorously. In the current period, we also face difficulties in testing the conditions under which increased financial repression leads to FDI restrictions because we have not seen large-scale reversions to state control of the banking sector.

While observational data make it challenging to test the symmetry of a financing constraints theory at this time, we are better positioned to examine a related question: is this theory path dependent? In particular, we might explore whether domestic firms, once integrated in production chains and ownership structures with foreign entities, become more likely to view their interests as closely aligned with those of global firms. A financing constraints theory of FDI suggests well-connected domestic firms view integration with MNEs, either directly through M&A or indirectly through supply chains, as central to their profitability when they do not receive state support through subsidized credit. Thus, business interests related to investment regulation may become increasingly path dependent; as domestic firms view their fortunes as progressively connected with those of multinationals, they may become reluctant to push for restrictions on such firms.

I briefly explore this possibility by examining how participation in global value chains corresponds with the propensity to enact restrictive changes to FDI policies. To do this, I return to UNCTAD's data on FDI restrictions that I introduced in Chapter 2. While I would prefer to examine variations in the correlates of FDI restrictions at the industry level, this is not possible given the limits of the data. Restrictions in the dataset often apply generally rather than by sector, and separation issues make it challenging to run analyses on restrictions at the industry level. Rather than using a country-year unit of analysis, I add all restrictive measures enacted by a country from 2000 to 2015 and estimate a cross-sectional analysis. I do this because having the country–time period unit of analysis allows me to include my preferred measure for banking sector repression, which I explain below.[30] Thus, my dependent variable, *Total Restrictive*

---

[30] My results for backward linkages are robust to a time-series cross-sectional analysis with year fixed effects.

Measures, is the number of restrictive FDI policies implemented within a country over the 2000–2015 time period.

To test the relationship between global value chain integration and restrictive regulations, I use *Average Backward Links*, which comes from the OECD's trade in value-added dataset and measures the backward participation in global value chains by measuring the percentage of total gross exports of a country that include foreign value added. I average this yearly variable across its values from 2000 to 2015. Countries that export goods and services and that rely on a large percentage of intermediate inputs from foreign firms are well integrated into disaggregated supply chains. I anticipate that, under these conditions, domestic firms will view their interests as overlapping with multinational firms and will therefore be less likely to support restrictive policies toward FDI.

In this analysis, I also include *Total Change in Net Interest Margin* to measure how competitive the domestic banking sector is. High values of *Net Interest Margin* indicate low levels of competition; as explained in greater detail in Chapter 4, this proxies for greater government direction of credit markets. I take the first difference of *Net Interest Margin* and then add this cumulative change over the 2000–2015 time period. Countries with high values for *Total Change in Net Interest Margin* have experienced decreased competitiveness in the banking sector over the time period studied, while countries with low values on the measure have experience increased banking sector competitiveness. Countries that had total changes in this measure at least one standard deviation above the mean include Russia, Argentina, and Brunei. Countries that experienced decreases in *Net Interest Margin* greater than one standard deviation below the mean include Mexico, Turkey, Romania, and Lithuania.

Because a hallmark of industrial policy-oriented FDI regulation is the simultaneous use of liberalizing and restricting investment measures, I also include *Total Liberal Measures*, which sums all liberal FDI policies enacted over the time period. Tables 8.1 and 8.2 include descriptive statistics and a list of countries included in the analysis. Because my dependent variable is a count and diagnostics indicate overdispersion, I employ a negative binomial regression. Table 8.3 reports results. I caution that this analysis is meant to be primarily suggestive in nature; more extensive statistical inference exercises are necessary before drawing strong conclusions from these data.

Table 8.1. *Descriptive statistics*

Variable	Mean	Standard Deviation	N
Total Restrictive Measures	2.532	3.665	62
Average Backward Links	25.533	10.555	62
Total Δ Net Interest Margin	−1.752	2.600	62
Total Liberal Measures	13.742	18.204	62

Table 8.2. *Included cases*

Argentina	Croatia	Indonesia	Netherlands	South Africa
Australia	Cyprus	Ireland	New Zealand	South Korea
Austria	Czech Republic	Israel	Norway	Spain
Belgium	Denmark	Italy	Peru	Sweden
Brazil	Estonia	Japan	Philippines	Switzerland
Brunei	Finland	Latvia	Poland	Taiwan
Bulgaria	France	Lithuania	Portugal	Thailand
Cambodia	Germany	Luxembourg	Romania	Tunisia
Canada	Greece	Malaysia	Saudi Arabia	Turkey
Chile	Hong Kong	Malta	Singapore	United Kingdom
China	Hungary	Mexico	Slovak Republic	United States
Colombia	Iceland	Morocco	Slovenia	Vietnam
Costa Rica	India			

As Model 1 shows, the pooled data show that countries with a greater degree of backward linkages are statistically significantly less likely to enact a restrictive measure on FDI. A one standard deviation increase in backward linkages, holding all else at the mean, is associated with a 47.16 percent decrease in the likelihood of enacting a restrictive measure. While the coefficient estimate for *Total Change in Net Interest Margin* is signed as expected, the parameter is not statistically significant. Over the time period, there is not enough evidence to conclude that increases in banking sector concentration lead to restrictions on FDI. However, this is not surprising given the compression of this variable in the time period in question. Unless and until there are examples of countries undergoing dramatic reimpositions of financial repression, it will remain challenging to test directly the symmetrical nature of a financing constraints theory of FDI liberalization. As expected, enacting liberal FDI measures is associated

Table 8.3. *Global value chains, banking and FDI restrictions*

	Model 1	Model 2	Model 3
	2000–2015	Before 2008	After 2009
Average Backward Links	−0.046**	−0.022	−0.046**
	(0.02)	(0.02)	(0.02)
Total Δ Net Interest Margin	0.072	−0.031	0.083
	(0.06)	(0.08)	(0.14)
Total Liberal Measures	0.027**	0.047**	0.054**
	(0.01)	(0.02)	(0.02)
AIC	245.341	158.563	198.245
BIC	255.977	169.199	208.881
N	62	62	62

Constant not reported. Standard error in parentheses.
$^*p < 0.05$, $^{**}p < 0.01$

with an increased probability of implementing restrictive measures as well. A one standard deviation increase in liberal FDI policies increases the likelihood of a restrictive measure by about 48.6 percent. This finding is consistent with a growing use of a combination of liberalizing and restrictive measures to enact industrial policies that discriminate between "beneficial" and "harmful" FDI.

Models 2 and 3 disaggregate the sample by reestimating the equation for 2000–2007 and 2009–2015. Splitting the sample in this way allows us to uncover any differences in explanatory variable effect before and after the global financial crisis. If we interpret the 2008 crisis as a global credit crunch that may have generated increased financing constraints for large domestic firms, we may expect that domestic firms would be especially unlikely to support FDI restrictions after the crisis. Indeed, we find that the coefficient estimate for *Average Backward Links* is not statistically significant before the crisis period, but it is after 2008. This provides us with some suggestive evidence that countries for which domestic firms are well integrated into global supply chains were less likely to pursue restrictions on FDI after the crisis. While these data do not provide direct evidence that domestic firms, motivated by the pecuniary advantages afforded by links to MNEs, pushed to maintain an open investment environment, they are consistent with such an argument.

Investment Screening and Firm Lobbying Efforts

The empirical exercises reported above suggest that integration into global value chains makes FDI restrictions less likely, but they do not isolate the behavior of firms in working to shape the regulatory environment. One window into firms' preferences over FDI policy today is to look at how business groups have responded to increased attempts to rein in FDI that is seen as being contrary to national security interests. As mentioned above, many countries have recently reinvigorated their inward investment screening processes, and they have largely justified these measures as important to prevent hostile governments from acquiring sensitive intellectual property. Foreign acquisitions that are frequently scrutinized on these grounds usually involve what is called dual-use technology, that is technology that has both commercial and military purposes. For example, aerospace and semiconductor technologies are often considered strategically important industries. Restricting FDI for national security purposes has natural supporters among relevant government officials, who view their interests as aligned with protecting state power, and ordinary citizens, who are likely to view investments from adversarial countries with suspicion.[31] Thus, it would seem that there would be very little domestic opposition to restrictions on FDI that can be reasonably claimed to invoke national security concerns.

However, the experience of the United States suggests that globally oriented domestic firms create interesting challenges for governments who may wish to tighten regulations on FDI for national security reasons. In many cases, these firms view M&A screening as burdensome and suggest that national security concerns serve mainly as useful rhetoric to legitimate restrictions. For instance, in the Lattice Semiconductors case, the domestic firm fought hard to obtain CFIUS approval and pointed to several measures it and its buyer were willing to make in order to decrease governmental security concerns.[32] When the US Senate sought to expand CFIUS authority to review outward investment in China, large US firms with substantial international presence,

---

[31] Chilton et al. (forthcoming); Meunier et al. (2014).

[32] David McLaughlin and Jonathan Browning, "Lattice Weighs Seeking Trump's Intervention on China Deal," *Bloomberg Politics*, August 29, 2017. www.bloomberg.com/news/articles/2017-08-29/lattice-said-to-weigh-seeking-trump-intervention-on-china-deal

such as GE and IBM, successfully lobbied hard to quash the proposal, citing the importance of providing US firms the opportunity to pursue outward FDI in order to facilitate global competitiveness.[33] Industry groups have been active in pushing back against both inward and outward FDI regulatory measures proposed on national security grounds. The Information Technology Industry Council also lobbied against expansions to CFIUS that would cover outward joint venture investments in China.[34] The conservative American Legislative Exchange Council (ALEC), a nonprofit advocacy organization of conservative legislators and private sector representatives, has a model legislative bill designed to push state legislatures to encourage the US federal government to reduce export controls on dual-use technology.[35]

The US example of attempts to increase scrutiny of foreign investment, particularly around sensitive technologies, shows that domestic firms and trade groups often push back aggressively to prevent such measures. To what extent does this case, as well as the cross-sectional quantitative data explored above, provide insights into whether the theory advanced in this book remains relevant to the politics of today? In general, the available evidence suggests that a financing constraints explanation of elite-led FDI liberalization has strong path-dependent tendencies. As firms pushed for more open investment environments in order to access the finance and supplier contracts that MNEs could provide, domestic firms become more globally oriented and progressively develop shared preferences with global firms rather than view MNEs as adversaries. This means politics around FDI and global production networks may pit governments and workers against firms that see their interests as more aligned with a global business class than with a national context. Because no country has reimposed broad financial repression regulations in recent years, it is more difficult to test whether increased use of state-subsidized financing leads to domestic firms once again viewing MNEs as competitors to keep out of local markets.

---

[33] Shawn Donnan, "Senators Ditch Plans to Review US Outward Investments," *Financial Times*, May 15, 2018.
www.ft.com/content/a1fcfeec-57cf-11e8-bdb7-f6677d2e1ce8

[34] Saleha Mohsin and Ben Brody, "A Top Senate Republican Slams Tech Lobby's CFIUS Bill Push," *Bloomberg Politics*, April 19, 2018.
www.bloomberg.com/news/articles/2018-04-19/top-senate-republican-cornyn-slams-tech-lobby-s-cfius-bill-push

[35] American Legislative Exchange Council (2012).

However, the quantitative analysis presented here suggests that domestic firms are unlikely to view their interests as distinct from foreign enterprises unless the global value chains they once participated in fell apart. While it once seemed unimaginable that global value chains would recede in importance, recent geopolitical events seem already to have negatively affected complex integration. The share of foreign value added in global trade, a leading indicator of global value chains, has begun to decline after 25 years of rapid growth.[36] The coming years will be an important out-of-sample test for the durability of a financing constraints theory of FDI regulation.

Future Directions

My analysis also opens new questions that demand further exploration. First, analysis from 2000 onward suggests that all countries, regardless of their banking sector structure, seem to face greater pressure to entice foreign investment than in prior years. At the same time, it seems that countries are engaging in complex policy changes, simultaneously liberalizing components of their investment law while placing greater restrictions in others. This increased complexity underscores the similarities in investment policy politics to the politics of trade. While most countries have steadily increased openness to foreign investment in recent decades, they have not done so unconditionally. Just as with trade, investment policies have substantial concentrated effects – both costly and beneficial – while they affect general publics only diffusely. These distributive dynamics, coupled with the highly technical and low salience nature of much of the regulatory space, generate opportunities for business elites to use their influence to fashion investment policy in their interests. Interest group dynamics are key to understanding why countries enact the constellation of investment policy regulations that they do.

This central insight – that investment policy is governed by interest group politics and that the domestic financing environment helps to structure firms' policy preferences – generates an expansive and exciting research agenda for future scholarship. Here, I briefly outline a few research extensions that I believe are most interesting theoretically and from a policy perspective.

---

[36] United Nations Conference on Trade and Development (2018b), 22.

Firm-Level Heterogeneity and Investment Preferences

First, the theory forwarded in this book is heavily influenced by recent developments in new-new trade theory that pushes analytic focus downward from country or industry to characteristics specific to the firm. While I use firm-level surveys to establish the characteristics of firms that make them more likely to lobby and also increase their propensity for perceiving themselves to be credit constrained, much more can be done empirically to explore how firm characteristics such as size, market share, and existing political and market connectivity influences both their policy preferences and their success at influencing regulations. Doing so will require creativity and substantial data collection efforts. However, using databases such as Orbis, which collects balance sheet data on over 200 million publicly traded and privately held firms, can enable scholars to measure external finance dependence at the firm level. This, paired with data on firm meetings with government officials, and the stock market performance of publicly traded firms in the aftermath of discrete policy changes can connect firm-level preferences more closely to political behavior and outcomes. Qualitative analysis that uses structured interviews with firms and policymakers, archival exploration of firm-lobbying behavior and correspondence with government officials, and fieldwork at major industry conventions can supplement quantitative analysis with grounded process-tracing.

MNE Policy, Market Concentration, and Innovation

Second, future research should explore the effect of MNE entry on market concentration, start-ups, and domestically produced and owned innovation. Above, I outline recent scholarship in economics that explores concentration's effects on profits, reinvestment, and inequality, primarily in the US context. More can be done to extend these analyses beyond the United States and to explore how policies toward foreign investment influence these effects. Attention to variations in investment policy and promotion strategy are essential here. Under what conditions does multinational entry exacerbate problems associated with increased market concentration? What policies provide complementary finance, technology, and skill upgrading that can foster rather than impede indigenous start-ups and innovation? How do the FDI-induced effects on concentration translate into economic and political inequality? What happens to interest group coalitions when multinationals become more prominent in economic life. Do they become more influential?[37] Or do they become easy targets for expropriation and scapegoating? What happens to the political influence of domestic firms under such conditions?

Emerging markets have increasingly been sources of FDI rather than just recipients. According to the most recent numbers, between 25 and 40 percent of FDI flows in a given year emanate from developing countries.[38] These investments are made more and more often by state-owned enterprises (SOEs) – just 1.5 percent of SOEs that invest abroad now own close to 10 percent of all foreign affiliates globally.[39] Especially as emerging markets such as China engage in outward FDI through strategic asset buying, for example, the China National Chemical Corporation's recent acquisition of the Swiss agribusiness company Syngenta, we see *global* consolidation of several industries and the expanded prominence of state-owned entities in markets beyond their own. How do these developments effect markups, labor share of income, and industry investment in research and development at a global level? How can governments construct effective antitrust policies when consolidation occurs globally? And what interest group politics undergird this policy space?

Sensitive FDI and Public Opinion

Third, this book explores elite-level politics investment policy formation because FDI regulation is rarely salient to mass publics. However, this does not undermine the idea that publics can, under certain circumstances, greatly influence FDI policy. Understanding the conditions under which publics are likely to be aware of and sufficiently mobilized around FDI policy is important because it can tell us when FDI politics will move from the quiet to the very loud. FDI policies may be entering the public conversation in a sustained and influential way, especially with global industry consolidation, growing concern about the monopoly status of many multinational firms, and acquisitions by SOEs of strategic assets. Indeed, the discussion above about FDI

---

[37] Malesky (2009).
[38] United Nations Conference on Trade and Development (2017).
[39] Ibid. xi.

screening and national security concerns underscores this point. Under what conditions might FDI policy become sufficiently salient to influence electoral politics? In the realm of corporate governance laws, Culpepper argues scandals can create windows of salience in which issues that are typically "quiet politics" temporarily achieve sufficient public interest to demand political accountability.[40] What conditions create windows of salience for FDI policy? Consider the increased frequency of CFIUS investigations and presidential blockage of inward investment in the United States, as discussed above. Along with the recent examples of Lattice and Qualcomm, 55 of 196 transactions investigated by CFIUS between 2014 and 2016 were withdrawn or rejected.[41] This is a sharp increase from historical patterns; from 2009 to 2011, CFUIS investigated 100 deals and 13 were withdrawn or rejected.[42] Survey experimental data suggest that US publics hold negative opinions of cross-border M&As when investing firms are from countries that are relatively closed to US investment.[43] However, more can be done to uncover whether these opinions have sufficient salience to influence voting behavior. While the nationality of investors may be important to opinion formation, industry characteristics such as sensitivity to national security and market concentration might be equally or more influential. Beyond M&As, we might consider whether such concerns lead to the cancellation of greenfield investment deals, and whether and under what conditions antipathy toward foreign firms may render the offering of investment incentives politically costly. In other words, under what conditions do FDI politics become "loud"? When publics drive policy, in which direction do they drive it?

It is important to develop better theoretical purchase over the relationship between FDI policy and public opinion for several reasons. As the previous section made clear, recent years have seen an increase in attempts to regulate MNE entry and activity more closely. While I provide some evidence that domestic firms that are globally oriented push back against these restrictive measures, a firm-driven financing constraints theory of FDI regulation does not completely explain where the demand for these regulations come from. Existing related

---

[40] Culpepper (2011).
[41] Committe on Foreign Investment in the United States (2016).
[42] Committe on Foreign Investment in the United States (2012).
[43] Chilton et al. (forthcoming).

research yields contradictory findings. The role of large firms in lobbying against these changes contradicts democracy-based theories of liberalization. At the same time, studies of investment incentives suggest politicians are rewarded for attracting foreign investment, either at the ballot box in democracies or from party leaders among single-party regimes.[44] But, as mentioned above, voters in the United States are likely to view foreign acquisitions unfavorably when the acquiring partner is domiciled in a country that has relatively illiberal economic policies.[45] None of these theories provides much analytic purchase over the politics that drive countries to embrace more complex strategies of regulation and promotion of varying types of FDI. Thus, more work remains to discover the conditions under which ordinary citizens view FDI policy as sufficiently salient to form opinions about it; when these opinions will drive political behavior and when the interests of smaller, less globally connected firms prevail over the interests of large, domestic, internationally engaged enterprises.

Beyond FDI

Finally, the theory articulated and tested in this book has implications for research outside the scholarship on FDI. First, scholars should consider how financing constraints theories might apply to other areas of economic policy, such as trade. Doing so will have the added benefit of helping to better integrate scholarship on FDI and trade into a united literature that explores the politics of global production, a development others have called for.[46] Thinking more broadly the financing constraints theory that undergirds this book has broader implications for how political scientists conceptualize and discuss power. While power is multidimensional, most theorists have emphasized four types of power: compulsory, institutional, structural, and productive power.[47] Less explored is the power of adaptation. In the context of FDI policy, politically connected firms have the resources necessary to adapt to changing global and local circumstances. Smaller firms do not. We can imagine other areas such as climate change in which the power

---

[44] Jensen and Malesky (2018).
[45] Chilton et al. (forthcoming).
[46] Pandya (2016).
[47] Barnett and Duvall (2005).

of adaption is particularly important for understanding survival. The characteristics associated with adaptive power may differ in various contexts. In armed conflict we often think of small forces as being more agile and capable of adapting to challenging environments. Scholarship on guerrilla groups often emphasize this. More abstractly, size is often associated with clumsiness and lack of agility. Widely shared metaphors often stress this "David versus Goliath" attitude. For example, the adaptive capacity of a small boat is much better than a large ocean liner when faced with an obstacle around which to maneuver. Yet, in other circumstances, adaptation requires investments, secure long-term cash flow, and patience.

We can do much more to explore, both theoretically and empirically, when it is beneficial to be small and agile versus large and well-resourced. By doing so, we can answer more fundamental questions about the ultimately normative questions regarding globalization-induced concentration and agglomeration versus opposing instincts wedded to local communities and small-scale activities. To echo a claim made much earlier in this book – the most influential cleavage in political economic life may not be based on factor of production or industrial activity, but instead on size. If so, scholars and policymakers must do more to make their empirical analyses relevant to publics that are concerned that globalization disadvantages small units over large and reinforces and accelerates preexisting inequalities rather than moderating them. In an age that is increasingly cynical toward economic integration and an open global society, the continued viability of a liberal world order may rest on the development of policy options that can reverse the worse excesses of globalization and protect small units from being overwhelmed by the benefits of bigness.

References

Abiad, Abdul, Detragiache, Enrica, and Tressel, Thierry. 2010. A New Database of Financial Reforms. *IMF Staff Papers*, 57(2), 281–302.

Abiad, Abdul, and Mody, Ashoka. 2005. Financial Reform: What Shakes It? What Shapes It? *American Economic Review*, 95(1), 66–88.

Acemoglu, Daron, and Guerrieri, Veronica. 2006 (August). Capital Deepening and Non-balanced Economic Growth. *Journal of Political Economy*, 116(3), 467–498.

Adler, Matthew, and Hufbauer, Clyde. 2008. *Policy Liberalization and FDI Growth, 1982 to 2006*. Working Paper Series 08-7. Washington, DC: Peterson Institute for International Economics.

Aguiar, Mark, and Gopinath, Gita. 2005. Fire-Sale Foreign Direct Investment and Liquidity Crises. *Review of Economics and Statistics*, 87(3), 605–618.

Aitken, Brian, Hanson, Gordon H., and Harrison, Anne E. 1997. Spillovers, Foreign Investment, and Export Behavior. *Journal of International Economics*, 43(1–2), 103–132.

Aitken, Brian, Harrison, Anne E., and Lipsey, Robert E. 1996. Wages and Foreign Ownership: A Comparative Study of Mexico, Venezuela, and the United States. *Journal of International Economics*, 40(3–4), 345–371.

Aizenman, Joshua. 2005. Opposition to FDI and Financial Shocks. *Journal of Development Economics*, 77, 467–476.

Akerlof, George A., and Romer, Paul M. 1993. Looting: The Economic Underworld of Bankruptcy for Profit. *Brookings Papers on Economic Activity*, 2, 1–73.

Alfaro, Laura, Chandra, Areendam, Kalemli-Ozcan, Sebnem, and Sayek, Selin. 2004. FDI and Economic Growth: The Role of Local Financial Markets. *Journal of International Economics*, 64(1), 89–112.

Alfaro, Laura, and Chen, Maggie. 2012. Surviving the Global Financial Crisis: Foreign Ownership and Establishment Performance. *American Economic Journal: Economic Policy*, 4(3), 30–55.

Alfaro, Laura, and Chen, Maggie X. 2018. Selection and Market Reallocation: Productivity Gains from Multinational Production. *American Economic Journal: Economic Policy*, 10(2), 1–38.

Alt, James, and Gilligan, Michael J. 1994. The Political Economy of Trading States: Factor Specificity, Collective Action Problems and Domestic Political Institutions. *Journal of Political Philosophy*, **2**, 165–92.

American Legislative Exchange Council. 2012 (October). *Resolution to Reform Export Control Regulation of Dual-Use and Defense Items*. Model Bill. ALEC.

Andrianaivo, Mihasonirina, and Yartey, Charles Amo. 2010. Understanding the Growth of African Financial Markets. *African Development Review*, **22**(3), 394–418.

Ang, James B. 2009. *Financial Development and Economic Growth in Malaysia*. London, UK: Routledge.

Antras, Pol. 2003 (May). *Firms, Contracts, and Trade Structure*. NBER Working Paper Series 9740. Cambridge, MA: National Bureau of Economic Research.

Arce, Moisés. 2008. The Repoliticization of Collective Action after Neoliberalism in Peru. *American Politics and Society*, **50**, 37–62.

Arndt, Heinz Wolfgang. 1971. Banking in Hyperinflation and Stabilisation. Pages 359–395 of: Glassburner, B. (ed.), *The Economy of Indonesia*. Ithaca, NY: Cornell University Press.

Arndt, Heinz Wolfgang, and Suwidjana, Njoman. 1982. The Jakarta Dollar Market. *Bulletin of Indonesian Economic Studies*, **28**, 35–65.

Asami, Tadahiro. 2000. Non-performing Loans in East Asia. *Institute for International Monetary Affairs Newsletter*, **8**(2), 1–8.

Asian Development Bank. 2005. *Improving the Investment Climate in Indonesia*. Asian Development Bank, Available at: www.adb.org/sites/default/ files/publication/29709/improving-investment-climate-ino.pdf

Association of Southeast Asian Nations. 1999 (November). *ASEAN Investment Report 1999: Trends and Developments in Foreign Direct Investment*. Jakara: ASEAN.

Athukorala, Prema-Chandra. 2003. Foreign Direct Investment in Crisis and Recovery: Lessons from the 1997–1998 Asian Crisis. *Australian Economic History Review*, **43**(2), 197–213.

Athukorala, Prema-Chandra. 2010. *Malaysian Economy in Three Crises*. Departmental Working Papers 2010–2012. Canberra: The Australian National University, Arndt-Corden Department of Economics.

Autor, David, Dorn, David, Katz, Lawrence F., Patterson, Christina, and Reenen, John Van. 2017. Concentrating on the Fall of the Labor Share. *American Economic Review*, **107**(5), 180–185.

Baker, Jonathan B., and Salop, Steven C. 2015. Antitrust, Competition Policy, and Inequality. *The Georgetown Law Journal Online*, **104**, 1.

Baldwin, Robert E. 1985. *The Political Economy of US Import Policy*. Vol. 2. Cambridge, MA: MIT Press.

Bandelj, Nina. 2008. Economic Objects as Cultural Objects: Discourse on Foreign Investment in Post-Socialist Europe. *Socio-Economic Review*, 6, 671–702.

Barkai, Simcha. 2016 (November). *Declining Labor and Capital Shares*. New Working Paper Series 2. Stigler Center for the Study of the Economy and the State. Chicago, IL: University of Chicago.

Barnett, Michael, and Duvall, Raymond. 2005. Power in International Politics. *International Organization*, 59(1), 39–75.

Bartels, Larry M. 2016. *Unequal Democracy*. 2nd ed. Princeton, NJ: Princeton University Press.

Beck, Nathaniel, and Katz, Jonathan N. 2011. Modeling Dynamics in Time-Series-Cross-Section Political Economy Data. *Annual Review of Political Science*, 14, 331–352.

Bihandi. 1995. *Financial Sector Deregulation: Banking Development and Monetary Policy – The Indonesian Experience*. Jakarta: Institut Bankir Indonesia.

Blalock, Garrick, and Gertler, Paul J. 2005. Foreign Direct Investment and Externalities: The Case for Public Intervention. Chap. 4, pages 73–106 of: Moran, Theodore H., Graham, Edward M., and Blostrӧm, Magnus (eds), *Does Foreign Direct Investment Promote Development?* Washington, DC: Institute for International Economics.

Blomstrom, Magnus, and Kokko, Ari. 1997. *How Foreign Investment Affects Host Countries*. International Economics Department Policy Research Working Paper 1745. Washington, DC: World Bank.

Blonigen, Bruce A., and Pierce, Justin R. 2016. *Evidence for the Effects of Mergers on Market Power and Efficiency*. Finance and Economics Discussion Series 2016-082. Board of Governors of the Federal Reserve System, https://doi.org/10.17016/FEDS.2016.082.

Bluedorn, John, Duttagupta, Rupa, Guajardo, Jaime, and Topalova, Petia. 2013 (August). *Capital Flows Are Fickle: Anytime, Anywhere*. Working Paper WP/13/183. Washington, DC: International Monetary Fund.

Borensztein, Eduardo, De Gregori, Jose, and Lee, Jong-Wha. 1998. How Does Foreign Direct Investment Affect Economic Growth. *Journal of International Economics*, 45(1), 115–135.

Brambor, Thomas, Clark, William Roberts, and Golder, Matt. 2006. Understanding Interaction Models: Improving Empirical Analyses. *Political Analysis*, 14, 63–82.

Brooks, Sarah M. 2004. Explaining Capital Account Liberalization in Latin America: A Transitional Cost Approach. *World Politics*, 56(3), 389–430.

Brooks, Sarah M. 2007. When Does Diffusion Matter? Explaining the Spread of Structural Pension Reforms across Nations. *Journal of Politics*, 69(3), 701–715.

Brooks, Sarah M., and Kurtz, Marcus J. 2012. Paths to Financial Policy Diffusion: Statist Legacies in Latin America's Globalization. *International Organization*, **66**, 95–128.

Brown, Cynthia J. 2002. Foreign Direct Investment and Small Firm Employment in Northern Mexico: 1987–1996. *Entrepreneurship and Regional Development*, **14**, 175–191.

Brown, Jeffrey R., and Huang, Jiekun. 2017. *All the President's Friends: Political Access and Firm Value*. Working Paper 23356. Cambridge, MA: NBER.

Bueno de Mesquito, Bruce, Smith, Alistar, Siverson, Randolph M., and Morrow, James. 2003. *The Logic of Political Survival*. Cambridge, MA: MIT Press.

Campello, Murillo, Graha, John R., and Harvey, Campbell R. 2010. The Real Effects of Financial Constraints: Evidence from a Financial Crisis. *Journal of Financial Economics*, **97**, 470–487.

Carkovic, Maria, and Levine, Ross. 2005. Does Foreign Direct Investment Accelerate Economic Growth? Chap. 8, pages 195–220 of: Moran, Theodore (ed.), *The Impact of Foreign Direct Investment on Development: New Measurements, New Outcomes, New Policy Approaches*. Washington, DC: Institute for International Economics.

Chair, Anusha, and Gupta, Nandini. 2008. Incumbents and Protectionisms: The Political Economy of Foreign Entry Liberalization. *Journal of Financial Economics*, **88**(3), 633–656.

Chilton, Adam S., Milner, Helen V., and Tingley, Dustin H. Forthcoming. Reciprocity and Public Opposition to Foreign Direct Investment. *British Journal of Political Science*.

Cho, Yoon Je. 2001. The Role of Poorly Phased Liberalization in Korea's Financial Crisis. Pages 157–187 of: Caprio, Gerard, Honohan, Patrick, and Stiglitz, Joseph E. (eds), *Financial Liberalization: How Far, How Fast?* Cambridge, MA: Cambridge University Press.

Chor, Davin, and Manova, Kalina. 2012. On the Cliff and Back? Credit Conditions and International Trade During Financial Crisis. *Journal of International Economics*, **87**, 117–133.

Chou, C. 1999. Indonesian Banks: Survival of the Fittest. Pages 35–72 of: Asian Development Bank (ed), *Rising to the Challenge in Asia: A Study of Financial Markets*. Manila, Philippines: Asian Development Bank.

Chwieroth, Jeffrey M. 2010. *Capital Ideas: The IMF and the Rise of Financial Liberalization*. Princeton, NJ: Princeton University Press.

Cihak, Martin, Demirguc-Kunt, Ash, Feyen, Erik, and Levine, Ross. 2012. *Benchmarking Financial Systems around the World*. Policy Research Working Paper Series Number 6175. Washington, DC: The World Bank.

Claessens, Stijn. 2006. Corporate Governance and Development. *The World Bank Research Observer*, 21(1), 91–122.

Claessens, Stijn, Djankov, Simeon, Fan, Joseph P. H., and Lang, Larry H. P. 2002. Disentangling the Incentive and Entrenchment Effects of Large Shareholdings. *Journal of Finance*, 57(6), 2741–2771.

Claessens, Stijn, Djankov, Simeon, and Lang, Larry H.P. 2000. The Separation of Ownership and Control in East Asian Corporations. *Journal of Financial Economics*, 58(1), 81–112.

Claessens, Stijn and Van Horen, Neeltje. 2012. Being a Foreigner Among Domestic Banks: Asset or Liability? *Journal of Banking and Finance*, 36(5), 1276–1290.

Cole, David C., and Slade, Betty F. 1999. *Building a Modern Financial System: The Indonesia Experience*. New York, NY: Cambridge University Press.

Committe on Foreign Investment in the United States. 2012. *Covered Transactions, Withdrawals, and Presidential Decisions 2008–2012*. Washington, DC: US Treasury Department, Available at: www.treasury.gov/resource-center/international/foreign-investment/Documents/CFIUS%20Stats%202008-2012.pdf

Committe on Foreign Investment in the United States. 2016. *Covered Transactions, Withdrawals, and Presidential Decisions 2008–2012*. Washington, DC: US Treasury Department. Available at: www.treasury.gov/resource-center/international/foreign-investment/Documents/CFIUS%20Stats%202008-2012.pdf

Cook, Malcolm. 2008. *Banking Reform in Southeast Asia: The Region's Decisive Decade*. Studies in the Growth Economies of Asia. New York, NY: Routledge.

Cornett, Marcia Millon, Guo, Lin, Khaksari, Shahriar, and Tenranian, Hassan. 2010. The Impact of State Ownership on Performance Differences in Privately-Owned Versus State-Owned Banks: An International Comparison. *Journal of Financial Intermediation*, 19(1), 74–94.

Crespo, Nuno, and Fontoura, Maria Paula. 2006. Determinant Factors of FDI Spillovers – What Do We Really Know? *World Development*, 35(3), 410–425.

Cruz, Ceci, Keefer, Philip, and Scartascini, Carlos. 2016. *The Database of Political Institutions 2015*. Database. Inter-American Development Bank, Available at: https://publications.iadb.org/handle/11319/7408.

Culpepper, Pepper. 2011. *Quiet Politics and Business Power: Corporate Control in Europe and Japan*. Cambridge, MA: Cambridge University Press.

Damijan, Joze P., Rojec, Matija, Majcen, Boris, and Knell, Mark. 2013. Impact of Firm Heterogeneity on Direct and Spillover Effects of FDI:

Micro-Evidence from Ten Transition Countries. *Journal of Comparative Economics*, **41**, 895–922.

de Backer, Koen, and Sleuwaegen, Leo. 2003. Does Foreign Direct Investment Crowd out Domestic Entrepreneurship? *Review of Industrial Organization*, **22**, 67–84.

DeBoef, Suzanna. 2001. Modeling Equilibrium Relationships: Error Correction Models with Strongly Autoregressive Data. *Political Analysis*, 1, 78–94.

Delhaise, P.F. 1998. *The Implosion of the Banking and Finance Systems*. Singapore: John Wiley & Sons.

Dell'Ariccia, Giovanni, Detragiache, Enrica, and Rajan, Raghuram. 2008. The Real Effect of Banking Crises. *Journal of Financial Intermediation*, **17**, 89–112.

Demirguc-Kunt, Asli, and Levine, Ross. 2001. *Financial Structure and Economic Growth: A Cross-Country Comparison of Banks, Markets, and Development*. Cambridge, MA: MIT Press.

Denisova, Irina, Eller, Markus, Frye, Timothy, and Zhuravskaya, Ekaterina. 2009. Who Wants to Revise Privatization? The Complementarity of Market Skills and Institutions. *American Journal of Political Science*, **103**(2), 284–304.

Denizer, Cevdet, Desai, Raj M., and Gueorguiev, Nikolay. 1998 (September). *The Political Economy of Financial Repression in Transition Economies*. Policy Research Paper 2030. Washington, DC: World Bank.

Desai, Mihir A., Foley, C. Fritz., and Forbes, K. 2008. Financial Constraints and Growth: Multinational and Local Firm Responses to Currency Depreciations. *Review of Financial Studies*, **21**(6), 2857–2888.

Desbordes, Rodolphe, and Vauday, Julien. 2007. The Political Influence of Foreign Firms in Developing Countries. *Economics and Politics*, **19**(3), 421–451.

Detragiache, Enrica, and Gupta, Poonam. 2004. *Foreign Banks in Emerging Market Crises: Evidence form Malaysia*. IMF Working Paper 04/129. Washington, DC: International Monetary Fund.

Djiwandono, J. Soedradjad. 2005. *Bank Indonesia and the Crisis: An Insider's View*. Singapore: Institute of Southeast Asian Studies.

Dobson, W., and Jacquet, P. 1998. *Financial Services Liberalization in the WTO*. Washington, DC: Institute for International Economics.

Doidge, Craig, Karolyi, G. Andrew, and Stulz, Rene M. 2004. Why Are Foreign Firms Listed in the U.S. Worth More? *Journal of Financial Economics*, **71**(2), 205–238.

Dominguez, Jorge I. 1982. Business Nationalism: Latin American National Business Attitudes and Behavior toward Multinational Enterprises.

Pages 16–68 of: Dominguez, Jorge I. (ed), *Economic Issues and Political Conflict: US–Latin American Relations.* London: Butterworth Science.

Doraisami, Anita. 2014. Macro-economic Policy Responses to Financial Crises in Malaysia, Indonesia and Thailand. *Journal of Contemporary Asia*, **44**(4), 581–598. doi:10.1080/00472336.2014.923636.

Dorobantu, Sinziana Paulina Ruxandra. 2010. *Political Competition and the Regulation of Foreign Direct Investment.* Ph.D. Dissertation. Duke University.

Driffield, Nigel, and Firma, Sourafel. 2003. Regional Foreign Direct Investment and Wage Spillovers: Plant Level Evidence from the Electronics Industry. *Oxford Bulletin of Economics and Statistics*, **65**(4), 453–474.

Dunning, John H. 1970. *Studies in International Investment.* London: Allen and Unwin.

Dunning, John H. 1988. The Eclectic Paradigm of International Production: A Restatement and Some Possible Extensions. *Journal of International Business Studies*, **19**(1), 1–31.

Dunning, John H. 2009. Location and the Multinational – A Neglected Factor? *Journal of International Business Studies*, **40**, 5–19.

Dunning, John H., and Rugman, Alan M. 1985. The Influence of Hymer's Dissertation on the Theory of Foreign Direct Investment. *American Economic Review*, **75**(2), 228–232.

Dyck, Andrew, and Zingales, Luigi. 2004. Private Benefits of Control: An International Comparison. *Journal of Finance*, **59**(2), 537–600.

Edwards, Sebastián. 1984. *The Order of Liberalization of the External Sector in Developing Countries.* Essays in International Finance 156. Princeton, NJ: Princeton University.

Ehrlich, Sean. 2011. *Access Points: An Institutional Theory of Policy Bias and Policy Complexity.* Oxford: Oxford University Press.

Eichengreen, Barry. 2001. Capital Account Liberalization: What Do the Cross-Country Studies Tell Us? *World Bank Economic Review*, **15**(3), 341–365.

Eichengreen, Barry, and Leblang, David. 2003. Capital Account Liberalization and Growth: Was Mr. Mahathir Right? *International Journal of Finance and Economics*, **8**(3), 205–224.

Eichengreen, Barry, and Mussa, Michael. 1998. Capital Account Liberalization and the IMF. *Finance and Development*, **35**(4), 16.

Elkins, Zachary, Guzman, Andrew T., and Simmons, Beth A. 2006. Competing for Captial: The Diffusion of Bilateral Investment Treaties, 1960–2000. *International Organization*, **60**(4), 811–846.

Engle, Robert F., and Granger, Clive W. J. 1987. Co-Integration and Error Correction: Representation, Estimation, and Testing. *Econometrica*, 55(2), 251–276.

Enoch, Charles, Frecuat, Olivier, and Kovanen, Arto. 2003. Indonesia's Banking Crisis: What Happened and What Did We Learn? *Bulletin of Indonesian Economic Studies*, 39(1), 75–92.

Ernst and Young. 2017. *Transactions 2017: Inbound M& Takes the Center Stage*.

European Bank for Reconstruction and Development. 2005. *Transition Report 2005: Business in Transition*. London: EBRD.

Evans, Peter. 1979. *Dependent Development: The Alliance of Multinational State and Local Capital in Brazil*. Princeton, NJ: Princeton University Press.

Evenett, Simon J., and Fritz, Johannes. 2016. *FDI Recovers? The 20th Global Trade Alert Report*. Global Trade Alert. Centre for Economic Policy Research, London.

Faccio, Mara. 2006. Politically Connected Firms. *American Economic Review*, 96(1), 369–386.

Feenstra, Robert C. 1999. Facts and Fallacies about Foreign Direct Investment. Pages 331–350 of: Feldstein, Martin (ed), *International Capital Flows*. Chicago, IL: University of Chicago Press and NBER.

Feenstra, Robert C., and Hanson, Gordon H. 1997. Foreign Direct Investment and Relative Wages: Evidence from Mexico's Maquiladoras. *Journal of International Economics*, 42(3–4), 371–393.

Feenstra, Robert C., and Taylor, Alan M. 2014. *International Economics*. 3 ed. New York, NY: Worth Publishers.

Feliciano, Zaida M., and Lipsey, Robert E. 2006. Foreign Ownership and Wages in the United States, 1987–1992. *Contemporary Economic Policy*, 24(1), 74–91.

Fernández, Andrés, Klein, Michael W., Rebucci, Alessandro, Schindler, Martin, and Uribe, Martín. 2015 (February). *Capital Control Measures: A New Dataset*. IMF Working Papers 15/80, Washington, DC: International Monetary Fund.

Fernández, Raquel, and Rodrik, Dani. 1991. Resistance to Reform: Status Quo Bias in the Presence of Individual-Specific Uncertainty. *American Economic Review*, 81(December), 1146–1155.

Figlio, David N., and Blonigen, Bruce A. 2000. The Effects of Foreign Direct Investment on Local Communities. *Journal of Urban Economics*, 48(2), 338–363.

Fisman, Raymond. 2001. Estimating the Value of Political Connections. *American Economic Review*, 91(4), 1095–1102.

Forbes, Kristin J., and Warnock, Francis E. 2012. Capital Flow Waves, Surges, Stops, Flight, and Retrenchment. *Journal of International Finance*, 88, 235–251.

Fraser Institute. 2015. *Economic Freedom of the World*, Available at: www.fraserinstitute.org/economic-freedom/dataset?geozone=world& year=2016&min-year=2&max-year=0&filter=0&page=dataset.

Frenkel, Jacob. 1982. The Order of Economic Liberalization: A Comment. In: Brunner, Karl, and Meltzer, Allan (eds), *Economic Policy in a World of Change*. Amsterdam: North-Holland.

Frieden, Jeffrey. 1981. Third World Indebted Industrialization: International Finance and State Capitalism in Mexico, Brazil, Algeria, and South Korea. *International Organization*, 35(3), 407–431.

Gandhi, Jennifer, and Przeworski, Adam. 2006. Cooperation, Cooptation, and Rebellion Under Dictatorship. *Economics and Politics*, 18(1), 1–26.

Gastanaga, Victor M., Nugent, Jeffrey B., and Pashamova, Bistra. 1998. Host Country Reforms and FDI Inflows: How Much Difference Do They Make? *World Development*, 26(7), 1299–1314.

Giger, Nathalie, and Kluver, Heike. 2016. Voting Against Your Constituents? How Lobbying Affects Representation. *American Journal of Political Science*, 60(1), 190–205.

Gilens, Martin, and Page, Benjamin I. 2014. Testing Theories of American Politics: Elites, Interest Groups, and Average Citizens. *Perspectives on Politics*, 12(3), 564–581.

Gilligan, Michael J. 1997. Lobbying as a Private Good with Intra-Industry Trade. *International Studies Quarterly*, 41(3), 455–474.

Girma, Sourafel, Greenaway, Sir David, and Wakelin, Katharine. 2001. Who Benefits from Foreign Direct Investment in the UK? *Scottish Journal of Political Economy*, 48(2), 119–133.

Goldstein, Judith. 2017. Trading in the Twenty-First Century: Is There a Role for the World Trade Organization? *Annual Review of Political Science*, 20, 545–564.

Golub, Stephen. 2003. Measures of Restrictions on Inward Foreign Direct Investment for OECD Countries. *OECD Economic Studies*, 36(1), 85–116.

Golub, Stephen S. 2009. Openness to Foreign Direct Investment in Services: An International Comparative Analysis. *The World Economy*, 32(8), 1245–1268.

Gonzalez-Garcia, Jesus, and Grigoli, Francesco. 2013. *State-Owned Banks and Fiscal Discipline*. IMF Working Paper Series 13/206. Washington, DC: International Monetary Fund.

Graham, Edward M., and Wada, Erika. 2000. Domestic Reform, Trade and Investment Liberalisation, Financial Crisis, and Foreign Direct Investment into Mexico. *The World Economy*, **23**(6), 777–797.

Granger, Clive W.J. 1969. Investigating Causal Relations by Econometric Models and Cross-spectral Methods. *Econometrica*, **37**(3), 424–438.

Grossman, Gene M., and Helpman, Elhanan. 1994. Protection for Sale. *American Economic Review*, **84**(September), 833–850.

Gupta, Nandini. 2005. Partial Privatization and Firm Performance. *The Journal of Finance*, **60**(2), 987–1015.

Gutierrez, German, and Pilippon, Thomas. 2017. Investmentless Growth: An Empirical Investigation. *Brookings Papers on Economic Activity*, **48**(2 (Fall)), 89–190.

Gwartney, James, Lawson, Robert, and Hall, Joshua. 2016. *Economic Freedom of the World: 2016 Annual Report*. Tech. rept. Fraser Institute.

Haber, Stephen, and Perotti, Enrico. 2007. *The Political Economy of Finance*. Mimeo, Stanford University.

Habir, A. 1984. Indonesia in 1983: Searching for Efficiency. *Southeast Asian Affairs*, 125–136.

Hacker, Jacob S., and Pierson, Paul. 2014. After the "Master Theory": Downs, Schattschnedier, and the Rebirth of Policy Focused Analysis. *Perspectives on Politics*, **12**(3), 643–662.

Haggard, Stephan. 1990. *Pathways from the Periphery*. Ithaca, NY: Cornell University Press.

Haggard, Stephan, and Kaufman, Robert R. 1995. *The Political Economy of Democratic Transitions*. Princeton, NJ: Princeton University Press.

Haggard, Stephan, Lee, Chung, and Maxfield, Sylvia (eds). 1993. *The Politics of Finance in Developing Countries*. Ithaca, NY: Cornell University Press.

Haggard, Stephan, and Maxfield, Sylvia. 1996. The Political Economy of Financial Internationalization in the Developing World. *International Organization*, **50**(1), 35–68.

Hall, Peter A., and Soskice, David (eds). 2001. *Varieties of Capitalism: The Institutional Foundations of Comparative Advantage*. Oxford: Oxford University Press.

Hansen, Wendy L., and Mitchell, Neil J. 2000. Disaggregating and Explaining Corporate Political Activity: Domestic and Foreign Corporations in National Politics. *American Political Science Review*, **94**(4), 891–903.

Hara, Fujio. 1991. Malaysia's New Economic Policy and the Chinese Business Community. *The Developing Economies*, **39**(4), 350–370.

Hardie, Iain, Howarth, David, Maxfield, Sylvia, and Verdun, Amy. 2013. Banks and the False Dichotomy in the Comparative Political Economy of Finance. *World Politics*, **65**(4), 691–728.

Harding, Torfinn, and Javorcik, Beata Smarzynska. 2012. Foreign Direct Investment and Export Upgrading. *Review of Economics and Statistics*, **94**(4), 964–980.

Harrison, Anne E., Love, Inessa, and McMillan, Margaret S. 2004. Global Capital Flows and Financing Constraints. *Journal of Development Economics*, **75**, 269–301.

Hausmann, Ricardo, and Fernández-Arias, Eduardo. 2000. *Foreign Direct Investment: Good Cholesterol?* IDB Publications (Working Papers) 6466. Washington, DC: Inter-American Development Bank.

Havranek, Tomas, and Irsova, Zuzana. 2011. Estimating Vertical Spillovers from FDI: Why Results Vary and What the True Effect is. *Journal of International Economics*, **85**, 234–244.

Hawkins, John, and Minhaljek, Dubravko. 2001. The Banking Industry in the Emerging Market Economies: Competition, Consolidation, and Systemic Stability: An Overview. Pages 1–44 of: Bank for International Settlements (ed), *The Banking Industry in Emerging Market Economies: Competition, Consolidation and Systemic Stability*, vol. 4. Basel: Bank for International Settlements.

Hays, Jude C., Freeman, John R., and Nesseth, Hans. 2003. Exchange Rate Volatility and Democratization in Emerging Market Countries. *International Studies Quarterly*, **47**, 203–228.

Helpman, Elhanan. 2006. Trade, FDI, and the Organization of Firms. *Journal of Economic Literature*, **XLIV**(September), 589–630.

Heritage Foundation. 2017. *Index of Economic Freedom*, Available at: www.heritage.org/index/explore.

Hewko, John. 2002. Foreign Direct Investment in Transitional Economies: Does the Rule of Law Matter? *East European Constitutional Review*, **11**(4), 71–79.

Hillman, Arye. 1982. Declining Industries and Political-Support Protectionist Motives. *The American Economic Review*, **72**(5), 1180–1187.

Hiscox, Michael. 2002. *International Trade and Political Conflict: Commerce, Coalitions and Factor Mobility*. Princeton, NJ: Princeton University Press.

Howell, Lewellyn D. *International Country Risk Guide Methodology*. The PRS Group, Available at www.prsgroup.com/wp-content/uploads/2012/11/icrgmethodology.pdf.

Hymer, Stephen H. 1960. *The International Operations of National Firms*. Cambridge, MA: MIT Press.

International Monetary Fund. 2012. *Liberalizing Capital Flows and Managing Outflows*. Washington, DC: IMF.

International Monetary Fund. 2014. *Annual Report on Exchange Arrangements and Exchange Restrictions*. Washington, DC: IMF.

Irsova, Zuzana, and Havranek, Tomas. 2013. Determinants of Horizontal Spillovers from FDI: Evidence from a Large Meta-Analysis. *World Development*, **42**, 1–15.

Jackson, James K. 2014. *The Committee on Foreign Investment in the United States (CFIUS)*. Washington, DC: Congressional Research Service.

Javorcik, Beata Smarzynska, and Spatareanu, Mariana. 2005. Disentangling FDI Spillover Effects: What Do Firm Perceptions Tell Us? Chap. 3, pages 45–72 of: Moran, Theodore H., Graham, Edward M., and Blostrom, Magnus (eds), *Does Foreign Direct Investment Promote Development?* Washington, DC: Institute for International Economics.

Javorcik, Beata Smarzynska, and Spatareanu, Mariana. 2008. To Share or Not to Share: Does Local Participation Matter for Spillovers from Foreign Direct Investment. *Journal of Development Economics*, **85**(1–2), 194–217.

Javorcik, Beata Smarzynska, and Spatareanu, Mariana. 2009. Tough Love: Do Czech Suppliers Learn from their Relationships with Multinationals? *Scandinavian Journal of Economics*, **111**(4), 811–833.

Jensen, Nathan M., Malesky, Eddy, Medina, Mariana, and Ozdemir, Ugur. 2014. Pass the Bucks: Credit, Blame, and the Global Competition for Investment. *International Studies Quarterly*, **58**(3), 433–447.

Jensen, Nathan M., and Malesky, Edmund. 2018. *Incentives to Pander: How Politicians Use Corporate Welfare for Political Gain*. Cambridge: Cambridge University Press.

Jesudason, James V. 1989. *Ethnicity and the Economy: The State, Chinese Business, and Multinationals in Malaysia*. Singapore: Oxford University Press.

Johnson, Simon, La Porta, Rafael, Lopez-de Silanes, Florencio, and Shleifer, Andrei. 2000. Tunneling. *American Economic Review*, **90**(2), 22–27.

Johnston, R. Barry. 1998. Sequencing Capital Account Liberalization. *Finance and Development*, **35**(4), 20–23.

Johnston, R. Barry, Darbar, Salim M., and Echeverria, Claudia. 1997 (November). *Sequencing Capital Account Liberalization: Lessons from the Experiences in Chile, Indonesia, Korea, and Thailand*. Washington, DC: International Monetary Fund.

Johnston, R. Barry, and Sundararajan, Vasudevan. 1999. *Sequencing Financial Sector Reforms: Country Experiences and Issues*. Washington, DC: International Monetary Fund.

KADIN. 2007 (16 July). *Kadin Indonesia Report on Business Concerns with the DNI.* Jakarta: KADIN.

Kalinova, Blanka, Palerm, Angel, and Thomsen, Stephen. 2010. *OECD's FDI Restrictiveness Index:* 2010 Update. OECD Working Papers on International Investment, 2010/03. Paris: OECD Publishing, Available at: http://dx.doi.org/10.1787/5km91p02zj7g-en

Kang, C. S Eliot. 1997. U.S. Politics and Greater Regulation of Inward Foreign Direct Investment. *International Organization,* 51(2), 301–333.

Kawai, Masahiro, and Takagi, Shinji. 2008. *A Survey of the Literature on Managing Capital Inflows.* Mandaluyong: Asian Development Bank.

Keele, Luke J., and DeBoef, Suzanna. 2008. Taking Time Seriously: Dynamic Regression. *American Journal of Political Science,* 52(1), 184–200.

Keller, Wolfgang, and Yeaple, Stephen. 2009. Multinational Enterprises, International Trade, and Productivity Growth: Firm-Level Evidence from the United States. *Review of Economics and Statistics,* 91(4), 821–831.

Kersting, Erasmus K., and Görg, Holger. 2017. Vertical Integration and Supplier Finance. *Canadian Journal of Economics,* 50(1), 273–305.

Kim, In Song. 2017. Political Cleavages within Industry: Firm-level Lobbying for Trade Liberalization. *American Political Science Review,* 111(1), 1–20.

King, Robert G., and Levine, Ross. 1993. Finance and Growth: Schumpeter Might Be Right. *Quarterly Journal of Economics,* 108(3), 717–737.

Kobrin, Stephen. 1987. Testing the Bargaining Hypothesis in the Manufacturing Sector in Developing Countries. *International Organization,* 57(3), 609–638.

Kobrin, Stephen J. 2005. The Determinants of Liberalization of FDI Policy in Developing Countries: A Cross-Sectional Analysis, 1992–2001. *Transnational Corprorations,* 14(1), 1–37.

Kochanek, Stanley A. 1996a. Liberalization and Business Lobbying in India. *The Journal of Commonwealth and Comparative Politics,* 34(3), 155–173.

Kochanek, Stanley A. 1996b. The Transformation of Interest Politics in India. *Pacific Affairs,* 68, 529–550.

Kono, Daniel Yuichi. 2008. Democracy and Trade Discrimination. *The Journal of Politics,* 70(4), 942–955.

Kose, M. Ayhan, Prasad, Eswar, and Taylor, Ashely D. 2011. Thresholds in the Process of International Financial Integration. *Journal of International Money and Finance,* 30(1), 147–179.

Kroszner, Randall S., Laeven, Luc, and Klingebiel, Daniela. 2007. Banking Crises, Financial Dependence, and Growth. *Journal of Financial Economics,* 84, 187–228.

Krueger, Anne. 1984. Problems of Liberalization. In: Harberger, A. (ed), *World Economic Growth*. San Francisco, CA: ICS Press.

Krugman, Paul. 2000. *Fire-Sale FDI*. Chicago, IL: University of Chicago Press. Chap. 2, pages 43–58.

Krusell, Per, and Ríos-Rull, José-Víctor. 1996. Vested Interests in a Theory of Growth and Stagnation. *Review of Economic Studies*, 63(April), 301–329.

La Porta, Rafael, de Silanes, Florencio Lopez, Shleifer, Andrei, and Vishny, Robert. 2000. Investor Protection and Corporate Governance. *Journal of Financial Economics*, 58, 3–27.

Lenz, Gabriel, and Sahn, Alexander. 2019. Achieving Statistical Significance with Covariates and without Transparency. Working Paper.

Levy-Yeyati, Eduardo, and Sturzenegger, Federico. 2005. Classifying Exchange Rate Reigmes. *European Economic Review*, 49(6), 1603–1635.

Lewis, Cleona. 1938. *America's Stake in International Investments*. Washington, DC: Brookings Institution Press.

Lewis, James A. 2019. *Learning the Superior Techniques of the Barbarians: China's Pursuit of Semiconductor Independence*. Washington, DC: Center for Strategic and International Studies, Available at: https://csis-prod.s3.amazonaws.com/s3fs-public/publication/190115_Lewis_Semiconductor_v6.pdf

Li, Quan. 2006. Democracy, Autocracy, and Tax Incentives to Foreign Direct Investors: A Cross-National Analysis. *Journal of Politics*, 68(1), 62–74.

Lipsey, Robert E. 2004. Home- and Host-Country Effects of Foreign Direct Investment. In: Baldwin, Robert E., and Winters, L. Alan (eds), *Challenges to Globalization: Analyzing the Economics*. Chicago, IL: University of Chicago Press, for National Bureau of Economic Research.

Lipsey, Robert E., Feenstra, Robert C., Hahn, Carl H., and Hatsopoulos, George N. 1999. The Role of Foreign Direct Investment in International Capital Flows. Pages 307–362 of: Feldstein, Martin (ed), *International Capital Flows*. Chicago, IL: University of Chicago Press.

Lipsey, Robert E., and Sjöholm, Fredrik. 2003. *Foreign Firms and Indonesian Manufacturing Wages: An Analysis with Panel Data*. Working Paper 9417. Cambridge, MA: National Bureau of Economic Research.

Lipson, Charles. 1985. *Standing Guard: Protecting Foreign Capital in the Nineteenth and Twentieth Centuries*. Berkeley, CA: University of California Press.

Little, Ian, Scitovsky, Tibor, and Scott, Maurice. 1970. *Industry and Trade in Some Developing Countries*. London: Oxford University Press.

MacIntyre, A. 1993. The Politics of Finance in Indonesia: Command, Confusion and Competition. Pages 123–164 of: Haggard, Stephen, Lee, Chung, and Maxfield, Sylvia (eds), *The Politics of Finance in Developing Countries*. Ithaca, NY: Cornell University Press.

Mai, Pham Hoang. 2004. *FDI and Development in Vietnam*. Singapore: Institute of Southeast Asian Studies.

Malesky, Edmund J. 2008. Straight Ahead on Red: How Foreign Direct Investment Empowers Subnational Leaders. *The Journal of Politics*, 70(1), 97–119.

Malesky, Edmund J. 2009. Foreign Direct Investors as Agents of Economic Transition: An Instrumental Variables Analysis. *Quarterly Journal of Political Science*, 4, 59–85.

Marchick, David M., and Slaughter, Matthew J. 2008. *Global FDI Policy: Correcting a Protectionist Drift*. New York, NY: Council on Foreign Relations.

Markusen, James R., and Venables, Anthony J. 1998. Multinational Firms and the New Trade Theory. *Journal of International Economics*, 46, 183–203.

Marshall, Monty G., Gurr, Ted Robert, and Jaggers, Keith. 2017. *Polity IV Project: Political Regime Characteristics and Transitions, 1800–2016*. University of Maryland, Centre for Systemic Peace, Available at: www.systemicpeace.org/inscr/p4manualv2016.pdf.

Mayer, Wolfgang. 1984. Endogenous Tariff Formation. *The American Economic Review*, 75(5), 970–985.

McKinnon, Ronald I. 1973. *Money and Capital in Economic Development*. Washington, DC: Brookings Institution Press.

McKinnon, Ronald L. 1991. *The Order of Economic Liberalization: Financial Control in the Transition to a Market Economy*. Baltimore, MD: The Johns Hopkins University Press.

Melitz, Marc. 2003. The Impact of Trade on Intra-Industry Reallocations and Aggregate Industry Productivity. *Econometrica*, 71(6), 1695–1725.

Menaldo, Victor, and Yoo, Daniel. 2015. Democracy, Elite Bias, and Financial Development in Latin America. *World Politics*, 67(4), 726–759.

Meunier, Sophie. 2014. 'Beggars Can't Be Choosers': The European Crisis and Chinese Direct Investment in the European Union. *Journal of European Integration*, 36(3), 283–302.

Meunier, Sophie, Burgoon, Brian, and Jacoby, Wade. 2014. The Politics of Hosting Chinese Direct Investment in Europe. *Asia-Europe Journal*, 12(1), 109–126.

Michaely, Michael. 1986. The Timing and Sequencing of Trade Policy Reform. In: Choksi, Armeane M., and Papageorgiou, Demetris. (eds), *Economic Liberalization in Developing Countries*. Oxford: Blackwell.

Michalet, Charles-Albert. 1997. France. Pages 359–376 of: Dunning, John H. (ed), *Governments, Globalization, and International Business*. Oxford: Oxford University Press.

Miller, Terry, Holmes, Kim R., and Feulner, Edwin J. 2013. *2013 Index of Economic Freedom*. Tech. rept. Heritage Foundation, Washington, DC.

Milner, Anthony. 2003. Asia-Pacific Perceptions of the Financial Crisis: Lessons and Affirmations. *Contemporary Southeast Asia*, 25(2), 284–305.

Milner, Helen V. 1987. Resisting the Protectionist Temptation: Industry and the Making of Trade Policy in France and the United States During the 1970s. *International Organization*, 41(4), 639–665.

Milner, Helen V. 1999. The Political Economy of International Trade. *Annual Review of Political Science*, 2, 91–114.

Milner, Helen V., and Kubota, Keiko. 2005. Why the Move to Free Trade? Democracy and Trade Policy in the Developing Countries. *International Organization*, 59, 107–143.

Milner, Helen V., and Yoffie, David B. 1989. Between Free Trade and Protectionsims: Strategic Trade Policy and a Theory of Corporate Trade Demands. *International Organization*, 43(2), 239–272.

Moran, Theodore H. 1978. Multinational Corporations and Dependency: A Dialogue for Dependentistas and Non-dependentistas. *International Organization*, 32(1), 79–100.

Moran, Theodore H. 2005. How Does FDI Affect Host Country Development? Using Industry Case Studies to Make Reliable Generalizations. Chap. 11, pages 281–314 of: Moran, Theodore H., Graham, Edward M., and Blostrӧm, Magnus (eds), *Does Foreign Direct Investment Promote Development?* Washington, DC: Institute for International Economics.

Mosley, Layna. 2003. *Global Capital and National Government*. Cambridge: Cambridge University Press.

Mosley, Layna, and Singer, David Andrew. 2009. The Global Financial Crisis: Lessons and Opportunities for International Political Economy. *International Interactions*, 35(4), 420–429.

Mukherjee, Bumba and Singer, David Andrew. 2010. International Institutions and Domestic Compensation: The IMF and the Politics of Capital Account Liberalization. *American Journal of Political Science*, 54(1), 45–60.

Narayanan, S. 1996. Fiscal Reform in Malaysia: Behind a Successful Experience. *Asian Survey*, 9(1), 869–881.

Noorbakhsh, Farhad, Paloni, Alberto, and Youssef, Ali. 2001. Human Capital and FDI Flows to Developing Countries: New Empirical Evidence. *World Development*, 29(9), 1593–1610.

Olson, Mancur. 1965. *The Logic of Collective Action: Public Goods and the Theory of Groups*. Cambridge, MA: Harvard University Press.

Organisation for Economic Co-operation and Development. 2010. *OECD Investment Policy Reviews: Indonesia 2010*, OECD Investment Policy Reviews, OECD Publishing, Paris, Available at: https://doi.org/10.1787/9789264087019-en

Organisation for Economic Co-operation and Development. 2013. *OECD Investment Policy Reviews: Malaysia, 2013*, OECD Investment Policy Reviews, OECD Publishing, Paris, Available at: www.oecd.org/investment/malaysia-investment-policy.htm.

Organisation for Economic Co-operation and Development. 2017. *FDI Regulatory Restrictiveness Index*, Available at: www.oecd.org/investment/fdiindex.htm.

Organisation for Economic Co-operation and Development, World Trade Organization, and World Bank Group. 2014 (19 July). *Global Value Chains: Challenges, Opportunities, and Implications for Policy*. Paris: OECD Publishing.

Osgood, Iain. 2017. The Breakdown of Industrial Opposition to Trade: Firms, Product Variety and Reciprocal Liberalization. *World Politics*, **69**(1), 184–231.

Osgood, Iain, Tingley, Dustin H., Bernauer, Thomas, Kim, In Song, Milner, Helen V., and Spilker, Gabriele. 2017. The Charmed Life of Superstart Exporters: Survey Evidence on Firms and Trade Policy. *Journal of Politics*, **79**(1), 133–152.

O'Sullivan, Mary. 2003. The Political Economy of Comparative Corporate Goverance. *Review of International Political Economy*, **10**(1), 23–72.

Owen, Erica. 2013. Unionization and Restrictions on Foreign Direct Investment. *International Interactions*, **39**(5), 723–747.

Owen, Erica. 2015. The Political Power of Organized Labor and the Politics of Foreign Direct Investment in Developed Democracies. *Comparative Political Studies*, **48**(13), 1746–1780.

Pagano, Marco, and Volpin, Paolo F. 2005. The Political Economy of Corporate Governance. *American Economic Review*, **95**(4), 1005–1030.

Pagano, Marco, and Volpin, Paolo F. 2006. "Alfred Marshall Lecture" Shareholder Protection, Stock Market Development, and Politics. *Journal of the European Economic Association*, **4**(2/3), 315–341.

PAIZ. 2006. *Polish Public Opinion Likes Foreign Investors*. Tech. rept. Warsaw: Polish Investment and Information Agency.

Palmer, I. 1978. *The Indonesia Economy Since 1965*. London: Cass.

Pandya, Sonal S. 2010. Labor Markets and the Demand for Foreign Direct Investment. *International Organization*, **64**(Summer), 389–409.

Pandya, Sonal S. 2013. *Trading Spaces: Foreign Direct Investment Regulation, 1970–2000*. Cambridge, MA: Cambridge University Press.

Pandya, Sonal S. 2014. Democratization and FDI Liberalization, 1970–2000. *International Studies Quarterly*, **58**, 475–488.

Pandya, Sonal S. 2016. Political Economy of Foreign Direct Investment: Globalized Production in the Twenty-First Century. *Annual Review of Political Science*, **19**, 455–475.

Parente, Stephen L., and Presott, Edward C. 1999. Monopoly Rights: A Barrier to Riches. *American Economic Review*, **89**(5), 1216–1233.

Pepinsky, Thomas. 2008. Capital Mobility and Coalitional Politics: Authoritarian Regimes and Economic Adjustment in Southeast Asia. *World Politics*, **60**(3), 438–474.

Pepinsky, Thomas. 2009. *Economic Crises and the Breakdown of Authoritarian Regimes: Indonesia and Malaysia in Comparative Perspectives*. New York, NY: Cambridge University Press.

Pepinsky, Thomas. 2012. *99 Problems (But a Crisis Ain't One) Political Business and External Vulnerability in Island Southeast Asia*. Working Paper 43. JICA Research Institute, Tokyo.

Pepinsky, Thomas. 2013a. The Domestic Politics of Financial Internationalization in the Developing World. *Review of International Political Economy*, **20**(4), 848–880.

Pepinsky, Thomas. 2013b. The Institutional Turn in Comparative Authoritarianism. *British Journal of Political Science*, 1–23.

Pinto, Pablo M. 2013. *Partisan Investment in the Global Economy: Why the Left Loves Foreign Direct Investment and FDI Loves the Left*. New York, NY: Cambridge University Press.

Pinto, Pablo M., and Pinto, Santiago M. 2008. The Politics of Investment Partisanship and the Sectoral Allocation of Foreign Direct Investment. *Economics and Politics*, **20**(2), 216–254.

Pop-Eleches, Grigore. 2009. *From Economic Crisis to Reform: IMF Programs in Latin America and Eastern Europe*. Princeton, NJ: Princeton University Press.

Prasad, Eswar, Rogoff, Kenneth, Wei, Shang-Jin, and Kose, M. Ayhan. 2003. *Effects of Financial Globalization on Developing Countries: Some Empirical Evidence*. IMF Occasional Paper 220. International Monetary Fund, Washington, DC.

Przeworski, Adam, and Wallerstein, Michael. 1988. Structural Dependence of the State on Capital. *American Political Science Review*, **82**(1), 11–30.

Qui, Larry D., and Wang, Shengzu. 2013. FDI Policy, Greenfield Investment, and Cross-Border Mergers. *Review of International Economics*, **19**(5), 836–851.

Quinn, Dennis P., and Inclan, Carla. 1997. The Origins of Financial Openness: A Study of Current and Capital Account Liberalization. *American Journal of Political Science*, 771–813.

Rajan, Raghuram G., and Zingales, Luigi. 1998. Financial Dependence and Growth. *American Economic Review*, 88(3), 559–586.

Rajan, Raghuram G., and Zingales, Luigi. 2003. The Great Reversals: The Politics of Financial Development in the Twentieth Century. *Journal of Financial Economics*, 69, 5–50.

Rajenthran, Arumugam. 2002 (October). *Indonesia: An Overview of the Legal Framework for Foreign Direct Investment*. Economics and Finance 4. Institute of Southeast Asian Studies, Singapore.

Ramirez, Carlos D., and Tan, Ling Hui. 2004. Singapore Inc. Versus the Private Sector: Are Government-Linked Companies Different? *IMF Staff Papers*, 51(3), 510–528.

Robertson, Graeme B., and Teitelbaum, Emmanuel. 2011. Foreign Direct Investment, Regime Type, and Labor Protest in Developing Countries. *American Journal of Political Science*, 55(3), 665–677.

Robison, Richard. 1996. The Middle Class and the Bourgeoisie in Indonesia. Pages 79–104 of: Robison, Richard, and Goodman, David. (eds), *The New Rich in Asia: Mobile Phones, McDonalds, and Middle Class Revolution*. London: Routledge.

Robson, Jake, and Loveless, Craig. 2013. Outlook for Foreign Investment in the Indonesian Banking Sector. *International Financial Law Review*, July, Available at: www.iflr.com/Article/3229284/Outlook-for-foreign-investment-in-the-Indonesian-banking-sector.html?ArticleId=3229284

Rodrik, Dani. 1998 (May). *Who Needs Capital-Account Convertibility?* Essays in International Finance 207. Department of Economics, Princeton University, Princeton, NJ.

Rodrik, Dani. 2008. *One Economics, Many Recipes: Globalization, Institutions, and Economic Growth*. Princeton, NJ: Princeton University Press.

Rohrscheider, Robert, and Whitefield, Stephen. 2004. Support for Foreign Ownership and Integration and Eastern Europe: Economic Interests, Ideological Commitments, and Democratic Context. *Comparative Political Studies*, 37(3), 313–339.

Rojas-Suárez, Liliana, and Mathieson, Donald J. 1993. *Liberalization of the Capital Account; Experiences and Issues*. IMF Occasional Paper 103. IMF, Washington, DC.

Roland, Gerard. 2000. *Transitions and Economics: Politics, Markets, and Firms*. Cambridge: MIT Press.

Ross Schneider, Ben. 2013. *Hierarchical Capitalism in Latin America: Busienss, Labor, and the Challenges of Equitable Development*. Cambridge, MA: Cambridge University Press.

Rosser, Andrew. 2002. *The Politics of Economic Liberalisation*. Richmond, VA: Curzon.

Rosser, Andrew. 2004. *Why Did Indonesia Overcome the Resource Curse?* IDS Working Paper 222. Institute of Development Studies, Brighton.

Rybczynski, Tadeusz. 1955. Factor Endowment and Relative Commodity Prices. *Economica*, **22**(88), 336–341.

Sadli, Mohammad. 1993. Recollections of My Career. *Bulletin of Indonesian Economic Studies*, **29**(1), 35–51.

Safarian, A. Edward. 1999. Host Country Policies Toward Inward Foreign Direct Investment in the 1950s and 1990s. *Transnational Corporations*, 8(2), 93–114.

Sato, Yuri. 2003. *Post-Crisis Economic Reform in Indonesia: Policy for Intervening in Ownership in Historical Perspective*. Research Paper 4. IDE.

Sato, Yuri. 2005. Bank Restructuring and Financial Institutional Reform in Indonesia. *The Developing Economies*, **43**(1), 91–120.

Schamis, Hector E. 1999. Distributional Coalitions and the Politics of Economic Reform in Latin America. *World Politics*, **51**(2), 236–268.

Scheve, Kenneth, and Slaughter, Matthew J. 2004. Economic Insecurity and the Globalization of Production. *American Journal of Political Science*, **48**(4), 662–674.

Schwab, Dan, and Werker, Eric. 2018. Are Economic Rents Good for Development? Evidence from the Manufacturing Sector. *World Development*, **112**(December), 33–45.

Scott, Peter, and Rooth, Tim. 1999. Public Policy and Foreign-Based Enterprises in Britain Prior to the Second World War. *The Historical Journal*, **42**(2), 495–515.

Searle, P. 1999. *The Riddle of Malaysian Capitalism: Rent-Seekers or Real Capitalists?* Sydney: Allen and Unwin.

Shambaugh, Jay C. 2004. The Effect of Fixed Exchange Rates on Monetary Policy. *Quarterly Journal of Economics*, **119**(1), 301–352.

Sharma, Shalendra D. 2001. The Indonesian Financial Crisis: From Banking Crisis to Financial Sector Reforms, 1997–2000. *Indonesia*, **71**, 79–110.

Simmons, Beth A., Dobbin, Frank, and Garrett, Geoffrey. 2006. Introduction: The International Diffusion of Liberalism. *International Organization*, **60**(4), 781–810.

Simmons, Beth A., and Elkins, Zachary. 2004. The Globalization of Liberalization: Policy Diffusion in the International Political Economy. *American Political Science Review*, **98**(1), 171–189.

Sinn, Hans-Werner. 1997. Foreign Direct Investment, Political Resentment and the Privatization Process in Eastern Europe. *Economic Policy*, 12(24), 179–210.

Soesastro, H. 1989. The Political Economy of Deregulation in Indonesia. *Asian Survey*, 29(9), 853–868.

Sorsa, P. 1997. *The GATS Agreement on Financial Services: A Modest Start to Multilateral Liberalization.* IMF Working Paper 97/55. International Monetary Fund, Washington, DC.

Stacey, Jeffrey. 2009. Creative Destruction? After the Crisis: Neoliberal Remodeling in East Asia. *Review of International Political Economy*, 16, 485–513.

Stone, Randall W. 2008. The Scope of IMF Conditionality. *International Organization*, 62(4), 589–620.

Stone, Randall W. 2011. *Controlling Institutions: International Organizations and the Global Economy.* New York, NY: Cambridge University Press.

Svedberg, Peter. 1978. The Portfolio-Direct Composition of Private Foreign Investment in 1914 Revisited. *Economic Journal*, 88(352), 763–777.

Swank, Duane. 1992. Politics and the Structural Dependence of the State in Capitalist Democracies. *American Political Science Review*, 86(March), 38–54.

Symons, Edward, and White, James. 1989. *Banking Law: Teaching Materials.* St. Paul, MN: West Publishing Company.

Tambunan, Tulus T. H. 2011. *Inward FDI in Indonesia and Its Policy Context.* Columbia FDI Profile Series. Vale Columbia Center on Sustainable International Investment, New York, NY.

Taylor, Christopher. 2000. The Impact of Host Country Government Policy on U.S. Multinational Investment Decisions. *World Economy*, 23, 635–648.

Teichman, Judith A. 1995. *Privatization and Political Change in Mexico.* Pittsburgh, PA: University of Pittsburgh Press.

Teichman, Judith A. 2001. *The Politics of Freeing Markets in Latin America.* Chapel Hill, NC: University of North Carolina Press.

Thelen, Kathleen. 2011. Varieties of Capitalism: Trajectories of Liberalization and the New Politics of Social Solidarity. *Annual Review of Political Science*, 15(2), 1–23.

Thomsen, Stephen. 1999. Southeast Asia: The Role of Foreign Direct Investment Policies in Development. Technical Report. OECD.

Thomsen, Stephen, and Mistura, Fernando. 2017. *Is Investment Protectionism on the Rise? Evidence from the OECD FDI Regulatory Restrictiveness Index.* Paris: OECD.

Thornton, Daniel L., and Batten, Dallas S. 1985. Lag Length Selection and Granger Causality. *Journal of Money, Credit and Banking*, **17**(2), 164–178.

Tienhaara, Kyla, and Ranald, Patricia. 2011 (July 12). Australia's Rejection of Investor-State Dispute Settlement: Four Potential Contributing Factors. *Investment Law and Policy News Bulletin*, **2011** (July). Available at: www.iisd.org/itn/2011/07/12/australias-rejection-of-investor-state-dispute-settlement-four-potential-contributing-factors/

Treasury of the Commonwealth of Australia. 2018. *Foreign Investment Review Board: Annual Report 2016–2017.*

Trefler, Daniel. 1993. Trade Liberalization and the Theory of Endogenous Protection: An Econometric Study of U.S. Import Policy. *The Journal of Political Economy*, **101**(1), 138–160.

Tripathi, Dwijendra. 2004. *The Oxford History of Indian Business.* New Delhi: Oxford University Press.

United Nations Conference on Trade and Development. 1998. *World Investment Report 1998: Trends and Determinants.* New York, NY: United Nations.

United Nations Conference on Trade and Development. 2000. *World Investment Report 2000: Cross-border Mergers and Acquisitions and Development.* New York, NY: United Nations.

United Nations Conference on Trade and Development. 2005a. *Economic Development in Africa: Rethinking the Role of Foreign Direct Investment.* New York, NY: United Nations.

United Nations Conference on Trade and Development. 2005b. *World Investment Report 2005: Transnational Corporations and the Internationalization of R&D.* New York, NY: United Nations.

United Nations Conference on Trade and Development. 2006. *World Investment Report 2006: FDI from Developing and Transition Economies – Implications for Development.* New York, NY: United Nations.

United Nations Conference on Trade and Development. 2009. *World Investment Report 2009: Transnational Corporations, Agricultural Production and Development.* New York, NY: United Nations.

United Nations Conference on Trade and Development. 2012. *World Investment Report 2012: Towards a New Generation of Investment Policies.* New York, NY: United Nations.

United Nations Conference on Trade and Development. 2013a. *Global Value Chains and Development: Investment and Value Added Trade in the Global Economy.* New York, NY: United Nations.

United Nations Conference on Trade and Development. 2013b. *World Investment Report 2013: Global Value Chains: Investment and Trade for Development.* New York, NY: United Nations.

United Nations Conference on Trade and Development. 2014. *World Investment Report 2014: Investing in the SDGs: An Action Plan.* New York, NY: United Nations.

United Nations Conference on Trade and Development. 2016a (April). *Investment Policy Monitor.* New York, NY: United Nations.

United Nations Conference on Trade and Development. 2016b (November). *Investment Policy Monitor: Investment Laws – A Widespread Tool for the Promotion and Regulation of Foreign Investment.* New York, NY: United Nations.

United Nations Conference on Trade and Development. 2016c. *World Investment Report 2016: Investor Nationality: Policy Challenges.* New York, NY: United Nations.

United Nations Conference on Trade and Development. 2017. *World Investment Report 2017: Investment and the Digital Economy.* New York, NY: United Nations.

United Nations Conference on Trade and Development. 2018a (March). *Investment Policy Monitor No. 19.* New York, NY: United Nations.

United Nations Conference on Trade and Development. 2018b. *World Investment Report 2018: Investment and New Industrial Policy.* New York, NY: United Nations.

United States Bureau of Economic and Business Affairs. 2013. *2013 Investment Climate Statement – Indonesia.* Washington, DC: United States State Department.

United States State Department. 1990. *1990 Country Commerce Guide – Malaysia.* Washington, DC: United States State Department.

Vadlamannati, Krishna Chaitanya, Cooray, Arusha, and Tamazian, Artur. 2014. What Drives FDI Policy Liberalization? An Empirical Investigation. *Regional Science and Urban Economics*, **49**, 179–189.

Vernon, Raymond. 1971. *Sovereignty at Bay.* New York, NY: Basic Books.

Vitalis, Robert. 1995. *When Capitalists Collide: Business Conflict and the End of Empire in Egypt.* Berkley, CA: University of California Press.

Walker, Edward T., and Rea, Christopher M. 2014. The Political Mobilization of Firms and Industries. *Annual Review of Sociology*, **40**(1), 281–304.

Wardhana, A. 1994. Financial Reforms: Achievements, Problems, and Prospects. Pages 79–93 of: McLeod, R. (ed), *Indonesia Assessment 1994: Finance as a Key Sector in Indonesia's Development.* Singapore: Research School of Pacific and Asian Studies and Institute for Southeast Asian Studies.

Wellhausen, Rachel L. 2013. Innovation in Tow: R&D FDI and Investment Incentives. *Business and Politics*, **15**(4), 467–491.

Wilkins, Mira. 1970. *The Maturing of Multinational Enterprise: American Business Abroad from 1914 to 1970*. Cambridge, MA: Harvard University Press.

Wilkins, Mira. 1989. *The History of Foreign Investment in the United States to 1914*. Harvard University Press.

Willliamson, John. 2000. What Should the World Bank Think About the Washington Consensus. *The World Bank Research Observer*, 15(2), 251–264.

Wilson, Sven E., and Butler, Daniel M. 2007. A Lot More to Do: The Sensitivity of Time-Series Cross-Section Analyses to Simple Alternative Specification. *Political Analysis*, 15(2), 101–123.

Winters, Jeffrey. 1996. *Power in Motion: Capital Mobility and the Indonesian State*. Ithaca, NY: Cornell University Press.

Woodhouse, Erik. 2003. The Guerra del Agua and the Cochabamba Concession: Social Risk and Foreign Direct Investment in Public Infrastructure. *Stanford Journal of International Law*, 39, 295–350.

World Bank. 2009. *Enterprise Surveys: Indonesia Country Profile 2009*. Database. World Bank, Washington, DC.

World Bank. 2017 (June). Global Financial Development Database (GFDD), distributed by the World Bank, Available at: https://datacatalog.worldbank.org/dataset/global-financial-development

Wright, Joseph. 2008. Do Authoritarian Institutions Constrain? How Legislatures Affect Economic Growth and Investment. *American Journal of Political Science*, 52(2), 322–343.

Yinug, Falan. 2009. Challenges to Foreign Investment in High-Tech Semiconductor Production in China. *Journal of International Commerce and Economics*, May, 1–30.

Yusof, Zainal Aznam, Hussin, Awang Adek, Alowi, Ismail, Lim, Chee Sing, and Singh, Sukhdave. 1994. Financial Reform in Malaysia. In: Caprio, Gerard, Atiyas, Izak, and Hanson, James A. (eds), *Financial Reforms: Theory and Experience*. Cambridge: Cambridge University Press.

Zarra-Nezhad, Mansour, Parseian, Sajjad, and Anvari, Ebrahim. 2012. Measuring Financial Repression in Selected Oil Exporting Countries. *Quarterly Journal of Quantitative Economics*, 8(4), 119–133.

Zingales, Luigi. 2017. Toward a Political Theory of the Firm. *Journal of Economic Perspectives*, 31(3), 113–130.

Index

Lightning Source UK Ltd.
Milton Keynes UK
UKHW020324060320
359877UK00005B/29